The Hope and Despair
of
Human Bioenhancement

Pontifical John Paul II Institute for Studies on Marriage and Family, Rome

Winner of the John Paul II Institute's 2017 *Sub Auspiciis* Award for the publication of outstanding dissertations

The Hope and Despair
of
Human Bioenhancement

*A Virtual Dialogue between the Oxford Transhumanists
and Joseph Ratzinger*

PASCHAL M. CORBY OFM CONV.

☙PICKWICK *Publications* · Eugene, Oregon

THE HOPE AND DESPAIR OF HUMAN BIOENHANCEMENT
A Virtual Dialogue between the Oxford Transhumanists and Joseph Ratzinger

Copyright © 2019 Paschal M. Corby. All rights reserved. Except for brief quotations in critical publications or reviews, no part of this book may be reproduced in any manner without prior written permission from the publisher. Write: Permissions, Wipf and Stock Publishers, 199 W. 8th Ave., Suite 3, Eugene, OR 97401.

Pickwick Publications
An Imprint of Wipf and Stock Publishers
199 W. 8th Ave., Suite 3
Eugene, OR 97401

www.wipfandstock.com

PAPERBACK ISBN: 978-1-5326-5394-0
HARDCOVER ISBN: 978-1-5326-5395-7
EBOOK ISBN: 978-1-5326-5396-4

Cataloguing-in-Publication data:

Names: Corby, Paschal M., author.

Title: The hope and despair of human bioenhancement : a virtual dialogue between the Oxford transhumanists and Joseph Ratzinger. / Paschal M. Corby.

Description: Eugene, OR : Pickwick Publications, 2019. | Includes bibliographical references and index.

Identifiers: ISBN 978-1-5326-5394-0 (paperback) | ISBN 978-1-5326-5395-7 (hardcover) | ISBN 978-1-5326-5396-4 (ebook)

Subjects: LCSH: Human body—Religious aspects—Christianity. | Theological anthropology—Christianity. | Technology—Religious aspects—Christianity. | Biotechnology—Religious aspects—Christianity.

Classification: BT741.3 .C67 2019 (paperback) | BT741.3 .C67 (ebook)

Manufactured in the U.S.A.   12/19/19

Dedication

For my parents, Max and Dora Corby,
and in memory of Professor Nicholas Tonti-Filippini (1956–2014)

Contents

Acknowledgments | ix
Introduction | xi

Part I—Philosophical Foundations

Chapter 1
Transhumanism and Human Enhancement according to the "Oxford School" | 3

Chapter 2
The Science of Enhancement | 29

Chapter 3
The Anthropological Question: The Human Person in Transhumanist Thought | 66

Chapter 4
The Philosophical Foundations of Transhumanism and the Positivist Reduction | 88

Chapter 5
Chanced or Purposeful?: Ratzinger's Response to Evolution | 115

Chapter 6
Technology and the Secularization of Hope | 144

Part II—Practical Applications

Chapter 7
Product or Gift?: The Hope and Despair of Selecting Children | 181

Chapter 8
The Case for Moral Enhancement: Unfit for the Future or Called to Love? | 218

Chapter 9
Should We Live Forever?: The Transhumanist Quest for Immortality versus Ratzinger's Hopeful Eschatology | 258

Conclusion | 285
Bibliography | 291
Index | 309

Acknowledgments

I EXTEND MY HEARTFELT thanks to all who contributed to the completion of this work:

To my brothers of the Order of Friars Minor Conventual; to provincials past (Fr. Patrick Greenough) and present (Fr. Michael Zielke), who allowed me to pursue doctoral studies; to the friars of the Australian Delegation of Our Lady, Help of Christians, for their encouragement and sacrifice; and to my former guardian (Fr. Timothy Kulbicki) and friars of Convento Sant'Antonio alla Vigna, Rome, for their friendship and support during the writing of my thesis.

To the professors and staff of the Pontifical John Paul II Institute in Rome: to Dr. Stephan Kampowski for his careful supervision of my thesis; to Monsignor Livio Melina, whose writings first awakened me to a new way of looking at issues of morality and bioethics; and to Monsignor Pierangelo Sequeri and his council for awarding me the 2017 *Sub Auspiciis* prize.

To my former colleagues of the John Paul II Institute in Melbourne: to Professor Nicholas Tonti-Filippini (1956–2014), to whose memory this work is dedicated, for his wisdom and goodness; to the former dean, Professor Tracey Rowland, for her faith and encouragement of my academic pursuits; and to Associate Professor Adam Cooper, Liet. Col. Toby Hunter, Anna Krohn, Dr. Gerard O'Shea, Dr. Anna Silvas, Dr. Colin Patterson, Dr. Conor Sweeney, and Dr. Owen Vyner, for their professionalilsm, spirited conversation, and gentle introduction into the art of teaching.

And to Joseph Ratzinger / Pope Benedict XVI, whose love for truth and defence of human dignity is an enduring inspiration.

Introduction

Why Transhumanism?

WHAT I REFER TO throughout this work as the transhumanist *project*, *cause*, or *movement* encompasses a range of proposals, from simple measures to the improbable and bizarre, that aim at enhancing the human condition, using medical technology to move human beings beyond their natural limitations. Nick Bostrom is representative of the transhumanist cause in contending that "current human nature is improvable through the use of applied science and other rational methods, which may make it possible to increase human health-span, extend our intellectual and physical capacities, and give us increased control over our own mental states and moods."[1] Such enhancement is often termed *transhuman* or *posthuman*, implying not only an augmentation of human abilities, but also a qualitative change that takes one beyond the human species.

In light of its futuristic aspirations, with limited actual application, transhumanism might not seem to warrant serious reflection. Before the presence of real bioethical dilemmas such as new threats to life, the unjust distribution of healthcare resources, and the perennial issues surrounding life at its beginning and end, devoting time to an improbable possibility might appear to be a distraction or a luxury that we can ill afford. Yet the prospect of transhumanism has caught the imagination of not a few contemporary bioethicists and philosophers, inspiring centers of research, and sparking a lively debate between its supporters and critics.

While first impressions suggest something remote and abstract, it soon becomes clear that the transhumanist proposal treats of real concerns that touch on the very meaning of human life. In asking why one

---

1. Bostrom, "In Defense of Posthuman Dignity," 202–3.

should take seriously the proposals of transhumanists, the prominent American bioethicist Leon Kass writes:

> It raises the weightiest questions of bioethics, touching on the ends and goals of the biomedical enterprise, the nature and meaning of human flourishing, and the intrinsic threat of dehumanization (or the promise of superhumanization). It compels attention to what it means to *be* a human being and to be active *as* a human being.[2]

In their pursuit to enhance and even transcend the current human condition, transhumanists caste shadows over the goodness of life and raise hopes for a bright and better future. Thus, even if many of its imaginative prospects do not eventuate, it demands a response here-and-now, for our hopes and aspirations define who we are. Accordingly, the primary concern of this work is not for the practicality of transhumanist claims, but a discernment of its worth as a proper object of human hope. In this context, hope becomes the *leitmotif* of this paper, in the context of a virtual dialogue between the Oxford Transhumanists and Joseph Ratzinger.

The Oxford Transhumanists

In presenting the transhumanist project, I will focus on what one might term the "Oxford School" of transhumanism, centered on the figures of Julian Savulescu and Nick Bostrom, and the Oxford Uehiro Centre for Practical Ethics (Uehiro Centre) and the Future of Humanity Institute (FHI) respectively.

Julian Savulescu (b. 1963) is an Australian philosopher and bioethicist, currently based at Oxford University as professor of practical ethics and director of the Uehiro Centre. He is the current editor in chief of the *Journal of Medical Ethics*. He is a graduate of medicine (Monash University), and completed a PhD under the supervision of renowned bioethicist Peter Singer. To date, Savulescu's main contribution to the field of human enhancement has been in the area of genetic selection of children, advocating selection of children with the best prospects of the best life, for which he coined the term "Procreative Beneficence." He also advocates biotechnology to enhance cognitive, physical (including doping in sport), and moral capacities. In this latter regard, he has coauthored with

---

2. Kass, "Ageless Bodies, Happy Souls," 10.

Ingmar Persson *Unfit for the Future: The Need for Moral Enhancement* (Oxford: Oxford University Press, 2012). More generally, he has coedited works with Ruud ter Meulen and Guy Kahane (*Enhancing Human Capacities*, Chichester: Wiley-Blackwell, 2011), and with Nick Bostrom (*Human Enhancement*, Oxford: Oxford University Press, 2009).

Nick Bostrom (b. 1973) is a Swedish philosopher, currently professor in the Faculty of Philosophy at Oxford University and founding director of the Future of Humanity Institute and of the Program on the Impacts of Future Technology within the Oxford Martin School. In addition to philosophy, Bostrom has a broad background covering fields of physics, computational neuroscience, and mathematical logic. His contribution to the transhumanist project is extensive, being an original signatory of *The Transhumanist Declaration* in 1988, and cofounder of the World Transhumanist Association. His major works include *Anthropic Bias: Observation Selection Ethics in Science and Philosophy* (New York: Routledge, 2002), *Global Catastrophic Risks* (with M. Ćirković, Oxford: Oxford University Press, 2008), and *Superintelligence: Paths, Dangers, Strategies* (Oxford: Oxford University Press, 2014).

In considering the influences on the Uehiro Centre and the Future of Humanity Institute, the analysis will extend beyond our two main protagonists, to include figures such as Guy Kahane (deputy director of the Uehiro Centre and FHI alumnus), Ingmar Persson (Uehiro consultant researcher), Anders Sandberg (research fellow for both the Uehiro Centre and FHI), Allen Buchanan (honorary fellow and Uehiro lecturer), Thomas Douglas (Uehiro research fellow), Jonathan Glover (honorary fellow and Uehiro lecturer), Rebecca Roache (FHI alumna) and Carl Shulman (FHI research associate).

Joseph Ratzinger

Joseph Ratzinger (b. 1927) is a German theologian and cleric, ordained priest in 1951, bishop in 1977 (as Archbishop of Munich and Freising), and elected pope in 2005 under the name Benedict XVI. Previously, he had served under his predecessor, John Paul II, as prefect for the Sacred Congregation for the Doctrine of the Faith (CDF) from 1981 until 2005.

His doctorate in theology, completed in 1953, was concerned with the ecclesiology of Saint Augustine, and his postdoctoral thesis, defended four years later, treated of Saint Bonaventure's theology of history. As professor of theology, Ratzinger taught at several German Universities: Bonn (1959–1963), Münster (1963–1966), Tübingen (1966–1969), and Regensburg (1969–1977). In 1972, together with Hans Urs von Balthasar and Henri de Lubac, he was cofounder of the theological journal *Communio*. He has published extensively, his scholarly reflections spanning a period of over fifty years.

Along with his collaboration with von Balthasar and de Lubac, Ratzinger derives inspiration from a number of influences, the most important being Augustine and Bonaventure, John Henry Newman, Romano Guardini, and Josef Pieper. Of these, Guardini and Pieper will feature prominently in this work in helping to trace Ratzinger's thought. I will also necessarily consider some more contemporary influences, including Hans Jonas and Robert Spaemann.

A Virtual Dialogue

I have subtitled this work "a virtual dialogue." Ratzinger does not write specifically on the theme of human enhancement (though there is evidence that he is aware of the topic).[3] In this sense the dialogue is virtual, drawing on what Ratzinger has written in other contexts and applying it to transhumanist claims. To this end, Ratzinger offers a rich source of material, with his breadth of interests and his historical sensibility, drawing on a range of topics and currents of thought. As D. Vincent Twomey, Ratzinger's former doctoral student at Regensburg, writes: "This capacity to listen with discernment, combined with his phenomenal erudition, makes him a superb partner in dialogue."[4]

However, there is a further sense in which this dialogue is virtual, which touches on a central thesis of this work. One need admit that there exists a certain incommensurability between transhumanists and Ratzinger. They often seem to speak different languages, to exist in different worlds. More properly, the world in which transhumanists present their position seems closed to a level of dialogue that Ratzinger deems

---

3. For example, in giving a Christian perspective to bioethics he asks: "What are the ethical limits to intervention in human genetics seeking not only 'radical' therapy for certain illnesses, but also having the chance to improve or, in any case, modify certain specific or individual characteristics?" Ratzinger, "Bioethics in the Christian Perspective," 10.

4. Twomey, introduction to Thornton and Varenne, *Essential Pope Benedict XVI*, xvi.

INTRODUCTION

to be crucial. Ratzinger's world of dialogue is far more expansive than the limitations of empirical science. He cannot be tied by the positivist constraints that characterize the transhumanist project. Nor will he be restricted by a secular totalitarianism that rejects religious insights and the idea of God as unreasonable or unphilosophical. For this reason, this current work will not be purely philosophical—or at least, not restricted to the philosophical categories that positive science imposes. Rather, it will take seriously Ratzinger's proposal to broaden the sphere of philosophical debate; to go beyond the limitations of empirical knowledge toward an understanding of reality, of the world and human nature, that is open to transcendence.

Fundamental to Ratzinger's approach is the Catholic insistence on the compatibility of faith and reason[5] that constitute the "two wings on which the human spirit rises to the contemplation of truth."[6] Reason is not in conflict with the nature of God, for God is himself reason, *logos*, word. Likewise, faith is not a substitute for reason, but is its salvation and "resuscitation."[7]

> Faith is not the resignation of reason in view of the limits of our knowledge; it is not a retreat into the irrational in view of the dangers of a merely instrumental reason. Faith is not the expression of weariness and flight but is courage to exist and an awakening to the greatness and breadth of what is real.[8]

Admittedly, Ratzinger is primarily a theologian. Furthermore, his theology is ecclesial, interpreting the revelation of God in Jesus Christ as entrusted to the church and contained in Sacred Scripture. But as Twomey notes, while he writes from an explicitly theological perspective,

---

5. The theme of faith and reason is present throughout Ratzinger's writings. See particularly his "Sorbonne Address" (1999) in Ratzinger, *Truth and Tolerance*, 162–83. Also his lecture as Benedict XVI in the Aula Magna of the University of Regensburg (2006) at http://w2.vatican.va/content/benedict-xvi/en/speeches/2006/september/documents/hf_ben-xvi_spe_20060912_university-regensburg.html.

6. John Paul II, *Fides et ratio*, n. 1.

7. "Consequently, man's listening to the message of faith is not the passive registering of otherwise unknown information, but the resuscitation of our choked memory and the opening of the powers of understanding which await the light of the truth in us. Hence, such understanding is a supremely active process, in which reason's entire quest for the criteria of our responsibility truly comes into its own for the first time. Reason's quest is not stifled, but is freed from circling helplessly in impenetrable darkness and set on its way." Ratzinger, "Truth and Freedom," 33.

8. Ratzinger, *Turning Point for Europe?*, 110.

he does so with attention to the breadth of philosophical questioning throughout history. His theological enquiry is attentive to the questions posed by a range of thinkers, "theologians and otherwise."[9] One would therefore be mistaken, writes Tracey Rowland, in thinking that Ratzinger is "fundamentally hostile to either philosophy or science."[10] If there is any hostility in Ratzinger, it is directed toward absolutizations of philosophy or science which, cut off from the guiding light of faith, promise more than they can provide. As Ratzinger himself writes: "Reason that is closed in on itself does not remain reasonable. . . . Reason needs revelation in order to be able to function as reason."[11]

Within the Key of Hope

This tension between the claims of a philosophical science and faith impacts on the question of hope. In this, Rowland draws our attention to Ratzinger's delineation of post-Enlightenment changes in the object of hope, away from God and even Marxist-style earthly utopias, toward what he identifies as a "new world order"[12] that pins its hopes on a rationality that is the product of technical science. Ratzinger writes:

> The criterion of rationality is taken exclusively from the experience of technological production based on science. Rationality is oriented to functionality, to effectiveness, and to an increase in the quality of life for all. This entails a use—indeed a domination—of nature that is problematic in view of the dramatic environmental problems our world now faces. But man's domination of his own self nonchalantly takes ever greater steps toward the realization of Aldous Huxley's vision. Man is no longer to be born in an irrational manner but is to be produced rationally. Man as a product is subject to the control of man. Imperfect individuals must be weeded out; the path of planning and production must aim at the perfect man. Suffering must disappear, and life is to consist of pleasure alone.[13]

---

9. Twomey, introduction to *Essential Pope Benedict XVI*, xiv.

10. Rowland, *Ratzinger's Faith*, 14.

11. Ratzinger, *Church, Ecumenism, and Politics*, 206.

12. Rowland, "Variations on the Theme of Christian Hope," 204; citing Ratzinger, *Values in a Time of Upheaval*, 156.

13. Ratzinger, *Values in a Time of Upheaval*, 157.

In this "new world order," biotechnology becomes the new hope, reduced, as Rowland interprets, "to something like trust in the future promises of genetic manipulation."[14] The relevance of this analysis to the transhumanist cause seems quite clear, with its projection of hope onto biotechnology and its quest to re-create human beings. Such is the inspiration for engaging Ratzinger in dialogue with transhumanists of the Oxford School; and to do so in the key of hope, subjecting transhumanism's optimism to a verification beyond technical viability.

Ratzinger does not object to biotechnology in itself, but to its unreasoned absolutization as the source of human hope. It is not his intention that humanity should remain in some primordial backwater, untouched by the advances of science. He is not threatened by human ingenuity, nor seduced by "the romanticism of pure nature."[15] He recognizes the blessings of technology and the legitimacy of human enhancement. He writes: "Anyone who looks even at only the last hundred years cannot deny that immense progress has been made in medicine, in technology, and in the understanding and harnessing of the forces of nature, and one may hope for further progress."[16]

The church in general appreciates the benefits of science as "*an invaluable service to the integral good of the life and dignity of every human being*,"[17] and recognizes the "great importance for the future of humanity" that flows from advances in genetics, medicine and biotechnologies.[18] However, this enthusiasm is qualified by the proviso that whatever technology we apply to human beings must be fitting to their nature, respectful of their end, and informed by reason. Ratzinger writes that the advance of humanity "becomes a rational project when one knows who man is, when one has found the measure of his humanity. Then technology becomes hope, when it takes its direction from the core of man's nature—the image of God in man."[19]

Accordingly, the question of human enhancement, even by means of biotechnology, may not be closed, provided that it does not subvert

---

14. Rowland, "Variations on the Theme of Christian Hope," 204.
15. Ratzinger, *Faith and the Future*, 97.
16. Ratzinger, *Values in a Time of Upheaval*, 25.
17. CDF, *Dignitas personae*, n. 3.
18. CDF, *Dignitas personae*, n. 37.
19. Ratzinger, *Faith and the Future*, 97–98.

human nature or compromise the human capacity for virtue.[20] There may indeed be a qualifiable difference between the radical proposals of transhumanists and more restrained bids to enhance human capacities. However, it is not my intention within this work to explore these differences, nor to decide on each proposal within the expansive repertoire of the transhumanist agenda, nor to suggest how far we may go in pursuing human development within the oftentimes confused distinction between therapy and enhancement. Rather, by working within the hermeneutic of hope, I propose to show that concealed behind the apparent optimism of the transhumanist cause for human enhancement is a form of despair that denies the greatness of the human spirit. In response, I invoke Ratzinger's determination that real hope can only operate through the grateful acknowledgment of what is given, an affirmation of the goodness of the human condition, (that transhumanism inherently undervalues), and an honest and willing acceptance of our limitations.

Outline

This work evolves in two parts. *Part 1* broadly deals with the philosophical foundations of the transhumanist project that underpin its hope for enhancement.

Chapter 1 offers an introduction to the terms of the transhumanist cause, developed within the context of a discussion of the contested distinction between therapy and enhancement, and of different concepts of enhancement and human flourishing, especially of the "welfarist" model that is proposed by some members of the Oxford School.

In an attempt to envisage the object of transhumanist hope, *chapter 2* sets forth a range of objectives of the transhumanist movement, specifically focusing on issues of cognitive enhancement, physical enhancement, mood enhancement, moral enhancement and lifespan extension.

Acknowledging the ambiguities of the transhumanist concept of enhancement and human flourishing, *chapter 3* explores the limitations of transhumanism's anthropology as deriving from an unqualified acceptance of the mechanisms of human evolution. This is evident in its materialist reduction, its denial of a substantive human nature, and its rejection of the human person's metaphysical distinction.

---

20. See Kraj, "Role of Virtue Ethics."

INTRODUCTION   xix

Chapter 4 more precisely deals with the philosophical foundations of transhumanism, tracing a path through Enlightenment rationalism, the positive reduction of science and technology, and the postmodern deconstruction. In dialogue with Ratzinger, transhumanism is seen to emerge from scientific positivism, which rejects *being* in favor of the *factum* of human products and the *faciendum* of human making. This contextualizes the transhumanist denial of a metaphysics of the human person and its embrace of a fluid concept of human nature as a work in progress. Ratzinger's response highlights the pathologies of a reason that is limited to what is humanly verifiable. He also aims at broadening the horizon of reality, moving beyond empirical knowledge and offering an apology for faith.

Chapter 5 engages Ratzinger in dialogue once more, in his offer of a more hopeful vision of the human person. He responds to the limitations of a strictly mechanical explanation of human beginnings, supplementing it with an account of the emergence of the human spirit, that founds the origins of human beings in an originating reason and directs them towards transcendence.

Finally, in *chapter 6*, Ratzinger highlights the dangers of a positivistic reduction that is wedded to a technological imperative void of moral responsibility. He further suggests that the conflation of reality into *techne* amounts to an immanentization or secularization of Christian hope. But despite its optimism in historical process and technology, Ratzinger exposes an underlying despair in this concept of hope: a despair that rejects contingency, despises gift, and craves control.

From these foundations, *part 2* pursues the thesis that transhumanism masks a fundamental despair for humanity, offering practical examples in the proposals to select children through genetic enhancement, to enhance morality, and to extend the human lifespan toward immortality.

In keeping with Ratzinger's diagnosis of a pathology of reason present in technology's dominion over the beginnings of human life, *chapter 7* considers the transhumanist proposal to select children through genetic engineering. A particular example is given in Julian Savulescu's theory of Procreative Beneficence. A critique drawn from various contemporary commentators highlights the negative impact of selection on the parent-child relationship, its transformation of the notion of responsibility, and its threat to the contingence of human origins. In upholding an imperative of contingency, Ratzinger speaks of the *necessity* of life proceeding from the context of conjugal love, in which children come forth not as an artifact of human engineering, but as gift, and thus as a proper object of hope.

Chapter 8 exposes the pessimism that permeates the transhumanist pursuit of moral bioenhancement, especially as espoused in Ingmar Persson and Savulescu's determination that human beings are "unfit for the future." The presumption of an evolutionary explanation of the limitations of human morality is revealed as a further example of the materialistic reduction of human nature, a denial of human freedom, and a withering of hope in the human capacity for transcendence. Engaging Ratzinger in dialogue once again, hope is restored through acknowledgment of the human power to love, as an affirmation of the goodness of self, the other, and the whole of creation. Love, with its proficiency for including the universal within the particular, is also offered as the means of overcoming the biases and indifferences that limit morality. Ultimately, it is offered as the fulfillment of our human nature, created in the image of God who is love. In this context, Ratzinger insists that we are never alone in our struggle to be moral, but are assisted by divine grace that makes us fit for a future of communion with God and neighbor.

In completing this exposition on the transhumanist mutilation of hope, *chapter 9* treats of transhumanism's utopian quest to overcome aging and extend earthly life toward immortality, departing from Nick Bostrom's imaginative *Fable of the Dragon Tyrant*. It is perhaps before the challenge of death that transhumanism's despair, with its denial of the human condition, is fully revealed. In response, contemporary critics propose the blessing of finitude as the means of appreciating the giftedness, seriousness, and beauty of life, of preserving the meaning of intergenerational relations, and of upholding human contingence. Ratzinger enters this dialogue by defending the capacity of human beings for transcendence, exposing the myth of the desirability of more of this life, and unmasking the quest for an earthly utopia as a distortion of our human nature and a mutilation of hope. The mystery of life and death escape positive categories, requiring the added light of faith to illumine our understanding and afford us true hope for the future.

Part I

Philosophical Foundations

Chapter 1

Transhumanism and Human Enhancement according to the "Oxford School"

IN THE INTRODUCTION TO their coedited work, *Human Enhancement*, Julian Savulescu and Nick Bostrom ask a fundamental question: "Are we good enough?" This is immediately followed by another: "If not, how may we improve ourselves?"[1] As the narrative continues, the transhumanist movement offers its own answer to these questions: (1) we are not good enough, and there is reason—indeed a moral duty—to improve ourselves; and (2) current advances in science and technology give us real hope of achieving that goal.

At the root of this imperative for enhancement is a sense of dissatisfaction with our human condition: a sense of something lacking, a frustration of our potential. In this, it would appear that transhumanists respond to a valid human experience. Discontentment and disappointment are part of every life. We all yearn for something more, desire to go further, strive to improve ourselves in one way or another. The human spirit has always striven toward self-improvement, and the historical advances in human culture would be unthinkable without this drive toward enhancement. The real question, however, is whether transhumanists like Savulescu and Bostrom interpret the experience of human dissatisfaction correctly, and whether their confidence in the methods of human enhancement, especially through biotechnology, corresponds to genuine human hope.

In moving toward answering these questions, this opening chapter offers an overview of the contemporary transhumanist scene. Beginning

---

1. Savulescu and Bostrom, "Human Enhancement Ethics," 1.

with a brief outline of the history of transhumanist thought, its adoption by the "Oxford School," and the definition of some key terms, it proceeds to a consideration of different approaches to enhancement, focusing mainly on the *welfare* or *well-being* model as proposed by the Oxford School.

What Is Transhumanism?

The term "transhumanism" appears for the first time in Julian Huxley's 1957 monograph *New Bottles for New Wine*. With Huxley, the transhuman state is envisaged as the apex of the evolutionary process, and its natural fulfillment,[2] defining evolution as "a history of the realization of ever new possibilities."[3] Through the explosion of knowledge from the modern era onwards—in the fields of psychology, science, archaeology, anthropology and history—human beings have embarked on a quest to help bring these possibilities to realization, considering human nature in its current, unrealized potential to be the new frontier of exploration.[4]

Motivating Huxley's determination to unleash humanity's true potential is the universal human experience of incompleteness and dashed hopes, marked by suffering and limitation. He writes:

> Up till now human life has generally been, as Hobbes described it, "nasty, brutish and short"; the great majority of human beings (if they have not already died young) have been afflicted with misery in one form or another—poverty, disease, ill-health, over-work, cruelty, or oppression. They have attempted to lighten their misery by means of their hopes and their ideals. The trouble has been that the hopes have generally been unjustified, the ideals have generally failed to correspond with reality.[5]

In the light of such unfulfilled prospects and dashed hopes, Huxley looks to the possibilities of science and technology as a means of

---

2. Moltisanti and Postigo Solana, "Transumanesimo," 203. "Il transumano, in sostanza, è per Huxley l'apice del processo evolutivo, il suo naturale compimento."

3. Huxley, *New Bottles for New Wine*, 13.

4. "We have pretty well finished the geographical exploration of the earth; we have pushed the scientific exploration of nature, both lifeless and living, to a point at which its main outlines have become clear; but the exploration of human nature and its possibilities has scarcely begun. A vast New World of uncharted possibilities awaits its Columbus." Huxley, *New Bottles for New Wine*, 14.

5. Huxley, *New Bottles for New Wine*, 16.

rationalizing hope; of transcending the wretchedness and ignorance of life toward an "existence based on the illumination of knowledge and comprehension."[6] It is at this point that Huxley proposes the term *transhumanism*: "man remaining man, but transcending himself, by realizing new possibilities of and for his human nature."[7]

Departing from Huxley's original musings, contemporary proponents of the transhumanist cause, encouraged by advances in science and technology, are confident of its realization. Together, Savulescu and Bostrom outline the prospects for human enhancement through technology:

> It seems likely that this century will herald unprecedented advances in nanotechnology, biotechnology, information technology, cognitive science, and other related areas. These advances will provide the opportunity fundamentally to change the human condition.[8]

While Huxley naïvely envisaged the transhumanist goal as "realizing new possibilities" for human nature, Savulescu and Bostrom are bold in setting their sights on changing the human condition: of going beyond human nature. Despite great risks, they contend that we should take advantage of the "enormous potential benefits" offered by technological enhancements to go beyond that which "can be achieved by low-tech means such as education, philosophical contemplation, moral self-scrutiny and other such methods."[9] As a founding member of the World Transhumanist Association (now Humanity+), and one of the original signatories of *The Transhumanist Declaration*,[10] Bostrom em-

---

6. Huxley, *New Bottles for New Wine*, 16.

7. Huxley, *New Bottles for New Wine*, 17. Huxley adds: "I believe in transhumanism: once there are enough people who can truly say that, the human species will be on the threshold of a new kind of existence, as different from ours as ours is from that of Pekin man. It will at last be consciously fulfilling its real destiny."

8. Savulescu and Bostrom, "Human Enhancement Ethics," 20–21.

9. Bostrom, "Human Genetic Enhancements," 496.

10. First drafted in 1988, the *Declaration* has undergone several revisions and modifications. The 2012 version declares: (1) Humanity stands to be profoundly affected by science and technology in the future. We envision the possibility of broadening human potential by overcoming aging, cognitive shortcomings, involuntary suffering, and our confinement to planet Earth. (2) We believe that humanity's potential is still mostly unrealized. There are possible scenarios that lead to wonderful and exceedingly worthwhile enhanced human conditions. (3) We recognize that humanity faces serious risks, especially from the misuse of new technologies. There are possible

bodies this hope of broadening human potential through technology. Indeed, he emphasizes "the enormous potential for genuine improvements in human well-being and human flourishing that are attainable *only* via technological transformation."[11] Consistent with Huxley's conception of humanity as the "new frontier of exploration," Bostrom envisages "hitherto inaccessible realms of value";[12] a world of experiences beyond our current limitations that is waiting to be explored.[13] These new experiences could constitute a radical change to our humanity. Accordingly, Bostrom expresses the transhumanist hope that the powers of science and technology will allow us to become posthuman: "beings with vastly greater capacities than present human beings have."[14]

---

realistic scenarios that lead to the loss of most, or even all, of what we hold valuable. Some of these scenarios are drastic, others are subtle. Although all progress is change, not all change is progress. (4) Research effort needs to be invested into understanding these prospects. We need to carefully deliberate how best to reduce risks and expedite beneficial applications. We also need forums where people can constructively discuss what could be done, and a social order where responsible decisions can be implemented. (5) Reduction of risks of human extinction, and development of means for the preservation of life and health, the alleviation of grave suffering and the improvement of human foresight and wisdom, be pursued as urgent priorities and generously funded. (6) Policy making ought to be guided by responsible and inclusive moral vision, taking seriously both opportunities and risks, respecting autonomy and individual rights, and showing solidarity with and concern for the interests and dignity of all people around the globe. We must also consider our moral responsibilities toward generations that will exist in the future. (7) We advocate the well-being of all sentience, including humans, nonhuman animals, and any future artificial intellects, modified life forms, or other intelligences to which technological and scientific advance may give rise. (8) We favor morphological freedom—the right to modify and enhance one's body, cognition, and emotions. This freedom includes the right to use or not to use techniques and technologies to extend life, preserve the self through cryonics, uploading, and other means, and to choose further modifications and enhancements. More and Vita-More, *Transhumanist Reader*, 54–55.

11. Bostrom, "History of Transhumanist Thought," 20. Emphasis added.

12. Bostrom, "Human Genetic Enhancements," 496.

13. "The range of thoughts, feelings, experiences, and activities that are accessible to human organisms presumably constitute only a tiny part of what is possible.... It is not farfetched to suppose that there are parts of this larger space that represent extremely valuable ways of living, feeling, and thinking." Bostrom, "Human Genetic Enhancements," 494.

14. Bostrom, "Human Genetic Enhancements," 493.

Transhuman versus Posthuman

In introducing the term *posthuman*, a distinction needs to be made. Bostrom refers to the transhuman (human+) as the "transitional human,"[15] existing between humanity in its extant form and its future shape.[16] A transhuman is one whose physical, intellectual and psychological capacities are enhanced with respect to present human capacities, but not to the point of creating a new species.[17] The idea of the transitional human flows from the conviction that the human condition is not constant, but is constantly evolving: adaptable, potential, and capable of change. Humanity as we possess it is merely a step in the process of development.[18]

Posthuman (human++), on the other hand, refers to a radically new state.[19] It is characterized by an amplification of one's capacities that exceeds "the maximum attainable by any current human being without recourse to new technological means"[20] in at least one of the following categories:

---

15. Moltisanti and Postigo Solana, "Transumanesimo," 204–5. "Il già citato Bostrom definisce *transumano*, o *umano transizionale*, l'essere umano avente 'capacità moderatamente potenziate' e in fase di transizione verso il *postumano*, vale a dire un soggetto le cui capacità fisiche, intellettuali e psicologiche oltrepasseranno in modo così radicale quelle dell'essere umano da non poter esserci confusione tra i due soggetti." Citing Bostrom, "Intensive Seminar on Transhumanism," Yale University, June 26, 2003.

16. Faggioni, "La natura fluida," 418. "Mentre il Transumanista e semplicemente qualcuno che sostiene il Transumanesimo, si dovranno chiamare 'Transumani' o 'Umani+', secondo Bostrom, gli esseri di transizione, gli umani moderatamente potenziati, le cui capacità sono intermedie fra quelle degli umani attuali e quelle degli umani futuri, i veri 'Post-umani' (gli 'Umani++' secondo Bostrom)."

17. Postigo Solana, "Transumanesimo e postumano," 272.

18. Moltisanti and Postigo Solana, "Transumanesimo," 203–4. "Il transumanesimo costituisce dunque un nuovo paradigma sul futuro dell'uomo, costruito a partire dall'opera di scienziati che provengono da diverse aree (Intelligenza Artificiale, Neurologia, Nanotecnologia e Biotecnologia applicata), filosofi e unomini di cultura, aventi tutti lo stesso obiettivo: alterare, migliorare la natura umana e prolungare la sua esistenza partendo dall'idea che la 'condizione umana' non sia costante e sostanzialmente inalterabile e che l'essere umano non sia quindi il prodotto finale della nostra evoluzione, ma solo una tappa precoce."

19. Faggioni, "La natura fluida," 418. "Il traguardo del Transumanesimo è la creazione di esseri postumani, radicalmente nuovi rispetto all'umanità come noi la conosciamo oggi, in una lotta tragica ed eroica contro il limite, la finitezza, la vulnerabilità."

20. Bostrom, "Why I Want to Be a Posthuman," 28–29.

- *healthspan*: the capacity to remain fully healthy, active, and productive, both mentally and physically;
- *cognition*: general intellectual capacities, such as memory, deductive and analogical reasoning, and attention, as well as special faculties such as the capacity to understand and appreciate music, humor, eroticism, narration, spirituality, mathematics, etc.;
- *emotion*: the capacity to enjoy life and to respond with appropriate affect to life situations and other people.[21]

This difference in capacities would constitute a new kind of being: a being with a different nature that would be literally post-human.[22] Thus, while the enhanced capacities of the transhuman signify a human being "in passage," the posthuman being "exceeds the human frontier, so much so as to no longer have the appearance of the *Homo sapiens* species."[23]

---

21. Bostrom, "Why I Want to Be a Posthuman," 29. Elsewhere, Bostrom writes: "Ultimately, it is possible that such enhancements may make us, or our descendants, 'posthuman,' beings who may have indefinite health-spans, much greater intellectual faculties than any current human being—and perhaps entirely new sensibilities or modalities—as well as the ability to control their own emotions." Bostrom, "In Defense of Posthuman Dignity," 203.

22. It must be admitted that Bostrom denies a strict separation between human and posthuman. He writes: "It does not follow, at least not in any obvious way, that a posthuman could not also remain a human being. Whether or not this is so depends on what meaning we assign to the word 'human.' One might well take an expansive view of what it means to be human, in which case 'posthuman' is to be understood as denoting a certain possible type of human mode of being." Bostrom, "Why I Want to Be a Posthuman," 49–50. However, this inclusion of the posthuman as a "type of human mode of being" is reflective of Bostrom's unwillingness to strictly define human nature, rather than a denial of the radical difference implied in the posthuman state. The fluid conception of human nature proposed by transhumanism will be discussed later.

23. Valera, "Posthumanism," 483. In this context, Valera draws a parallel with other contemporary movements (e.g., *post*-modern, *post*-romantic, *post*-structuralist, etc.) that claim "to overtake a reality that appears as antiquated, as if the 'post' . . . should necessarily indicate a situation of positive development, a possible release from an oppressive and limiting condition" (481). The parallel seems legitimate, especially in light of the dissatisfaction with the human lot that characterizes and motivates the transhumanist-posthumanist project.

Enhancement

Human enhancement is in some ways synonymous with the process of transhumanism. Enhancement can refer to both the enhanced state that is desired, and the means by which one moves toward it.[24] Accordingly, Allen Buchanan distinguishes enhancement according to *type* and *mode*.[25]

Type refers to the human capacities that biomedicine seeks to enhance, including cognitive function, physical strength, length of life, emotional control, and moral powers. Buchanan writes:

> Biomedical enhancements can make us smarter, have better memories, be stronger and quicker, have more stamina, live much longer, be more resistant to disease and to the frailties of ageing, and enjoy richer emotional lives. They may even improve our character or at least strengthen our powers of self-control.[26]

With even greater imagination and enthusiasm Bostrom adds:

> The enhancement options being discussed include radical extension of human health-span, eradication of disease, elimination of unnecessary suffering, and augmentation of human intellectual, physical, and emotional capacities. Other transhumanist themes include space colonization and the possibility of creating superintelligent machines, along with other potential developments that could profoundly alter the human condition.[27]

The *mode* of bioenhancement refers to the kinds of technology employed to reach the above-mentioned goals. Bostrom describes transhumanism as "a loosely defined movement" that employs "an interdisciplinary approach to understanding and evaluating the opportunities for enhancing the human condition and the human organism opened up by the advancement of technology."[28] The various disciplines include drug therapy, eugenic selection of embryos through preimplantation genetic

---

24. Giglio, *Human Enhancement*, 9–10. "Nel parlare di *enhancement* si fa riferimento sia a dei mezzi, ossia le applicazioni tecnologiche e le metodologie di potenziamento funzionale di parti del corpo, che a delle finalità, cioè il potenziamento di capacità o di caratteristiche individuali, e infine a un progetto più ampio, il miglioramento dell'uomo."

25. Buchanan, *Better than Human*, 5.

26. Buchanan, *Better than Human*, 4.

27. Bostrom, "Human Genetic Enhancements," 493.

28. Bostrom, "Human Genetic Enhancements," 493.

diagnosis (PGD), genetic manipulation (e.g., transgenesis) of gametes and embryos, nanotechnology, and brain-computer interfaces.

PGD allows for genetic screening of embryos created through *in vitro* fertilization (IVF). It is currently used to screen embryos according to sex and the existence of some gene-linked diseases. It is proposed that the same process could be used to screen "for genes that are likely to result in better than normal capacities."[29] Transgenesis involves the introduction of foreign genes that code for desired capacities in other species into the human genome. Nanotechnology aspires to develop further the science of prosthesis and implants, moving beyond artificial limbs and pacemakers toward "silicon chips and other electrical and computer prosthetic devices or implants."[30] Such technology could be utilized to enhance memory and vision, "to create artificial blood cells with greater life, durability, and oxygen carrying capacity," and indeed "to reconstruct and enhance all parts of the human body."[31] Finally, the combination of neuroscience and computer technology promises a range of possibilities for cognitive enhancement. "Already, chips have been introduced into human beings for the purposes of tracking and computer-assisted control of biological functions,"[32] and brain-computer interface technologies are "helping people who have lost their sight or their ability to move their limbs."[33] It is suggested that such technology can be further developed to enable "direct mind-reading and thought-sharing across human minds," as well as "uploading of human minds to artificially intelligent systems"[34] as a means of "cheating" death.

The feasibility of many of these techniques is yet to be proven. However, Bostrom is hopeful that the combination of already available technologies "could profoundly transform the human condition," predicting that the possibility of human enhancement will become an ever greater reality in the near future as "these and other anticipated technologies come online."[35]

---

29. Buchanan, *Better than Human*, 6.
30. Harris, *Enhancing Evolution*, 57.
31. Savulescu, "Human Prejudice," 214.
32. Savulescu, "Human Prejudice," 214.
33. Buchanan, *Better than Human*, 6.
34. Savulescu, "Human Prejudice," 214.
35. Bostrom, "History of Transhumanist Thought," 10. Bostrom makes a list of existing and imminent technologies: "Virtual reality; preimplantation genetic diagnosis; genetic engineering; pharmaceuticals that improve memory, concentration,

Theories of Enhancement

While the transhumanist project focuses mainly on biomedical enhancements, its supporters insist that such technology exists in continuity with non-biomedical forms which have enriched humanity in the past and have furthered the course of evolution. Literacy, numeracy, science and technology have each contributed to human flourishing, and made for a wealthier and more productive society.[36] Thus, rather than attempting a precise definition of enhancement, transhumanists generally cast their net widely to include all means which improve the human lot. In the words of Buchanan, enhancement is "ubiquitous."[37]

It is therefore supposed that "there is no morally significant difference between novel biomedical enhancements and all the other more familiar ways of enhancing."[38] Accordingly, Buchanan argues against what he calls a form of "biomedical enhancement exceptionalism," defined as "the dogmatic assumption that because an enhancement involves biotechnologies (pills, computers, fiddling with embryos, etc.) it's somehow off the moral scale."[39] He suggests that the moral challenges associated with biomedical enhancement have been associated with every previous enhancement initiative.[40]

In particular, it is proposed that biomedical enhancement, in its dependence on biotechnology, is consistent with the advances fostered by

---

wakefulness, and mood; performance-enhancing drugs; cosmetic surgery; sex change operations; prosthetics; anti-ageing medicine; closer human-computer interfaces: these technologies are already here or can be expected within the next few decades."

36. Buchanan, *Better than Human*, 10. He adds: "The great historical enhancements—the agrarian revolution, institutions, literacy, numeracy, and computers—have affected us profoundly; they've radically transformed human life and made us who we are" (24).

37. Buchanan, *Beyond Humanity?*, 38.

38. Savulescu and Bostrom, "Human Enhancement Ethics," 3. Cf. Bostrom, "In Defense of Posthuman Dignity," 213: "From the transhumanist standpoint, there is no need to behave as if there were a deep moral difference between technological and other means of enhancing human lives."

39. Buchanan, *Better than Human*, 10.

40. Buchanan, *Better than Human*, 24. Buchanan writes: "Every one of the historical nonbiomedical enhancements has created moral challenges—in many cases the same ones that biomedical enhancement will create. Neither the problem of bad unintended consequences, nor the worry about worsening existing injustices is unique to *biomedical* enhancements. In fact, these problems arise for technologies generally, not just enhancement technologies."

technology itself. As Savulescu and Bostrom write: "In one sense, *all* technology can be viewed as an enhancement of our native human capacities, enabling us to achieve certain effects that would otherwise require more effort or be altogether beyond our power."[41] They challenge those who object to human enhancement through biotechnology to demonstrate how it is essentially different from other acceptable forms; to "distinguish the problematic new types of enhancements from the unobjectionable use of shoes, clothes, tea, sleep, PDAs, literacy, forklifts, and the bulk of contemporary medicine."[42]

In taking up this challenge, Elena Colombetti suggests that such examples do not make sufficient distinction between enhancements and tools: that while shoes and forklifts enhance human performance, they remain, as tools, extraneous to the human subject—something that cannot be claimed for the effects of drugs and changes to the genome.[43] Kass makes a similar point. While acknowledging that many things in our lives are filtered or mediated through modern technology (e.g., telephones, internet, etc.), without us becoming overtly inauthentic or dehumanized in the process, he notes that they remain external to us. We can objectify them, see them working on us, and are free to distance ourselves from them.[44] But it is not so with biotechnological interventions that touch the very core of our being.

The Welfarist Approach to Enhancement

In continuity with this expansive vision of enhancement, Savulescu, together with Sandberg and Kahane, proposes a so-called "welfarist" definition of human enhancement. The welfarist model rests on a distinction between *functional* and *human* enhancements. In the first instance, functional enhancement concerns "the enhancement of some capacity or

---

41. Savulescu and Bostrom, "Human Enhancement Ethics," 2.

42. Savulescu and Bostrom, "Human Enhancement Ethics," 3.

43. "It would be more interesting," she writes, "to refer to vaccination, because of the change it causes in the organism, but here, too, we forget a critical distinction, which is the fact that a vaccination facilitates the organism to develop its own antibody. It is like a sort of training: a vaccine helps the body to prepare in advance the defence against some illnesses or diseases as it could be obtained after a successful fight against an illness. It is not at all an enhancement beyond the boundaries of a therapeutic purpose." Colombetti, "Contemporary Post-Humanism," 370.

44. Kass, "Ageless Bodies, Happy Souls," 23.

power (e.g., vision, intelligence, health)."[45] This seems to be the position taken by Bostrom. With Roache, he speaks of the enhancement of basic human capacities.[46] He defines enhancement as any "intervention that improves the functioning of some subsystem of an organism beyond its reference state; or that creates an entirely new functioning or subsystem that the organism previously lacked."[47] An improved subsystem is a more efficiently functioning one. In this functional model, enhancement is measured against the reference state of what is "the normal, healthy state of the subsystem, i.e., the level of functioning of the subsystem when it is not 'diseased' or 'broken' in any specific way."[48] He speaks of enhancements of self-control and concentration; of the ability to manage stress and to be an independent thinker; of withstanding pain and metabolic regulation.[49]

In highlighting the functional bias of this approach to enhancement, Savulescu et al. alert us to the specific focus "on *capacities, moods,* or *functions* that might be improved by the pharmacological (or other) intervention—'improved' in the sense of facilitating *more* of whatever it

---

45. Savulescu et al., "Well-Being and Enhancement," 3. Cf. Buchanan, *Beyond Humanity?*, 57: Enhancement is the "improvement of a capacity or function, with no assumption that this means an improvement in well-being overall, either for the individual who is enhanced or for society." And again: "A biomedical enhancement is a deliberate intervention, applying biomedical science, which aims to improve an existing capacity that most or all normal human beings typically have, or to create a new capacity, by acting directly on the body or brain. One advantage of this definition is that it helps us to avoid a simple mistake: thinking that an enhancement by definition makes one better off. Enhanced hearing, in a noisy environment, might make an easily distracted person worse off. Enhanced memory, unless accompanied by enhanced capacities to control the activation of memories or the management of their psychological effects, might also be problematic" (23).

46. Bostrom and Roache, "Ethical Issues in Human Enhancement," 120.

47. Bostrom, "Dignity and Enhancement," 179.

48. Bostrom, "Dignity and Enhancement," 179. However, having apparently established an objective standard by which enhancement can be measured, Bostrom immediately relativizes the reference state according to several potential parameters: "It could refer to the state that is normal for some particular individual when she is not subject to any specific disease or injury. This could either be age-relative or indexed to the prime of life. Alternatively, the reference state could be defined as the 'species-typical' level of functioning." Accordingly, Bostrom concludes that "when we say 'enhancement,' unless we further specify these and other indeterminacies, we do not express any very precise thought" (179).

49. Bostrom, "Dignity and Enhancement," 180.

is that the function normally does."⁵⁰ But an objection is raised that *more* does not always correspond to *better*, and that not all functional improvements are necessarily good for people.⁵¹ They even speak of diminishment as a form of enhancement, highlighting "cases in which 'subtractive' interventions—that is, interventions geared toward weakening a given capacity or function—might plausibly contribute to individual welfare enhancement."⁵²

Therefore, in contrast to a functional model of enhancement, *human* enhancement looks to "the enhancement of a human being's life."⁵³ In the determination of the ethics of enhancement, Savulescu et al. suggest that it is this concept of human enhancement that is important, since one does not simply look to changes in individual capacities, but must consider the effect of those changes on a human life.⁵⁴ While functional enhancements regard the capacities of individual systems, human

---

50. Earp et al., "When Is Diminishment," 2.

51. Earp et al., "When Is Diminishment," 4; Savulescu et al., "Well-Being and Enhancement," 6. For example, he suggests that enhancing the survival chances of a permanently unconscious patient may not correspond to his intrinsic good.

52. Earp et al., "When Is Diminishment," 2. Mention is made of Ashley, a child born with static encephalopathy, a severe brain impairment that left her unable to walk, talk, eat, sit up, or roll over, whose parents wanted to stunt her growth through a combination of oestrogen therapy and surgery to remove her uterus and breast buds, arguably in order to improve her quality of life. The authors write: "While parts of the treatment and even the motivations behind it may certainly be called into question, it is at least plausible to think that reducing Ashley's growth, all things considered, would count in favor of her own best interests. For example, Ashley's parents suggested that her smaller size would make it easier to carry her around, thus allowing her to participate more fully in the activities of daily living." Earp et al., "When Is Diminishment," 4. Cf. Liao et al., "Ashley Treatment."

53. Savulescu et al., "Well-Being and Enhancement," 3.

54. It would seem that there is general consensus on this point. Buchanan, who himself favors a functional interpretation of enhancement, nonetheless concedes that while an "enhancement is an improvement of some particular capacity," it is "not necessarily something that makes us better off *overall*." He adds: "Even when an enhancement would make you better off overall, it doesn't follow that you should undertake it. Sometimes, the right thing to do isn't the thing that improves your own situation—especially if doing so wrongly disadvantages someone else or if the improvement comes at the cost of violating some important moral rule or has the effect of undermining your character." Buchanan, *Better than Human*, 6. Kass, who fits neither the welfarist nor functional camps, similarly contends that the prospect of biomedical enhancement not only raises ethical issues of the proper ends of biotechnology, but more importantly concerns "the nature and meaning of human flourishing." Kass, "Ageless Bodies, Happy Souls," 10.

enhancement concerns "the goodness of a person's life, that is, his or her well-being."[55] Accordingly, they propose the *welfarist* definition of human enhancement, comprising "any change in the biology or psychology of a person which increases the chances of leading a good life in the relevant set of circumstances."[56]

Following the same logic, disability is defined as "any state of a person's biology or psychology which decreases the chance of leading a good life in the relevant set of circumstances."[57] This definition attempts to steer a course midway between *medical* and *social* models of disability: between disabilities defined as "conditions that are abnormal and negatively deviate from normal human species' functioning"[58] and disabilities considered disadvantageous because of social prejudice. The welfarist approach does not accord any moral significance to normal functioning, but neither does it reduce well-being and disability to mere social factors.[59] Admitting that the welfarist approach "does not use explicit evaluative and normative terms,"[60] Savulescu and Kahane nonetheless insist that the concept of well-being is inherently normative since well-being is intrinsically valuable.[61]

Within this broad definition, in which any reduction in well-being is constitutive of a disability, we are all "disabled" in some way.[62] From

55. Savulescu et al., "Well-Being and Enhancement," 7.

56. Savulescu et al., "Well-Being and Enhancement," 7.

57. Savulescu et al., "Well-Being and Enhancement," 12. Savulescu and Kahane elsewhere offer a more precise definition: "According to the welfarist account of disability, 'disability' should refer to any stable physical or psychological property of subject S that leads to a significant reduction of S's level of wellbeing in circumstances C, excluding the effect that this condition has on wellbeing that is due to prejudice against S by members of S's society." Savulescu and Kahane, "Disability," 45.

58. Savulescu and Kahane, "Disability," 45.

59. Savulescu and Kahane, "Disability," 45.

60. Savulescu and Kahane, "Disability," 46.

61. "When something reduces someone's wellbeing, then what is intrinsically bad is the harm it does—the reduction of wellbeing"; "If something leads to a reduction in someone's wellbeing, then that thing is bad for that person." Savulescu and Kahane, "Disability," 46.

62. "We all suffer from disabilities which are conditions inherent to our nature (biological, psychological or other) which either reduce the value of our lives or which make it more difficult to realize (in the sense that that [sic] they reduce the chances that we will achieve) a good life. Poor concentration, poor memory, poor visuospatial skills, poor emotional intelligence are just like asthma, a lame foot, pigheadedness and weakness of will. They are all disabilities on this definition." Savulescu et al., "Well-Being and Enhancement," 14.

the transhumanist perspective we are all "handicapped" by our human limitations: "restricted physical and mental capabilities, uncontrollable emotional and psychic disturbances, disease, and ultimately death."[63] Thus, merely *being* is reason enough to seek enhancement or improvement of one's situation. As Lomanno adds: "Any human limit is seen by transhumanists to be a flaw rather than simply a condition of the species."[64] And the diverse paths that lead us toward overcoming our "disabilities," all considered to be enhancements, are deemed equivalent. Accordingly, Savulescu et al. perceive no essential difference between procedures that aim at (1) the medical treatment of disease, (2) increasing natural human potential, and (3) *superhuman* enhancements (posthuman or transhuman).[65] In their opinion, each path can and should be legitimately pursued, and simply judged according to their capacity to increase well-being.

According to Savulescu, it is the connection with well-being and human goods that makes the welfarist model superior to alternative models of enhancement. In this context, he extends his criticism beyond the functional approach, taking aim also at models defined as the *sociological pragmatic*, the *ideological*, and the *therapy-enhancement* (not medicine) distinction.

In the first place, through its objectification of well-being as ethically normative, the welfarist model claims to avoid the relativism of the sociological pragmatic model. According to a *sociological pragmatic* approach, enhancement has no essential meaning since the value of human performance is determined by social, historical and cultural values. Ethically, therefore, there is no ground for judging the relative preferences of particular enhancements between given cultures. An enhancement is ethical when it is valued as such.

Furthermore, in its openness to anything which increases well-being, it is claimed that the welfarist approach avoids the so-called constraints—the "overly narrow or mistaken conception of human well-being"[66]—of the *ideological* approach. In Savulescu's analysis, the ideological approach, grounded in a particular metaphysical or spiritual

---

63. Lomanno, "Possibilities and Problems of Transhumanism," 59.
64. Lomanno, "Possibilities and Problems of Transhumanism," 64.
65. Savulescu et al., "Well-Being and Enhancement," 8.
66. Savulescu et al., "Well-Being and Enhancement," 8.

conception of the human person, canonizes "contentious value claims"[67] of what constitutes the human good, on the basis of which individual enhancements are judged. In contrast, the welfarist model, grounded not in ideology but in well-being, is open to something more than lists of value claims.

> It singles out well-being as one dimension of value that is constitutive of genuine human enhancement. But it leaves open substantive and contentious questions about the nature of well-being, and important empirical questions about the impact of some treatment on well-being.[68]

Finally, with its loose definition of well-being and disability, and its broad concept of enhancement as anything which increases the value of a person's life,[69] the welfarist model renders the distinction between therapy and enhancement irrelevant. Those who insist on a distinction between treatment/therapy and enhancement define enhancement as "going beyond health-restoring treatment or health."[70] In the definition of the President's Council, *therapy* concerns "the use of biotechnical power to treat individuals with known diseases, disabilities, or impairments, in an attempt to restore them to a normal state of health and fitness," while *enhancement* "is the directed use of biotechnical power to alter, by direct intervention, not disease processes but the 'normal' workings of the human body and psyche, to augment or improve their native capacities and performances";[71] to make us "better than well," as Michael Sandel puts it.[72] In its recourse to advances in biotechnology, modern medicine may use similar means to those proposed by transhumanism, but its goal is different: not to perfect human potentials, but "for the purposes of preventing and curing disease, reversing disabilities, and alleviating suffering."[73]

While some transhumanists are willing to admit a distinction between therapy and enhancement, they nonetheless downplay its ethical significance.[74] Thus Buchanan writes:

67. Savulescu et al., "Well-Being and Enhancement," 4.
68. Savulescu et al., "Well-Being and Enhancement," 7.
69. Savulescu et al., "Well-Being and Enhancement," 8.
70. Savulescu et al., "Well-Being and Enhancement," 4.
71. President's Council on Bioethics, *Beyond Therapy*, 13.
72. Sandel, "Case Against Perfection," 71.
73. President's Council on Bioethics, *Beyond Therapy*, 12.
74. "If we think of disease as an adverse departure from normal functioning, and

The mere fact that an intervention is an enhancement rather than a therapy does nothing to show that it is impermissible, or even morally problematic. Numeracy, literacy, and computers are all cognitive enhancements, but that doesn't count against them at all, morally speaking.[75]

They also object to strict terms of reference, as, for example, in restricting the "ends of medicine" to "treating and preventing disease, restoring normal functioning, and offering comfort and care for those who are ill or disabled."[76] Such "essentialist talk," as Buchanan calls it, confuses moral analysis. It does not allow an independent appraisal of the merits of enhancement. The claim that enhancement is not a legitimate end of medicine adds nothing to its moral evaluation.[77]

Transhumanists thus assert that the distinction between therapy and enhancement is ethically problematic "only for those who maintain that this distinction has practical or normative significance."[78] Since they themselves deny such significances, transhumanists remain unaffected by the distinction. As Bostrom and Roache write:

> Transhumanists hold that we should seek to develop and make available human enhancement options in the same way and for the same reasons that we try to develop and make available options for therapeutic medical treatments: in order to protect and expand life, health, cognition, emotional well-being, and other states or attributes that individuals may desire in order to improve their lives.[79]

In other words, whether an intervention is classified as a therapy or an enhancement, the goal is the same: the improvement of a person's life

---

therapy as aimed at preventing or curing disease, then the contrast with enhancement is clear: Enhancement aims to augment or improve normal functioning. In that sense, it aims to go beyond therapy." Buchanan, *Better than Human*, 5.

75. Buchanan, *Beyond Humanity?*, 26.

76. Buchanan, *Beyond Humanity?*, 27. An example of the mentality criticized by Buchanan is provided by Francis Fukuyama, who, in upholding the distinction between therapy and enhancement writes: "The original purpose of medicine is, after all, to heal the sick, not to turn healthy people into gods." Fukuyama, *Our Posthuman Future*, 208.

77. Buchanan, *Beyond Humanity?*, 27.

78. Bostrom and Roache, "Ethical Issues in Human Enhancement," 122.

79. Bostrom and Roache, "Ethical Issues in Human Enhancement," 122–23.

relative to their current condition. Accordingly, there is no significant moral difference between the two.

Objections to the Welfarist Approach

Relativism and Lack of Distinction

In response to Savulescu's welfarist model, several questions arise: Is it really normative for ethical enquiry? Does it succeed in distinguishing itself from other models? Does it offer a realistic vision of well-being and human flourishing?

In the first instance, it might be contended that the welfarist model fails to be normative for ethics, especially since well-being is afforded no substantive or normative content. In this context, Jürgen Habermas notes that contemporary concepts of well-being have been weakened by the rejection of a metaphysics of human nature in favor of a plurality of provisional and relative conceptions "of the 'good life' according to one's own abilities and choices."[80] But Habermas contends that this liberal approach, fully developed in the political liberalism of John Rawls, does not in itself mean the renunciation of "normative concerns."[81] Similarly, while rejecting intransigent claims to knowledge of human nature as divisive and intolerant, Italian philosopher Francesco Remotti recognizes the need to move "beyond relativism" (*oltre il relativismo*) toward a form of stabilization that avoids absolutes.[82] As evidence in the current context, one notes the attempts of Savulescu and Kahane to identify certain commonly held values that impinge on the goodness of life: the value of significant relationships and achievements, the presence or absence of pleasure and pain.[83] They also refer to what Buchanan et al., following Rawls, call "all-purpose" goods:[84] "traits that are valuable regardless of which kind of life a person chooses to live—valuable on all plausible conceptions of well-being."[85]

80. Habermas, *Future of Human Nature*, 2.

81. Habermas, *Future of Human Nature*, 3.

82. Remotti, *Contra natura*, 255.

83. Savulescu and Kahane, "Disability," 48.

84. Buchanan et al., *From Chance to Choice*, 174.

85. "They give us greater all-round capacities to experience a vast array of lives. Examples include memory, self-discipline, patience, empathy, a sense of humor, optimism, and just having a sunny temperament." Savulescu et al., "Well-Being and

But on what grounds are such goods decided? Why choose these particular goods and omit others that have traditionally been upheld: the goodness of life which is to be preserved, the goodness of raising and educating children, the good of religion in knowing the truth of God? And who decides what constitutes a good? When practically applied to the question of enhancement, one might ask, together with the church's magisterium: "who would be able to establish which modifications were to be held as positive and which not, or what limits should be placed on individual requests for improvement since it would be materially impossible to fulfil the wishes of every single person."[86] It is suggested that any attempt to respond to these questions could only "derive from arbitrary and questionable criteria" that prejudice "the will of some over the freedom of others," of the strong over the weak, amounting to "*an unjust domination of man over man.*"[87] Thus, in the determination of goods, the welfarist model is not only prone to the same relativism that it criticizes in other models, but also dangerously poised as a threat to human equality and the common good.

Regarding the question of its distinction, Francesca Giglio contends that the welfarist model is simply a variant of functionalism, in which better function equates with better life.[88] Despite protestations that the welfarist model is primarily concerned with enhancements that affect the goodness or well-being of a person's life, those enhancements are inevitably reduced to functional enhancements. Thus, in Savulescu's definition, enhancement constitutes an increased capacity: "to enhance any state of a person's biology or psychology which increases the chance of leading a

---

Enhancement," 11. Bostrom and Sandberg also offer a list of traits that promote individual well-being, including emotional well-being, freedom from severe or chronic pain, friendship and love, long-term memory, mathematical ability, awareness and consciousness, musicality, artistic appreciation and creativity, literary appreciation, confidence and self-esteem, healthy pleasures, mental energy, ability to concentrate, abstract thinking, longevity, and social skills. Bostrom and Sandberg, "Wisdom of Nature," 394.

86. CDF, *Dignitas personae*, n. 27.

87. CDF, *Dignitas personae*, n. 27.

88. Giglio, "*Enhancement*," 29. "La '*Welfarist Definition of Human Enhancement*' proposta da Julian Savulescu, sintetizzabile nell'equazione *miglor funzionamento = vita migliore*, sembra poter offrire la prospettiva mediante la quale penetrare il disegno del potenziamento tecnologico, inteso dai sostenitori non solo come lecito, ma moralmente obbligatorio."

good life."[89] In Giglio's critique, this reduction of well-being to function is symptomatic of an anthropology which diminishes the human person to his physiology; that does not take seriously his rational and spiritual nature.[90]

The inherent relativism (as noted above) of the welfarist model of enhancement has further consequences. In the first place, in its open-endedness it tends toward the infinite without any clear end-point in view. In this context, Kampowski makes a more nuanced distinction between therapy and enhancement than discussed to date. While therapy has in nature a point of reference by which interventions are judged to be better or worse, there is no such point of reference for enhancement.[91] In the absence of such criteria, the only norm for enhancement seems to be that "more is better."[92] But clearly, such is not always the case.[93]

The other consequence is that unfettered enhancement overlooks an essential human characteristic: that of the limits inherent to human ontology.[94] It has already been noted, and *Dignitas personae* confirms, that proposals of human enhancement through genetic engineering "exhibit a certain dissatisfaction or even rejection of the value of the human being as a finite creature and person."[95] But, as Giglio explains, when embraced

---

89. Savulescu, "Justice, Fairness, and Enhancement," 325. Cf. Landeweerd, "Asperger's Syndrome," 208.

90. Giglio, "*Enhancement*," 32. "Pensare ad un miglioramento della nostra natura in termini meramente funzionali è frutto di un'antropologia di carattere riduzionistico che esaurisce l'uomo nella fisiologia, mentre è davvero umano il bene che proviene dalla riflessione razionale dell'uomo su se stesso e sui suoi limiti, e sulla capacità di darsi dei fini."

91. Kampowski, *Ricordati della nascita*, 188. The President's Council similarly caution against "uncertain goals and absent natural standards, once one proceeds 'beyond therapy.'" President's Council on Bioethics, *Beyond Therapy*, 287.

92. "L'unico principio che orienta gli interventi oltre la terapia sembra essere questo: *se un poco è buono, di più è meglio.*" Kampowski, *Ricordati della nascita*, 188–89.

93. Kampowski gives the example of extending one's lifespan toward immortality. Drawing on the thought of Hans Jonas and Robert Spaemann, he contends that *more* life does not equate to a *better* life; that, in the absence of death, memory, passion for life, and intergenerational relations, as well as hopes for the future, would all be adversely affected. This will be discussed further in chapter 9.

94. Giglio, "*Enhancement*," 31. Cf. Moltisanti and Postigo Solana, "Transumanesimo," 221: "nell'età della tecnica perde sempre più consistenza, fino quasi a sfumare, un concetto che invece è centrale per comprendere appieno l'esperienza umana: il 'limite.'"

95. CDF, *Dignitas personae*, n. 27.

in free and dialectical self-reflection, the human person's limits are "the source of meaning and of values."[96] From this flows human rationality, constitutive of human nature, according to which human beings truly know themselves.[97] By inference, the denial of human limits should be considered irrational, a denial of truth, and meaningless. Accordingly, *Dignitas personae* advocates the need "of education in accepting human life in its concrete historical finite nature."[98] The recognition of our human limits is a concept that will be developed further in this work, being central to the anthropology of Joseph Ratzinger and fundamental to a vision of human hope that offers a realistic vision of human flourishing.

Enhancement and Perfectionism

In admitting the inherent functional bias within the transhumanist project, one may proceed to a further criticism: that it is essentially a project of perfectionism,[99] or of what Sandel refers to as "a Promethean aspiration to remake nature, including human nature, to serve our purposes and satisfy our desires."[100] Take as an example the following vision of Bostrom in which he envisages "aesthetic and contemplative pleasures whose blissfulness vastly exceeds what any human being has yet experienced": of beings with enhanced maturity and personal development due to "the opportunity to live for hundreds or thousands of years with full bodily and psychic vigor"; of beings with brilliant minds and enhanced intelligence, capable of reading books in seconds, of engaging in complex philosophical thought, and of producing artistic masterpieces; of beings capable of loving with a "love that is stronger, purer, and more secure than any human being has yet harbored."[101]

---

96. Giglio, "*Enhancement*," 31.

97. "Il limite costituisce tuttavia, per l'uomo, fonte di senso e di valori poiché, grazie all libertà egli può vivere tale condizione in modo dialettico, riflettendo intorno a se stesso: questa capacità, non riducibile a funzione, si identifica con la 'razionalità,' forma propria e vera natura dell'essere umano." Giglio, "*Enhancement*," 31.

98. CDF, *Dignitas personae*, n. 27.

99. Moltisanti and Postigo Solana, "Transumanesimo," 209. "Come ben si evince dal contenuto della *Dichiarazione*, l'obiettivo prioritario del transumanesimo consiste nel favorire lo sviluppo scientifico e tecnologico, considerato quale fattore fondamentale per il perfezionamento dell'essere umano."

100. Sandel, "Case Against Perfection," 78.

101. Bostrom, "Human Genetic Enhancements," 494–95.

True, not all transhumanists are as enthusiastic as Bostrom. Buchanan, for instance, offers a more sober account of the possibilities of enhancement, claiming "to steer a steady course between hysterical loathing and breathless optimism."[102] He dismisses the bioconservative charge of perfectionism as naïve,[103] stressing that there is a vast difference between the desire to *better* oneself and to *master* oneself. He then advances the more restrained view that enhancement does not aim at perfection but at survival, arguing that enhancement is necessary to maintain the *status quo*, to "help us sustain the good we now enjoy or, to put it negatively, prevent things from getting worse":[104] to slow the effects of aging and enhance immunity via tissue regeneration and tumor gene suppression; to reduce the risk of escalating violence through the moral enhancement of impulse control, enhanced sympathy, altruism, and moral imagination; to enhance our ability to extract nutrients from foods due to food shortage; to enhance fertility in light of increasing rates of infertility; to enhance the body's capacity for thermal regulation in face of climate change; to enhance immunity against virulent infectious diseases more easily spread in an era of globalization; or to develop skin cell resistance to cancer in light of a depleted ozone layer.[105] In this, Buchanan attempts to "turn the tables," so to speak, in the debate. "The reasonable alternative to the 'anti-enhancement' stance is not the 'pro-enhancement' stance but rather 'anti-anti-enhancement'—the rejection of the admonition to forego enhancement entirely."[106] According to this view, humanity cannot afford not to enhance. Its future existence depends on it. The desperate, pessimistic undertones in this argument open a different perspective to the foundations of transhumanist hope.

Enhancement and Eugenics

Yet, despite these protestations, the specter of perfectionism looms large over the transhumanist project. *Dignitas personae* speaks of a "eugenic mentality" (*eugeneticum mentis habitum*) both implicit in, and encouraged

---

102. Buchanan, *Better than Human*, 24.
103. Buchanan, *Better than Human*, 9; Buchanan, *Better than Human*, 79.
104. Buchanan, *Better than Human*, 77.
105. Buchanan, *Better than Human*, 77–78; Buchanan, *Beyond Humanity?*, 56.
106. Buchanan, *Beyond Humanity?*, 14.

by, attempts to enhance the human lot through genetic engineering.[107] Here too, transhumanists are quick to defend themselves against the suspicion of a eugenic agenda,[108] attempting to normalize eugenics[109] and drawing a distinction between the public and coercive eugenic practices of the past and a new eugenics of consent and cooperation.[110] In developing this final point, Savulescu attempts to distinguish his principle of *procreative beneficence* (see chapter 7) from the old eugenics.

> Eugenics is selective breeding to produce a better *population*. A *public interest* justification for interfering in reproduction is different from Procreative Beneficence which aims a producing the best child, of the possible children, a couple could have. This is an essentially private enterprise. It was the eugenics movement itself which sought to influence reproduction, through involuntary sterilization, to promote social goods.[111]

The implication is that a *privatized* or *free-market* eugenics, free from coercion, should be accepted as a legitimate reproductive choice.[112]

---

107. CDF, *Dignitas personae*, n. 27.

108. "Another source of unease about genetic intervention are the perceived parallels between current discussions of enhancement and the coercive eugenics programmes of the last century, and the idea that enhancement may foster beliefs about some people being fundamentally inferior to others (this latter concern is sometimes expressed as the concern that enhancement would undermine human dignity). Advocating enhancement, however, has no necessary link with coercive eugenics, nor with the belief that some people are fundamentally inferior to others." Bostrom and Roache, "Ethical Issues in Human Enhancement," 148.

109. "There are many methods, low- and high-tech, by which we influence the character of new persons being brought into the world. At one end of the spectrum, mate choice has an obvious effect on what our children will be like, and the quality of prospective offspring is one factor that can influence our choice of romantic partners. According to evolutionary psychology, sexual attraction is often keyed to a subconscious assessment of the genetic quality of a potential mate (along with other factors). These factors can also be taken into account when we consciously deliberate to select among romantic prospects. We can also achieve 'eugenic' objectives by exerting choice over the timing of conception—for example, by taking into account the increasing risk of birth defects associated with conceiving at an older age." Savulescu and Bostrom, "Human Enhancement Ethics," 10.

110. "Savulescu argues instead that he advocates a new kind of eugenics that is essentially different from the early eugenics movement: what was particularly objectionable about that movement, he says, was the coercive imposition of a state-approved vision for a healthy population." Güell Pelayo, "Post-humanist Embryo," 429.

111. Savulescu, "Procreative Beneficence," 424.

112. Bostrom adds: "Transhumanists argue that the best way to avoid a *Brave New*

But as Sandel suggests, the concern over eugenics is not limited to public policy and state coercion, but is more deeply rooted in an attitude that views human life as a commodity. It is a more subtle form of coercion that penetrates to the very heart of our thinking about others. "The problem with eugenics and genetic engineering is that they represent the one-sided triumph of wilfulness over giftedness, of dominion over reverence, of moulding over beholding."[113]

As Habermas adds, this "triumph" of our dominion over human nature, that through genetic engineering allows scientists "to take evolution in their own hands," portends a loss of distinction between the subjective and the objective, between the *naturally grown* and the *made*.[114] He warns that this dedifferentiation threatens "our ethical self-understanding as a species in a way that could also affect our moral consciousness"[115]—transforming our "moral landscape," as Sandel expresses it, by radically altering our concepts of humility, responsibility, and solidarity[116]—and hindering our capacity "to conceive of ourselves as the authors of our own lives and as equal members of the moral community."[117]

Enhancement and Giftedness

Thus, the idea advanced by Sandel is that the charge of perfectionism and eugenics is not primarily aimed at particular enhancements or human traits, but concerns a fundamental attitude toward the goodness of being. The distortion "lies less in the perfection it seeks than in the human disposition it expresses and promotes."[118] In the first place, Sandel

---

World is by vigorously defending morphological and reproductive freedoms against any would-be world controllers. . . . Because people are likely to differ profoundly in their attitudes toward human enhancement technologies, it is crucial that no single solution be imposed on everyone from above, but that individuals get to consult their own consciences as to what is right for themselves and their families." Bostrom, "In Defense of Posthuman Dignity," 206.

113. Sandel, "Case Against Perfection," 85.

114. "What is at stake is a dedifferentiation, through biotechnology, of deep-rooted categorical distinctions which we have as yet, in the description we give ourselves, assumed to be invariant." Habermas, *Future of Human Nature*, 42.

115. Habermas, *Future of Human Nature*, 42.

116. Sandel, "Case Against Perfection," 86.

117. Habermas, *Future of Human Nature*, 42.

118. Sandel, "Case Against Perfection," 80.

criticizes the striving for perfection as being dismissive of the giftedness of our being.

> To acknowledge the giftedness of life is to recognize that our talents and powers are not wholly our own doing, despite the effort we expend to develop and to exercise them. It is also to recognize that not everything in the world is open to whatever use we may desire or devise. Appreciating the gifted quality of life constrains the Promethean project and conduces to a certain humility. It is in part a religious sensibility. But its resonance reaches beyond religion.[119]

As Sandel notes, the acknowledgment of the giftedness of life, though symphonic with religious faith in a creator God, does not presume a religious foundation and can equally be upheld by secular values.[120]

Kass similarly takes up this concept of gift. He contends that "we need more than generalized appreciation for nature's gifts. We need a particular regard and respect for the special gift that is our own given nature."[121] In this he adds something important to Sandel's argument, recognizing two meanings to the word *given*: (1) as "bestowed as gift," as Sandel intends it; and (2) as something "granted."[122] It is in this second sense that human nature can be regarded as gift, bestowed on us, and of fixed and defined content. He adds:

> In short, only if there is a human givenness, or a given humanness, that is also *good* and worth respecting, either as we find it or as it could be perfected without ceasing to be itself, does the "given" serve as a *positive* guide for choosing what to alter and what to leave alone. Only if there is something precious in the given—beyond the mere fact of its giftedness—does what is given serve as a source of restraint against efforts that would degrade it.[123]

---

119. Sandel, "Case Against Perfection," 78.

120. This in spite of objections by the likes of Peter Singer, who doubts that the concept of life as "gift" can be explained independently of belief in God. "If there is no God, life can only be a gift from one's parents. And if that is the case, wouldn't we all prefer parents who try to make the gift as good as possible, rather than leaving everything to chance?" Singer, "Parental Choice," 279.

121. Kass, "Ageless Bodies, Happy Souls," 20.

122. Kass, "Ageless Bodies, Happy Souls," 19–20.

123. Kass, "Ageless Bodies, Happy Souls," 20.

As this study proceeds, it will be noted that several factors prevent transhumanists from accepting the giftedness of human nature, particularly in their denial of a Giver and refutation of a substantive human nature. Behind both denials stands the transhumanist conception of nature that is typically negative. Bostrom writes:

> Transhumanists counter that nature's gifts are sometimes poisoned and should not always be accepted. Cancer, malaria, dementia, ageing, starvation, unnecessary suffering, and cognitive shortcomings are all among the presents that we would wisely refuse. Our own species-specified natures are a rich source of much of the thoroughly unrespectable and unacceptable—susceptibility for disease, murder, rape, genocide, cheating, torture, racism. The horrors of nature in general, and of our own nature in particular, are so well documented that it is astonishing that somebody as distinguished as Leon Kass should still in this day and age be tempted to rely on the natural as a guide as to what is desirable or normatively right. We should be grateful that our ancestors were not swept away by the Kassian sentiment, or we would still be picking lice off each other's backs.[124]

As a reflection of the contradictions that plague human nature, there is no denying the reality of Bostrom's point: nature, and human nature in particular, can frequently be *nasty* and *brutish*. But as the basis for a genuine anthropology and ethics, Bostrom's vision is particularly gloomy. It would thus seem to be a precarious foundation on which to set transhumanist hopes for humanity.

Summary

From this opening chapter, it appears that while projected as an aspiration, a hope, for the future—the "new frontier" of exploration—the transhumanist movement is in reality propelled by a sense of frustration with our current lot. The sense of dissatisfaction for the present human condition—the sense that we are "not good enough"—gives birth to the transhumanist dream that opens toward a posthuman future.[125] Thus, from the beginning, one can identify a tension between aspirations of hope and dissatisfaction, which provides the rationale for this current

---

124. Bostrom, "In Defense of Posthuman Dignity," 205.

125. Faggioni, "La natura fluida," 418. "Il sogno transumanista nasce dall' insoddisfazione per la condizione umana naturale."

work, and in which I suggest that transhumanism's hope is a façade for profound despair for the limitations that define our human nature.

Problems have also been identified in defining the object or goal of transhumanist hope. Without a precise definition of enhancement, encapsulated within the vague outlines of the welfarist approach, the ends of human enhancement remain unclear and its ethical evaluation plagued by relativism. Thus, rather than being the foundation of a concept of well-being, such imprecision is an obstacle to an understanding of human flourishing and genuine hope.

Chapter 2

The Science of Enhancement

IN FILLING OUT THE object of transhumanist hope, this chapter examines five key projects for human enhancement: cognitive enhancement, physical enhancement, mood enhancement, moral enhancement, and lifespan extension.

Cognitive Enhancement

Transhumanists of the "Oxford School" are united in their definition of cognitive enhancement: "Cognitive enhancement may be defined as the amplification or extension of core capacities of the mind through improvement or augmentation of internal or external information-processing systems."[1] Enhancements could target any of the cognitive faculties: perception, attention, understanding, memory, reasoning, and coordination of motor outputs,[2] as well as "planning, problem solving, and self-monitoring."[3] According to this broad definition, any improvement in cognitive function may be regarded as an enhancement, without creating extraordinary or super-human cognitive capacities, but also without requiring the correction of a pathology or dysfunction.

---

1. Sandberg and Savulescu, "Social and Economic Impacts," 93; Bostrom and Roache, "Smart Policy," 138; Sandberg, "Cognition Enhancement," 71; Bostrom and Sandberg, "Cognitive Enhancement," 311.

2. Bostrom and Sandberg, "Cognitive Enhancement," 312.

3. Housden et al., "Cognitive Enhancing Drugs," 113.

Modes of Cognitive Enhancement

Cognitive enhancements are differentiated according to the mode of technological intervention, as either *internal* (pharmacological modifications, genetic interventions, transcranial magnetic stimulation, and neural implants) or *external* (schooling, writing, software, ultraportable computers, and memory arts).[4] Otherwise, they are differentiated as *conventional* (education, mental techniques, neurological health, and external systems) or as *unconventional* (drugs, implants, and direct brain-computer interfaces).[5] Indeed, one of the first steps in the transhumanist project is to demythologize the specter of biotechnological enhancements by presenting them within the context of conventional techniques. The newer, more radical proposals for cognitive enhancement are posed in continuity with the established forms of education,[6] with methods of mental training,[7] and the use of external aids such as

---

4. Sandberg and Savulescu, "Social and Economic Impacts," 94.

5. Sandberg and Savulescu, "Social and Economic Impacts," 94.

6. "[Cognitive enhancement] exists within a broad spectrum of practices, some of which have been practiced for thousands of years. The prime example is education and training, where the goal is often not only to impart specific skills or information, but also to improve general mental faculties such as concentration, memory, and critical thinking." Sandberg, "Cognition Enhancement," 72.

7. Including memorization and visualization techniques, mnemonics and rhyming, as well as yoga, martial arts, meditation. "General mental activity—'working the brain muscle'—can improve performance and long-term health, while relaxation techniques can help regulate the activation of the brain." Bostrom and Sandberg, "Cognitive Enhancement," 315. "Training specific cognitive skills by increasing blood to certain neural networks through cognitive problem solving may also be beneficial to overall cognitive function." Housden et al., "Cognitive Enhancing Drugs," 121.

calculators and computers,[8] as well as with the cognitively enhancing effects of nutrition,[9] exercise,[10] sleep,[11] and health promotion.[12]

Of the internal modes of cognitive enhancement, attention is drawn to the wide acceptance of certain drugs to enhance concentration and memory. In the first place there are stimulants such as nicotine and caffeine. These work "by increasing neuronal activation or by releasing neuromodulators, facilitating the synaptic changes that underlie learning."[13] Note is also made of the popularity of herbal remedies and other supplements to improve memory.[14] From there, it is considered a small step to the acceptance of other pharmaceuticals that have been shown to enhance cognition in healthy individuals:[15] drugs such as Modafinil, developed for the treatment of narcolepsy, and Methylphenidate (Ritalin), used in the treatment of Attention Deficit Hyperactivity Disorder (ADHD).[16] The

---

8. "Progress in computing and information technology has vastly increased our ability to collect, store, analyze, and communicate information. External hardware and software supports now routinely give humans beings [sic] effective cognitive abilities that in many respects far outstrip those of our biological brains. Another important area of progress has been in 'collective cognition'—cognition distributed across many minds." Bostrom and Roache, "Smart Policy," 139.

9. For example, studies suggest that supplementing a mother's diet during pregnancy with docosahexaenoic acid (DHA), and infant formulas with the same, can improve cognitive performance and IQ in children. Bostrom and Sandberg, "Cognitive Enhancement," 320. It is also noted that an "easy and cheap approach to increasing cognitive functioning is to treat the two billion people worldwide suffering from iodine deficiency, the world's most common cause of preventable mental impairment." Bostrom and Roache, "Smart Policy," 146.

10. Maslen et al., "Pharmacological Cognitive Enhancement," 1.

11. Housden et al., "Cognitive Enhancing Drugs," 121.

12. "Improving general health has cognition-enhancing effects. Many health problems act as distracters or directly impair cognition. Improving sleep, immune function, and general conditioning promotes cognitive functioning." Bostrom and Sandberg, "Cognitive Enhancement," 314.

13. Bostrom and Sandberg, "Cognitive Enhancement," 316.

14. In addition to the popularity of Ginkgo biloba, the authors note: "In an ordinary supermarket or health food store we can find a veritable cornucopia of energy drinks and similar preparations, vying for consumers hoping to turbo-charge their brains." Bostrom and Roache, "Smart Policy," 138.

15. "Indeed, some neuroscientists do not believe there is a great difference between taking methylphenidate or Modafinil and drinking coffee. Therefore, the idea of enhancing cognition in healthy people is not a new one, and using pharmacological tools is certainly not the only way to achieve improvements in cognitive skill." Housden et al., "Cognitive Enhancing Drugs," 121.

16. Maslen et al., "Pharmacological Cognitive Enhancement," 1.

use of such drugs is already a phenomenon among university students seeking to increase alertness, aid concentration,[17] and improve examination performance,[18] and among certain professionals such as pilots[19] and academics.[20]

With advances in the scientific understanding of the cognitive faculties, the hope is to develop specifically nootropic (or "smart") drugs with the potential to enhance cognition.[21] Increasingly, research is being directed toward drugs related to the cholinergic system[22] due to its involvement in focusing attention and encoding memory.[23] "The goal is to develop drugs that not only allow the brain to learn quickly, but which also facilitate selective retention of the information that has been learned."[24]

Beyond drugs, there is the possibility of enhancing cognition through other biotechnologies. One example is Transcranial Magnetic Stimulation (TMS), which aims to "increase or decrease the excitability of the cortex, thereby changing its level of plasticity."[25] Another is the potential offered by genetic technology. It has already been demonstrated that memory can be genetically enhanced in rats and mice.[26] However, transferring such successes into the human population is not straightforward.

17. Housden et al., "Cognitive Enhancing Drugs," 118.
18. Bostrom and Roache, "Smart Policy," 142.
19. "Modafinil, a drug that combats narcolepsy and induces wakefulness more generally, has been shown to enhance the performance of airplane pilots, commercial and military." President's Council on Bioethics, *Beyond Therapy*, 104.
20. "Academic staff, as well as students, are taking cognitive-enhancing drugs, as reported by an informal survey, to counteract the effects of jet lag, to enhance productivity or mental energy, and to deal with demanding and important mental challenges." Housden et al., "Cognitive Enhancing Drugs," 118.
21. Examples include cholinergic agonists, drugs of the piracetam family, ampakines, and consolidation enhancers. Bostrom and Sandberg, "Cognitive Enhancement," 316.
22. Examples of acetylcholinesterase inhibitors include donepezil, rivastigmine, and galantamine. Maslen et al., "Pharmacological Cognitive Enhancement," 4.
23. "There is a relationship between the functional loss of the neurotransmitter acetylcholine and memory loss. This loss of acetylcholine production in the brain can be compensated for by cholinesterase inhibitors, which are drugs that stop the breakdown of acetylcholine in the synapse by the enzyme cholinesterase." Housden et al., "Cognitive Enhancing Drugs," 116.
24. Bostrom and Sandberg, "Cognitive Enhancement," 317.
25. Bostrom and Sandberg, "Cognitive Enhancement," 318.
26. Sandberg, "Cognition Enhancement," 75.

Even though the "cellular machinery of memory appears to be highly conserved in evolution,"[27] the genetics of intelligence is complicated and variable, suggesting that "genetic enhancement of intelligence through direct insertion of a few beneficial alleles is unlikely to have a big enhancing effect."[28]

Existing external methods of cognitive enhancement include external hardware (pen and paper, calculators, personal computers) and software systems that help "display information, keep multiple items in memory, and perform routine tasks."[29] However, future developments in technology promise more intimate links between external systems and human users through the creation of what is referred to as an *exoself*, "embedding the human within an augmenting 'shell' such as wearable computers or virtual reality, or through smart environments in which objects are given extended capabilities."[30] It is suggested that the external-internal divide can be further bridged by the creation of brain-computer interfaces. Technology has developed to the point of being able to implant electrodes in brains, and to design computers that can interpret the brain's signals. Clinically, such technology is already utilized in cochlear implants to cure deafness, stands behind ongoing research into artificial retinas,[31] and offers hope as a treatment for paralysis.[32] It is also proposed that the technology could be directed toward creating new senses as an enhancement of the cognitive faculty of perception: an extension of the spectral range of the human eye to include ultraviolet light,[33] or

---

27. Sandberg, "Cognition Enhancement," 76.
28. Sandberg, "Cognition Enhancement," 76.
29. Bostrom and Sandberg, "Cognitive Enhancement," 320.
30. Bostrom and Sandberg, "Cognitive Enhancement," 320. They add: "Given the availability of external memory support, from writing to wearable computers, it is likely that the crucial form of memory demand on humans in the future will increasingly be the ability to link information into usable concepts, associations, and skills rather than the ability to memorize large amounts of raw data. Storage and retrieval functions can often be offloaded from the brain, while the knowledge, strategies, and associations linking the data to skilled cognition cannot so far be outsourced to computers to the same extent (321).
31. Bostrom and Sandberg, "Cognitive Enhancement," 321.
32. "Early experiments on humans have shown that it is possible for profoundly paralyzed patients to control a computer cursor using just a single electrode implanted in the brain." Bostrom and Sandberg, "Cognitive Enhancement," 321.
33. Sandberg, "Cognition Enhancement," 78.

the creation of magnetic sensitivity.³⁴ While technology is currently limited, there exist future prospects for even more direct brain-computer interfaces, such as uploading human minds to artificially intelligent systems, as well as the possibility of "direct mind-reading and thought-sharing across human minds."³⁵

Reasons for Cognitive Enhancement

Proponents of cognitive enhancement outline both its individual and collective benefits. At the individual level it is suggested that increased cognition both reduces risks (social, economic, and physical) and enhances prospects.³⁶ At the societal level, it is claimed that cognitive enhancement could improve the economy by reducing losses and increasing individual welfare.³⁷ Such predictions work on the basis that if small, widespread decreases in intelligence (e.g., through lead-contaminated water) have been associated with a general economic downturn, then "it is plausible that a small *increment* would have positive effects of a similar magnitude."³⁸

It is also argued that cognitive enhancements offer particular benefits for employment, not only in terms of the ethically problematic context of securing an advantage over other applicants or employees, but more persuasively as a benefit to certain occupations: occupations that include high risks and stress (such as soldiers, pilots, workers in the oil industry, or those working at great heights), or those that involve irregular hours or require extended periods of awareness (such as shift workers, nurses and drivers). It is even suggested that cognitive enhancements might become obligatory in professions of heightened responsibility, such as doctors and pilots.³⁹

Ultimately, cognitive enhancement is proposed as a means of fulfilling individual goals and enhancing general well-being. Such goals could include "to perform better at work, to learn a skill or language quicker, to

34. Sandberg, "Cognition Enhancement," 79.
35. Savulescu, "Human Prejudice," 214.
36. Bostrom and Roache, "Smart Policy," 140.
37. Sandberg and Savulescu, "Social and Economic Impacts," 95.
38. Sandberg and Savulescu, "Social and Economic Impacts," 98; Bostrom and Roache, "Smart Policy," 141. Cf. Bostrom and Ord, "Reversal Test," 656–79.
39. Sandberg and Savulescu, "Social and Economic Impacts," 103.

decrease the need for rest in leisure time, or even just to experience one's mind as 'sharper.'"[40] Proponents of enhancement adopt a quite liberal attitude in this regard. It is even noted that among current users of cognitive enhancements, beyond reasons of study and employment, there are some who use simply in order "to facilitate completion of household chores."[41]

Ethical Concerns of Cognitive Enhancement

Needless to say, a range of ethical concerns are raised in relation to the prospect of cognitive enhancement. In the first place is the question of *safety* and *effectiveness*. In the case of pharmaceutical enhancements this includes the significant risk of side effects, not only due to the specific action of the drugs involved, but also related to broader effects of a physiological or psychological nature. The significance of such risks is heightened when one considers that the effectiveness of these treatments is currently limited and their future prospects somewhat speculative. However, enhancement proponents justify such risks on the basis of personal autonomy. They look to cosmetic surgery as setting a precedent. "The consensus is that patient autonomy overrides at least minor medical risks even when the procedure does not reduce or prevent morbidity."[42] It is suggested that a similar model be adopted for medical cognitive enhancements, with the consumer weighing risks and benefits according to their "personal goals" and "way of life."[43]

Concerns related to personal authenticity are also raised in objection to cognitive enhancement. It is feared that, in relying on technology to enhance cognitive capacity, one would not *own* his or her achievements. Stephan Kampowski gives the example of an air traffic controller using cognitive enhancing medications in order to remain alert over long periods of time. In raising the flag of inauthenticity, Kampowski suggests that such enhancement signifies a form of dehumanization. In the first instance, it dehumanizes through substituting technology for virtue.[44]

40. Maslen et al., "Pharmacological Cognitive Enhancement," 3.
41. Maslen et al., "Pharmacological Cognitive Enhancement," 3.
42. Bostrom and Sandberg, "Cognitive Enhancement," 323.
43. Bostrom and Sandberg, "Cognitive Enhancement," 323.
44. Kampowski, *Ricordati della nascita*, 194. He adds: "Qui la tecnologia ci appare come una scorciatoia che ci promette di ottenere qualche effetto su noi stessi senza

> It would mean asking a whole professional group to abdicate their humanity in order to be allowed to exercise their profession. It would mean to ask of them that their job performance be no longer the result of their own excellence or virtue bur rather the result of a pill.[45]

Kampowski suggests that our age is particularly susceptible to replacing "virtue—human excellence—by technology to get results without efforts."[46] He gives the examples of taking pills to increase strength without exercise, to lose weight without curbing intake, or to plan a family (through contraception) without abstinence. To this list he adds the desire to know (through cognitive enhancement) without learning. "Hence we seek the solution in a pill or a similar technological device that saves us the trouble of forming ourselves by our own volitional control. Technology can be the easy shortcut. The danger with shortcuts is that sometimes they make us miss our aim."[47]

Kampowski then suggests a second way in which cognitive enhancement might be considered as dehumanizing, in diminishing the subject to the status of a machine. We pump more into the person in order to get more results. Thus, in the example given, the air traffic controller is drugged-up in order to make him more productive. But in response Kampowski asks:

> Could it ever be licit to ask people to perform a job in which they are no longer allowed to be human? If the job is so complex that it can no longer be done by one "unenhanced" human being, then maybe it should be broken down, so that it can be done by two or three. What should not be done is to treat human beings as if they were machines.[48]

In this sense, authenticity demands an acknowledgment of human limitations and a willingness to act in solidarity with others.

Proponents of enhancement approach the question of authenticity from a different perspective. Savulescu and others begin by asking whether or not an intervention "helps a person to achieve her autonomous

---

passare per l'esercizio della disciplina o della virtù, anzi rendendolo superfluo" (195).

45. Kampowski, "Technology, Virtue, and the Brave New World," 559.
46. Kampowski, "Technology, Virtue, and the Brave New World," 559.
47. Kampowski, "Technology, Virtue, and the Brave New World," 560.
48. Kampowski, "Technology, Virtue, and the Brave New World," 559.

goals."[49] In this interpretation, if a cognitive enhancement could "help an individual to concentrate better so that he or she can achieve the goals he or she values, this acts in service of authenticity rather than undermines it."[50] It is therefore argued that enhancement is not a passive process of letting something happen, but of actively pursuing a certain goal which the intervention enables. Similarly, Bostrom and Anders Sandberg maintain that "shortcuts to excellence" are acceptable when higher goals are sought. They give the example of learning mathematics, in which in early stages the use of calculators is banned in order for students to grasp the basics of arithmetic, but are allowed later on, once the basics have been mastered, in order for students to progress to more advanced concepts. On this basis, they suggest "that cognitive enhancement aimed at extending and completing a person's talents may promote authenticity by offloading irrelevant, repetitive, or boring tasks and enabling a person to concentrate on more complex challenges that relate in more interesting ways to his or her goals and interests."[51]

Concerns about authenticity and virtue also find expression in the objection that cognitive enhancement is a form of cheating and against fair play. Leon Kass writes:

> Yet in those areas of human life in which excellence has until now been achieved only by discipline and effort, the attainment of those achievements by means of drugs, genetic engineering, or implanted devices looks to be "cheating" or "cheap." We believe—or until only yesterday believed—that people should work hard for their achievements. "Nothing good comes easily."[52]

Kass would seem to suggest that students taking Modafinil and Ritalin in order to improve examination performance are guilty of cheating. However, proponents of enhancement disagree. In the first place, Bostrom and Sandberg contend that the substance of cheating "depends on the agreed game rules for different activities."[53] They use the analogy of sport: "To pick up the ball with one's hands is cheating in golf and soccer, but not in handball or American football."[54] When applied to the

49. Maslen et al., "Pharmacological Cognitive Enhancement," 5.
50. Maslen et al., "Pharmacological Cognitive Enhancement," 5.
51. Bostrom and Sandberg, "Cognitive Enhancement," 326.
52. Kass, "Ageless Bodies, Happy Souls," 21.
53. Bostrom and Sandberg, "Cognitive Enhancement," 328.
54. Bostrom and Sandberg, "Cognitive Enhancement," 328.

context of school exams, the determination of cheating will depend on the aims of education.

> If school is to be regarded as a competition for grades, then enhancers would arguably be cheating. . . . But if school is seen as being significantly about the acquisition of information and learning, then cognitive enhancements may have a legitimate and useful role to play.[55]

While Kampowski agrees that education is not only about achieving good grades, he baulks at the idea that it is simply a matter of acquiring information. It is also about learning discipline and mastery of self, of assimilating information and internalizing it.[56]

The second point raised by transhumanists about cognitive enhancement and cheating draws on a differentiation between *positional* and *intrinsic* goods. "A positional good is one whose value is dependent on others not having it."[57] If cognition is considered a positional good, an object of competition with others, then enhancement could be considered a form of cheating.[58] However, proponents of cognitive enhancement deny that cognition is merely a positional good. "They are also intrinsically desirable: their immediate value to the possessor does not entirely depend on other people lacking them. Having a good memory or a creative mind is normally valuable in its own right, whether or not other people also possess similar excellences."[59]

---

55. Bostrom and Sandberg, "Cognitive Enhancement," 328.

56. "In un esame non conta soltanto il buon voto, ma conta molto di più lo studio e la disciplina. In questo modo, lo studente non impara soltanto la materia, ma impara anche il dominio di sé, la disciplina che ogni studio serio comporta." Kampowski, *Ricordati della nascita*, 195.

57. Sandberg, "Cognition Enhancement," 83.

58. Bostrom and Sandberg add: "If cognitive enhancements were purely positional goods, then the pursuit of such enhancements would be a waste of time, effort, and money. People might become embroiled in a cognitive 'arms race,' spending significant resources merely in order to keep up with the Joneses. One person's gain would produce an offsetting negative externality of equal magnitude, resulting in no net gain in social utility to compensate for the costs of the enhancement efforts." Bostrom and Sandberg, "Cognitive Enhancement," 328.

59. Bostrom and Sandberg, "Cognitive Enhancement," 328; Sandberg, "Cognition Enhancement," 83.

Physical Enhancement

The prospect of physical enhancement is usually discussed in the context of doping in sport. While the transhumanist project for enhancement goes beyond this controversy, it serves to highlight the possibilities for physical enhancement and introduces some of the ethical concerns surrounding it. It can also serve as a case study for human enhancement in general, as noted in *Beyond Therapy*.[60]

Modes of Physical Enhancement

In the first instance, interventions are directed toward the enhancement of existing physical powers: to increase muscle mass, prolong endurance, or sharpen eyesight. These may range from specialized training regimes and protein-rich diets,[61] to elective surgery,[62] prosthetic devices,[63] and designer drugs. In the context of enhancements in sport, most attention is drawn to the latter. While international sporting authorities are vigilant against the use of performance enhancing drugs, voices of dissent exist among enhancement supporters.[64]

Among those drugs currently banned in sport, though demonstrably the most effective for physical enhancement, three main categories may be identified. First, there is human growth hormone (HGH), a pituitary hormone that has effects on physical stature and bulk. Clinically, HGH has been used "in attempts to enhance muscle size and strength, especially in the elderly."[65] It is also routinely used as a treatment for dwarfism and other growth-related disorders, but its *therapeutic* use has also been extended "to help the normally short to become taller."[66] HGH effects muscle growth only indirectly. It works through promoting the liver's secretion of insulin-like growth factor 1 (IGF–1), which has

---

60. President's Council on Bioethics, *Beyond Therapy*, 106.
61. Miah, "Physical Enhancement," 267.
62. "One example of this is laser eye surgery, which was famously utilized by world champion golfer Tiger Woods." Miah, "Physical Enhancement," 270.
63. Miah, "Physical Enhancement," 269.
64. Savulescu et al., "Why We Should Allow Performance Enhancing Drugs"; Savulescu and Foddy, "Le Tour."
65. President's Council on Bioethics, *Beyond Therapy*, 120.
66. President's Council on Bioethics, *Beyond Therapy*, 104.

anabolic effects through the promotion of muscle and organ growth.[67] A variant of IGF-1 is produced directly by muscles (mIGF-1) "in response to stretching the muscles during exercise."[68] This muscle variant acts locally to enhance and repair muscle and is therefore not detected in the blood stream.

Another physically enhancing drug is erythropoietin (EPO). EPO is naturally produced by the body as a stimulant to the production of red blood cells. A synthetic form of EPO (rHuEPO) can be injected to increase the body's haematocrit, thus augmenting the oxygen-carrying capacity of blood. This approach is another indirect means of muscle enhancement, "not by enlarging muscle size but by increasing muscle endurance."[69] The use of EPO follows earlier attempts at "blood doping" through autologous transfusions, in which blood taken from athletes was separated, the red blood cells concentrated, and then re-infused into the athletes' blood stream.[70]

Finally, there are the commonly used and well-known anabolic steroids.[71] These testosterone-like hormones function both locally to promote muscle development, as well as centrally on the pituitary to increase levels of HGH. "Used in combination with weight training and special diets, they can greatly increase muscle size and strength."[72] New generation steroids include the selective androgen receptor modulators (SARMs). These are designed to target specific tissues, thus minimizing the global side effects of steroids.[73]

An alternative form of physical enhancement is what may be referred to as *neurophysical* enhancement. As Bennett Foddy explains, it fits somewhere between pure physical enhancement (e.g., to increase muscle strength) and cognitive enhancement (to enhance memory or attention). The uniqueness of neurophysical enhancements is that they "target neural systems—particularly systems in the peripheral nervous system, which exists outside the brain—as a means of improving physical

---

67. Miah, "Physical Enhancement," 271.
68. President's Council on Bioethics, *Beyond Therapy*, 115.
69. President's Council on Bioethics, *Beyond Therapy*, 120.
70. President's Council on Bioethics, *Beyond Therapy*, 121.
71. Oral forms of anabolic steroids include *Anadrol* (oxymetholone), *Winstrol* (stanozolol), and *THG* (tetrahydrogestrinone). Injectable varieties include *Durabolin* (nandrolone) and *Equipoise* (boldenone).
72. President's Council on Bioethics, *Beyond Therapy*, 121.
73. Miah, "Physical Enhancement," 270.

performance."⁷⁴ Typical of neurophysical enhancers are stimulants such as amphetamines, cocaine, and caffeine, which facilitate attention and quicken reactivity.⁷⁵ They are effective in stimulating "both the central nervous system, increasing alertness and general brain activity, and the sympathetic nervous system, increasing heart rate, sweating, and blood pressure."⁷⁶ It is also suggested that caffeine may help "to mobilize fat stores during exercise in some individuals, increasing their endurance by making more fuel available for the muscles."⁷⁷ However, it is unclear whether this effect is direct or mediated by the nervous system. While Foddy primarily focuses on neurophysical enhancements as they impact on sport, he acknowledges their relevance to "skill-based pursuits outside of competitive sports, such as in aviation, musical performance, construction or in factory work"⁷⁸—activities which could potentially benefit from enhancements of concentration, motor-memory tasks, and the ability to track moving objects.

Furthermore, the prospects of physical enhancement could be served by advances in genetic technology. For example, with the determination of the DNA sequence of IGF-1, experiments on mice have shown that the introduction of genes coding for the growth factor into mouse cells via viral vectors has resulted in increased muscle mass.⁷⁹ Transferring this technology to humans, it may be possible to introduce muscle-enhancing genes directly into muscles, into the muscle precursor stem cells (which would then be transferred into the muscle), or even into the human embryo itself.⁸⁰

In the practical application of this technology, it is suggested that "genes encoding growth factors may be used to improve regeneration of sports-related injuries, including muscle injuries, ligament and tendon ruptures, meniscal tears, cartilage lesions, and bone fractures."⁸¹ As well as genes coding for muscle strength, "gene doping" could also target genes

---

74. Foddy, "Enhancing Skill," 313.
75. President's Council on Bioethics, *Beyond Therapy*, 110-11.
76. Foddy, "Enhancing Skill," 315.
77. Foddy, "Enhancing Skill," 315.
78. Foddy, "Enhancing Skill," 313.
79. President's Council on Bioethics, *Beyond Therapy*, 116.
80. President's Council on Bioethics, *Beyond Therapy*, 118.
81. Haisma, "Physical Enhancement," 260.

coding for EPO (in order to increase endurance), for vascular endothelial growth factor (VEGF), myostatin, and endorphins.[82]

A further application of genetic technology for physical performance could come through genetic screening. With the identification of multiple genes associated with health and fitness, it may be possible in the future to identify potential athletes or select them for particular sports.[83] Alternatively, knowledge of the genetic makeup of athletes may allow sports technicians to devise individual training regimes that complement the athlete's genetic predisposition.[84]

Finally, with genetic technology there is also the prospect of going beyond the enhancement of existing physical powers, toward creating new ones. Through transgenesis of animal genes into the human genome, technology could create humans with extraordinary capacities: "the hearing of dogs, the visual acuity of hawks, the night vision of owls, or even be able to navigate by sonar employed from bats."[85]

Ethical Concerns of Physical Enhancement

The risks of drug-enhanced physical strength are well documented. The use of HGH is associated with an increased risk of developing diabetes, cardiovascular disease, hypertension, osteoarthritis, abnormal hypertrophy of organs, as well as muscle, joint, and bone pain.[86] The increased haematocrit and thickening of blood associated with EPO use increases the risk of thrombosis, and the subsequent danger of heart disease, stroke, and embolism (cerebral or pulmonary).[87] In addition to the risk of sudden cardiac death, the side effects of anabolic steroids include hepatic tumors, hypertension, infertility, mood swings, and psychological dependence.[88]

When we consider the possibility of genetic enhancement, the risks become potentially even graver. These risks stem both from the genetic

82. Tamburrini and Tännsjö, "Enhanced Bodies," 275.

83. "Genetic screening at an early age may indicate the greatest potential for a specific child to develop into a top athlete and a specific training programme may be designed." Haisma, "Physical Enhancement," 260.

84. Haisma, "Physical Enhancement," 260.

85. Savulescu, "Human Prejudice," 213–14.

86. Miah, "Physical Enhancement," 271.

87. Miah, "Physical Enhancement," 271–72.

88. President's Council on Bioethics, *Beyond Therapy*, 137.

information that is transferred and the vector used.[89] In the first instance, beyond the unpredictability of gene expression in the individual, there is also the risk of transferring the genetic modification to offspring, especially in cases of germline alterations.[90] In the latter case, it is suggested that gene doping might constitute an environmental risk due to the genetic, chemical, or viral nature of the vector.[91]

In continuity with objections leveled at cognitive enhancement, the prospect of physical enhancement also raises ethical issues related to autonomy, self-realization, authenticity, fairness and equality, justice, coercion, the meaning of sport, and the dignity of human effort and activity. Integral to some of these objections is the distinction, already noted above, between positional and intrinsic goods. Even transhumanists will acknowledge that "the benefits of many physical enhancements . . . seem to have a very large positional component."[92] The value of being stronger, taller, faster, etc., exists in relation to others who do not possess them.[93]

This positional nature of physical goods seems to be intensified when they are achieved through means other than human effort. While some might claim an intrinsic value to the spectacle of "the sheer bullocking power"[94] of human strength at any cost, it doesn't seem to be what most people value in human achievements. As members of the

89. Haisma, "Physical Enhancement," 261.

90. Tamburrini and Tännsjö, "Enhanced Bodies," 276.

91. "Gene doping implies environmental risks as genetically modified athletes may have genetically modified cells or excreta that contain the gene transfer vector. People in close contact with the athlete might be exposed to the gene." Tamburrini and Tännsjö, "Enhanced Bodies," 276.

92. Bostrom and Roache, "Ethical Issues in Human Enhancement," 132.

93. Bostrom illustrates this with the example of stature: "There is evidence that being tall is statistically advantageous, at least for men in Western societies. Taller men earn more money, wield greater social influence, and are viewed as more sexually attractive. Parents wanting to give their child the best possible start in life may rationally choose a genetic enhancement that adds an inch or two to the expected length of their offspring. Yet for society as a whole, there seems to be no advantage whatsoever in people being taller. If everybody grew two inches, nobody would be better off than they were before. Money spent on a positional good like length has little or no net effect on social welfare and is therefore, from society's point of view, wasted." Bostrom, "Human Genetic Enhancements," 501.

94. A reference to journalist David Owen's comment on Ben Johnson's drug-assisted "victory" in the men's 100m at the 1988 Seoul Olympics. Owen admitted his "guilty secret" that he found the spectacle of Johnson's power "just about the most exciting 10 seconds of sport I have ever witnessed." Owen, "Chemically Enhanced," quoted in Bostrom and Roache, "Ethical Issues in Human Enhancement," 129.

President's Council stress, the dignity of the performance of those who rely on enhancing drugs "seems less real, less one's own, less worthy of our admiration."[95] The performance is the result of external agents, not the fruit of disciplining the body and cultivating gifts.

While it is acknowledged that the science and technology that underpin such enhancements are themselves the products of human ingenuity, and for that reason might constitute an element of authenticity, in the separation of bodily effort and physical enhancement we risk "losing sight of why excellence is worth seeking at all, and hence what excellence really is, and how we pursue it as human beings, not as artifacts."[96]

Mood Enhancement

The idea of using drugs to enhance one's mood, to "drown sorrows" or "lift spirits," is not new. As the President's Council writes: "Alcohol, in different measures, can accomplish both."[97] In addition, caffeine, amphetamines, opioids, barbiturates, benzodiazepines, cannabis, and other psychopharmaceuticals are all potentially mood enhancing.[98] However, the mood altering effects of such agents is often nonspecific, temporary, and prone to tolerance.

Modes of Mood Enhancement

Today, the prospect of mood enhancement is given new hope through the development of pharmaceuticals which are specific for affect: "drugs (such as beta-adrenergic blockers) that numb the emotional sting typically associated with our intensely bad memories, and 'mood brighteners' (such as serotonin reuptake inhibitors) that lift and stabilize our general disposition and make us feel good (or better) about ourselves."[99] The latter are not only effective in treating symptoms of depression but also, in the words of psychiatrist and novelist Peter Kramer, of helping individuals feel "better than well." In *Listening to Prozac*, Kramer recounts

---

95. President's Council on Bioethics, *Beyond Therapy*, 140.
96. President's Council on Bioethics, *Beyond Therapy*, 156.
97. President's Council on Bioethics, *Beyond Therapy*, 207.
98. Liao and Roache, "After Prozac," 245; Berghmans et al., "Scientific, Ethical, and Social Issues," 161.
99. President's Council on Bioethics, *Beyond Therapy*, 207.

stories of patients who, though cured of their depression, seek to remain on Prozac (Fluoxetine) in order to deal with everyday stressful situations and maintain a certain level of psychological well-being.[100] Interpreting this phenomenon, Bostrom and Roache write:

> Prozac, as well as relieving their medical condition, had—in their view—improved various aspects of their personality which had never been classed as part of their illness: shy patients had become more outgoing and assertive, compulsive patients had become more relaxed and easy-going, and those with low self-esteem had become more confident.[101]

The hopes of mood enhancement advocates are further encouraged by advances in neuroscience and neurotechnology, including the production of *neuroceuticals*, "highly efficient synthetic neuromodulators that could target specific subreceptors in well-defined neural circuits."[102] When added to the ever-expanding field of genetic research, such technology could lead to the development of so-called *geneceuticals*: drugs that seek to modify the expression of the genes that code for emotion. The specificity of such drugs would potentially create more efficient results with fewer side effects.[103]

With technological advances in the areas of physics and neurochemistry, the prospect of mood enhancement therapies also goes beyond drugs.[104] Transcranial magnetic stimulation (TMS) and deep-brain stimulation (DBS) already have a place in the treatment of some medically intractable neuropsychiatric illnesses. It is suggested that these mood-enhancing effects may be transferrable to a wider population.[105]

---

100. Kramer gives the example of Tess: "After about eight months off medication, Tess told me she was slipping. 'I'm not myself,' she said. New union negotiations were under way, and she felt she could use the sense of stability, the invulnerability to attack, that Prozac gave her. Here was a dilemma for me. Ought I to provide medication to someone who was not depressed?." Kramer, *Listening to Prozac*, 10.

101. Bostrom and Roache, "Ethical Issues in Human Enhancement," 133.

102. Earp et al., "If I Could Just Stop Loving You," 7; Berghmans et al., "Scientific, Ethical, and Social Issues," 157.

103. Liao and Roache, "After Prozac," 245.

104. Berghmans et al., "Scientific, Ethical, and Social Issues," 156–57.

105. It should be noted, however, that "deep brain stimulation in healthy volunteers seems very futuristic. Implantation is a surgical technique that would not be considered ethical in healthy people because of the considerable risks associated with the procedure." Berghmans et al., "Scientific, Ethical, and Social Issues," 157.

Ethical Concerns of Mood Enhancement

Predictably, the idea of employing sophisticated mood-altering technology and pharmaceuticals to enhance the general population provokes ethical considerations. It raises questions about the determination of "normal" mental health (as distinct from both disease and normal variants),[106] and about the "grey area" between treatment and enhancement.[107] This grey area is confounded by the range of normal human affect,[108] and the social construction of some conditions.[109] In this context, advocates of mood enhancement tend to exploit the inexact differentiation between disease and variant, of therapy and enhancement. It is suggested that in the imprecise world of human emotions, we are not dealing with a perfect, well-harmonized system that would be threatened by interventions. For example, Guy Kahane maintains that "our emotional lives were never in some pristine natural state that mood enhancers might corrupt."[110] They are "already awry," in which case mood enhancement offers a possible solution.[111]

---

106. It is claimed that "there is no simple discontinuity between the characteristic mood of patients with diagnosable mood disorders and the range of moods found in the general population." Berghmans et al., "Scientific, Ethical, and Social Issues," 155.

107. Schermer and Bolt, "What's in a Name?," 181.

108. "Traits like shyness and aggression are manifested in people to varying degrees, with correspondingly various effects on the way the person in question lives his or her life." Bostrom and Roache, "Ethical Issues in Human Enhancement," 133.

109. It is noted "that historical, cultural, and societal factors play a role in the conceptualization of mood, the demarcation of psychiatric illnesses and diagnoses (i.e., depression, manic depressive disorder, anxiety disorders, social phobia, etc.), and different societal ways of dealing with suffering individuals." Berghmans et al., "Scientific, Ethical, and Social Issues," 158. In a contemporary example, it is suggested that the diagnosis of ADHD, and the expansion of its diagnostic criteria, has been subject to social conditioning. In this context, Schermer and Bolt note a difference between the "insider's perspective" of their condition, oftentimes regarding it as a normal variant and even embracing its positive aspects, and the "outsider's perspective," which tends more and more to focus on aspects of "underperformance." "It is from this outsider's perspective that the sociological study of Conrad and Potter describes the expansion of ADHD as 'the medicalization of underperformance.' They show how the criteria for ADHD have been extended over the years to include more people, and to include adults as well as children." Schermer and Bolt, "What's in a Name?," 186. Cf. Conrad and Potter, "From Hyperactive Children to ADHD Adults."

110. Kahane, "Reasons to Feel," 174.

111. Kahane, "Reasons to Feel," 166.

There are other concerns regarding the risks posed by indiscriminate mood enhancement to individuality, personality, and authenticity through *ad hoc* prescription of mood-enhancing medication. It is suggested that the shortcut offered by mood-enhancing technologies would bypass, to our detriment, much of what is human in our struggle with a range of emotions. The following observation by Kass is representative of such concerns:

> In most of our ordinary efforts at self-improvement, either by practice or training or study, we sense the relation between our doings and the resulting improvement, between the means used and the end sought. There is an experiential and intelligible connection between means and ends; we can see how confronting fearful things might eventually enable us to cope with our fears. We can see how curbing our appetites produces self-command. . . . In contrast, biomedical interventions act directly on the human body and bring about their effects on a subject who is not merely passive but who plays no role at all. He can at best *feel* their effects *without understanding their meaning in human terms.*[112]

In response, while conceding the value of conventional means of dealing with difficulties, proponents of mood enhancement value the end state above the means used to achieve it.[113] They also relativize concerns regarding authenticity. Though acknowledging situations in which emotional authenticity could be compromised by the use of drugs, they choose to highlight those instances in which mood-altering medication helps people "to find their 'true self.'"[114] From this they draw the conclusion that "in some cases the use of drugs can help a person live *more* authentically."[115]

---

112. Kass, "Ageless Bodies, Happy Souls," 22.

113. "Well, even if we concede that certain means of achieving an improvement can add value to the end state, the end state may have value independently of the means by which it is achieved, meaning that bringing about the end state using less valuable means is better than not bringing it about at all." Bostrom and Roache, "Ethical Issues in Human Enhancement," 135.

114. Bostrom and Roache, "Ethical Issues in Human Enhancement," 136. For example, some of Kramer's Prozac patients "identified with their on-drug persona and viewed their earlier 'natural' state as a long-lasting aberration, an alien condition that they had never been able to escape."

115. Bostrom and Roache, "Ethical Issues in Human Enhancement," 136.

Concern is also expressed regarding the effect of mood enhancement on "our understanding of what it means to be a person, to be healthy and whole, to do meaningful work, and to value human life in its imperfection."[116] In this context it is noted that mental health, and well-being in general, depends on a range of *contrast experiences*: sadness, grief, and suffering existing alongside feelings of happiness and joy.[117] The "interweaving" of highs and lows, strengths and weaknesses, is deemed essential to the determination of one's character and identity, and "constitutes in its interplay of light and dark much that is of value and significance in human existence."[118]

Perhaps in recognition of this fuller meaning of the human experience, that "both positive and negative feelings are important for human beings, individually and socially, for survival, aspiration, achievement, prosperity, and communal life,"[119] advocates of mood enhancement have suggested applications beyond making the subject feel better.[120] As Roache and Matthew Liao write: "There are many reasons why we might seek to induce feelings we lack in order to experience a particular emotion or to experience it more fully."[121] In this context, it is suggested that drugs could be used to facilitate appropriateness of mood or feelings that "may be expected or required by our social roles and relationships":[122] to help us feel sad when sadness is called for; to share in the joys of another; to foster feelings of love toward one's spouse or child.[123]

116. Berghmans et al., "Scientific, Ethical, and Social Issues," 153.

117. Berghmans et al., "Scientific, Ethical, and Social Issues," 161. The President's Council make a similar point: "There appears to be a connection between the possibility of feeling deep unhappiness and the prospects for achieving genuine happiness. If one cannot grieve, one has not truly loved. To be capable of aspiration, one must know and feel lack." President's Council on Bioethics, *Beyond Therapy*, 299.

118. Parker, "Best Possible Child," 281. Parker draws this insight from Shakespeare's *All's Well That Ends Well*, act IV, scene 3: "The web of our life is of mingled yarn, good and ill together; our virtues would be proud if our faults whipp'd them not, and our crimes would despair if they were not cherish'd by our virtues."

119. Berghmans et al., "Scientific, Ethical, and Social Issues," 161.

120. "Might it be possible to generally increase our responsiveness to our affective reasons—both positive and negative?" Kahane, "Reasons to Feel," 175.

121. Liao and Roache, "After Prozac," 246.

122. Liao and Roache, "After Prozac," 246.

123. "There are occasions when emotions that seem appropriate for certain circumstances are not forthcoming, for a variety of psychological or physiological reasons. For example, we may want to be happy for a friend who is getting married, but we may be too stressed to enjoy the friend's wedding celebration. Or we may have

Kahane admits that the concept of *negative* mood enhancement "may sound like an oxymoron"; or perhaps "some perverted invention for masochists."[124] But he suggests that enhancing one's capacity to experience negative emotions could be both therapeutic[125] and a means of bringing harmony and balance to one's natural disposition.[126] It may offer a means of conforming to affective reason in order to feel what we ought. "It might be best to directly feel grief in response to a loss," he concedes, "but if some emotional inhibition prevents this, it would still be better to feel grief by artificial means, than not to feel grief at all."[127]

Enhancement and Love

The unease some feel at the idea of manufacturing feelings of grief is compounded by the prospect of manipulating feelings of love. Proponents of such enhancement begin from a biological basis of emotions.

From the perspective of brain science, "love is a 'complex neurobiological phenomenon' that has been wired into our biology by the forces

---

neurological incapacities that prevent us from feeling a range of affective states. Being able to regulate or induce certain feelings in appropriate circumstances can help us in several ways. We might feel better just by being able to experience emotions that should come naturally. It can be frustrating not to be able to experience joy when one knows one should, and when all those around one seem joyful.

Moreover, we arguably owe the people to whom we stand in close personal relationships certain emotional responses—not because those responses promote their welfare directly or indirectly, but because we cannot relate to them in the way we should unless we have such responses. For example, instead of feeling spontaneous love for their newborn child, it is common for mothers—perhaps owing to postpartum depression—to feel instead estrangement and resentment. Or, step- or adoptive parents might really want to love their step- or adopted children, but find it very difficult to do so. On these occasions, it can be frustrating not to be able to exhibit the kind of love that children need. If pills that could induce the feelings associated with parental love were available, this might enable one to provide the kind of love that children need, thereby relieving this frustration. Indeed, in being able to induce parental love that one does not feel spontaneously, one may also be able at least partially to fulfil a duty to love a child." Liao and Roache, "After Prozac," 246.

124. Kahane, "Reasons to Feel," 175.

125. "When we say that someone has finally managed to grieve some childhood loss only after years of therapy, and treat this as an achievement, we implicitly recognize the value of such negative mood enhancement." Kahane, "Reasons to Feel," 175.

126. "Indeed some people might be endowed with a strong cheerful disposition that is inappropriate to their life circumstances." Kahane, "Reasons to Feel," 175.

127. Kahane, "Reasons to Feel," 171.

of evolution."[128] This science of love is underpinned by systems in the brain that code for lust, attraction, and attachment.[129] Each subsystem is "characterized by discrete yet interrelated behavioral repertoires, neural circuits, and changes in hormone levels."[130] For *lust* these include the hormones estrogen and testosterone; for *attraction*, adrenaline, dopamine and serotonin; for *attachment*, the neuropeptide oxytocin and vasopressin.[131] While it is not claimed that love is reducible to such mechanisms, it is suggested that the chemicals and the pathways involved both shape and respond to feelings of love and attachment.[132]

Of the chemicals identified, oxytocin provides particular interest for the science of pair bonding. The effects of oxytocin are numerous. It fosters altruism, empathy and trust, and enables eye-contact and "mind-reading."[133] It also has the propensity to reduce anxiety and fear, stress and tension.[134] Added to these general features, oxytocin has a specific role in partner bonding.[135] Together with dopamine, "oxytocin signals elicited during the early romantic phase of a relationship and during sexual interaction are likely to act as learning signals: they help imprint details of the partner, positive emotional associations and relationship-related

---

128. Earp et al., "If I Could Just Stop Loving You," 6.

129. "The lust system promotes mating with a range of promising partners; the attraction system guides us to choose and prefer a particular partner; and the attachment system fosters long-term bonding, encouraging couples to cooperate and stay together until their parental duties have been discharged." Earp et al., "Natural Selection," 581.

130. Earp et al., "If I Could Just Stop Loving You," 7.

131. "Many of the brain regions associated with romantic love in humans are rich in receptors for oxytocin and vasopressin." Earp et al., "Natural Selection," 581.

132. Earp et al., "Medicalization of Love," 324.

133. Liao and Roache note that "test subjects given the prosocial hormone oxytocin were more willing to share money with strangers, and to behave in a more trustworthy way," and that the same hormone "appears to improve the capacity to read other people's emotional state, which is important for empathy." Liao and Roache, "After Prozac," 246–47. Cf. Zak et al., "Oxytocin is Associated"; Zak et al., "Oxytocin Increases Generosity"; Domes et al., "Oxytocin Improves 'Mind-Reading.'"

134. "In one study, Swiss researchers showed that nasally inhaled oxytocin can reduce stress levels and promote more positive communication between couples engaged in an argument." Earp et al., "Natural Selection," 564. Cf. Ditzen et al., "Intranasal Oxytocin."

135. Savulescu and Sandberg, "Neuroenhancement," 36.

habits."[136] It is thus associated with recognition of loved ones[137] and linked with positive memories which strengthen bonding.[138] Release of oxytocin is further increased by body contact,[139] which not only confirms feelings of intimacy between partners, but also helps in the formation of mother-child bonds and augments nursing behavior.

It is proposed that knowledge of the science of love could assist couples experiencing difficulties in their relationships.[140] Highlighting the real problems of separation and divorce, especially when children are involved, proponents of enhancement make a case for helping couples in any way possible, including the use of so-called "love drugs" like oxytocin.[141] In its practical application to human relationships, it is hoped that oxytocin could be used to foster openness and cooperation between partners, increase mutual understanding, and enhance positive attitudes. Along with other drugs which mimic processes of attraction, it could be used to trigger the process of imprinting, reinforcing "pair bonds by giving the right drugs to subjects while they are in close contact with their partner."[142] Thus, it is claimed that love drugs do not seek to create love magically, but simply to "help it along by acting on the underlying substrates of attachment, or by promoting more empathic states of mind."[143] In this context, proponents claim that the use of "neurolove potions"

---

136. Savulescu and Sandberg, "Neuroenhancement," 36. See also Earp et al., "Natural Selection," 582.

137. "Administering oxytocin enhances recognition of face identities, but not non-social stimuli." Earp et al., "Natural Selection," 581. Cf. Rimmele et al., "Oxytocin Makes a Face."

138. "In humans, brain regions activated by seeing beloved people (either partners or children) appear to correspond to regions with oxytocin, vasopressin and dopamine receptors." Savulescu and Sandberg, "Neuroenhancement," 36.

139. Brian Earp notes that oxytocin is commonly referred to as "the cuddle chemical" in popular literature. Earp, "Love and Other Drugs," 17.

140. According to Earp, this includes the majority of marriages. "Of those marriages that *do* last, only some fraction can be fairly described as 'happy'—and possibly none at all reach the heights of connubial bliss we read about in fairy tales." Earp, "Love and Other Drugs," 14.

141. See Wudarczyk et al., "Could Intranasal Oxytocin Be Used to Enhance Relationships?"

142. Savulescu and Sandberg, "Neuroenhancement," 36.

143. Earp et al., "Medicalization of Love," 326.

could exist in continuity with, and morally equivalent to, a range of acceptable methods that aim at enhancing the *chemistry* between couples.[144]

Moving in the opposite direction, it is suggested that the same neural subsystems could be targeted by "anti-love" pharmaceuticals in order to inhibit or diminish feelings of attachment, love, lust, and sexual attraction in specific, problematic situations.[145] Possible *anti-lust* agents include Selective Serotonin Reuptake Inhibitors (SSRIs), oral naltrexone, and androgen blockers as currently used in the chemical castration of sex-offenders. Research into *anti-attraction* interventions is guided by clinical findings which show that levels of serotonin (5–HT) transporter protein during moments of physical attraction are similar to levels observed in cases of Obsessive-Compulsive Disorder (OCD). It is therefore suggested that OCD medications might be effective anti-attraction agents. Finally, *anti-attachment* techniques primarily aim to block the effects of oxytocin, but also of vasopressin which plays a similar role in bond formation.

Prospective benefactors of such "enhancement" would primarily include victims of violent relationships: individuals (usually women) caught in cycles of violence and emotional dependence which renders them powerless to end the relationship. In such situations, love-diminishing therapies might assist the victim to sever emotional ties with her abusive partner.[146] Other situations that might benefit from such therapies include:

- Romantic love for someone other than one's spouse;
- Unrequited love that leads to despair or suicidal thoughts and behaviors;
- Delusive love, as in erotomania;
- Spurned love that leads to violence or other harmful acts, such as abuse of children during a marital separation;

---

144. "There is a long history to the use of love potions. Alcohol is the commonest love drug. We have always tried to use chemistry to influence the chemistry between people. Neurolove potions will just be more effective. There is no morally relevant difference between marriage therapy, a massage, a glass of wine, a fancy pink, steamy potion and a pill. All act at the biological level to make the release of substances like oxytocin and dopamine more likely." Savulescu and Sandberg, "Neuroenhancement," 37.

145. Earp et al., "Brave New Love," 4–12.

146. Earp et al., "Brave New Love," 7.

- An older person's uncontrollable sexual attraction for a child;
- Incestuous love;
- Love for a cult leader.[147]

Cautiously (or reluctantly) added to this list are cases of homosexual attraction,[148] limited to adults who voluntarily request the intervention, free of homophobic pressures or religious bigotry.[149] However, despite this particular reservation, the overall prospect of anti-love biotechnology is enthusiastically embraced, even suggesting that in certain cases it could constitute a moral duty, such that "to deny its use would be inhumane."[150]

Moral Enhancement

In continuity with both cognitive and mood enhancement, and relying on its scientific basis, moral enhancement is variously defined as "the acquisition of morally better motives,"[151] or as having "those dispositions which make it more likely that you will arrive at the correct judgement of what it is right to do and more likely to act on that judgement."[152]

147. Earp et al., "If I Could Just Stop Loving You," 5.

148. Ibid., 13. In this case, transhumanists fall victim to their own liberal perspective. Though seemingly allergic to the idea of a "conversion" from homosexual attraction, they are nonetheless bound to the liberal ideology, including a liberal conception of mood enhancement, in which "individuals should have the freedom to alter their own brain states—through drugs or other means—in order to pursue their personal goals or realize their conception of the good life, so long as they do not harm or infringe upon the rights of others." Earp et al., "Natural Selection," 562.

149. Earp et al., "Brave New Love," 11. However, the authors insist that such cases would be rare. "Even though we think that mature individuals—that is, individuals who have not been brainwashed, who are competent to reason about their own goals and values, and who are meaningfully autonomous in their decision making—should be permitted to modify themselves pharmacologically in the ways we have described, it does not follow that there are no other reasons why societies might justifiably seek to manage (or restrict access to) certain mind- and self-altering substances. In the case of technologies used to alter sexual preferences or orientation, especially, one has to remember that religious indoctrination, community pressures, stigma, and a host of other powerful social forces may undermine the robust freedom of thought that is ordinarily deemed to be necessary for genuine autonomy. 'In practice,' therefore, the justifiable use of such technology may be comparatively rare."

150. Earp et al., "If I Could Just Stop Loving You," 6.

151. Douglas, "Moral Enhancement via Direct Emotion Modulation," 161.

152. Persson and Savulescu, "Moral Enhancement," 406. However, Persson and Savulescu betray themselves as moral relativists when they add: "What constitutes

Modes of Moral Enhancement

The science of moral enhancement proceeds along two lines: (1) through enhancing one's capacity to reason (cognitive enhancement); and (2) by direct modulation of one's emotions.

In the first instance, it is suggested that morality could be supported by cognitive enhancement through sharpening moral discernment, improving memory, or correcting cognitive errors and biases, enhancing one's capacity to reason and make judgments essential for growing in virtue and overcoming vice. Such is the opinion of Allen Buchanan[153] and John Harris.[154] There is also the possibility of mood enhancement to augment one's capacity for sympathy and empathy, which, when combined with cognitive enhancement, could "improve our capacity for moral imagination—for vividly entertaining possibilities other than the status quo, or for fully appreciating the impact of our actions on others."[155]

But since moral capacity lags behind cognitive skill, some individuals within the transhumanist movement are wary of cognitive enhancement. Among them, Julian Savulescu and Ingmar Persson are concerned that cognitive enhancement will put more power in the hands of already morally deficient human beings.[156] They rightly insist that moral formation cannot be compared to acquisition of empirical knowledge, since moral formation involves more than learning information. It requires the internalization of moral doctrines that become expressed in action: a difficult process which is never complete and always threatened by human freedom.[157] In this they find agreement with Jürgen Habermas, who notes

---

moral enhancement will depend on the account one accepts of right action." But if concepts of right and wrong are relative to one's acceptance, without an objective foundation, it seems impossible to speak of moral "enhancement." In this context one could only speak of "change," without the moral categories of better or worse.

153. Buchanan, *Beyond Humanity?*, 75.

154. Harris, "Moral Enhancement and Freedom," 102–11.

155. Buchanan, *Better than Human*, 169. Cf. Buchanan, *Beyond Humanity?*, 76.

156. As they write: "The progress of science is in one respect for the worse by making likelier the misuse of ever more effective weapons of mass destruction, and this badness is increased if scientific progress is speeded up by cognitive enhancement, until effective means of moral enhancement are found and applied." Persson and Savulescu, "Perils of Cognitive Enhancement," 174.

157. "This is shown not only by how few people live up to more demanding doctrines, for example, those that require the sacrifice of a substantial part of their welfare to save the life of strangers, but more emphatically by the frightening speed with which people, when political conditions allow it, are capable of regressing to

that moral behavior (or lack thereof) is not derived from memory or knowledge, but from the will. As Habermas writes: "The cynical acceptance of an unjust world, the normality of repression for so many people, is evidence not of a deficit in *knowledge* but of a corruption of the *will*. The human beings who could know better do not *want* to understand."[158]

Savulescu and Persson give the example of racism. As a remnant of the evolutionary distrust of strangers, it is suggested that human beings *encode* individuals by race "via computational processes that appear to be both automatic and mandatory,"[159] and that these processes continue to function in spite of our realization of the falsity of racism. Since the enhancement of intelligence or reason is not enough to overcome such moral impoverishment, Persson and Savulescu are skeptical of the capacity of cognitive enhancement alone to improve morality. They, therefore, seek other means to counter natural tendencies and biases, to "speed up" the process of internalization of moral doctrines, to enhance motivation and overcome the limitations of altruism.[160] They seek the direct biomedical modulation of emotions by means of genetic engineering and drug therapy.

In this context, Thomas Douglas speaks of the biomedical mitigation of "counter-moral emotions."[161] In noting the biological links between violent aggression and serotonergic neurotransmitters,[162] it is suggested

---

barbarous behavior, which one had hoped humanity had left behind for good. Every new generation has to go through a strenuous moral training anew. Consequently, there is a widening gap between what we are practically able to do, thanks to modern technology, and what we are morally capable of doing, though we might be somewhat more morally capable than our ancestors were." Persson and Savulescu, *Unfit for the Future*, 106–7.

158. Habermas, *Future of Human Nature*, 8. Habermas highlights the insufficiency of knowledge for moral action with the following example: "If morality could move the will of the knowing subject *solely* through good reasons, then we could not explain that desolate condition against which Kierkegaard as critic of the contemporary age directed his barbs again and again—the condition of an enlightened and morally self-righteous, but deeply corrupt Christian society" (7).

159. Persson and Savulescu, "Perils of Cognitive Enhancement," 168.

160. Persson and Savulescu, *Unfit for the Future*, 105; Persson and Savulescu, "Getting Moral Enhancement Right," 130.

161. Douglas, "Moral Enhancement," 233.

162. "There has long been evidence from adoption and twin studies of a genetic contribution to aggression, and there is now growing evidence implicating a polymorphism in the monoamine oxidase A gene, and, at the neurophysiological level, derangements in the serotonergic neurotransmitter system." Douglas, "Moral Enhancement," 233.

that serotonin could be used to suppress aggressive behavior,[163] as well as enhancing fair-mindedness and willingness to collaborate.[164] Similarly, in its association with feelings of trust, oxytocin could be therapeutic in overcoming xenophobic aversions and enhancing moral cooperation.[165] Furthermore, in noting that women as a whole have a greater capacity for altruism than men, and are less likely to harm others,[166] Persson and Savulescu suggest that men could be morally enhanced by using biomedical means to make them "more like women," at least in terms of empathy and aggression.[167] Along the posthuman trajectory, there is also the prediction of enhancing individuals toward a *supra-personal* moral status.[168] Through the enhancement of altruism, self-control and intelligence, superior forms of cooperation are envisaged, with morally enhanced beings replacing existing political and legal institutions and the current economic market.

However, critics of Persson and Savulescu within the transhumanist circle note a contradiction in their favoring of moral enhancement over cognitive enhancement. For example, Elizabeth Fenton highlights an inconsistency that while Persson and Savulescu reject the cognitive solution, the moral enhancements that they envisage are themselves dependent on cognitive advancements.[169] The question therefore arises as to whether scientific advancements, aided by cognitive enhancements, are simply the cause of the problems that face humanity, or whether they could also be the solution. As a practical example Fenton suggests that

163. Persson and Savulescu, "Unfit for the Future?," 498.

164. Persson and Savulescu, "Moral Enhancement," 404.

165. Persson and Savulescu, "Unfit for the Future?," 498.

166. Persson and Savulescu, "Moral Enhancement," 408.

167. Persson and Savulescu, "Getting Moral Enhancement Right," 130. In expressing his concerns over human enhancement, Francis Fukuyama notes a blunting of sexual difference already in play with the frequent prescription of mood-altering drugs, making women more assertive and aggressive and men more subdued and compliant. He writes: "There is a disconcerting symmetry between Prozac and Ritalin. The former is prescribed heavily for depressed women lacking in self-esteem; it gives them more of the alpha-male feeling that comes with high serotonin levels. Ritalin, on the other hand, is prescribed largely for young boys who do not want to sit still in class because nature never designed them to behave that way. Together, the two sexes are gently nudged toward that androgynous median personality, self-satisfied and socially compliant, that is the current politically correct outcome in American society." Fukuyama, *Our Posthuman Future*, 51–52.

168. See Douglas, "Human Enhancement," 473–97.

169. Fenton, "Perils of Failing to Enhance," 148.

resolutions to the global environmental crisis could be provided by enhanced scientists figuring out "ways to reverse the effects of carbon, or invent more efficient forms of transport, or more adept economists who can sell alternative energy to brighter politicians."[170] And Harris adds that while there is no assurance that such solutions will be forthcoming, it would be reckless to deny a cognitively enhanced morality the chance of becoming reality.[171]

Objections to Moral Enhancement

Foremost among criticisms of moral enhancement is the pervasive concern that human autonomy would be compromised through biotechnology. Critics suggest that human beings who have been motivationally enhanced to make moral decisions would not truly be free to choose, and that their actions could not be attributed to them as their own. For instance, members of the President's Council warn:

> By medicalizing key elements of our life through biotechnical interventions, we may weaken our sense of responsibility and agency. And, technologies aside, merely regarding ourselves and our activities in largely genetic or neurochemical terms may diminish our sense of ourselves as moral actors faced with genuine choices and options in life.[172]

As noted above, Leon Kass questions the authenticity of enhancements that bypass human effort. Through recourse to biological interventions that act directly on one's emotions and motivations, Kass suggests that the subject is alienated from his experiences that are "mediated by unintelligible forces."[173] He writes that one "can at best *feel* their effects

---

170. Fenton, "Perils of Failing to Enhance," 150. Harris similarly ponders "the benefits that might accrue from accelerating science via cognitive enhancement, including the rapid development of antidotes to engineered diseases and other bio-weapons and biohazards, better insights into how to combat the worst effects of climate change, and reliable methods of predicting asteroid strikes and developing methods of diverting the asteroids, to identify just a few of the dangers that we may hope will prove amenable to a scientific or technological 'fix.'" Harris, "Moral Enhancement and Freedom," 109–10.
171. Harris, "Moral Enhancement and Freedom," 110.
172. President's Council on Bioethics, *Beyond Therapy*, 92.
173. Kass, "Ageless Bodies, Happy Souls," 22.

without understanding their meaning in human terms."[174] While acknowledging that many things in our lives are filtered or mediated through modern technology (e.g., telephones, internet, etc.) without us becoming overtly inauthentic or dehumanized in the process, he notes that they remain external to us. We can objectify them, see them working on us, and are free to distance ourselves from them.[175] But it is not so with biotechnological interventions that touch the very core of our being.

From the other side of the transhumanist debate, John Harris insists that moral freedom must include the "freedom to fall." Drawing on the words of Milton's God in *Paradise Lost*, who made humanity "just and right, sufficient to have stood, though free to fall,"[176] he insists that the capacity to stand firm and to fall are intimately connected;[177] that the "sufficiency to stand is worthless, literally morally bankrupt, without freedom to fall."[178] He argues this on the basis that moral proficiency is not a matter of "being better at being good," but of recognizing the good and knowing how to pursue it. Freedom exists as the space between knowing and doing, and it is within this space that virtue is able to

---

174. Kass, "Ageless Bodies, Happy Souls," 22. He adds: "With biotechnical interventions that skip the realm of intelligible meaning, we cannot really own the transformations nor experience them as genuinely ours. And we will be at a loss to attest whether the resulting conditions and activities of our bodies and our minds are, in the fullest sense, our own as human" (24).

175. Kass, "Ageless Bodies, Happy Souls," 23.

176. Milton, *Paradise Lost*, book 3, in Harris, "Moral Enhancement and Freedom," 103.

177. Harris writes: "A very fundamental problem, which has not been much discussed in the literature on moral enhancement, is that the sorts of traits or dispositions that seem to lead to wickedness or immorality are also the very same ones required not only for virtue but for any sort of moral life at all." Harris, "Moral Enhancement and Freedom," 104. Fukuyama makes a similar point in highlighting the complexity of the evolved human organism. "For all our obvious faults, we humans are miraculously complex products of a long evolutionary process—products whose whole is much more than the sum of our parts. Our good characteristics are intimately connected to our bad ones: If we weren't violent and aggressive, we wouldn't be able to defend ourselves; if we didn't have feelings of exclusivity, we wouldn't be loyal to those close to us; if we never felt jealousy, we would also never feel love. Even our mortality plays a critical function in allowing our species as a whole to survive and adapt (and transhumanists are just about the last group I'd like to see live forever). Modifying any one of our key characteristics inevitably entails modifying a complex, interlinked package of traits, and we will never be able to anticipate the ultimate outcome." Fukuyama, "Transhumanism," 43.

178. Harris, "Moral Enhancement and Freedom," 110.

flourish, and the choice for the good is capable of existing as a real choice. He therefore suggests that the manipulation of moral choice would infringe on the freedom to choose in moral deliberation.

Persson and Savulescu respond by insisting that moral bioenhancement would not make us any less free than those people who are already morally virtuous and strive to do good.[179] They suggest that enhancement of impulse control and altruism, of the willingness to make sacrifices and cooperate, would not compromise freedom or autonomy, but could in fact foster them.[180] Even in extreme cases in which the freedom to commit grave crimes is deliberately removed, it is claimed that the benefits would outweigh the loss, since "the value of human well-being and respect for the most basic rights outweighs the value of autonomy."[181] But in reality Persson and Savulescu do not limit restrictions to freedom to extreme cases. In the eventuality of safe moral enhancements being developed, they believe that "there are strong reasons to believe that their use should be obligatory, like education or fluoride in the water, since those who should take them are least likely to be inclined to use them."[182]

Lifespan Extension

Life expectancy has changed over time, with estimates that "the average human lifespan has nearly tripled over the course of human history."[183] The most dramatic increase occurred over the past 150 years, since the height of the industrial revolution, during which time "life expectancy has increased at a steady two years per decade."[184] Due to the rapid nature of this change, it is deemed that the increase "is primarily due to social and technological developments rather than any evolutionary changes in

---

179. Persson and Savulescu, "Getting Moral Enhancement Right," 128.
180. Persson and Savulescu, "Moral Enhancement," 417.
181. Persson and Savulescu, "Moral Enhancement," 416.
182. Persson and Savulescu, "Perils of Cognitive Enhancement," 174.
183. Barazzetti, "Looking for the Fountain of Youth," 335.
184. Bond, "Enhancing Human Aging," 435. During the period 1840–1900, the single most important contributing factor in the increase of life expectancy was a reduction in child mortality. After 1960, it was the decline in premature mortality in mid-life (between 45 years and 65 years). Since 1990, evidence suggests that "changes in the patterns of late-life mortality (aged 65 years or over) from cardiovascular disease has continued the increase in life expectancy" (438).

human biology."[185] Such developments include an increase in income and wealth, availability of education, improvements in nutrition and sanitation, and advances in medicine.[186] The interplay of these developments "brought about a progressive reduction of infant and child mortality which eventually resulted in the increase in life expectancy at birth."[187] Buoyed by these trends, transhumanists envisage the possibility of extending life well beyond its current limits, of halting the process of aging, and of even reaching toward immortality.

However, transhumanist hopes for life extension are not merely about numbers of years, but of lives "characterized by health and good quality of life."[188] Christine Overall expresses the prospect in these words:

> What is important in extended life is the exploration of one's talents, capacities, and potential. It is likely that as lives get longer, the content of individuals' goals will change, and people will play a larger variety of roles (familial, domestic, community, work, and volunteer functions) during their lifetimes. Like today, people will undertake new tasks, projects, and interests at different life stages, but if those life stages are longer, then the range of tasks, projects, relationships, and interests can become broader.[189]

Bostrom and Roache express it in terms of a comparison between our current capacities over a lifespan of eighty years, and those of a possible extended future: between "mastering a musical instrument, learning a foreign language, meeting one's grandchildren, sailing around the world, and building one's own house" and the possibility of "mastering every musical instrument in the orchestra, writing a book in each of all the major languages, planting a new garden and seeing it mature, teaching

---

185. Bostrom and Roache, "Ethical Issues in Human Enhancement," 123.

186. The specific contribution of medical science to increasing life expectancy since 1900 has been estimated to be three to five years. Bond, "Enhancing Human Aging," 439.

187. Barazzetti, "Looking for the Fountain of Youth," 335.

188. Barazzetti and Reichlin, "Life Extension and Personal Identity," 398. Bostrom writes: "The goal, of course, is to radically extent people's active health-spans, not to add a few extra years on a ventilator at the end of life." Bostrom, "Transhumanist Values," 13.

189. Overall, "Lifespan Extension," 392.

one's great-great-grandchildren how to fish, travelling to Alpha Centauri, or just seeing history unfold over a few hundred years."[190]

Future Prospects of Lifespan Extension

While to date increases in life expectancy have been the result of a "complex interaction between genes, the physical and social environment, and chance,"[191] it seems that future prospects will increasingly rely on medical technology, either to bolster the body's immune response to diseases that threaten life, or to counteract the process of aging itself. In their pursuit of a radical extension of life, transhumanists pin their hopes on the latter of these two options. As Bostrom and Roache write:

> If the processes of senescence are left unchecked, then there comes a point in each individual's life where cellular damage accumulates to such a degree that pathology and death become inevitable. Preventing and curing specific diseases can only have a limited impact on life expectancy in a population that already lives as long as people do in the industrialized world.[192]

Many scientists believe that the mechanisms of cellular biology, in which cells lose their ability to replicate and to replace dead or damaged tissue, "simply reflect a particular evolutionary strategy for species survival, one that is neither necessary nor immutable."[193] Seen as a biological process, human aging is thus amenable to therapeutic intervention and control. As Larry Temkin writes:

> In principle, then, it seems that we could manipulate our DNA, so that all of our cells continually replaced themselves as older ones were damaged, wore out, or died; or that we could employ stem cells to perform such functions. In this way, we might become biological versions of the Ship of Theseus, maintaining

---

190. Bostrom and Roache, "Ethical Issues in Human Enhancement," 125.
191. Bond, "Enhancing Human Aging," 438.
192. Bostrom and Roache, "Ethical Issues in Human Enhancement," 123.
193. Temkin, "Is Living Longer Living Better?," 352. From the perspective of evolution, "nature has relatively little stake in keeping us alive beyond our reproductive years. Insofar as we may speak of our lives having a point, it is to be carriers of DNA. Having passed that on to the next generation, we are dispensable." Meilaender, *Should We Live Forever?*, 4.

ourselves in peak condition, presumably at a developmental stage of our choosing.[194]

If that were indeed achievable—if the process of cell aging could be arrested[195]—then a virtual immortality would be possible.[196]

To this end, science has already made some hopeful discoveries. For example, experiments on certain animals and life-forms (e.g., yeast, worms, fish, rats, and mice) has demonstrated a "significant lengthening of lifespan" through caloric restriction.[197] When applied to humans, there is preliminary evidence that "caloric restriction might slow down or reduce some age-related physiological changes."[198] Alternative strategies to combat the effects of aging include the use of certain hormones,[199]

---

194. Temkin, "Is Living Longer Living Better?," 352.

195. Not everyone believes that it is possible. For example, Dino Moltisanti and Elena Postigo Salana suggest that it may be possible to slow the process of cellular aging, but not to stop it altogether: "Le possibilità di ampliamento delle aspettative di vita mediante l'uso di terapie geniche o metodi biologici che permetterebbero di bloccare l'invecchiamento cellulare. Attualmente questo non è possibile: si può forse rallentare il processo, ma non fermarlo." Moltisanti and Postigo Solana, "Transumanesimo," 211.

196. Barazzetti speaks of "virtual" immortality "since death would come from accidents, homicides or suicides, rather than from progressive decline in performance and fitness with advancing age." Barazzetti, "Looking for the Fountain of Youth," 338–39. In the same light, Bostrom and Roache comment: "Were it not for aging, our risk of dying in any given year might be like that of somebody in their late teens or early twenties. Life expectancy would then be around 1,000 years." Bostrom and Roache, "Ethical Issues in Human Enhancement," 124.

197. Barazzetti, "Looking for the Fountain of Youth," 339.

198. Barazzetti, "Looking for the Fountain of Youth," 339. The author adds: "These observations are highly encouraging and strongly suggest that caloric restriction, regardless of the fact that it may increase longevity, is likely to improve general health and well-being in elderly human beings. However, a few studies are currently investigating the quality of life and potential 'pitfalls' of long-term caloric restriction in human beings. Potential negative side effects may include hypotension, infertility, bone thinning and osteoporosis, and psychological conditions such as depression and irritability." Accordingly, the development of interventions which mimic the effects of caloric restriction are proposed (e.g., pharmaceuticals, hormones, genetic manipulation), thus avoiding the negative effects of reducing food and calories.

199. Examples include growth hormone (GH), insulin-like growth factor 1 (IGF-1), dehydroepiandrosterone (DHEA), melatonin, testosterone, progesterone, and oestrogen. Barazzetti, "Looking for the Fountain of Youth," 340. Cf. President's Council on Bioethics, *Beyond Therapy*, 178: "The rates of production of certain hormones (particularly testosterone and estrogen) decline sharply in one's later years, and these declines are closely related to the loss of muscle mass that accompanies aging and to a series of other age-related declines."

THE SCIENCE OF ENHANCEMENT 63

agents against oxidative damage,[200] and therapies deriving from stem cell research.[201] The anti-aging effects of rapamycin[202] and the anti-diabetes drug metformin[203] are being currently trialled. Yet another potential therapy involves the activation of telomerase, an enzyme which is protective against telomere[204] degradation or shortening which is associated with the aging process.[205] Following the same logic, genetic manipulation could target telomeres to prevent their degradation. Alternatively, DNA from "animals that have a significantly longer lifespan than humans, such as turtles and rockfish,"[206] or from organisms that appear to be immortal, such as hydras and certain forms of jellyfish[207] (e.g., *Turritopsis nutricula*, *Turritopsis dohrnii*), could be transferred into the human genome via transgenesis or their stem cells utilized.

    200. "For many years, there has been ample (if indirect) evidence that oxygen free radicals—oxygen molecules that have one unpaired electron, and that are therefore chemically very active—produced as inevitable by-products of the body's various functions, cause gradual deterioration of many of the body's cells and tissues. These oxygen free radicals perform some important metabolic functions, but they can also disrupt protein synthesis and repair (especially in mitochondria) and can cause minor errors in DNA replication that accumulate over time." President's Council on Bioethics, *Beyond Therapy*, 177. The age-retarding effects of antioxidants have been shown in studies on worms, mice and fruit flies. Cf. Barazzetti, "Looking for the Fountain of Youth," 341.

    201. "Cloned human embryonic stem cells, appropriately reprogrammed, might be used for constant regeneration of organs and tissue." Harris, "Intimations of Immortality," 59.

    202. Ehninger et al., "Longevity, Aging and Rapamycin."

    203. Reddy, "Scientists' New Goal"; Knapton, "World's First Anti-Ageing Drug."

    204. Telomeres form the tips of chromosomes.

    205. "There is growing evidence that telomere shortening limits the regenerative potential of organ cells during aging and chronic disease. Telomere shortening affects organ regeneration at cellular level and limits the pool of regenerating cells by activation of a senescence programme in cells with critically short telomeres. The possibility of using telomerase activation, to extend the regenerative potential of cells during aging and chronic disease, depends on the effects of telomerase activity on tumor formation." Barazzetti, "Looking for the Fountain of Youth," 341. Cf. President's Council on Bioethics, *Beyond Therapy*, 179.

    206. Savulescu, "Human Prejudice," 212.

    207. See Nebel and Bosch, "Evolution of Human Longevity," 730–31; Rich, "Can a Jellyfish."

Objections to Lifespan Extension

A response to the quest for lifespan extension might consider two points: (1) its feasibility, and (2) its desirability. In terms of the latter, Gilbert Meilaender makes a distinction between the desire to live longer and the legitimacy of that desire. "That we often desire, even greedily desire, longer life is clear; whether what we desire is truly desirable is harder to say."[208] The legitimacy of this desire will be discussed in more detail in chapter 9.

The question of feasibility, however, directly challenges the scientific foundations on which the quest for lifespan extension is based. Despite observational studies that point to the positive effects of caloric restriction on human health and aging,[209] other techniques remain theoretical, with no current therapeutic application. Experimental findings of age-retardation remain at the level of animal studies[210] or observations in human tissue cultures.[211] A recent report that experimental gene therapy has resulted in increased telomere length in the leukocytes of a human subject has been met with caution.[212]

However, even if it were proved possible to slow the aging process in humans, it would be likely to have uneven effects, not only between individuals, but also within the individual subject. For age retardation to be desirable it requires a general and coordinated slowing of the aging process that involves all body systems. Otherwise, a mere increase

---

208. Meilaender, *Should We Live Forever?*, ix.

209. Kurzweil and Grossman, "Bridges to Life," 5. Cf. Nikolich-Zuglich and Messaoudi, "Mice and Flies and Monkeys Too."

210. Hildt, "Living Longer," 180. However, as the President's Council cautions, the findings of animal studies cannot be easily translated to human beings since "we are not simply more complicated versions of worms, flies, or mice." President's Council on Bioethics, *Beyond Therapy*, 180.

211. Conger, "Telomere Extension Turns Back Aging Clock."

212. The announcement was made on the website of the American biotech firm Bioviva, claiming that Elizabeth Parrish, CEO of Bioviva USA Inc., had become "the first human being to be successfully rejuvenated by gene therapy, after her own company's experimental therapies reversed 20 years of normal telomere shortening." Bioviva, "First Gene Therapy." However, despite the claim that if could boost immunity by adding up "20 years of health onto the leukocytes," critics have underlined that the link between telomere length, health and mortality is yet to be established. Grens, "First Data."

in longevity could result in a proportionally longer period of frailty and decline.²¹³ Accordingly, further caution is advised.

> Given that age-retardation sets out to alter not just this organ or that tissue but the entire (putative) coordinated biological clock of a most complex organism, caution and modest expectations are proper leavens for zeal, especially as the love of longer life needs little encouragement to embrace false hopes of greater time on earth.²¹⁴

Summary

From this overview of the transhumanist project, especially as developed by individuals of the Oxford School, two of the dynamics already identified in the previous chapter have been confirmed: (1) transhumanism's discontentment with the limitations of the human condition, and (2) its confidence in the prospects of technology to transcend them.²¹⁵ It has also demonstrated the wide-ranging prospects for human enhancement, in the application of biotechnology to make us smarter and stronger, to be happier and morally responsible, and to live longer. While there is nothing new in human beings struggling against their limitations, and history is littered with various successes and enhancements, the current era is buoyed by advances in science and technology that promise new and more efficient means for achieving that end. As a representative of the transhumanist movement puts it, "for the first time we have scientific knowledge that has the potential for transforming ourselves perhaps more profoundly—and certainly more deliberately—than ever before."²¹⁶ And for transhumanists, such potential turns to hope.

---

213. "Indeed, the period of debility could be lengthened not only absolutely (as it would be on the model of a rubber band being stretched) but also relative to the whole lifespan, and, in either case, virtually everyone who survives past eighty or ninety might come to expect ten to fifteen years of severely diminished capacity. All the scenarios for *happy* life-extension depend on technologies that will keep *all* the body's systems going for roughly the same duration, after which time they will shut down more or less simultaneously." President's Council on Bioethics, *Beyond Therapy*, 183.

214. President's Council on Bioethics, *Beyond Therapy*, 183.

215. What Elena Colombetti identifies as "the idea that the present condition of human beings is miserable and that the self transcendence is only a matter of scientific knowledge and techniques." Colombetti, "Contemporary Post-Humanism," 369.

216. Buchanan, *Beyond Humanity?*, xi.

Chapter 3

The Anthropological Question

The Human Person in Transhumanist Thought

From the outset it was noted that transhumanism emerges from the conviction that human beings in their current form are incomplete, improvable, "a work-in-progress, a half-baked beginning that we can learn to remould in desirable ways."[1] In this context, transhumanists assume a particular stance in relation to evolution, recognizing both the limitations of the evolutionary process and opportunities for further development. They consider human enhancement to be in continuity with evolution, either by giving it a helping hand or by correcting its shortcomings; to move human beings further along evolution's trajectory by replacing natural selection with technological enhancement. According to a popular transhumanist mantra: "Transhumanism is a way of thinking about the future that is based on the premise that the human species in its current form does not represent the end of our development but rather a comparatively early phase."[2]

Departing from the theory of evolution, individual transhumanists vary in the respect they show for the evolutionary process, but in each instance there is the perception that evolution has somehow failed to prepare human beings for the modern world. As Bostrom writes: "Human nature is in an evolutionary disequilibrium; our evolved dispositions are not adapted to the contemporary fitness landscape and do not maximize

---

1. Bostrom, "Human Genetic Enhancements," 493.
2. *Transhumanist FAQ*, n. 3.0.

the inclusive fitness of current individuals."[3] In making sense of this disequilibrium, he employs the "evolution heuristic," which basically involves asking why the human organism has evolved in its current form, and why it does not possess certain qualities which today we might consider beneficial. Together with Anders Sandberg, Bostrom offers three explanations: changed trade-offs, value discordance, and evolutionary restrictions. I will consider each in turn.

The Evolution Heuristic

Changed Trade-Offs

It is hypothesized that human beings evolved as hunter-gatherer tribesmen in the African savannah, very different in its environment from the demands of the modern world.[4] The principle of *changed trade-offs* asserts that the adaptions that favored fitness for survival within the "Environment of Evolutionary Adaptedness" (EEA)—that is, the environment in which human beings evolved—do not necessarily retain their evolutionary advantage today. Two ways are identified in which trade-offs have changed in the contemporary context: (1) through the availability of new resources that weren't available before; and (2) through a change in demands placed on the human organism in the current environment. The two are interrelated.

Changed resources, especially those related to nutrition, are marked between life today and that in the EEA when food was scarce and energy conservation essential. In the past, trade-offs favored the metabolic demands of immunity over those of brain development and mental activity. However, in today's context, with decreased demands on the immune response (through better hygiene and effective antimicrobial agents), as well as a more stable (though unequally distributed) nutrition, more energy is potentially available for brain function. Indeed, the contemporary context places greater demands upon abstract thought, for literacy and numeracy, and for concentration over longer periods, than in the past. According to Bostrom and Sandberg, this change in resources

---

3. Bostrom, "Future of Human Evolution," 6.

4. "Hunting, gathering of fruits and nuts, courtship, parasites, and hand-to-hand combat with wild animals and enemy tribes were element of the EEA; speeding cars, high levels of trans fats, concrete ghettos, and tax return forms were not." Bostrom and Sandberg, "Wisdom of Nature," 381.

and demands "suggests opportunities for enhancement by readjusting trade-offs that are no longer optimal,"[5] providing that the human organism can be released from its evolved limitations through technological intervention.

Applying the same logic, transhumanists identify evolutionary adaptions that have become disadvantageous in the current context. Thus, it is suggested that human beings evolved to have an easily distracted attention, advantageous in protecting oneself from surrounding threats, but disadvantageous in the contemporary setting in which sustained concentration to certain tasks is required.[6] Similarly maladaptive is the evolved craving for high-calorie foods and propensity for fat storage which, though beneficial in times of food shortage, is responsible for significant health problems in contemporary society. Other examples include the "fight-or-flight" response, that while advantageous in protecting oneself against predators in the past, is today linked to problems of stress and anxiety; and the sensitivity of anti-parasite immune cells, which in the absence of parasitic threats in the modern context, may trigger allergies.[7]

In order to close the gap between the trade-offs of the past and present needs, new forms of adaption are required. In this, transhumanists see a role for technological enhancement to *retune* the trade-off to a point that corresponds to our changing needs.[8] It does not require that we possess the wisdom or the engineering skills to repeat what evolution has achieved, but rather to *tweak* the result toward something better adapted to contemporary demands.[9]

---

5. Bostrom and Sandberg, "Wisdom of Nature," 389–90.

6. In this context Bostrom and Sandberg note: "It has been suggested that ADHD is a form of 'response-readiness' that was more adaptive in past environments," but which is maladaptive in today's world. Bostrom and Sandberg, "Wisdom of Nature," 390.

7. Earp et al., "When Is Diminishment," 5.

8. Bostrom and Sandberg, "Wisdom of Nature," 381.

9. Bostrom and Sandberg use the analogy of tuning a car, contending that "it is much harder to design and build a car from scratch than it is to fit an existing car with a new set of wheels or make some other tweaks to improve functioning in some particular setting." Bostrom and Sandberg, "Wisdom of Nature," 379.

Value Discordance

By *value discordance*, transhumanists refer to a discordance between evolution's objectives and human values;[10] a discrepancy between our notions of happiness and evolution's indifference.[11] The example is given of fertility regulation through contraceptive technology. Contraception stands in conflict with evolutionary fitness which depends upon one's ability to reproduce, according to which nature has engineered an intrinsic link between sex and reproduction. However, in the current context, this evolutionary tactic comes into conflict with certain human values: the desire to plan one's family, to be free to pursue a career without the burden of children, to engage in sexual activity without the risk of pregnancy.

A related value discordance concerns our conceptions of love and marriage. While it is suggested that feelings of love between a couple may have constituted an evolutionary advantage for ensuring the care of offspring, evolution has not equipped us to be faithful to the lifelong, monogamous relationships that we expect of marriage today.[12] This value discordance between our human biological and psychological nature, "designed by the blind hand of natural selection" and "forged into us over thousands of generations by the fires of evolution," and our human values regarding marriage, "shaped by relatively recently-developed conscious concerns about human flourishing, well-being, justice, and so on," is exacerbated by the contemporary context, including the above-mentioned separation of sex and reproduction through contraceptive technology, which has made fidelity even more difficult.[13] In this context, mood and love enhancing drugs that promote fidelity are deemed to represent a form of "biological liberation" from the constraints imposed on us by evolution.[14]

Finally, a value discordance exists between our concern for old age and Mother Nature's neglect of her elderly children.[15] Evolution selects

10. Bostrom and Sandberg, "Wisdom of Nature," 393.

11. As Savulescu and Sandberg write: "Evolution does not promote human happiness except as a side effect. Pleasure, joy and love all appear to have evolved as adaptations to promote fitness rather than ends in themselves. To us humans, however, they (and many other life goals) are often far more important than the survival of our genes." Savulescu and Sandberg, "Neuroenhancement," 32.

12. Earp et al., "Natural Selection," 570.

13. Earp, "Love and Other Drugs," 14.

14. Savulescu and Sandberg, "Neuroenhancement," 41.

15. Buchanan, *Better than Human*, 32.

for reproductive fitness. However beyond reproductive age, selective pressures diminish to nothing.

> Simply put, evolution does not regard what occurs to the progenitors once they have successfully reproduced. There are no selective forces holding them together, and their biological programme ceases to have positive functionality. Their systems of repair fail, their positive functions pass beyond optimal efficiency and can become antagonistic, and inexorable degeneration to death occurs.[16]

This evolutionary indifference toward the elderly is at odds with our desire for a long and healthy life. Transhumanists thus look to biotechnology to provide the processes of repair and regeneration that are lacking in evolution's repertoire, to find a "cure" for aging, and move us toward immortality.

Evolutionary Restrictions

While achieving some remarkable feats, evolution relies on primitive tools, which when compared to the promise of modern science and technology, is recognized as a restriction to the evolutionary potential of human beings. In this perspective, the "wisdom of nature" is replaced by the power of technology.

Along with evolution's "fundamental inability" to produce specific traits due to lack of resources, Bostrom and Sandberg note two other restrictions to the evolutionary process that could potentially be overcome through technology: (1) due to "entrapment in a local optimum," in which evolution "sometimes gets stuck on solutions that are locally but not globally optimal";[17] and (2) due to an "evolutionary lag," which recognizes that it takes many generations for a specific trait to develop.

In terms of entrapment, Allen Buchanan speaks of "Local Optimality Traps."

> From the standpoint of evolution, to say that a trait is optimal means that no further *incremental* changes in the organism's genes can improve the traits contribution to reproductive fitness. Optimal doesn't mean unimprovable. It only means "the best that can be done, from the standpoint of reproductive

---

16. Horrobin, "Value of Life Extension," 421.
17. Bostrom and Sandberg, "Wisdom of Nature," 399.

fitness, *given that this is where we are now and that we have to proceed incrementally.*"[18]

Buchanan suggests that we are currently caught in such an optimality trap; that under natural selection we have reached a pinnacle of reproductive fitness that doesn't allow us to develop further, even though under different circumstance we could have reached higher capacities.

Evolutionary lag, on the other hand, refers to factors that limit the speed of evolution, such as the rate of mutation and the time required to create genetic diversity.[19] Since such factors are inherent to the process of evolution, which is unable to correct itself, the "wisdom of nature" is shown to be wanting. An opening therefore exists for bioenhancement "to solve some of the problems that were intractable to blind evolution"[20]—to "clean up the unwanted residue" of the "Pleistocene hangover"[21]—thinking backward from the desired goal and applying the necessary genetic modifications. Quoting Francis Fukuyama: "As 'transhumanists' see it, humans must wrest their biological destiny from evolution's blind process of random variation and adaptation and move to the next stage as a species."[22]

The Elimination of Human Difference

However, while transhumanism finds its rationale in evolution, its concept of the human person is somewhat removed from the humanist anthropology which underpins evolutionary theory. The difference lies in the appreciation of humanity's place within, and its distinction from, the world. As Maurizio Faggioni explains, while classical evolutionary theory regards human beings as "the point of arrival and the apex of an ascending movement," transhumanists have purged evolution of its anthropocentrism and has robbed humanity of any special significance.[23]

---

18. Buchanan, *Better than Human*, 43–44.
19. Bostrom and Sandberg, "Wisdom of Nature," 403.
20. Bostrom and Sandberg, "Wisdom of Nature," 399.
21. Buchanan, *Better than Human*, 36.
22. Fukuyama, "Transhumanism," 42.
23. Faggioni, "La natura fluida," 406-7. "L'evoluzionismo classico, in parte ancora erede del pensiero greco e cristiano, continuava a considerare l'uomo come il punto di arrivo e l'apice di un movimento ascendente che portava dal più semplice al più complesso, ma al nostro tempo, un evoluzionismo purgato dall'antropocentrismo e da ogni traccia di finalismo antropico, ha definitivamente spodestato l'uomo dal fastigio della storia della vita sul pianeta."

In the humanist interpretation, the process of evolution is seen as increasing humanity's distinction from the world. The human being is gradually purified and separated from nature, "*eliminating the animal and the machine from his image.*"[24] In contrast, the process of transhumanism, especially in its posthuman aspirations through the hybridization of person and machine, of the human mind and technology, is leading toward a new *alterity*—a diffusion of human distinctness and a blurring of boundaries.[25] As Luca Valera explains, this is the real goal of posthumanism: not simply a hyper-technologized humanity, but the "elimination" and "fluidization" of differences, and "the annihilation of all the boundaries that make 'human' a human being."[26]

This denial of human distinction, and the elimination of boundaries, ultimately amounts to "the negation of man,"[27] or of what C. S. Lewis prophetically refers to as his *abolition*:[28] of the human person treated as an artifact, as a mere "natural object," or "as raw material for scientific manipulation to alter at will."[29] Lewis warns against this end, troubled by the prospect of human beings assuming full control over themselves through eugenics, pre-natal conditioning, and "by an education and propaganda based on a perfect applied psychology."[30] The end would be

---

24. Tintino, "From Darwinian to Technological," 388.

25. Pepperell, "Posthumans and Extended Experience," 34: "Humanists might regard humans as distinct beings, in an antagonistic relationship with their surroundings. Posthumanists, on the other hand, regard humans as embodied in an extended technological world." Cf. Marchesini, "Ruolo delle alterità nella definizione dei predicati umani," 54: "Nella visione postumanista l'umano non è più pertanto l'emanazione o l'espressione dell'uomo bensì il risultato dell'ibridazione dell'uomo con le alterità non uname."

26. Valera, "Posthumanism," 483. With Vittoradolfo Tambone, Valera adds: "The posthuman being, the post-mankind, has indeed lost the characteristics of the human being, traditionally understood, hybridized and contaminated by other living things. Posthumanism is characterized, so, for the accentuation given to the plasticity of the human body, in the sense that, due to the hybridization with technology, the post-human being can have his own bodily identity in a relatively arbitrary way, thereby embodying the generally postmodern concept of fluid identity. In this sense, the posthuman era is characterized as the era of the *end of the differences.*" Valera and Tambone, "Goldfish Syndrome," 361–62.

27. Valera and Tambone, "Goldfish Syndrome," 362.

28. Lewis, *Abolition of Man*, 65. Ratzinger adopts and develops Lewis's insights in *A Turning Point*, 34–40.

29. Lewis, *Abolition of Man*, 73.

30. Lewis, *Abolition of Man*, 60.

something like that sought by the transhumanist projects: "We shall have 'taken the thread of life out of the hand of Clotho'[31] and be henceforth free to make our species whatever we wish it to be."[32]

The Alienation of the Body

Morphological Freedom

The elimination of the boundaries that define what is *human* begins with the body.[33] Transhumanists propose morphological freedom as "an extension of one's right to one's body,"[34] and as a means of self-expression, realized "through what we transform ourselves into."[35] In this context, Sandberg twists the concept of human nature, in which bodily integrity is replaced by "self-definition and a will to change."[36] Accordingly, he insists that morphological freedom does not threaten humanity, but allows it to be more fully expressed.[37]

However, morphological freedom means that the body is no longer something *given*. The body ceases to be the irreducible basis of individuality and identity. It does not have an essential relationship to the human subject. Instead, it is extrinsic to the person, arbitrarily related,

---

31. Clotho, a goddess from Greek mythology, and one of the three "Fates," is a spinner who spins the thread of human life. The length of the spun thread determines how long each person's life will be.

32. Lewis, *Abolition of Man*, 60. However, Lewis warns that "the power of Man to make himself what he pleases means, as we have seen, the power of some men to make other men what *they* please." Ibid., 60. And that "if man chooses to treat himself as raw material, raw material he will be: not raw material to be manipulated, as he fondly imagined, by himself, but by mere appetite, that is, mere Nature, in the person of his de-humanized Conditioners" (73–74).

33. "Here, the body as a signpost limit (and, therefore, as an identity) becomes the first element to be replaced in a posthuman ontology." Valera and Tambone, "Goldfish Syndrome," 359–60.

34. Sandberg, "Morphological Freedom," 56. Sandberg writes: "From the right to freedom and the right to one's own body follows that one has a right to modify one's body. If my pursuit of happiness requires a bodily change—be it dying my hair or changing my sex—then my right to freedom requires a right to morphological freedom" (57).

35. Sandberg, "Morphological Freedom," 59.

36. Sandberg, "Morphological Freedom," 60.

37. Sandberg, "Morphological Freedom," 63.

redundant and replaceable.[38] As Maria Russo and Nicola di Stefano note: "If anatomy is no longer a destiny, but the result of a decision that is constantly revocable, the body turns into prosthesis of the Self that is forever in search of an identity. The body is now seen as a sketch, a draft to be corrected."[39]

Of course, this alienation of the body does not begin with the transhumanist movement. It has deep philosophical roots in rationalist idealism. Cartesian dualism reduced the human person to thought and consciousness, existing as "a sort of inhabitant in a body"[40] or ghost within a machine. Accordingly, the body was not recognized as defining the human person, and human dignity was narrowed to the exercise of rationality. In time, thought itself came to be conceived as "a disembodied computable process,"[41] requiring a material substrate, but not necessarily of human flesh.[42] Following this logic, transhumanism envisages novel interactions between human beings and technology: intelligent machines, "*disembodied consciousness, mind uploading* (or *downloading*), [and] unconditional openness to otherness as a source of 'constitution of identity.'"[43] In consequence, the body becomes "a changeable and replaceable substrate; and technology becomes a feature of human ontology."[44]

Furthermore, transhumanism's de-emphasizing of the human body can be viewed as being consistent with postmodernism's aversion toward "exclusive categorization," especially with regard to culture and gender.[45] One recognizes practical expressions of this in the areas of ar-

38. Valera, "Posthumanism," 485.
39. Russo and Di Stefano, "Post-Human Body and Beauty," 459.
40. Colombetti, "Contemporary Post-Humanism," 372.
41. Colombetti, "Contemporary Post-Humanism," 372.

42. Max More writes: "While a few transhumanists believe that the self is tied to the current, human physical form, most accept some form of functionalism, meaning that the self has to be instantiated in *some* physical medium but not necessarily one that is biologically human—or biological at all." More, "Philosophy of Transhumanism," 7.

43. Valera, "Posthumanism," 484. Cf. Moltisanti and Postigo Solana, "Transumanesimo," 216: "I transumanisti si spingono addirittura più in là nell'affermare che potrebbero essere persone anche delle macchine che fossero apparentemente intelligenti. Questo *riduzionismo funzionalista* ha portato a considerare la persona soltanto da una prospettiva efficientistica, ossia un ente che produce atti di ragione."

44. Colombetti, "Contemporary Post-Humanism," 372.
45. Murillo, "Does Post-Humanism Still Need Ethics?," 471.

tificial reproduction and sexual ethics.⁴⁶ The advent of asexual means of reproduction, alienated from the body, makes sexual difference redundant. Similarly, instead of being something given along with the body, it is suggested that one's sexuality can be chosen and crafted at will. As a result, the boundaries "between what is given and what is the result of self-determination, between what is a technical product and what is properly human,"⁴⁷ are dissolved. In the end, the category of the human is itself surpassed: "a remnant of the past which is doomed to disappear."⁴⁸

Materialist Reduction

Paradoxically, the de-corporealization of the human subject is simultaneously a type of materialist or mechanistic reduction. In eliminating the complex reality of the human person, transhumanism adopts modernity's materialist conception of the human body as a kind of machine.⁴⁹ As Max More admits: "With few exceptions, transhumanists describe themselves as materialists, physicalists, or functionalists."⁵⁰ In this mechanistic view, materialism attempts to explain complex human faculties such as reason, thought and emotion in terms of chemical processes, which, when adopted by the transhumanist agenda, can be manipulated or augmented so as the enhance the human organism. As Bostrom writes: "If human beings are constituted by matter that obeys the same laws of physics that operate outside us, then it should in principle be possible to learn to manipulate human nature in the same way that we manipulate external objects."⁵¹

However, serious objections are leveled at this materialist reduction that lies at the heart of transhumanist thought. In the first instance, one could sight the objection of Hans Jonas that materialism's reductionist logic cannot fully appreciate living beings. In its dissection of bodies to their constituent parts, it treats them as dead matter. For this reason,

46. Russo and Di Stefano, "Post-Human Body and Beauty," 459.
47. Russo and Di Stefano, "Post-Human Body and Beauty," 459.
48. Murillo, "Does Post-Humanism Still Need Ethics?," 471.
49. In this context Bostrom quotes from Julien Offray de La Mettrie, *L'Homme Machine*, in which the eighteenth-century French physician and materialist philosopher asserts that "man is but an animal, or a collection of springs which wind each other up"; in Bostrom, "History of Transhumanist Thought," 3.
50. More, "Philosophy of Transhumanism," 7.
51. Bostrom, "History of Transhumanist Thought," 3.

Jonas refers to materialism as an "ontology of death."[52] Another objection concerns the reduction of nature to function. If function, and not rational *nature*, defines the human person,[53] then those members of the human species who lack the physical equipment for function are denied their status as persons, while certain animals (e.g., higher primates) and intelligent machines become potential candidates,[54] thus further confounding human significance and difference.[55] Once the concept of the person is determined in terms of functioning rationality, one is rendered incapable of recognizing the intrinsic, ontological dignity of every human being. And once the ontological foundation that makes humans different from every other living being is removed, human beings become merely quantitatively different from other beings (e.g., more complex), and dignity becomes merely subjective (e.g., quality of life, capacity for autonomy etc.).[56] It is to these considerations that I now turn.

---

52. Jonas, *Phenomenon of Life*, 11.

53. Moltisanti and Postigo Solana, "Transumanesimo," 216: "Nella teoria transumanista si tende quindi a produrre una eliminazione della realtà personale nella sua completezza, riducendola esclusivamente alla sfera materiale e in particolare all'esercizio di determinate funzioni, prima tra tutte quella razionale. Come ben sappiamo, nell'età Moderna si produsse una deriva dall'*esse* all'*agere*, vale a dire il passaggio dal concetto di persona umana ontologicamente fondato a quello operazionale (o attualistico)."

54. Moltisanti and Postigo Solana continue: "è persona umana soltanto chi ragiona (qui e ora), non è persona umana chi non ragiona più o non ancora (embrioni, feti, disabili mentali gravi, soggetti in stato vegetativo persistente o anche in coma, ecc.); inoltre, secondo questa prospettiva, lo statuto personale può essere attribuito ad esseri non umani che apparentemente sono in grado di esercitare attività razionali (certi primati superiori)." "Transumanesimo," 216.

55. Jeff McMahan illustrates this with a differentiation between an anencephalic human and a chimpanzee: "An anencephalic infant is a mindless biological organism belonging to the human species. A chimpanzee is a conscious being whose organism belongs to a different species. If one is not an organism but is essentially an embodied mind, one's relation to the chimpanzee may be closer and more significant that one's relation to the anencephalic infant. For one's relation to the infant is only that one *has* an organism that is, like the anencephalic organism, biologically human. But one's relation to the chimpanzee is that one *is*, like the chimpanzee, an embodied mind. The chimpanzee, in short, is of the same kind that one essentially is, whereas the anencephalic infant is only of the same kind that one's organism is." McMahan, *Ethics of Killing*, 225–26.

56. Moltisanti and Postigo Solana, "Transumanesimo," 217.

The Diminishment of the Human Significance

The loss of human distinction is evident in the thought of Savulescu. In his apology for human enhancement, Savulescu takes aim at the "folk view" of our special significance as human beings:[57] what Bernard Williams refers to as the "human prejudice."[58] Savulescu enumerates certain characteristics of this prejudice:

- we privilege human beings in our ethical thought;
- we think that what happens to human beings is more important than what happens to other creatures;
- we think that human beings as such have a claim on our attention and care in all sorts of situations in which other animals have less or no claim on us.[59]

In defending the human prejudice, Williams does not seek justification in metaphysical principles or from a cosmic point of view.[60] Rather, he suggests that it is justified simply because we care more about human beings. According to Savulescu's interpretation, Williams invokes "internal reasons" or a "desire-based" account of normative reasons.[61] He insists that this human preference is different in character from other prejudices like racism or sexism, for the human prejudice requires no further rationalization or justification. The significance to the words "It's a human being" is enough.

Savulescu, however, rejects this distinction, likening human prejudice to a "club privilege,"[62] or worse still, to a form of "speciesism" that favors human interests over the interests of nonhuman animals: a prejudice that in the opinion of Peter Singer, on whom Savulescu leans, has no rational foundation other than biological membership.[63] With

---

57. Savulescu, "Human Prejudice," 216.
58. Williams, "Human Prejudice," 135–54.
59. Savulescu, "Human Prejudice," 217.
60. Williams writes: "If there is no such thing as the cosmic point of view, if the idea of absolute importance in the scheme of things is an illusion, a relic of a world not yet thoroughly disenchanted, then there is no other point of view except ours in which our activities can have or lack a significance." Williams, "Human Prejudice," 137.
61. Savulescu, "Human Prejudice," 224.
62. Savulescu, "Human Prejudice,", 220.
63. Singer likens speciesism to "a prejudice no better founded than the prejudice of white slaveowners against taking the interests of their African slaves seriously." Singer,

Singer, Savulescu rejects the human prejudice in favor of "personism," in which what matters morally is not membership in the species, but specific properties that we value in human persons, such as rationality and self-consciousness, the capacity for preferences and ability to visualize oneself as extending across time.⁶⁴ To the extent that other animals (or posthuman beings) express these properties, we have reason to care for them also. One might note a consistency here with the reductionist view of human nature and the loss of distinction between humans, other animals and machines, as outlined above.

In contrast to the desire-based, internal reasoning of the human prejudice, personism favors "value-based" or "external reasons" for the moral significance of individuals in which not all human qualities are deemed to be morally relevant.⁶⁵ In addition to rationality and self-consciousness, the capacity for preferences and for self-extension across time, Savulescu provides a list of values that include "the badness or goodness of suffering, indignity, achievement, warm and sincere human relations, knowledge, development of skills, and talents."⁶⁶ It is suggested that it is these capacities which afford moral status and value to members of the species, and give a normative sense to what is human. Consequently, enhancement of such values would make individuals *more* human, offering incentive and even obliging "an evolution to posthumanism."⁶⁷

Practical Ethics, 55–56. Contradicting Williams, Singer makes a deliberate parallel between speciesism and other "isms" such as racism and sexism. Singer, "Speciesism and Moral Status," 572.

64. Savulescu, "Human Prejudice," 221.

65. Savulescu, "Human Prejudice," 226. Savulescu suggests that there is inconsistency and a lack of rational development surrounding our profession of what we value. For example, he suggests that there are many who claim to value membership of the human species, but whose behavior suggests otherwise. Concretely, when faced with a situation in which permanently unconscious human beings are trapped in a burning building, he proposes that few would risk their lives attempting to save them. According to Savulescu, this response reveals that we don't value human beings as such, but "the characteristics that make them persons" and "our special relations with them." He further adds: "This is revealed by our practices of letting brain damaged human beings die and even killing them: those in a persistent vegetative state, sufferers from severe brain injury or advanced dementia. These are human beings but we do not value their lives when we disconnect their feeding tubes." Thus, Savulescu concludes: "It is true that people believe that merely being a human being matters, but they are mistaken. It is other properties of being a human being that really matter" (228).

66. Savulescu, "Human Prejudice," 225.

67. Persson and Savulescu, "Moral Transhumanism," 668.

However, without offering an account of how we should reason these values or come to hold them as normative—i.e., without a metaphysical basis for value claims[68]—there is the danger that the values proposed by Savulescu will themselves degenerate into Williams-like preferences,[69] void of normative significance.

In contrast, Robert Spaemann defends a form of personism that is metaphysically founded. He argues that biological membership *is* morally significant and that it engages reason: not as a crude reality, but at the level of a shared history and common genealogy. As he explains, members of the human species "are not merely exemplars of a kind; they are kindred, who stand from the outset in a personal relation to one another."[70] Being a person is not determined by specific qualities, valued and verified, but by belonging to the human family through genealogical connections. "There is only one admissible criterion for human personhood," he writes: "belonging biologically to the human family."[71] According to Spaemann, the separation of the *personal* from the *biological*, implicit in Singer's personism, is an attempt to put personality over and above human animality; as if human animality was "mere animality" and not "the medium of personal realization."[72]

While Savulescu is willing to admit some significance to membership of the human species, arguing "that humanity or the member of

68. In a "value-based" account there is no room for metaphysics or a cosmic point of view. Indeed, Savulescu belittles reference to a cosmic order as favoring a human prejudice that is "typical among the uneducated and the religiously dogmatic." Savulescu, "Human Prejudice," 229.

69. Savulescu unwittingly acknowledges as much when he writes: "We can simply value, because we desire them, culture, intelligence, and technology with no commitment to the cosmic order of things." Savulescu, "Human Prejudice," 227.

70. Spaemann, *Persons*, 240.

71. Spaemann, "Begotten, Not Made," 297.

72. Spaemann, *Persons*, 240. "What this separation of the biological from the personal fails to grasp, is that personhood is situated in the *life* of human beings. Fundamental biological functions and relations are not apersonal; they are specifically personal performances and interactions. Eating and drinking are personal acts (*actus humani*, as the scholastics said, not merely *actus hominis*). They are embedded in rituals, they provide the focus of many forms of community life, they stand at the center of many cults. Something similar applies to sexual intercourse. Here, too, the biological function is integrated in a personal context, often as the highest form of expression of a relation between persons. The kinship-connections of mothers and fathers to sons and daughters, of grandparents to grandchildren, of siblings and cousins to one another, are not merely a biological given, but personal relations of a typical kind, relations which as a rule last for life" (239).

the species *homo sapiens* is a rough placeholder that typically includes a range of properties which we value,"[73] he nonetheless maintains that it is the properties themselves that are morally significant. In this context, he refers to the significance of family ties, comparing human partiality to the special ties between husband and wife, parent and child.[74] However, Savulescu insists that such connectedness can only justify a weak preference for human beings. It does not determine the substance of our obligations.

But in this interpretation there seems to be a confusion between obligation and benevolence. For instance, Spaemann argues that while *amor benevolentiae* is determined by the intrinsic properties of beings, obligations (toward kin and close connections) are established by a hierarchy within the *ordo amoris*. In the first instance, the imperative toward benevolence is awakened by the realization that one exists along with the other as beings on a *common horizon*.[75] "Other humans are unequivocally given to us as 'things-in-themselves,' as real in the strong sense of the word."[76] Our benevolent consideration of other human beings is not determined by an instinctual biological solidarity, uniting us as a species. Rather, it exists in the recognition that "others stand in a relationship with themselves, that is, they are selves."[77]

However, the disparity between the infiniteness of benevolence, the individual existence of the other,[78] and the finiteness of the moral subject means that, in practice, this imperative needs to be relativized. This is precisely what happens in the *ordo amoris*, in which one's obligation toward others is hierarchically determined according to the closeness of one's relationship. Since human limitations dictate that giving to one corresponds to taking or withholding from another, family, friends, neighbors, and fellow citizens place a deeper claim upon our time and action

---

73. Savulescu, "Human Prejudice," 229.

74. "There are some reasons to believe that there are special ties, albeit much weaker than humanists want to assert, between members of the family of man. Human beings share a biological, genetic connection, just like family members. Indeed, the genetic differences between humans are small. There is a common history. Our physical and psychological attributes, despite conspicuous dissimilarities, are much more similar at the deepest level. We can understand the actions and behavior of people from radically different cultures." Savulescu, "Human Prejudice," 233.

75. Spaemann, *Happiness and Benevolence*, 106.

76. Spaemann, *Happiness and Benevolence*, 114.

77. Spaemann, *Happiness and Benevolence*, 114.

78. "Persons *are* only as individuals." Spaemann, *Happiness and Benevolence*, 110.

than do those who are distant or unknown. Thus, in the choice between saving the life of one's own child and the life of another, Spaemann does not hesitate in saying that he would choose the life of his child. "And I would need the forgiveness of the one, who by this decision, was lost. Forgiveness, not in its narrower, moral sense, since I have no guilt."[79]

By insisting on the limited significance of partiality, Savulescu both weakens the bonds that exist between human beings, and expands moral responsibility beyond members of the human race; and this dynamic is encouraged by a value-based account of moral significance and his reduction of "intrinsic properties" to self-consciousness and functional rationality. Interpreted kindly, it means that just as a father, despite his special attachment to his child, also has obligations toward the stranger, so members of the human family should extend their concern beyond the human species.[80] But taken to its logical end, it signifies division, loss of solidarity, and abandonment of the more vulnerable members of the human family.

Redefining Human Dignity

The transhumanist denial of a definable human nature not only signifies the loss of human distinction, but also has implications for human dignity. With a value-based concept of human significance, the concept of human dignity is stripped of any ontological or metaphysical foundations. Traditionally, respect for human dignity, like the recognition of human rights,[81] is rooted in human nature. As Spaemann explains:

79. Spaemann, *Happiness and Benevolence*, 111. As Spaemann acknowledges elsewhere, this decision stands in contrast to that of Peter Singer who "thinks that, if two children are drowning and I can only save one, then the fact that one of them is my own should not matter for the question as to which one I should save. I would have to save the one who, because of his great talents and special qualities, promises to increase the improvement of the world in a higher degree." But as Spaemann objects, this attitude is "an attempt to take God's viewpoint and to devalue creaturely relations. As if we know by what the world is improved! It certainly is not improved by people who imagine themselves to bear the responsibility for the universe." Spaemann, *Love*, 18.

80. Savulescu, "Human Prejudice," 232. "Other humans are like our children and non-human persons are like strangers. Even if we care more about humans, we should still care about non-human persons. Why? Because we do value the properties which non-human beings instantiate."

81. As Fukuyama explains: "Underlying this idea of the equality of rights is the belief that we all possess a human essence that dwarfs manifest differences in skin color, beauty, and even intelligence. This essence, and the view that individuals therefore

> If talk of human rights is to have any meaning at all, then it implies that the claim to such rights is not bestowed by other humans but comes to the being which asserts the claim from the being itself. "From the being itself" can only mean: on account of its nature. If, for the grounding of human dignity, some empirical quality or other was required beyond the simple belonging to the human species, then the recognition of a human as a human would be dependent on others who defined these qualities and decided on their presence or absence in individual cases. But that would mean that the real essence of human rights, namely the independence from such definitions and judgments of others, would be lost.[82]

While admitting that human dignity is not determined by biology, Spaemann insists that dignity flows from biological membership in the sense that it is a relational concept; from belonging to a species that is, by nature, free and rational. "It is therefore irrelevant," he adds, "whether an individual member of the family does already have, or still has, or has ever had at all those properties that cause us to speak of person, i.e., those properties which bring dignity phenomenally to appearance."[83]

Thus, the recognition of dignity cannot be determined by the presence of an empirically determined property.[84] But this is precisely what Bostrom attempts to do with his conception of dignity as a *quality*: "a kind of excellence admitting of degrees and applicable to entities both within and without the human realm";[85] a kind of virtue (though not necessarily moral virtue); "an ideal, which can be cultivated, fostered, respected, admired, promoted, etc."[86] Individuals will necessarily vary in such qualities and have more or less dignity accordingly. By extension, dignity may also be ascribed to nonpersons.

Bostrom distinguishes dignity as a quality from both dignity as a "moral status" and dignity as associated with concepts of "worthiness"

---

have inherent value, is at the heart of political liberalism." Fukuyama, "Transhumanism," 42.

82. Spaemann, *Happiness and Benevolence*, 115.

83. Spaemann, *Love*, 28.

84. "Dignity is not a property among other empirical data. Nor should we say that it is a human right to have one's own dignity respected. Dignity is rather the transcendental ground for the fact that human beings have rights and duties." Spaemann, *Love*, 27.

85. Bostrom, "Dignity and Enhancement," 173.

86. Bostrom, "Dignity and Enhancement," 175.

or "honor."[87] The first distinction (moral status) regards human dignity (*Menschenwürde*) as the foundation of equality and human rights. In the second instance, dignity corresponds to social rank or status, conferred either by merit, effort, or according to a supposed intrinsic value (e.g., the aristocrat or Brahmin). In admitting of gradation, this interpretation of dignity lacks the concept of equality that is essential to the prior definition.[88]

In speaking of dignity as a quality, Bostrom attempts to go beyond both these definitions. In developing his theory, he claims to draw on "the sensitive linguistic and phenomenological analysis provided by Aurel Kolnai."[89] In Bostrom's interpretation, Kolnai asserts that dignity "contains both descriptive and evaluative components, and may not be in any simple way reducible to more basic moral predicates."[90] Dignity exists as a virtue among other virtues, marked by certain characteristics: qualities of composure, calmness, restraint, and reserve; of distinctness and distance that make one invulnerable and inaccessible to corruption and subversion; of serene self-sufficiency and restrained self-assertion with which "the dignified quietly defies the world."[91]

While acknowledging that dignity as a quality could conceivably be compromised by enhancement,[92] Bostrom nonetheless focuses on its

---

87. Bostrom, "In Defense of Posthuman Dignity," 209.

88. Bostrom, "Dignity and Enhancement," 176.

89. Bostrom, "Dignity and Enhancement," 177. Cf. Kolnai, "Dignity," 251–71. In responding to Bostrom's thesis, Charles Rubin suggests that Kolnai "would seem to be an odd source for the case for transhumanism. A Hungarian-born philosopher who converted to Catholicism after reading G. K. Chesterton, Kolnai spent much of his career as an expatriate. Trained in phenomenology by Husserl, Kolnai articulated a politics of 'Christian imperfectionism' and a powerful anti-utopianism, a politics not at all well suited to a thoroughgoing project to remake human nature." Rubin, "Commentary on Bostrom," 207.

90. Bostrom, "Dignity and Enhancement," 177.

91. Kolnai, "Dignity," 253–54. Quoted in Bostrom, "Dignity and Enhancement," 178–79.

92. "For instance, a greatly increased capacity for empathy and compassion might (given the state of this world) diminish our composure and our self-contained serenity, leading to a reduction of our Dignity as a Quality. Some enhancements that boost motivation, drive, or emotional responsiveness might likewise have the effect of destabilizing a dignified inner equilibrium. Enhancements that increase our ability rapidly to adapt to changing circumstances could make us more susceptible to 'destructive or corruptive or subversive interference' and undermine our ability to stand firm and quietly defy the world." Bostrom, "Dignity and Enhancement," 180.

potential for increasing dignity.[93] He suggests that "self-made" human beings possess more dignity than those who merely accept their fate. In this he is encouraged by Kolnai's determination that compliance and adaptability are prototypically undignified attributes, significant of what Kolnai terms the "meretricious" person, who "wallows in his dependence on his environment" and substitutes his preferences for "alien wants and interests."[94] In contrast, those who defy their lot, who assume authorship of their life project, may potentially enhance their dignity.

The concept of dignity as a quality allows Bostrom to confer dignity across species, to include nonhuman animals and even inanimate objects. However, he differentiates the dignity attributed to nonhumans (or non-persons) from that attributed to humans.[95] In making the distinction, he draws on a concept of Stephen Darwall.[96] Darwall differentiates two kinds of respect: "recognition respect" and "appraisal respect." In the first instance, recognition respect concerns the consideration given to moral agents. As Bostrom interprets, this is what is presumably meant by respect for *Human Dignity*. "We owe this respect to all people equally, independently of their moral character or any special excellences that they might have or lack."[97] On the other hand, appraisal respect considers the "positive characteristics or excellences that we attribute to his character, especially those that belong to him as a moral agent."[98]

Bostrom uses Darwall's categories to make a further distinction, between a limited and narrowly defined dignity that demands appraisal respect, and dignity in a wider, inclusive sense, that calls for mere recognition respect. In this wider sense, almost anything can be recognized as an object of respect. The demand for such respect is, in Bostrom's own

---

93. "Consider, for example, enhancements in executive function and self-control, in concentration, or in our ability to cope with stressful situations; further, consider enhancements of mental energy that would make us more capable of independent initiative and that would reduce our reliance on external stimuli such as television; consider perhaps also enhancement of our ability to withstand mild pains and discomforts, and to more effectively self-regulate our consumption of food, exercise, and sleep." Bostrom, "Dignity and Enhancement," 180.

94. Kolnai, "Dignity," 265–66. Quoted in Bostrom, "Dignity and Enhancement," 184.

95. Bostrom, "Dignity and Enhancement," 199.

96. Darwall, "Two Kinds of Respect," 36–49.

97. Bostrom, "Dignity and Enhancement," 199.

98. Bostrom, "Dignity and Enhancement," 199.

words, ubiquitous. "What is limited," he suggests, "is not the supply but our ability to appreciate it."[99]

Bostrom expresses the same idea using the categories of "quiet" values and "loud" values. Quiet values correspond to dignity as a quality in an extended sense, inclusive of subtle and non-domineering values. Without such values, Bostrom suggests that the world would be sterile and impoverished. "The quiet values add the luminescence, the rich texture of meaning, the wonder and awe, and much of the beauty and nobility of human action."[100] Loud values, in contrast, have a narrower scope, are "more starkly prudential or moral," and "tend to dominate the quiet values in any direct comparison." Such loud values encompass categories that one normally associates with concepts of human dignity: "alleviation of suffering, justice, equality, freedom, fairness, respect for Human Dignity, health and survival, and so forth."[101] Bostrom insists that in recognizing dignity as a quality, both loud and quiet values have their place. But in addressing what he perceives as an imbalance in favor of the loud in other models of human dignity, he relativizes their importance through adherence to aesthetic values that "might depend crucially on our subjective conscious responses."[102]

Through this broadened concept of dignity and the relativization of loud values, Bostrom's concept of dignity as quality has profound ethical implications. In the first place, by narrowing the pool of candidates for recognition respect to human persons defined as moral agents, a significant part of the human species is excluded: human embryos, anencephalic babies, individuals in a state of persistent unconsciousness, those suffering advanced dementia. Furthermore, with an ever-expanding respect for nonhumans and inanimate objects, the respect due to those humans excluded from the narrow definition of human dignity is even further diminished. This withering of respect is evident when Bostrom acknowledges that within the broad category of appraisal respect the "ethical fades . . . into the aesthetic (and perhaps into the sentimental), and it is not clear that there exists any sharp line of demarcation."[103]

---

99. Bostrom, "Dignity and Enhancement," 200.
100. Bostrom, "Dignity and Enhancement," 201.
101. Bostrom, "Dignity and Enhancement," 200.
102. Bostrom, "Dignity and Enhancement," 201.
103. Bostrom, "Dignity and Enhancement," 200.

This blurring of ethical boundaries is to be expected. Without a metaphysical basis for human nature, human dignity becomes a fluid concept, void of universal significance. As Brad Gregory explains, "in a society riven by fundamental disagreement about what 'human' means," fuelled by an academic climate which views the idea of human nature as "an oppressive, essentialist chimera,"[104] notions of human dignity and human rights are incapable of forming the basis of a shared morality. Instead, the recognition of human dignity becomes a matter of the will,[105] and in a democratic society, of the will of the majority (or at least of the loudest and most persuasive voices).

Summary

On the basis of the evolution heuristic, we are left with a being whose nature is devoid of any normative content. There is no ultimate reason why human beings should have evolved as they did; nothing special or final about their current form.[106] Holding no claim on our allegiance, there is no moral imperative to continue as we are; no "principled reasons to remain human if we can create creatures, or evolve into creatures, fundamentally 'better' than ourselves";[107] no objection to enhancements that "would alter or destroy human nature."[108]

A practical consequence of this development is that the meaning of enhancement is further eroded. Without a normative concept of human nature, enhancement makes little sense and our strivings to improve

---

104. Gregory, *Unintended Reformation*, 19.

105. As Moltisanti and Postigo Solana write: "Ma non c'è uguaglianza se non sulla base del riconoscimento della dignità come qualità intrinseca al puro essere uomo: se la dignità indica una qualità che si può perdere o possedere, se non è pensata in termini ontologici, ma nei termini morali dell'esercizio della ragione e della volontà umane, allora non vi è dubbio che la dignità varia e l'uguaglianza si frantuma." Moltisanti and Postigo Solana, "Transumanesimo," 218.

106. Max More writes: "Transhumanists regard human nature not as an end in itself, not as perfect, and not as having any claim on our allegiance. Rather, it is just one point along an evolutionary pathway and we can learn to reshape our own nature in ways we deem desirable and valuable." More, "Philosophy of Transhumanism," 4.

107. Harris, *Enhancing Evolution*, 40. Harris likens the attempt to preserve our current human nature to "the absurdity of our common ape ancestors in Africa getting together with a simian agenda to block evolution so that simian nature would be preserved as 'the common heritage of simian kind.'"

108. Buchanan, *Beyond Humanity?*, 138.

ourselves are without direction. The fluidity of human nature, and the freedom to create ourselves according to our wishes, renders "any concrete proposal for improvement vague and imprecise."[109] As Valera clearly identifies, "becoming needs Being as its foundation."[110] Enhancements require a given structure in which to adhere, in the absence of which we can only speak of change. In the words of José Murillo: "Freedom uprooted from nature can no longer aspire to improve nature. It can only aspire to reconfigure it over and over again, as it pleases."[111] And in the end, such reconfiguration of nature is not only without limit, but essentially without meaning as well.

---

109. Murillo, "Does Post-Humanism Still Need Ethics?," 475. Leon Kass makes the same point: "If, however, we can no longer look to our previously unalterable human nature for a standard or norm of what is good or better, how will anyone know what constitutes an improvement?" Kass, *Life, Liberty and the Defense of Dignity*, 132.

110. Valera, "Posthumanism," 484.

111. Murillo, "Does Post-Humanism Still Need Ethics?," 477.

Chapter 4

The Philosophical Foundations of Transhumanism and the Positivist Reduction

IN LIGHT OF THE preceding discussion, this chapter seeks to root transhumanist anthropology within the broader context of secular humanism, exploring transhumanism's philosophical roots in Enlightenment thought. With its rationalistic worldview, positivistic tendencies and presumption of the eclipse of God, secular humanism found in the theory of evolution a plausible explanation for the origins of the human species, and through the exaltation of the scientific method, thought it could achieve comprehensive knowledge of the human person and the world without recourse to religious myth or revelation.

Introducing the thought of Ratzinger, I will sketch a genealogy of the modern scientific mindset from which transhumanism emerges, tracing a path through its turn toward historical thinking and its reduction of reality to that which human beings can fathom and reproduce. This embrace of positivism helps explain modernity's rejection of being and the transhumanist denial of the distinctiveness of human nature. In response, Ratzinger highlights the restrictiveness of positive knowledge, proposing in its place an expansion of the contours of reality, offering an apology for the legitimacy of faith, and relativizing the positive claim.

Roots in Secular Humanism and Postmodern Reductionism

Transhumanism's embrace of the evolutionary heuristic fits within a broader philosophical system that, by Bostrom's own admission, has its roots in rational humanism.[1] The transhumanist movement draws specifically on the Enlightenment's encouragement of human enhancement through knowledge that goes beyond the limitations imposed by mythology and religion,[2] its exaltation of human rationality and its promotion of science, as well as its humanistic concern for human welfare and individual liberties.[3] In this context, Bostrom notes the important contribution of certain individuals: figures such as Giovanni Pico, Francis Bacon, Isaac Newton, Thomas Hobbes, John Locke, and Immanuel Kant. Significantly, Pico (1463–1494) asserted that the human form is not given or fixed, but is shaped by the individual,[4] while Bacon (1561–1626) advocated mastery over nature through scientific enquiry. All contributed to a form of rationalism that would ultimately canonize empirical science and critical reason as the only sources of knowledge about humanity and the world, and would pin its hopes on the seemingly endless possibilities offered by scientific development.[5]

According to Gerald McKenny, modern medicine emerges from this mindset as a purely practical science, dedicated to relieving "the human condition of subjection to the whims of fortune or the bonds of

---

1. Bostrom, "History of Transhumanist Thought," 2.

2. In this context, Bostrom notes a turning point in the emergence of Renaissance humanism which "encouraged people to rely on their own observations and their own judgment rather than to defer in every matter to religious authorities." Bostrom, "History of Transhumanist Thought," 2.

3. Bostrom, "History of Transhumanist Thought," 3–4.

4. Bostrom, "History of Transhumanist Thought," 2. Bostrom quotes from Pico's *Oration on the Dignity of Man* (1486): "We have made you a creature neither of heaven nor of earth, neither mortal nor immortal, in order that you may, as the free and proud shaper of your own being, fashion yourself in the form you may prefer. It will be in your power to descend to the lower, brutish forms of life; you will be able, through your own decision, to rise again to the superior orders whose life is divine."

5. "Ma senza alcun dubbio la Rivoluzione Scientifica e il pensiero moderno costituiscono una svolta, sia nel modo di fare scienza, sia nella visione dell'uomo. In particolare, per quanto riguarda il ruolo della scienza, con David Hume, Isaac Newton, Thomas Hobbes e Francis Bacon, si pongono le basi di un razionalismo che enfatizza lo sviluppo scientifico e che è sempre ottimista sulle sue possibilità." Moltisanti and Postigo Solana, "Transumanesimo," 206.

natural necessity."[6] He refers to this objective as the "Baconian project," inspired by the writings of Bacon and René Descartes (1596–1650), encouraged by the possibilities of modern technology, and ordered toward eliminating human suffering and expanding choice. The traditional teleological reading of nature with its hierarchy of ends was thus replaced by a "conception of nature as a law-governed mechanism, susceptible to human control and neutral with regard to ends—an order, therefore, which permits human control for the purposes of human preservation and well-being."[7]

Transhumanism may be read in continuity with this project, with its confidence in empirical science and exaltation of human reason over nature. However, the genealogy of transhumanism is complicated by the postmodern relativization of Enlightenment claims. In tracing the roots of postmodernity, Luis Miguel Pastor and José Ángel García-Cuadrado contend that confidence in scientific progress represents just one "soul" of the modern project. Alongside it there exists another current that exalts freedom in the place of truth, using science as a means to recreate reality.[8] In drawing out the difference between these two movements within modernism, Pastor and García-Cuadrado write:

> One especially identifies the human person with his consciousness, while the other identifies him with his freedom; one adores reason, whereas the other has traits of irrationality and nihilism. One seeks a new human being based on the old, and achieved through a purification by reason; the other wants to make a new human being through the transforming force of the will. One attempts to base the independence of the human person on the self-sufficiency of his all-knowing reason; the other bases it on the autonomy of his will, a will that proposes its own truth.[9]

In this reading, postmodernism is interpreted as the triumph of the nihilist or existential soul of modernity. Accordingly, postmodernity is not the negation of modernity, but its "radicalization" or "natural evolution." From this nihilistic root, postmodernism emerges with its characteristic allergy to metaphysics, its abandonment of rational systems, its relativism and skepticism. It signals "the end of the certainties and great

---

6. McKenny, *To Relieve the Human Condition*, 2.
7. McKenny, *To Relieve the Human Condition*, 18.
8. Pastor and García-Cuadrado, "Modernity and Postmodernity," 340.
9. Pastor and García-Cuadrado, "Modernity and Postmodernity," 340.

stories" that typified modernism in its rationalist form, and ushers in "a more liquid concept of the human being and society."[10]

In this continuity between aspects of modernity and postmodernism, in addition to its roots in Enlightenment philosophy, one can recognize transhumanism's accommodation of postmodern concepts. As already noted, transhumanism adopts the fluidity of postmodernist anthropology, emptied of any meaningful content. With the "death of God"[11] and metaphysics, the outlines of what is specifically human becomes blurred. From the existential point of view, human beings are defined by what they *choose*, more than by what they *are*, or even by what they *think*. But since postmodernity lacks the capacity to discern between choices, the human significance quickly degenerates into relativism and indifference.

Accordingly, the concept of what is human is given no normative value, dismissed as a construct "without empirical grounding in the findings of science."[12] There is no such thing as the human *project*, with the consequence that humanity is vulnerable to the whims of science and technology.[13] As Pastor and García-Cuadrado note, while modernism "attempted to *reduce* the human essence to pure culture, history, economics or biology," postmodernity "seeks to rebuild the human being as an ateleological reality where the outlines of the human evaporate completely."[14] And this is precisely where the transhumanist project fits, especially in its posthumanist leanings, in dissolving the human specificity, deconstructing human beings and attempting to create them anew;[15] of pursuing a Dionysian-like course of creating something out of nothing. A parallel may therefore be drawn between the transhumanist project and Nietzsche's efforts to "overcome" humanity in pursuit of

---

10. Valera, "Posthumanism," 482.

11. According to Nietzsche's "madman," having "killed" God allows human beings to move beyond their limitations. "There was never a greater deed—and whoever is born after us will on account of this deed belong to a higher history than all history up to now!" Nietzsche, *Gay Science*, 3 [125] 120.

12. Gregory, *Unintended Reformation*, 19.

13. Murillo, "Does Post-Humanism Still Need Ethics?," 473.

14. Pastor and García-Cuadrado, "Modernity and Postmodernity," 349.

15. But as Steven Jensen notes, this is the fundamental error of transhumanism, attempting to create what can only be received. "We do not create our end or good; it is received from our nature." Jensen, "Roots of Transhumanism," 522.

the *Overman* (*Übermensch*).¹⁶ Indeed, Brad Gregory does not hesitate in claiming that through the application of technology, especially genetic manipulation, transhumanism seeks "the deliberate self-elimination of human beings."¹⁷

Genealogy of the Contemporary Scientific Attitude

With his keen perception of philosophical trends, Ratzinger highlights the pervasive nature of scientism that has infected contemporary thought and made the transhumanist project possible.¹⁸ Thus, in helping to further trace transhumanism's philosophical foundations, I will follow his presentation of the genealogy of the scientific mentality, in its movement toward the rejection of metaphysics and its embrace of philosophical positivism. In his *Introduction to Christianity*, Ratzinger sketches a rough two-stage process through adoption of the historical approach and a turn toward technical thinking.

The First Stage: The Birth of the Historical Approach

The Rejection of Being

Ratzinger's point of departure is the Scholastic conviction that "being is truth" (*verum est ens*), or, in an alternative formulation, "all that is real is true" (*omne ens est verum*). In this Ratzinger is consistent with the thought of Thomas Aquinas, which he often reads through the lens of Josef Pieper (1904–1997).¹⁹ Aquinas asserts: "Being cannot be known

---

16. Nietzsche, *Thus Spoke Zarathustra*, I [3] 5. Several critics make this parallel, e.g., Murillo, "Does Post-Humanism Still Need Ethics?," 471; Colombetti, "Contemporary Post-Humanism," 368. Bostrom, however, denies a direct link with Nietzsche's thought. Bostrom, "History of Transhumanist Thought," 4.

17. Gregory, *Unintended Reformation*, 19.

18. "Characteristic of our contemporary scientific attitude, which moulds, whether we like it or not, every single individual's feeling for life and shows us our place in reality, is the limitation to 'phenomena,' to what is evident and can be grasped. We have given up seeking the hidden 'initselfness' of things and sounding the nature of being itself; such activities seem to us to be a fruitless enterprise; we have come to regard the depths of being as, in the last analysis, unfathomable. We have limited ourselves to our own perspective, to the visible in the widest sense, to what can be seized in our measuring grasp." Ratzinger, *Introduction to Christianity*, 58.

19. It might be noted that Ratzinger has a somewhat ambiguous relationship with

without the true";[20] and Pieper interprets: "The truth of a thing is not some 'property' that could equally be missing. Indeed, the reason for a thing's *being* is the same as for its *truth*."[21]

Adopting the Thomistic assertion of the truth of being, Ratzinger grounds his ontology in God's nature as spirit and intellect, who created all things by thinking them. In the first place, this signifies that *all things are known by God*. As Pieper interprets, the affirmation of divine omniscience signifies that there is nothing in being that is intrinsically irrational or unknowable.[22] For Ratzinger, this grounding of all things in divine knowledge also means that God's knowledge is creative; that for God "thinking and making are one and the same thing. His thinking is a creative process. Things are, because they are thought."[23]

Thus, all being stands in relation to a knowing mind and is orientated toward it.[24] This truth has anthropological implications. While the

---

Saint Thomas. He was no fan of pre-conciliar neo-Thomism with its "cramped thinking" and "excessively one-sided zeal" (Ratzinger, *Theological Highlights of Vatican II*, 41–42). In his memoirs, Ratzinger recalls his dissatisfaction with "rigid, neo-scholastic Thomism" of his seminary formation, that "no longer asked questions" but defended itself passionately against further enquiry (Ratzinger, *Milestones*, 44). Commenting on his time as a young professor and *peritus* at the Second Vatican Council he writes: "I was of the opinion that scholastic theology, in the form it had come to have, was no longer an instrument for bringing faith into the contemporary discussion. It had to get out of its armor; it also had to face the situation of the present in a new language, in a new openness" (Ratzinger, *Salt of the Earth*, 73). In contrast, he professes to be "a decided Augustinian," attracted to the great Bishop of Hippo insofar as he is "a counterweight to Thomas Aquinas" (*Salt of the Earth*, 33, 60). Against the perceived "impersonalism" of Scholasticism, Ratzinger identifies with "the passionate, suffering, questioning man" that he finds in Augustine (*Milestones*, 44; *Salt of the Earth*, 61). In this context, Ratzinger's engagement with Thomas is often mediated by Pieper, who exists as a significant influence on Ratzinger's thought, and with whom he maintained a longstanding friendship (de Gaál, *Theology of Pope Benedict XVI*, 152). Indeed, Pieper's thinking reverberates throughout Ratzinger's writings, "particularly in his treatments of the theological virtues, of hope and history and of faith and reason," which are precisely those areas in where Ratzinger is closest to Aquinas (Rowland, *Benedict XVI*, 16).

20. "Ens non potest intelligi sine vero." Aquinas, *Quaestiones disputatae de veritate*, I, 1 ad 3.

21. Pieper, "Truth of All Things," 29.

22. Pieper, "Truth of All Things," 43.

23. Ratzinger, *Introduction to Christianity*, 59.

24. Pieper, "Truth of All Things," 35. Cf. *STh.*, I, q. 16, a. 1. "True in an absolute sense are all things insofar as they are ordered toward the knowing mind on which their being depends."

truth of things exists primarily in the mind of God, Aquinas insists that it also exists in human minds.[25] But things are humanly knowable and apprehensible because they are first known and apprehended by an Other; or, as Ratzinger is want to say, "since all being is thought, all being is meaningful, *logos*, truth. It follows from this traditional view that human thinking is the rethinking of being itself, rethinking of the thought that is being itself."[26]

Against this background, Ratzinger identifies the initial movement away from metaphysics toward history in the thought of the Italian philosopher Giambattista Vico (1668–1744). "Against the Scholastic equation *verum est ens* (being is truth) he advocates his own formula, *verum quia factum*. That is to say, all that we can truly know is what we have made ourselves."[27] This path away from the truth of being toward the truth of the *factum* was paved, not by a lack of faith in God as Creator, but by a lack of faith in the human person's capacity to perceive the truth in things. The Copernican Revolution had challenged the traditional perception of the ordering of the cosmos. With the development of the telescope, the long-held belief that the world and humankind were placed at the center of the universe was shattered. Thus deceived by the powers of human observation, Descartes began by doubting the reality of external things, concluding in the third of his *Meditations* that only what can be perceived *clearly* and *distinctly* is true.[28] Spinoza (1632–1677) further rejected the idea of truth in being, declaring things to be "mute" and reducing truth to the content of statements.[29] Finally, Kant (1724–1804) "labelled the

---

25. "Res autem dicitur vera per comparationem ad intellectum divinum et humanun." Aquinas, *Quaestiones disputatae de veritate*, I, 6. As Pieper interprets: "The truth of all things consists in their being known by God and being knowable by man; all things are knowable for man, however, only *because* they are already known by God. The lucidity which from the creative knowledge of the divine *Logos* flows into things, together with their very being—yes, even *as* their very being—this lucidity alone makes all things knowable for the human mind." Pieper, "Truth of All Things," 52–53.

26. Ratzinger, *Introduction to Christianity*, 59. Pieper writes: "In view of human cognition, 'all things are true' means precisely that they stand revealed, open, intelligible—by reason of the primordial light emanating from the *Logos*, by reason of God's creative knowledge." Pieper, "Truth of All Things," 53.

27. Ratzinger, *Introduction to Christianity*, 59.

28. Pieper, "Truth of All Things," 26; Descartes, *Meditations on First Philosophy*, 29: "So I now seem to be able to lay it down as a general rule that whatever I perceive very clearly and distinctly is true."

29. Pieper, "Truth of All Things," 17.

principle of the truth of all things 'sterile' and 'tautological,'"[30] denying the human mind's capacity to contemplate being.

The Turn toward History

Thus alienated from truth, the enquiring mind turned instead to the *factum*: to that which has been made and immediately exists. Accordingly, knowledge was limited to the realm of demonstrable human activity, within the fields of mathematics and history,[31] and the world was rethought within the historical context. With Hegel and Comte, ontology was understood as a historical unfolding. Marx applied the same logic to economics. In the field of the natural sciences, Darwin's theory reduced human origins to a historical process of evolution and change. Thus, unlike the immovable stability of the created world, the modern world was marked by movement and expansion.

Theology also fell victim to this changing historicism.[32] With the advent of archaeology and source theory, the idea of history expanded beyond traditional biblical interpretations, stretching into an unknown past. As Guardini notes, the new historical consciousness posed serious questions for faith: "Can God really work within history if modern science and philosophy offer a true understanding of the world? Can God direct the universe providentially, can he be the Lord of Grace? Can he enter into history and become a Man?"[33] With the relativization of all historical events, the significance of the Incarnation *in the fullness of time* (see Gal 4:4), central to the biblical vision of history, was reduced to yet another event.[34] The change in mentality also stands behind the quest for

---

30. Pieper, "Truth of All Things," 19. In this, Pieper sees the influence of Baumgarten and Wolff, fathers of the German Enlightenment, who reduce "the truth of all things" to simply mean "that all existing things are real, nothing more," and in which "reality" and "being real" concern the "tangible, factual and objective." Reality, therefore, conforms to "structured reason," meaning that "every thing has to make sense, all that exists and occurs has to have some rational explanation" (24–25).

31. Ratzinger, *Introduction to Christianity*, 61.

32. Ratzinger, *Introduction to Christianity*, 62.

33. Guardini, *End of the Modern World*, 48.

34. "The single historical event lost its unique significance under the immense weight of historical facts and under the impact of the new conviction that time was unlimited. The multiplicity of historic phenomena allowed a unique importance to no one event; rather all events were viewed as having an indifferent significance and value." Guardini, *End of the Modern World*, 32–33.

the "historical Jesus," presumed to be buried beneath centuries of theologizing. As Ratzinger writes, it was thought that "everything supernatural, everything pertaining to the mystery of God that surrounded Jesus, was merely the embellishment and exaggeration of believers."[35] Only when everything was reduced to historical scrutiny would the true figure of Jesus be revealed.[36]

Furthermore, in a limitless universe, God no longer had his dwelling place in the heavens.[37] With the de-mystification of nature, cosmological proofs of God's existence were rejected. Descartes retreated to an ontological argument, which, with the abandonment of ontology and metaphysics, became equally unsatisfactory. Thus, God could not be known with certainty. In the end, Kant, who, as noted above, denied the human person's capacity to contemplate being, could merely postulate God's existence without engaging human reason.[38] Through a similar process, human beings lost their place of privilege within the world and history. With the new cosmology, they no longer found themselves at the center of the universe. According to Guardini, this new position was both humanity's exaltation and its debasement. *Torn* from the center of the world, and from God's universal gaze, human beings became autonomous, "raised up against God, exalted at his expense."[39] At the same time, however, they became no different from any other living being. They lost their special significance.

For his part, Ratzinger notes further anthropological implications in the relativization of being to time, suggesting that the modern notion of being's dependence on time destroys normative concepts of human nature.[40] The interpretation of being *in* time finds expression in two con-

---

35. Ratzinger, "Guardini on Christ," 53.

36. But as Ratzinger adds, quoting Guardini's preface to *The Lord*: "The figure and mission of Jesus are 'forever beyond the reach of history's most powerful ray,' because 'their ultimate explanations are to be found only in that impenetrable territory which he calls *my Father's will*.'" Ratzinger, "Guardini on Christ," 54; quoting Guardini, *Lord*, xvi.

37. Guardini, *End of the Modern World*, 44.

38. In his *Critique of Practical Reason*, Kant reduces the existence of God and the immortality of the soul to postulates of practical reason: noumenal, beyond the realm of human reasoning, but necessary conditions for the moral life. Kant, *Critique of Practical Reason*, bk. 2, ch. 2 [IV and V], 155–67.

39. Guardini, *End of the Modern World*, 46.

40. "The decisive turning point lies with Hegel, since which being and time have been more and more intertwined in philosophical thinking. Being itself is now

tradictory movements. In one interpretation, truth is understood within the context of an evolutionary process: particular truths are thought of as individual moments, reconciled and assimilated within the whole. Truth is an act of becoming. There is, therefore, no definable difference between true and untrue.

> Truth becomes a function of time; the true is not that which simply *is* true, for truth is not simply that which *is*; it is true for a time because it is part of the becoming of truth, which *is* by becoming. This means that, of their very nature, the contours between true and untrue are less sharply defined; it means above all that man's basic attitude toward reality and toward himself must be altered. In such a view, fidelity to yesterday's truth consists precisely in abandoning it, in assimilating it into today's truth; assimilation becomes the form of preservation.[41]

In the opposite direction, a Marxist ideology seeks not reconciliation of truth but revolution;[42] not assimilation but transformation. The recognition of being in time is not a process of identifying the strands of truth already present, but of constantly moving forward toward its realization. In this conception, all proclamations of truths are guarded with suspicion, as expressions of vested interests that impede progress. Accordingly, truth "must be sought at every step of history because anything that is designated as enduring truth is in direct contradiction with the logic of history."[43]

As Ratzinger notes, both conceptions of being in time have profound philosophical consequences for our appreciation of the truth of the human person. One is left asking: "Is there, in the course of historical time, a recognizable identity of man with himself? Is there a human

---

regarded as time; the logos becomes itself in history. It cannot be assigned, therefore, to any particular point in history or be viewed as something existing in itself outside of history; all its historical objectifications are but movements in the whole of which they are parts." Ratzinger, *Principles of Catholic Theology*, 16.

41. Ratzinger, *Principles of Catholic Theology*, 16.

42. While the vagaries of the perfect, classless society constitute the Marxist reconciliation, Marx is more concerned with defining revolution as the process of its accomplishment than with a description of the content of its end. As Jonas writes: "Everything is therefore focused on the revolution and its stages, that is, on the process of *bringing about* the new order. Contrary to the earlier utopias, it is the *coming*, not the *being*, of utopia about which Marxism has something to say." Jonas, *Imperative of Responsibility*, 179. Cf. Kampowski, *Greater Freedom*, 96.

43. Ratzinger, *Principles of Catholic Theology*, 17.

'nature'? Is there a truth that *remains* true in every historical time because it *is* true?"[44]

The Second Stage: The Turn toward Technical Thinking

Ratzinger identifies the second stage of the intellectual revolution of the modern era as moving away from the *factum*, the thing made, toward the *faciendum*, the process of making.[45] He identifies this shift in emphasis with the words of Marx: "So far philosophers have merely interpreted the world in various ways; [now] it is necessary to change it."[46] As Ratzinger interprets, in the turn toward technical thinking truth does not exist in *being*, nor in "accomplished deeds," but simply in changing and molding reality. Thus truth is tied to action; history is replaced by *techne*, by process and demonstration.

What emerged was a positivistic philosophy in which knowledge is restricted to what is verifiable, reproducible, and demonstrable.[47] Positivism is historically associated with the French philosopher Auguste Comte (1798–1857), who Ratzinger engages through the critique of Henri de Lubac in *The Drama of Atheist Humanism*.[48] Comte distin-

---

44. Ratzinger, *Principles of Catholic Theology*, 17.

45. "Translated into the language of the philosophical tradition, this maxim meant that *verum quia factum*—what is knowable, tending toward truth, is what man has made and what he can now contemplate—was replaced by the new programme *verum quia faciendum*—the truth with which we are now concerned is feasibility." Ratzinger, *Introduction to Christianity*, 63.

46. "Die Philosophen haben die Welt nur verschieden interpretirt; es kommt aber darauf an, sie zu verändern." Marx, "Theses on Feuerbach" (1845), thesis XI; cited in Ratzinger, *Introduction to Christianity*, 63. These emblematic words are engraved upon Marx's tomb at Highgate Cemetery in London.

47. See A. J. Ayer's "principal of verification." Ayer (1910–1989) wasn't concerned so much with the truth or falsity of a proposition, as with its significance, according to which something is significant if it is empirically verifiable, or elsewise tautological. "We say that a sentence is factually significant to any given person, if, and only if, he knows how to verify the proposition which it purports to express—that is, if he knows what observations would lead him, under certain conditions, to accept the proposition as being true, or reject it as being false. If, on the other hand, the putative proposition is of such a character that the assumption of its truth, or falsehood, is consistent with any assumption whatsoever concerning the nature of his future experience, then, as far as he is concerned, it is, if not a tautology, a mere pseudo-proposition." Ayer, *Language, Truth and Logic*, 16.

48. Ratzinger, *Faith and the Future*, 14.

guishes three stages in the evolution of thought: the "theological-fictive," the "metaphysical-abstract," and the "positive." According to this distinction, the theological or fictitious stage encompasses the whole history of religions, progressing through stages of fetishism, polytheism and theism. The metaphysical or abstract stage seeks a reconciliation between theology and physics. It exists as an intermediate phase between the theological-fictive and the scientific-positive. The latter, as the endpoint of human knowledge, seeks answers to reality entirely within the domain of physics.[49]

With the evolution of positivism, Comte sought to answer all of humanity's needs; to offer a blueprint for life.[50] Not restricted to the empirical sciences, its scientific method was applied to all forms of reality, offering answers to questions of anthropology, morality, and philosophy in general.[51] The consequences for human thought were dramatic. As Ratzinger notes, the triumph of positivism means

> that the entire realm of values, the entire realm of what "is above us," drops out of the sphere of reason, that the sole binding standard for reason and thus for man, politically as well as individually, becomes what "is under him," namely, the mechanical forces of nature that can be manipulated experimentally.[52]

In practice, this means that correctness of method and experiment take the place of the quest for truth. In terms of morality it means that "man no longer acknowledges any moral authority outside of his calculations."[53] In the case of philosophy, the question that stands at the beginning of all philosophical enquiry, "What *is* it?" is replaced by its pragmatic surrogate "How does it function?"[54] When wedded to a materialist philosophy, positivism becomes a form of scientism which reduces all knowledge to the exact and quantitative knowledge of calculation and experimentation, and deems all other knowledge claims to

---

49. Lubac, *Drama of Atheist Humanism*, 140.

50. Lubac, *Drama of Atheist Humanism*, 136.

51. Ratzinger notes that, with Wittgenstein's success in the field of linguistics in the twentieth century, positivism "has now very largely taken possession of philosophy." Ratzinger, *Faith and the Future*, 26–27.

52. Ratzinger, *Church, Ecumenism, and Politics*, 213.

53. Ratzinger, "Europe in the Crisis of Cultures," 351.

54. As Ratzinger translates, "reason abandons the question about the truth and investigates nothing more than feasibility. In doing so, it has fundamentally abdicated as reason." Ratzinger, *Church, Ecumenism, and Politics*, 150.

be nonrational.⁵⁵ In this context, Ratzinger recognizes the fulfillment of Comte's prediction that a "physics of man" would one day replace metaphysics: a return to a form of pagan materialism in which "everything is to become 'physics' again."⁵⁶

The Philosophical Limits of Positivism

However, Ratzinger is not convinced that this development represents progress for human thought. Rather than a liberation, he insists that the triumph of positivism makes human beings prisoners of their own methods.⁵⁷ In entrusting themselves only to that which they can personally verify, they are cut off from reality, limited in their capacity to engage the world and others. Their world becomes smaller, more contained and immediate. Indeed, Ratzinger suggests that one "who can no longer transcend the limits either of his consciousness or of his speech fundamentally can no longer speak of anything at all."⁵⁸ Ratzinger's critique to this point is consistent with Eric Voegelin's identification of positivism as a form of Gnosticism, alongside other gnostic variants including progressivism, scientism, and Marxism.⁵⁹ Without suggesting a dependence, Voegelin's influence on Ratzinger's thought is real. Ratzinger himself acknowledges his appreciation of Voegelin's contribution in a personal note on the occasion of the latter's eightieth birthday in 1981, in which he admits to being "fascinated" (*fasziniert*) and "stimulated" (*befruchtet*) by the philosopher's work.⁶⁰

---

55. Ratzinger, *Church, Ecumenism, and Politics*, 197.

56. Ratzinger, *Truth and Tolerance*, 178. Elsewhere he writes: "Auguste Comte called for a physics of man: gradually, even the most difficult object of nature—man—must become scientifically comprehensible, that is, subordinate to the knowledge of the natural sciences. Thus one would see through man in precisely the same way as one has already seen through matter." Ratzinger, *Turning Point*, 37–38.

57. Ratzinger, *Faith and the Future*, 27.

58. Ratzinger, *Faith and the Future*, 80.

59. Voegelin, *New Science of Politics*, 164.

60. The full text of Ratzinger's letter to Voegelin is contained in a note to D. Vincent Twomey's introduction to *The Essential Pope Benedict XVI*: "It was as a great surprise as it was a joy for me to receive your philosophical meditation, which you kindly sent to me with a personal dedication, in which you intend to awaken such a necessary and such a very fragile consciousness of the imperfect in opposition to the magic of the Utopian. Even since your small book, *Science, Politics and Gnosticism*, came into my hands in 1959, your thinking has fascinated and stimulated me, even though I

Voegelin characterizes the whole of modernity as gnostic,[61] originating in the gnostic speculations of Joachim of Fiore (c. 1135–1202).[62] As Voegelin describes, Gnosticism is a program of demystification, consistent with the modernist cause of "immanentizing" reality: "an attempt at bringing our knowledge of transcendence into a firmer grip than the *cognitio fidei*, the cognition of faith, will afford," and of drawing God "into the existence of man."[63] This is attempted at various levels: (1) the intellectual, as a "form of speculative penetration of the mystery of creation and existence"; (2) the emotional, as a "form of an indwelling of divine substance in the human soul"; and (3) the volitional, as a "form of activist redemption of man and society."[64] Each in its own way seeks a form of utopian divinization, but in the absence of God.[65]

Atheism and the Eclipse of God

This process of immanentization ultimately meant the eclipse of God in contemporary philosophy. The question of God, unable to find a foothold in the narrow constraints of positivistic verification, is denied a hearing within contemporary debate. The genealogy of this eclipse is long, having its roots in nominalism's univocal conception of *being*, reducing God to a Being alongside other beings. Adherents of the school of Radical

---

was unfortunately unable to study it with the thoroughness I would have wished." The original text of the letter in German can be found at http://voegelinview.com/benedict-and-voegelin/.

61. Voegelin, *New Science of Politics*, 133.

62. Voegelin, *New Science of Politics*, 110–13. The gnostic influence of Joachim of Fiore provides another point of confluence between Voegelin and Ratzinger. In his postdoctoral *Habilitationsschrift*, Ratzinger treats of Saint Bonaventure's theology of history, especially in his attempt to come to terms with Joachim's novel and disturbing understanding of history that was dividing the Franciscan Order of his time. See Ratzinger, *Theology of History in St. Bonaventure*.

63. Voegelin, *New Science of Politics*, 124.

64. Voegelin, *New Science of Politics*, 124.

65. Voegelin writes: "Gnostic speculation overcame the uncertainty of faith by receding from transcendence and endowing man and his intra-mundane range of action with meaning of eschatological fulfilment. In the measure in which this immanentization progressed experientially, civilizational activity became a mystical world of self-salvation. The spiritual strength of the soul which in Christianity was devoted to the sanctification of life could now be diverted into the more appealing, more tangible, and, above all, so much easier creation of the terrestrial paradise." *New Science of Politics*, 129.

Orthodoxy attribute this initiative to John Duns Scotus (c.1266–1308), whose abandonment of the universal form in favor of the individual[66] favored the substitution of univocity for analogy,[67] and opened the way to the "rationalist abolition of the qualitative distance between God and creatures."[68] When combined with the nominalism of William of Occam (c.1285–c.1348), whose famous *razor* advised against multiplying entities beyond necessity in explaining natural phenomena, "the intellectual pieces were in place, at least in principle, for the domestication of God's transcendence and the extrusion of his presence from the natural world."[69] With the development of the natural sciences, probing the mystery of being, challenging the accepted worldview and finding no evidence of God's existence, the reasonableness of faith was further brought into question.[70] Finally, with the advent of empirical positivism as the only means of investigating reality, the eclipse of God was complete.

Consistent with this trend, transhumanism treats the God-question as something irrelevant or superfluous.[71] As heir to positivistic thinking, it limits truth to what is realizable and concrete. Bostrom thus contrasts humanity's "realistic" future through enhancement and technology with religious eschatology, comparing the latter's "symbolism" to fantastic stories about dragons and wizards.[72] Consistent with Bostrom's slight against

---

66. Interpreting Scotus, Dupré writes: "What distinguishes one being from another of the same kind and makes it this rather than another—the *forma individualis*—is itself a form, rather than being a mere quantification of a universal *species* singuralized by the principle of indeterminacy.... Individuality, then, far from being a mere sign of contingency, constitutes the supreme form, and perfect knowledge consists in knowing the individual form." Dupré, *Passage to Modernity*, 38–39.

67. Milbank, *Beyond Secular Order*, 28.

68. Milbank, *Beyond Secular Order*, 30.

69. Gregory, *Unintended Reformation*, 38.

70. In the traditional view, in which God was envisaged as existing outside of the empirical world, this lack of "evidence" was no obstacle to faith. As Gregory writes: "It is self-evident that a God who by definition is radially distinct from the natural world could never be shown to be unreal via empirical inquiry that by definition can only investigate the natural world." *Unintended Reformation*, 32.

71. Brice de Malherbe speaks of the "absence of God as Creator" (*l'absence de Dieu en tant que Créateur*) that signifies the transhumanist project. de Malherbe, "Créer ou revêtir l'homme nouveau," 33.

72. "Traditionally, the future of humanity has been a topic for theology. All the major religions have teachings about the ultimate destiny of humanity or the end of the world. Eschatological themes have also been explored by big-name philosophers such as Hegel, Kant, and Marx. In more recent times the literary genre of science fiction

THE PHILOSOPHICAL FOUNDATIONS OF TRANSHUMANISM 103

the relevance of religion, transhumanists seek more concrete means for assuring a future for humanity. Max More thus speaks in terms of "a type of nonreligious philosophy of life that rejects faith, worship, and the supernatural, instead emphasizing a meaningful and ethical approach to living informed by reason, science, progress, and the value of existence in our current life."[73] While a few individuals bother to present a case against God—Allen Buchanan, for instance, notes that "Darwin debunked the argument for the existence of God, by cataloguing the 'clumsy, wasteful, blundering' works of nature"[74]—for the majority, the question of God does not enter and a happy agnosticism prevails.

Ratzinger, however, denies the sustainability of such a neutral stance.[75] Contrary to the presumption of secular humanism, he insists that "the unbeliever is not to be understood undialectically as a mere man without faith."[76] Despite protestations to the contrary, neither the agnostic nor the professed atheist is immune to the question of God. He claims that "atheism's dismissal of the subject of God is only apparent, that in reality it represents a form of man's concern with the question of God."[77] Just as the believer chooses to believe in the midst of doubts,

---

has continued the tradition. Very often, the future has served as a projection screen for our hopes and fears; or as a stage setting for dramatic entertainment, morality tales, or satire of tendencies in contemporary society; or as a banner for ideological mobilization. It is relatively rare for humanity's future to be taken seriously as a subject matter on which it is important to try to have factually correct beliefs. There is nothing wrong with exploiting the symbolic and literary affordances of an unknown future, just as there is nothing wrong with fantasizing about imaginary countries populated by dragons and wizards. Yet it is important to attempt (as best we can) to distinguish futuristic scenarios put forward for their symbolic significance or entertainment value from speculations that are meant to be evaluated on the basis of literal plausibility. ... We need realistic pictures of what the future might bring in order to make sound decisions." Bostrom, "Future of Humanity," 42.

73. More, "Philosophy of Transhumanism," 4.

74. Buchanan, *Better than Human*, 30. He claims further that "the nasty, brutish, and long process by which beneficial genes spread through populations" speaks against divine providence (37).

75. Ratzinger, *Christianity and the Crisis of Cultures*, 89: "When faced with the question of God, man cannot permit himself to remain neutral. All he can say is Yes or No—without ever avoiding all the consequences that derive from this choice even in the smallest details of life. Accordingly, we see that the question of God is ineluctable; one is not permitted to abstain from casting one's vote."

76. Ratzinger, *Introduction to Christianity*, 45.

77. "However vigorously he may assert that he is a pure positivist, who has long left behind him supernatural temptations and weaknesses and now accepts only what

so too the non-believer "remains threatened" by the claims of belief; haunted by the words "Yet perhaps it is true."[78]

This admission of doubt relativizes the absolutism of positive claims, and at the same time provides space for dialogue between believers and unbelievers. In this context Ratzinger seeks a qualification of the Enlightenment dictum that justified morality *etsi Deus no daretur*, "even if God did not exist." In its day it aimed to establish a rational basis for morality amid confessional differences among believers. Today, in order to save humanity from alienating itself within positivistic claims, Ratzinger suggests that "we must invite our agnostic friends to be receptive to a morality *si Deus daretur*, 'if God existed.'"[79] What does this mean in practice? Ratzinger suggests that to act *quasi Deus daretur* means "to live as though one had an unlimited responsibility; as though justice and truth were not only programmes, but a living existent power to which one has to render an account." It means "to act as though the human being next to me were not just some chance product of nature, of no great ultimate importance, but an embodied thought of God, an image of the Creator whom he knows and loves."[80] It means to acknowledge each other's transcendence and eternal significance.

However, confessed atheist Paolo Flores d'Arcais interprets Ratzinger's proposal as an attempt to subvert reason to Christian faith. He sees it as a threat to the achievements of the Enlightenment that liberated reason from religious doctrine, and a return to a notion of absolutes: a "Constantinian restoration" of faith, ethics and politics.[81] Francesco Remotti similarly reproaches Ratzinger for imposing "truths" that are extraneous to human reason; of offering a "complete and definitive" model of humanity, not as the product of human reasoning, but as consigned to the church from above for the benefit of humankind.[82] According to their

---

is immediately certain, he will never be free of the secret uncertainty about whether positivism really has the last word." Ratzinger, *Introduction to Christianity*, 104.

78. "That 'perhaps' is the unavoidable temptation it cannot elude, the temptation in which it, too, in the very act of rejection, has to experience the unrejectablility of belief. In other words, both the believer and the unbeliever share, each in his own way, doubt *and* belief, if they do not hide from themselves and from the truth of their being. Neither can quite escape either doubt or belief." Ratzinger, *Introduction to Christianity*, 46–47.

79. Ratzinger, *Values in a Time of Upheaval*, 111.

80. Ratzinger, "Beyond Death," 14.

81. Flores d'Arcais, *La sfida oscurantista*, 49, 70.

82. Remotti, *Contra natura*, 257.

combined reasoning, any presumption to the fullness of reason is a threat to tolerance and relativism as foundational to a pluralist, democratic society.[83] Rejecting absolute or supra-cultural truth claims, they prefer an agnosticism that "gropes in the dark" in search of stability. Within a culture of relativism, claims to truth can only be offered as humble hypotheses, based on reason and observation, and open to critique and revision.[84] The assertion of absolute truth is caricatured as an imposition of one's opinions on others; as a desperate attempt to secure stability (whether in God, reason, nature, or history); as originating from the fear of having one's own convictions and power undermined.[85]

But in proposing an attitude *as if God existed*, Ratzinger's point seems to be much less imposing. In a postmodern society in which neither Christian faith nor secular rationality can claim universal acceptance, he maintains that both sides need to recognize their limits and learn from each other. In this context Ratzinger speaks of certain *pathologies of religion* that need to be "purified and structured by reason."[86] But he also identifies *pathologies of reason* (see below) that require the sobering wisdom of religious tradition.

Thus, rather than limiting philosophical discussion, Ratzinger desires a broadening of its horizons that allows the question of God to be raised. This includes the intellectual honesty to acknowledge the influence of the Judeo-Christian faith at the foundation of western democratic societies, and to admit that the very concept of "Europe" flows from the synthesis of Israel's faith and Greek culture as realized in Christianity.[87] He relativizes the inflated differences between the Enlightenment and Christianity. In the first place, he presents Christianity as its own form of enlightenment in continuity with the Socratic and the Old Testament prophetic confrontation with the cult of idols.[88] It represents a victory of demythologization, of knowledge and of truth. From this perspective, writes Ratzinger, Christians have from the beginning considered their

83. Ratzinger and Flores d'Arcais, "Controversia su Dio," 118.
84. Remotti, *Contra natura*, 5.
85. Remotti, *Contra natura*, 256.
86. Ratzinger, "That Which Holds the World Together," 77.
87. Ratzinger, *Church, Ecumenism, and Politics*, 216–17. He adds: "The Renaissance attempt to distil and restore the Greek element in a pure form by removing the Christian element is just as hopeless and absurd as the more recent attempt to manufacture a de-Hellenized Christianity" (217).
88. Ratzinger and Flores d'Arcais, "Controversia su Dio," 109.

faith to be universal; as a message to be preached to all peoples: "not as a specific religion that overcomes and displaces others, not on the basis of some kind of religious imperialism, but as the truth that renders mere appearance superfluous."[89] Accordingly, he denies a subversion of reason to Christianity. Rather, in holding on to the illumination of faith, Ratzinger persists in his attempt to expand the boundaries of rational debate.

In further rebuking Christianity's threat to enlightened ideals, he maintains that the enshrinement of inviolable human rights did not begin with the Enlightenment, but flowed from the Christian culture that gave birth to it, claiming that if the basis of inviolable rights is restricted to civil legislation, and thus to human choice, they are by definition changeable and the very notion of inviolability destroyed.[90] While acknowledging the unique contribution of the modern era in shaping Western culture—"the relative separation of church and state, freedom of conscience, human rights, and reason's responsibility for itself"—he suggests that a radicalization of these elements in the form of an autonomous reason "which no longer recognizes anything but itself" must be avoided "by holding fast to the foundations of reason in reverence for God and for the fundamental moral values that come from the Christian faith."[91] Accordingly, the influence of faith is not simply an historical anecdote, but a necessary and ongoing reality.

In this, Ratzinger finds broad support from Jürgen Habermas, with whom he met to discuss the pre-political foundations of the free democratic state in a public dialogue organized by the Catholic Academy of Bavaria on January 19, 2004.[92] While upholding the autonomy and self-legitimization of the secular constitutional state, "independent of religious and metaphysical traditions,"[93] Habermas recognizes that the postmodern skepticism toward the rational basis of society, and its aversion for a

---

89. Ratzinger, *Truth and Tolerance*, 170.

90. Ratzinger and Flores d'Arcais, "Controversia su Dio," 141. Ratzinger offers this in response to Flores d'Arcais's denial of the modern state's dependence on Christian values, his determination that a constitutional democracy can justify its own existence and decisions, his presumption that inviolable rights have their origin in Enlightenment rationality, and his confidence that laws that are constitutionally enshrined cannot be easily or arbitrarily changed by popular opinion.

91. Ratzinger, *Church, Ecumenism, and Politics*, 219.

92. Published as *The Dialectics of Secularization: On Reason and Religion* (2006).

93. Habermas, "Pre-political Foundations," 29.

THE PHILOSOPHICAL FOUNDATIONS OF TRANSHUMANISM 107

"universally obligatory concept of a good and exemplary life,"[94] threatens the stability of the modern state. He therefore acknowledges the appeal of religion and "a transcendent point of reference"[95] as providing a way through the confusion. Unlike Flores d'Arcais and Remotti, Habermas does not seem threatened by this trend, insisting that "it is in the interest of the constitutional state to deal carefully with all the cultural sources that nourish its citizens' consciousness of norms and their solidarity."[96] Instead of sidelining religion and enforcing secular reason, he is open to the "cognitive challenge" of religion.[97] Philosophy, he says, "has good reasons to be willing to learn from religious traditions."[98] In this regard, he notes philosophy's assimilation of "genuinely Christian ideas,"[99] noting the important "translation of the concept of 'man in the image of God' into that of the identical dignity of all men that deserves unconditional respect."[100] While celebrating the secularization of knowledge, freed from the monopolization of religious doctrine, Habermas insists that the tolerance of the democratic state demands real dialogue between believers and non-believers. In turn, this demands that religious convictions are not disregarded as irrelevant, but are granted "an epistemological status that is not purely and simply irrational."[101]

94. Habermas, "Pre-political Foundations," 43.

95. Habermas, "Pre-political Foundations," 37.

96. Habermas, "Pre-political Foundations," 46.

97. Habermas, "Pre-political Foundations," 38.

98. Habermas, "Pre-political Foundations," 42. Ratzinger takes it a step further, claiming that "reason that is closed in on itself does not remain reasonable, just as the state that tries to become perfect becomes tyrannical. Reason needs revelation in order to be able to function as reason." Ratzinger, *Church, Ecumenism, and Politics*, 206.

99. He gives examples of "responsibility, autonomy, and justification; or history and remembering, new beginning, innovation, and return; or emancipation and fulfilment; or expropriation, internalization, and embodiment, individuality and fellowship." Habermas, "Pre-political Foundations," 44.

100. Habermas, "Pre-political Foundations," 45.

101. Habermas, "Pre-political Foundations," 51. As Habermas notes, this has implications for public discourse. "The neutrality of the state authority on questions of world views guarantees the same ethical freedom to every citizen. This is incompatible with the political universalization of a secularist world view. When secularized citizens act in their role as citizens of the state, they must not deny in principle that religious images of the world have the potential to express truth. Nor must they refuse their believing fellow citizens the right to make contributions in a religious language to public debates. Indeed, a liberal political culture can expect that the secularized citizens play their part in the endeavors to translate relevant contributions from the religious language into a language that is accessible to the public as a whole" (51–52).

Thus, while arriving at this conclusion from a different starting point, Habermas seems to be in harmony with Ratzinger's desire to expand the horizon of rational dialogue. In the context of the debate over human enhancement, it is therefore unfortunate that the question of God is to a great extent left aside, or raised only superficially in response to the charge of "playing God," dismissed by transhumanists as a substitute for reason and an avoidance of real engagement in debate.[102] However, this escape into the mystery of God is by no means Ratzinger's way of engaging faith and reason.[103] For him, faith in God has more significance than belief in his existence. It also concerns the nature of reality itself. To believe means that reality goes beyond what is seen or heard or touched. It means going beyond oneself and one's immediate perceptions, offering an alternative means of access to reality in an expanded view of the world.[104] Such belief does not undermine the certainty of positivistic knowledge. Rather, it relativizes it, broadening the horizons of knowledge by challenging the positivistic reduction to the *faciendum*, to what human beings can make themselves, and saving them from the destructive power of the works of their hands.

The Insufficiency of Knowledge over Understanding

Challenging the absoluteness of positivistic knowledge, Ratzinger draws a distinction between knowledge and understanding, between "*ratio* (reason in relation to the empirical, to the realm of what can be done), and *intellectus* (reason that contemplates the deeper strata of being)."[105] He also draws on Heidegger's categories of thought as *calculating* (concerned with making) and thought as *reflective* (concerned with meaning).[106] In its exclusive concern for empirical knowledge, positivism considers the questioning of "why," intrinsic to the theological and metaphysical

---

102. Coady, "Playing God." See also Buchanan, *Better than Human*, 13–14; Bostrom and Sandberg, "Cognitive Enhancement," 327; Sandberg, "Cognition Enhancement," 82–83.

103. Ratzinger, *Turning Point*, 110.

104. Ratzinger, *Introduction to Christianity*, 50.

105. Ratzinger, *Values in a Time of Upheaval*, 110. Pieper, borrowing from Aquinas (*STh.*, I, q. 59, a. 1), further distinguishes *ratio* as the power of "discursive thinking," from *intellectus* as the capacity for "simple intuition." Pieper, *Happiness and Contemplation*, 74.

106. Ratzinger, *Introduction to Christianity*, 71.

approaches, to be "childish" and "adolescent."[107] Emancipated from such "puerile" concerns, positivism instead aims to discover the laws by which things happen.[108]

Without denying the validity of positivist knowledge, Ratzinger nonetheless questions the reasonableness of abandoning the search for understanding. He rejects the idea that human beings can or should ever give up asking why. In so doing, he draws a distinction between knowledge of the *faciendum* on one hand, and metaphysical truths, belief or faith on the other. He writes:

> The penetrating "perhaps" that belief whispers in man's ear in every place and in every age does not point to any uncertainty *within* the realm of *Machbarkeitswissen*;[109] it simply queries the absoluteness of this realm and relativizes it, reminding man that it is only *one* plane of human existence and of existence in general, a plane that can only have the character of something less than final.[110]

Knowledge of the *faciendum*, according to Ratzinger, is intrinsically positivistic, limited to what is measurable and functional. It follows, however, that such knowledge is not concerned with truth. It does not "inquire what things are like on their own and *in themselves*, but only whether they will function *for us*."[111] Structural knowledge, therefore, cannot penetrate to the essence of reality. As a young Ratzinger wrote in critique of *Gaudium et spes* and its attitude toward technology: "To

---

107. Lubac, *Drama of Atheist Humanism*, 158.

108. "In the positive state, on the other hand, 'our understanding, gradually emancipated,' does not perplex itself with all kinds of curious and vain 'whys'; it no longer wonders what are the causes of phenomena but strives to ascertain the laws according to which they happen." Lubac, *Drama of Atheist Humanism*, 159.

109. In the English text, *Machbarkeitswissen* is misleadingly translated as "practical knowledge," the knowledge of moral discernment, which is usually contrasted with speculative knowledge. Instead, Ratzinger here intends *Machbarkeitswissen* as knowledge of what is makeable, of what is practicable or able to be produced, which stands in contrast to the reality of being. (I acknowledge the assistance of Prof. Stephan Kampowski in awakening me to this mistranslation.)

110. Ratzinger, *Introduction to Christianity*, 70. The original states: "Das bohrende Vielleicht, mit dem der Glaube den Menschen allerorten und jederzeit in Frage stellt, verweist nicht auf eine Unsicherheit *innerhalb* des Machbarkeitswissens, sondern es ist die Infragestellung der Absolutheit dieses Bereichs, seine Relativierung als *eine* Ebene des menschlichen Seins und des Seins überhaupt, die nur den Charakter von etwas Vorletztem haben kann." Ratzinger, *Einführung in das Christentum*, 81.

111. Ratzinger, *Introduction to Christianity*, 75.

decipher the physical structure of things is not the same thing as to decode the meaning of existence itself. Rather, it introduces us to the enigmatic character of existence in its full mystery and thus shows us the riddle of our own existence."[112]

Belief or faith, on the other hand, is not concerned with the calculable and the positivistic.[113] Contrary to rationalistic prejudice, faith is not provisional knowledge, "a diluted form of natural science, an ancient or medieval preparatory stage that must vanish when the real thing turns up."[114] Nor is it some enigmatic system of knowledge, "a colossal edifice of numerous supernatural facts, standing like a curious second order of knowledge alongside the realm of science."[115] Rather, Ratzinger defines faith as "an existential attitude, a fundamental decision about the direction of life."[116] It is the "disclosure" of a greater reality, open to those who love and trust.[117] It is the acknowledgment that being, including the human person's being, is beyond the measurable and the calculable. In the realm of that which cannot be "laid on the table" and dissected by scrutiny, faith seeks to understand being itself, not knowledge of its products. According to this rationale Ratzinger writes that "the tool with which man is equipped to deal with the truth of being is not *knowledge* but *understanding*: understanding of the meaning to which he has entrusted himself."[118] Accordingly, the differences between understanding (faith) and knowledge do not constitute a contradiction. Ordinarily, faith does not impose on human reason, but rather serves to awaken and recall it to itself.[119] The two come into conflict only when they fail to respect their differences and intrude on each other's domain.

112. Ratzinger, *Theological Highlights of Vatican II*, 234.

113. As Ratzinger insists: "It can never become that, and in the last analysis it can only make itself ridiculous it if tries to establish itself in those forms." Ratzinger, *Introduction to Christianity*, 77.

114. Ratzinger, *Faith and the Future*, 29.

115. Ratzinger, *Faith and the Future*, 30.

116. Ratzinger, *Faith and the Future*, 35. In this context, Ratzinger recalls the paradigmatic faith of Abraham. "He let go of what was safe, comprehensible, calculable, for the sake of what was unknown. But he did this in response to a single word from God. . . . The word he had heard was more real to him than all the calculable things he could hold in his hand. He trusted in that which he could not yet see and thus became capable of new life, of breaking out of rigidity" (40).

117. Ratzinger, *Faith and the Future*, 30.

118. Ratzinger, *Introduction to Christianity*, 77.

119. Ratzinger, "*Evangelium Vitae*," 1.

In Ratzinger's analysis, rational discourse is impoverished by the current imbalance between knowledge and understanding, in which everything is reduced to the narrow confines of *ratio*. He suggests that Heidegger was justified in his concern "that in an age in which calculating thought is celebrating the most amazing triumphs man is nevertheless threatened, perhaps more than ever before, by thoughtlessness."[120] For all the knowledge gained through technical and scientific thinking, humanity as a whole has not progressed in understanding. By restricting knowledge to what is practicable, human beings risk losing themselves and the reason for their existence. As Ratzinger writes, "Man does not live on the bread of practicability alone; he lives as *man* and, precisely in the intrinsically human part of his being, on the word, on love, on meaning."[121] Love, word, meaning, and other realities like the transcendentals of truth, goodness, and beauty, constitute what is truly human and cannot be reduced to positive categories. To take just one example, Ratzinger highlights the impossibility of the mathematical mind to comprehend the "superfluous wonder" of beauty, its extravagance surpassing explanation by calculation.[122] In the end, he insists that positivism is incapable of extinguishing belief; that it cannot annihilate the human search for meaning and the yearning for transcendence, because faith, in its seeking for understanding, corresponds to the truth of human nature.[123]

A Pathology of Reason

Added to its impoverishment of the human spirit, Ratzinger claims that the absolutism of positivism blunts human reason.[124] In the context of

---

120. Ratzinger, *Introduction to Christianity*, 71.

121. Ratzinger, *Introduction to Christianity*, 72–73. He continues: "Meaning is the bread on which man, in the intrinsically human part of his being, subsists. Without the word, without meaning, without love he falls into the situation of no longer being able to live, even when earthly comfort is present in abundance."

122. Ratzinger, *Introduction to Christianity*, 154.

123. "For man is more generously proportioned than the way Kant and the various post-Kantian philosophies see him or will allow him to be. Kant himself ought to have found a place for this, somehow or other, among his postulates. The longing for the infinite is alive and unquenchable within man. None of the attempted answers will do; only the God who himself became finite in order to tear open our finitude and lead us out into the wide spaces of his infinity, only he corresponds to the question of our being." Ratzinger, *Truth and Tolerance*, 137.

124. Ratzinger, *Values in a Time of Upheaval*, 110.

knowledge devoid of understanding he speaks of certain *pathologies of reason*[125] or of a *hubris* of reason that presumes to be self-sufficient.[126] He claims that reason that is limited to the empirical domain is a disabled reason, blind to everything that is nonmaterial, to God and the human spirit.

Ratzinger identifies this pathology of reason particularly in positivism's attitude toward the beginnings of human life. It is evident in two ways. In the first place there is an inherent contradiction in the interpretation of the scientific data surrounding the beginning of life. In the absence of any metaphysical foundation that would confirm its existence as an individual being (the soul being indemonstrable and therefore a meaningless concept in positivistic thought), the developing human is reduced to nothing more than an aggregate of cells. But the scientific data itself points to the existence of something more. Under Ratzinger's direction the Congregation for the Doctrine of Faith writes:

> Certainly no experimental datum can be in itself sufficient to bring us to the recognition of a spiritual soul; nevertheless, the conclusions of science regarding the human embryo provide a valuable indication for discerning by the use of reason a personal presence at the moment of this first appearance of a human life.[127]

In other words, the self-directed development of the human embryo suggests a purpose and teleology that cannot be reduced to chemistry and algorithms. In acknowledging this personal presence, Robert Spaemann recognizes an imperative to "regard what has been conceived by human beings and develops autonomously into an adult human form as 'someone' and not as 'something.'"[128]

Furthermore, in the recognition that scientific knowledge cannot exhaust the reality of the human person, one must seek further understanding, deeper insights into the mystery of human life. This has already been noted in the revelation of the goodness of the human person's creation in the image of God, confirmed and elevated in the Incarnation of the Divine Word. Looking to *Dignitas personae* one reads:

---

125. Ratzinger, "That Which Holds the World Together," 77.
126. Ratzinger, "That Which Holds the World Together," 78.
127. CDF, *Donum vitae*, I, 1. Cf. CDF, *Dignitas personae*, n. 5.
128. Spaemann, "Begotten, Not Made," 297.

This new dimension does not conflict with the dignity of the creature which everyone can recognize by the use of reason, but elevates it into a wider horizon of life which is proper to God, giving us the ability to reflect more profoundly on human life and on the acts by which it is brought into existence.[129]

However, this ability to reflect more profoundly is only possible if human beings are willing to go beyond the confines of positivist thought. In the absence of evidence to the contrary, one must again be troubled by the possibility of the "perhaps." Just as Ratzinger encourages openness to a morality "as if God existed," so *Donum vitae* insists that "the human being is to be respected and treated *as* a person from the moment of conception."[130] The probability, even the mere possibility, that this "group of cells" constitutes a human person demands inviolable respect.[131] This whispering voice of doubt must be given chance to speak, free from the deafening clamor of positivistic demands.

Thus, in the context of bioethical questions which touch on the very meaning of human life, answers cannot be sought in knowledge of biology or physics alone. As Ratzinger insists, biologists and physicians must not be left alone in finding answers to these questions, but must "seek enlightenment and comfort in society from those felt to be more competent in regard to what is human."[132] While not hesitating in his acknowledgment that, as a scientific method, positivism "is unbelievably useful and absolutely necessary for the mastery of the problems of ever-developing humanity," Ratzinger nonetheless insists that "as a philosophy of life [it] is intolerable and the end of humanity";[133] that it "is adequate in the technical domain," but that when it is universalized it "mutilates man."[134]

Summary

Through a critical engagement of the principles of secular humanism, especially in its guise of scientific positivism, the philosophical roots of the transhumanist movement have been more clearly identified.

129. CDF, *Dignitas personae*, n. 7.
130. CDF, *Donum vitae*, I, 1. Emphasis added.
131. Ratzinger and Flores d'Arcais, "Controversia su Dio," 133.
132. Ratzinger, "Bioethics in the Christian Perspective," 10.
133. Ratzinger, *Faith and the Future*, 81.
134. Ratzinger, "Europe in the Crisis of Cultures," 351.

Ratzinger's response primarily consists in a rejection of the absolutization of the secular program, specifically in its narrow conception of reality and its positive reduction of meaning to praxis. He maintains that in the absence of the nonmaterial dimension of reality, everything is inevitably reduced to matter; that without the acknowledgment of a creating Spirit, or of a world infused with reason and purpose, the human person inevitably stands over matter, molding and manipulating it in order to "liberate" its divine potential. In this perspective, he no longer has "God behind him as something that had gone before him but only in front of him as something to be creatively effected by him, as his own better future."[135] Humanity's God-given *dominion* over the fruits of creation (see Gen 1:28) is thus transformed into power and *domination*. Ratzinger identifies the pathological effects of this materialist reduction in our attitude toward the goodness of humanity, in our relation to self and others, and in our connection with the world.

---

135. Ratzinger, *Introduction to Christianity*, 109.

Chapter 5

Chanced or Purposeful?

Ratzinger's Response to Evolution

Originating Logos

IT HAS BEEN ESTABLISHED that the project of transhumanism is founded in evolutionary theory, employing the evolution heuristic to explain why human beings evolved in their present-day form and limitations. The heuristic concerns the mechanics of the evolutionary process and human beings in their biological constitution. In this context it has something interesting to say, but it surely does not exhaust the reality of the human person. Consistent with the important distinction between knowledge and understanding, there are further and deeper questions that escape its methodology. Why do human beings exist at all? From where do they come? What is the meaning of their life? The evolution heuristic has no answer to these questions.

    Ratzinger insists that theories of evolution must be judged, not only in terms of empirical evidence, but according to the reason and logic that underpins them. As a rule, the transhumanist account of evolution affords no place for an originating reason. Although Bostrom and Sandberg offer lip service to the wisdom of a "master craftsman,"[1] their

---

1. "If we do not understand why a very complex evolved system has a certain property, there is a considerable risk that something will go wrong if we try to modify it. The case might be one of those where nature does know best. Like an over-ambitious tinkerer with merely superficial understanding of what he is doing while he

evolutionary heuristic is devoid of any guiding reason. Buchanan's evaluation would seem more honest, when he insists that "evolution is not like a Master Engineer; it is more like a morally insensitive, blind, tightly shackled tinkerer."[2] Evolution doesn't follow a plan. Rather, it responds to short-term problems, not in a conscious manner, but through natural selection. Its products are never complete, constantly evolving and adapting to their environment. "The designing that evolution accomplishes through natural selection isn't just nonconscious," writes Buchanan; "it's downright unintelligent."[3]

In consequence, the existence of the world, including humanity, is interpreted as the result of chance. No reason or intelligence stands at its origins. In this context, Ratzinger identifies the thought of Jacques Monod (1910–1976). In *Chance and Necessity*, the French biologist and Nobel Prize winner asserts that human evolution may be compared to a lottery.[4] In doing so, he draws on the traditional concept of humanity's contingency. Whereas faith had always interpreted contingency as an expression of the freedom in which we were created[5]—there being no necessity for our existence—Monod sees it as evidence of our accidental existence. Evolution, accordingly, is not guided by reason or a divine will. Instead, it is a haphazard process that stumbles across existence and leaves much to be desired.

---

is making changes to the design of a master craftsman, the potential for damage is considerable and the chances of producing an all-things-considered improvement are small." Bostrom and Sandberg, "Wisdom of Nature," 406. Buchanan, however, rails against the "master engineer" analogy. "It smacks of pre-Darwinian religious thought about the created world—the previously dead and buried, but recently resurrected argument from intelligent design. The only difference is that the evolutionary version of the master engineer analogy substitutes natural selection for God's creative genius." For Buchanan this resemblance is particularly disturbing "because the Darwinian revolution was supposed to have overthrown the argument from intelligent design." Buchanan, *Better than Human*, 28.

2. Buchanan, *Beyond Humanity?*, 2. In a particularly dark and despairing evaluation of evolution, Buchanan writes: "It's not about human improvement or even human well-being, and when it does happen to achieve what's good for us the means it uses are typically ghastly. It's fickle, in that it shapes species and then discards them. The only reliable prediction about evolution we can make is that all species go extinct eventually." Buchanan, *Better than Human*, 49.

3. Buchanan, *Better than Human*, 28.

4. Monod, *Le hasard et la nécessité*, 178–79.

5. In the realm of faith, Ratzinger notes that the realization of our contingency becomes prayer: "I did not have to exist but I do exist, and you, O God, wanted me to exist." Ratzinger, *In the Beginning*, 53.

It is precisely these aspects of chance and the absence of originating reason that form the basis of Ratzinger's critique. He rejects as meaningless the idea that rationality proceeds as "a chance by-product of irrationality and floating in an ocean of irrationality";[6] that "the whole of nature's concerto has grown up and developed from a few random murmurs of noise."[7] Instead, he holds to the primacy of *logos*: of the origins of being in thought; of an intellectual structure at the foundation of what exists.[8] He contends that living creation points to a rationality at the basis of all being, that it exhibits the traces of Reason in its intelligence and design, and that, through the discoveries of science, it does so "more luminously and radiantly today than ever before."[9]

According to Ratzinger, to assert that this intelligence and order is the result of chance not only belies evidence, but also undermines the very foundations of rationality itself.[10] Human nature is rational because it proceeds from Reason. Human beings are able to reason because rationality exists in all that surrounds them.[11] The idea that rationality evolves from nothing is unsustainable, and ultimately leads to uncertainty, moral confusion, and irrationality. Indeed, without an original Reason, human reason would not be reason at all. It would be groundless, arbitrary, and ultimately dangerous.

Furthermore, Ratzinger maintains that our thinking is nothing other than a rethinking of the originating Thought.[12]

> This means nothing else than the conviction that the objective mind we find present in all things, indeed, as which we learn increasingly to understand things, is the impression and expression of subjective mind and that the intellectual structure that being possesses and that we can *re*-think is the expression of a creative *pre*-meditation, to which they owe their experience.[13]

6. Ratzinger, *Truth and Tolerance*, 181.
7. Ratzinger, *Truth and Tolerance*, 151.
8. Ratzinger, *Introduction to Christianity*, 152.
9. Ratzinger, *In the Beginning*, 56.
10. "As a general rule, whenever the Big Bang is seen as the primordial beginning of the universe, the measure and foundation of reality is no longer reason but the irrational; then reason, too, is only a by-product of the irrational that has come about through 'chance and necessity,' indeed, by mistake, and to that extent is itself ultimately something irrational." Ratzinger, *Church, Ecumenism, and Politics*, 149.
11. Ratzinger, *Introduction to Christianity*, 155.
12. Ratzinger, *Introduction to Christianity*, 153.
13. Ratzinger, *Introduction to Christianity*, 152.

This capacity to rethink Thought is also the mark of humanity's distinction and greatness. For unlike lesser animals, the human person knows "the *essence* of things," and thus "gains access to the totality of the universe as well."[14]

To recognize the presence of an originating Thought at the beginning of all things is also to recognize that this Thought is creative. As Ratzinger writes: "To believe in creation means to understand, in faith, the world of becoming revealed by science as a meaningful world that comes from a creative mind."[15] Accordingly, belief in creation is not the negation of evolution. It simply acknowledges that evolution is unable to explain *why* we and the world exist. While it can explain physical processes and material causations, it cannot explain final causes. The natural sciences are limited to the observable, the explicable, and the quantifiable.[16] The domain of faith, on the other hand, is "greater, broader, and deeper,"[17] seeking an ultimate meaning for our existence. Thus, even with the emergence of evolutionary theory, creation retains its relevance, offering a "better hypothesis": "a fuller and better explanation than any of the other theories."[18]

Therefore, according to Ratzinger, the debate about the human origins cannot be reduced to a choice between *either* creation *or* evolution, because the two theories seek to answer different questions. The account of creation, in which the human person is formed from the dust of the earth, and animated by the breath of God, "does not in fact explain how human persons come to be but rather what they are."[19] It concerns who human beings are in their origin and their vocation or project. The theory of evolution, on the other hand, attempts to explain the biological development of human beings. "But in so doing it cannot explain where the 'project' of human persons comes from, nor their inner origin, nor

---

14. Pieper, "Truth of All Things," 90. In this context Pieper quotes Aquinas: "Anima intellectiva, quia est universalium comprehensiva, habet virtutem ad infinita." *STh.*, I, q. 76, a. 5.

15. Ratzinger, "Belief in Creation," 140.

16. "It is the affair of the natural sciences to explain how the tree of life in particular continues to grow and how new branches shoot out from it." Ratzinger, *In the Beginning*, 56.

17. Ratzinger, *In the Beginning*, 17.

18. Ratzinger, *In the Beginning*, 17.

19. Ratzinger, *In the Beginning*, 50.

their particular nature. To that extent we are faced here with two complementary—rather than mutually exclusive—realities."[20]

However, this is precisely where the problem lies today. Evolution has moved beyond the bounds of the natural sciences and has become an all-embracing philosophy, attempting to explain the whole of reality. Christoph Schönborn quotes Ratzinger as writing:

> Today a new stage of the debate has been reached, inasmuch as "evolution" has been exalted above and beyond its scientific content and made into an intellectual model that claims to explain the whole of reality and thus has become a sort of "first philosophy." Whereas the Middle Ages had attempted a "derivation of all science from theology" (Bonaventure), we can speak here about a derivation of all reality from "evolution," which believes that it can also account for knowledge, ethics, and religion in terms of the general scheme of evolution.[21]

In making this observation, Ratzinger does not endorse a return to the medieval synthesis. He admits of no contradiction between faith and the independence of "the scientific hypothesis of evolution."[22] He accepts the findings of natural science, insisting that "no one will be able to cast serious doubt upon the scientific evidence for micro-evolutionary processes."[23] What he objects to, however, is the absolutization of the evolutionary claim, its transformation into a *philosophia universalis* to the exclusion of every other explanation.[24] In other words, he rejects the unreasonable transition from microevolution, which concerns the intracellular, biological processes of evolution, to macroevolution, as an attempt to explain the origins of the universe and the whole of reality.[25] Accordingly, Ratzinger claims that the substance of the current debate is not faith and science, but philosophy. Again, it is not a question of

---

20. Ratzinger, *In the Beginning*, 50.
21. Schönborn, foreword to *Creation and Evolution*, 9.
22. Schönborn, foreword to *Creation and Evolution*, 10.
23. Ratzinger, *Truth and Tolerance*, 179.
24. Ratzinger, *Truth and Tolerance*, 180.
25. Brad Gregory makes a similar point: "But evolutionary biology cannot extrapolate on *scientific* grounds from microcausal mechanisms of genetic mutation, for example, to evaluative judgments about the putative lack of meaning, order, and purpose in the evolutionary process as a whole or in the universe as such. *That* move requires extrascientific interpretation and atheistic faith commitments." Gregory, *Unintended Reformation*, 66.

choosing between faith in creation or the theory of evolution. Rather, the question is whether or not adherents to the theory of evolution are willing to admit its philosophical limitations and accept the deeper significance of meaning that creation offers.

In this context, Ratzinger insists that belief in creation offers something more.

> Confronted with the fundamental question, which cannot be answered by evolutionary theory itself, of whether meaninglessness or meaning [*Sinn*] prevails, this belief expresses the conviction that the world as a whole, as the Bible says, comes from the Logos, that is, from creative mind [*Sinn*] and represents the temporal form of its self-actuation.[26]

Accordingly, Ratzinger can speak of an alternative "enlightenment" in the form of the biblical accounts of creation when compared to the creation stories of other traditions. In particular, he admits the influence of the Babylonian creation story, *Enuma Elish*. According to this story of the beginning of things, creation was the result of a struggle between opposing forces: between Marduk, the god of light, and the primordial dragon. Overcoming the dragon, Marduk formed heaven and earth from its sundered body, and human beings from its blood. As Ratzinger interprets, the image is foreboding. "At the very origin of the world lurks something sinister, and in the deepest part of humankind there lies something rebellious, demonic, and evil."[27] And he admits that it is reflective of the irrationality and despair that often marks our experience in this world.

In contrast, Ratzinger's notes that the biblical accounts of creation are marked by temperateness and rationality, revealing "that the world was not a demonic contest but that it arose from God's Reason and reposes on God's Word";[28] that the universe "is not the product of darkness and unreason," but instead "comes from intelligence, freedom, and from the beauty that is identical with love."[29] This recognition of Reason at the beginning of all things gives a particular orientation to life. It not only pacifies human beings' oppressive and irrational fears about the gods and the powers of darkness, but also establishes an order and reason that guarantees them freedom and responsibility.

26. Ratzinger, "Belief in Creation," 139.
27. Ratzinger, *In the Beginning*, 12.
28. Ratzinger, *In the Beginning*, 14.
29. Ratzinger, *In the Beginning*, 25.

The Christian faith further confirms the presence of an originating Reason. In the Prologue of the Gospel of John we read: "In the beginning was the Word, and the Word was with God, and the Word was God.... All things were made through him, and without him was not anything made that was made" (John 1:1, 3). Christian faith is faith in the primacy of God's *logos*. It is the recognition that thought and meaning are not chance by-products of being, but that, on the contrary, "all being is a product of thought and, indeed, in its innermost structure is itself thought."[30] This originating Reason finds its full and personal expression in Christ, God's *logos* made flesh (see John 1:14).[31] And, as Ratzinger insists, this personal dimension reveals that "the original thought, whose being-thought is represented by the world, is not an anonymous, neutral consciousness but rather freedom, creative love, a person."[32] The personal nature of the originating Reason that stands behind our creation bestows purpose and meaning to our existence: a firm foundation on which to stand, a past on which to build, and hope for a future that is based on something sure. As Ratzinger writes:

> Only when we know that there is Someone who did not make a blind throw of the dice and that we have not come from chance but from freedom and love can we then, in our unnecessariness, be grateful for this freedom and know with gratitude that it is really a gift to be a human being.[33]

In the last analysis, our origin in a creating Reason assures us of a meaning within our contingency. We are not a mistake or chance event, but are the products of the divine will, the fruit of a great love.[34]

The Human Distinction

Whether or not we recognize Reason at the origin of all things also has consequences for the appreciation of human nature. As has been noted,

---

30. Ratzinger, *Introduction to Christianity*, 152.

31. "When the Gospel of John names Christ the Logos... it means to say that the very foundation of being is reason, and that reason is not a random by-product of the ocean of irrationality from which everything actually sprang." Ratzinger, *Church, Ecumenism, and Politics*, 148.

32. Ratzinger, *Introduction to Christianity*, 158.

33. Ratzinger, *In the Beginning*, 53–54.

34. Ratzinger, *In the Beginning*, 57.

in its post-modernist interpretation and abandonment of metaphysical principles, transhumanism rejects a definable human nature. Ratzinger, by contrast, adheres to what Savulescu rather dismissively defines as an "ideological" concept of human nature. Emerging from an originating Thought, human nature is purposeful and teleological. It has content that is normative and universal.

We recall that Remotti claims that it is in the nature of human beings to "grope in the darkness";[35] that we are united in ignorance, seeking stability not in absolutes and universals, but in tolerance and acceptance of difference. Ratzinger, however, disagrees. Human beings are not united by darkness, but according to a light that shines from within; according to a universal capacity to recognize the truth about what it means to be human. According to Ratzinger, this question is fundamental to our existence. In response to the question "What is the human being?" Ratzinger writes:

> This question is posed to every generation and to each individual human being, for in contrast to the animals our life is not simply laid out for us in advance. What it means for us to be human beings is for each one of us a task and an appeal to our freedom. We must each search into our human-beingness afresh and decide who or what we want to be as humans. In our own lives each one of us must answer, whether he or she wants to or not, the question about being human.[36]

The existentialist idea of deciding "who or what we want to be," which could fit nicely within both Remotti's relativism as well as the transhumanist philosophy of self-determination and morphological freedom, is in Ratzinger prefaced and conditioned by the need to "search into our human-beingness." In other words, our self-determination (enhancement, transcendence) is rooted in what we already are—in what has been received as nature. The human person's origin and his or her destiny are not, as Bostrom would have us believe, unconnected.[37] And contrary to Buchanan's claim, the idea of giftedness does not negate the possibility of

---

35. Remotti, *Contra natura*, 13.
36. Ratzinger, *In the Beginning*, 42.
37. Bostrom writes that human dignity "consists in what we are and what we have the potential to become, not in our pedigree or our causal origin. What we are is not a function solely of our DNA but also of our technological and social context. Human nature in this broader sense is dynamic, partially human-made, and improvable." Bostrom, "In Defense of Posthuman Dignity," 213.

enhancement.[38] Rather, giftedness requires appreciation of the gift, and the wisdom to use it well. It can be developed and enhanced, but always in accordance with the logic with which it is given and received. As noted, this is precisely where the transhumanist project fails, for in denying the givenness of human nature, they have no foundation, no basis, no logic on which to build.

In this search into our human-beingness, Ratzinger seeks a definition of the human person within the stories of our origins, especially as revealed through the Judeo-Christian tradition. Convinced that the mechanisms of evolution cannot hope to exhaust the complex truth of the human person, Ratzinger defends the place of faith in anthropological discussion, in its penetration of reality, and its understanding of truths that go deeper than mere knowledge.

For Ratzinger, only faith can perceive the specifically spiritual nature of human beings. A crudely materialistic evolutionism, that "regards spirit and life in its ascending forms as an incidental mould on the surface of the material world," must be contrasted with a spiritually defined worldview which "regards spirit as the goal of the process and, conversely, matter as the prehistory of the spirit."[39] According to the materialist worldview, the origin of our spiritual nature is essentially meaningless. In Marxist philosophy the question of origins is deemed a distraction, a "mere curiosity."[40] What matters to human beings is not their origins but what they make of themselves. The human spirit does not proceed from a creative mind, but is released through the efforts of human beings to conquer nature. Not looking back, human beings march into the future—a future created by themselves.

A spiritually defined worldview, on the other hand, recognizes that matter is teleologically orientated toward the spirit. The spirit is created. It cannot be reduced to a product of development, "even though it comes

38. Buchanan, *Beyond Humanity?*, 77.

39. Ratzinger, "Belief in Creation," 141.

40. In response Ratzinger writes: "No, the question *does* have influence, and Marx would not take so much trouble to eliminate it if it were otherwise. We must emphasize that here the Marxist system leads to a ban on questioning. It rules out the old basic questions by referring to their alleged sociological conditioning. Here lies the methodical inflexibility of this whole way of thinking, which imposes quite definite limits on rationality itself. Within its self-generated structure, the Marxist system draws a line between allowed and disallowed questions. Human thinking gets dogmatic spoon feeding from the system, but then that is exactly in line with the general demands that the system (the Party) makes on humans." Ratzinger, *In the Beginning*, 97–98.

to light by way of development."⁴¹ Ratzinger contends that this distinction allows the theological conception of the special creation of the human person to coexist with evolutionary theory. In the concept of the immediate creation of the soul by God, "spirit does not enter the picture as something foreign, as second substance in addition to matter; the appearance of spirit . . . means rather that an advancing movement arrives at the goal that has been set for it."⁴²

For the human person, this goal is a special likeness to God. His special creation signifies God's will that human beings should know him. Thus, in the process of evolution, Ratzinger identifies a critical moment:

> The clay became man at that moment in which a being for the first time was capable of forming, however dimly, the thought "God." The first Thou that—however stammeringly—was said by human lips to God marks the moment in which spirit arose in the world. Here the Rubicon of anthropogenesis was crossed. For it is not the use of weapons or fire, not new methods of cruelty or of useful activity, that constitute man, but, rather, his ability to be immediately in relation to God.⁴³

Human beings are distinguished from other animals by their capacity to think about God and to pray.⁴⁴ Thus, according to Ratzinger, the human person is not simply *homo rationalis*, but *homo orans*. This attention to the spiritual nature of human beings in the relation to their Creator further underlines the limitations of evolutionary theory to explain the human complexity. With anthropogenesis determined by "the rise of the spirit," the moment of humanity's emergence cannot be comprehended by paleontology, nor "excavated with a shovel."⁴⁵ It is a profoundly per-

---

41. Ratzinger, "Belief in Creation," 141.

42. Ratzinger, "Belief in Creation," 141.

43. Ratzinger, "Belief in Creation," 142. Borrowing the language of Teilhard de Chardin, Ratzinger offers another image of the emergence of the human spirit: "Teilhard de Chardin once remarked that it is in the nature of evolution to produce ever better eyesight. If we take up this thought, we can describe man accordingly as that stage in the creation, that creature, then, for whom the vision of God is part and parcel of his very being." Ratzinger, *Eschatology*, 154.

44. Ratzinger, *In the Beginning*, 48. Cf. Ratzinger, "Concerning the Notion," 451: "The spirit is that being which is able to think about, not only itself and being in general, but the wholly other, the transcendent God. This is perhaps the mark that truly distinguishes the human spirit from other forms of consciousness found in animals, namely, that the human spirit can reflect on the wholly other, the concept of God."

45. Ratzinger, "Belief in Creation," 142.

sonal and relational moment that the theory of evolution cannot hope to explain.

Taken from the Earth

Thus, in the development of his anthropology, Ratzinger begins: "We are told that God formed the man of dust from the ground."[46] Reflecting on this initial act of human creation through the formation of the human body, Ratzinger contends that there is "something at once humbling and consoling":[47] humbling in the sense that "we are told: You are not God, you did not make yourself and you do not rule the universe; you are limited. You are a being destined for death, as are all things living; you are only earth";[48] consoling in that "we are all *one* humanity, formed from God's *one* earth."[49] In this image of our creation, there exists a fundamental equality between all human beings; not only a contemporaneous equality, but an equality across the centuries. We are equal in our origin, but also equal in our end, destined to return to the dust of the earth (see Gen 3:19). Death, the inescapable reality of human mortality and limitations, is therefore an original guarantor of human equality and solidarity.

Formed by the Breath of God, Created in His Image

"The Lord God formed man of dust from the ground, and breathed into his nostrils the breath of life; and man became a living being" (Gen 2:7). From the humility of our earthly origins we are enlivened by God's life-giving breath. On account of this second creative step, Ratzinger reflects that the human person cannot be reduced to physical origins. He is more than the product of the mechanical process of evolution; "more than just a product of the available genes and DNA, but comes directly from God."[50]

---

46. Ratzinger, *In the Beginning*, 42.
47. Ratzinger, *In the Beginning*, 42.
48. Ratzinger, *In the Beginning*, 42–43.
49. Ratzinger, *In the Beginning*, 44.
50. Ratzinger, *God and the World*, 77. Livio Melina expresses this dynamic as a tension within the human person, existing both "sopra la terra" (above the earth) and "sotto il cielo" (under heaven): "Se si riferisce quest'incerta posizione alla vita umana, si deve rilevarne la simultanea dimensione di continuità e di trascendenza rispetto alle altre forme viventi. Da un lato l'uomo appare il coronamento di uno sforzo di compimento 'dal basso' dell slancio vitale, proprio dell'evoluzione della materia. Anche

In the first place, this infusion of the divine breath gives a particular form to the human person and lends a special dignity to the human body. The body is not estranged from the soul. Rather, together body and soul from a unity that is the human person. As prefect of the Congregation for the Doctrine of Faith, Ratzinger affirmed:

> By virtue of its substantial union with a spiritual soul, the human body cannot be considered as a mere complex of tissues, organs and functions, nor can it be evaluated in the same way as the body of animals; rather it is a constitutive part of the person who manifests and expresses himself through it.[51]

Furthermore, the presence of the divine breath bestows a special dignity on the human person, different to all other living beings: a difference that cannot be eliminated or erased. As Ratzinger writes:

> It is most important to see this special creation by God in order to perceive the uniqueness and value of man and, thereby, the basis of all human rights. This gives man a reverence for himself and for others. God's breath is within him. He sees that he is not just a combination of biological building blocks, but a personal conception of God.[52]

As a "personal conception of God," created in his image (see Gen 1:27), the human person is unique among created beings, and from the beginning exists in special relationship with the Divine. While the bond between God and every other living creature is by nature generic and mediated, human beings enjoy a personal and immediate relationship with

---

tomisticamente l'embrione umano ricapitola le forme cosmiche sostanziali ascendenti. D'altro canto, la possibilità della riflessione nell'uomo importa una distanza dalla realtà vivente immediata. Ciò che dal basso appare come una meta dell'evoluzione, considerato nella prospettiva del fine raggiunto, si rivela, 'dall'alto,' come il senso che finalisticamente muove tutto il dinamismo." Melina, *Corso di Bioetica*, 80–81.

51. CDF, *Donum vitae*, Intro. 3.

52. Ratzinger, *God and the World*, 77. And again: "Human life stands under God's special protection, because each human being, however wretched or exalted he or she may be, however sick or suffering, however good-for-nothing or important, whether born or unborn, whether incurably ill or radiant with health—each one bears God's breath in himself or herself, each one is God's image. This is the deepest reason for the inviolability of human dignity, and upon it is founded ultimately every civilization. When the human person is no longer seen as standing under God's protection and bearing God's breath, then the human being begins to be viewed in utilitarian fashion." Ratzinger, *In the Beginning*, 45.

their Creator.⁵³ Each is known and loved by God personally and called into communion with him.⁵⁴ In this context, Thomas Aquinas identifies a special dignity of human nature as being created "for attaining to the Word."⁵⁵ As a rational and intellectual nature, human nature is inherently capable of knowing God and responding to his love. The fullness of this capacity is revealed in the Incarnation of God's Son, in which God himself assumes a human nature. In the Word made flesh, God and humanity are definitively joined. As the Fathers of the Second Vatican Council write: "By his incarnation the Son of God has united himself in some fashion with every man,"⁵⁶ shedding light on his mystery,⁵⁷ confirming his goodness, and raising him to "a divine dignity."⁵⁸

Tomasz Kraj thus confirms that human dignity and rights are rooted in this "particular relationship with God," through our twofold creation in the image of God and divine adoption, and as such "rights are proper to the human person not because someone (e.g., a human authority or community) granted them; it is the very existence (the creation) of the human being which is the basis of rights."⁵⁹ Or, as one reads in *Dignitas personae*, "there is an intrinsic connection between the

---

53. Melina, *Corso di Bioetica*, 85: "Questa distinzione è colta dalla teologia dell'immagine: la persona umana è in un rapporto unico e singolare con Dio. Mentre tutti gli altri esseri viventi sono in una relazione generica e mediata col Creatore, l'essere umano, ogni essere umano, si trova in una relazione di immediatezza personale con Lui."

54. Ratzinger, *In the Beginning*, 45.

55. *STh.*, III, q. 4, a. 1. Aquinas's reflection on the uniqueness of human nature occurs in the midst of pondering why it (as opposed to another nature) was assumed by the Son of God.

56. Vatican Council II, *Gaudium et spes*, n. 22.

57. "The truth is that only in the mystery of the incarnate Word does the mystery of man take on light." Ibid., n. 22. In this regard Ratzinger writes: "Pilate is correct when he says: 'Behold the man.' In him, in Jesus Christ, we can discern what the human being, God's project, is, and thereby also our own status. In the humiliated Jesus we can see how tragic, how little, how abased the human being can be. In him we can discern the whole history of human hate and sin. But in him and in his suffering love for us we can still more clearly discern God's response: Yes, that is the man who is loved by God to the very dust, who is so loved by God that he pursues him to the uttermost toils of death. And even in our own greatest humiliation we are still called by God to be the brothers and sisters of Jesus Christ and so to share in God's eternal love." Ratzinger, *In the Beginning*, 57–58.

58. Vatican Council II, *Gaudium et spes*, n. 22.

59. Kraj, "Magisterium and Modern Genetics," 631.

ontological dimension and the specific value of every human life."[60] Thus, the presence of God's breath dwelling within the human person is the source of human unity. The solidarity between human beings that begins with our common creation from the dust of the earth, and the equality that is foundational to our species, are confirmed and strengthened by God's loving gaze upon us.

Human Dependence and Transcendence

Enlivened by the divine breath, "each person stands in direct relationship with God."[61] This relationship is not limited to the beginning, to the moment of "in-breathing," but is dynamic and evolving. It is a relationship marked by a twofold dependence and transcendence: the dependence of originating in the dust of the earth, and the transcendence to "pass beyond material creation."[62] In this sense, the human person is unique.

In the first place, the human person's dependence involves the acknowledgment of his or her limitations; the acceptance of finitude. As Ratzinger writes: "He must recognize that he is not self-sufficient and autonomous. He must give up the lie of unrelatedness and of arbitrariness. He must say Yes to his neediness, Yes to the other, Yes to creation, Yes to the limits and precepts of his own essence."[63] To this one might add that human beings must say Yes to their human nature, to that which has been given and which they cannot create themselves. Clearly, this vision of humanity in its dependence and limitations is the antithesis of the transhumanist ideal, with its denial of the given and its arbitrary

---

60. CDF, *Dignitas personae*, n. 5.
61. Ratzinger, *God and the World*, 76.
62. Ratzinger, *God and the World*, 77.
63. Ratzinger, *Church, Ecumenism, and Politics*, 255. Ratzinger writes that the human person's refusal to say Yes to his or her creation is the root of his alienation and sin. "Here we can at once say that at the very heart of sin lies human beings' denial of their creatureliness, inasmuch as they refuse to accept the standard and the limitations that are implicit in it. They do not want to be creatures, do not want to be subject to a standard, do not want to be dependent. They consider their dependence on God's creative love to be an imposition from without.... Human beings who consider dependence on the highest love as slavery and who try to deny the truth about themselves, which is their creatureliness, do not free themselves; they destroy truth and love. They do not make themselves gods, which in fact they cannot do, but rather caricatures, pseudogods, slaves of their own abilities, which then drag them down." Ratzinger, *In the Beginning*, 70–71.

searching for novelties. Against such an ideal Ratzinger adds: "He who can merely choose between arbitrary options is not yet free." Rather, "he is free who has become one with his essence, one with the truth itself."[64]

Dependence, humility, and the acceptance of limits, is therefore the condition of human freedom and transcendence. In their dependence, human beings do not withdraw into the finite, but become "infinite precisely in the recognition of limits."[65] In their relationship with God, human beings recognize that they are created for something more. Indeed, they will not be satisfied with anything less than communion with the Divine. This capacity for transcendence thus puts a lie to the reductionist claims of materialism. Human beings are not only dust, the product of an evolutionary process. They are also spirit, reaching toward infinity and the totality of being.[66]

Accordingly, Ratzinger writes:

> We do not understand man when we ask only where he comes from. We understand him only when we also ask where he can go. Only from his height is his essence really illuminated. And only when this height is perceived does there awaken an absolute reverence for man that considers him still holy even in his humiliation. Only from there can we really learn to love the human condition [*Menschsein*] in ourselves and in the other.[67]

In this sense, Ratzinger could agree with transhumanists that human greatness is not limited to the present but is defined by the future. But unlike transhumanists, Ratzinger defines the content of this future and the goal toward which we are moving. It is not an open future in which human beings decide their own end and the means by which they will reach it. Rather, it is a future that is the fulfillment of our nature as created beings. Human beings are "most profoundly human when they step out of themselves and become capable of addressing God on familiar terms"; "when they discover their relation to their Creator."[68] Thus, our future is union with God: a communion of love. Such is the object of human hope. In Ratzinger's words, hope is "the finding of a 'you' that upholds me

---

64. Ratzinger, *Church, Ecumenism, and Politics*, 255.
65. Ratzinger, *Church, Ecumenism, and Politics*, 255.
66. As Pieper writes: "For the finite spirit, although it is only a 'fragment' of being, by the very fact that it is spirit, is related to the whole of reality." Pieper, *Happiness and Contemplation*, 41.
67. Ratzinger, *Images of Hope*, 58–59.
68. Ratzinger, *In the Beginning*, 48.

and amid all the unfulfilled—and in the last resort unfulfillable—hope of human encounters gives me the promise of an indestructible love that not only longs for eternity but also guarantees it."[69] At the same time, with our end identified as love, the means of our "enhancement" is also defined. It is in our capacity to love that we fulfill our potential: love of God, love of neighbor, love of self.

Created for Relation, Created for Love

The original communion of the human person with God reveals a further truth about human nature: human beings are not created to be alone; they are created for relation; they are made for love.[70] Ratzinger writes:

> The image of God means, first of all, that human beings cannot be closed in on themselves. Human beings who attempt this betray themselves. To be the image of God implies relationality. It is the dynamic that sets the human being in motion toward the totally Other. Hence it means the capacity for relationship.[71]

This capacity for relationship is also a fundamental need, since "no one can live of or for himself or herself alone."[72] No one can live *of* himor herself alone. This fact is inscribed in the reality of our origins. No one can give birth to him- or herself. No one is the source of his or her own being. In the mechanics of sexual reproduction, each is conceived through the union of his or her parents, each is carried in the womb of his or her mother. And while new biotechnologies, assisted and asexual means of reproduction, and the prospect of artificial wombs, admittedly blur the contours of this dependence, they cannot remove it completely. For, as Ratzinger writes, we are by nature not only *of* others, but also *for* others.

> We receive our life not only at the moment of birth but every day from without—from others who are not ourselves but who nonetheless somehow pertain to us. Human beings have their selves not only in themselves but also outside of themselves: they live in those whom they love and in those who love them and to whom they are "present." Human beings are relational,

---

69. Ratzinger, *Introduction to Christianity*, 80.
70. Ratzinger, *God and the World*, 111.
71. Ratzinger, *In the Beginning*, 47.
72. Ratzinger, *In the Beginning*, 72.

and they possess their lives—themselves—only by way of relationship. I alone am not myself, but only in and with you am I myself. To be truly a human being means to be related in love, to be *of* and *for*.[73]

This relationality, intrinsic to human nature, seems to stand in contrast to biotechnologies on which the transhumanist project depends. It has been noted how methods of assisted and asexual reproduction confuse human relationality, by introducing others (physicians, technicians, gamete donors, surrogates, etc.) at the origins of life.[74] But at the same time, this amplification of relationships is also a denial of their importance, for there seems to be nothing essential in the relationship of mother and father. They become relative concepts that can be just as easily "filled" by science and technique.

Dependence on others is further diminished in the transhumanist concept of forming or creating oneself. The human person seizes control of his or her life's project, including the "morphological freedom" to shape body and nature at will. However, in this trivialization of relationships, the individual stands alone, distant, inaccessible to others. At its roots, therefore, transhumanism is a lonely business, and in denying our dependence on others it can only increase our sense of loneliness by seeking happiness in ways that cannot fulfill us. In placing our hope in personal control over our life, we lose something essential to our nature: the joy that comes through dependence and our fulfillment in love.

Awakened to Love

The vocation to love presumes a prior reality. Human beings are capable of loving because they have been loved first. As Ratzinger writes: "Only the 'yes' that is given to me by someone else makes me capable for my

---

73. Ratzinger, *In the Beginning*, 72.

74. Kass, for example, notes that the confusion of origins implicit in many forms of artificial reproductive technology undermines traditional attempts to "defend the integrity of marriage, kinship and especially the lines of origin and descent" that has been enshrined in taboos against incest and prohibitions against adultery. "These time-honored restraints implicitly teach that clarity about who your parents are, clarity in the lines of generation, clarity about who is whose, are the indispensable foundations of a sound family life, itself the sound foundation of civilized community. Clarity about your origins is crucial for self-identity, itself important for self-respect." Kass, *Life, Liberty and the Defense of Dignity*, 99–100.

part of addressing this 'yes' to myself, in and with the other."[75] Through an honest search into our origins we hear this "yes" addressed to us. We discover not simply that there is "such a thing as objective meaning but that this meaning knows me and loves me, that I can entrust myself to it like the child who knows that everything he may be wondering about is safe in the 'you' of his mother."[76]

According to Ratzinger, the form of the relationship between mother and child, especially during the prenatal period, is illustrative of the human vocation to love.

> The being of another person is so closely interwoven with the being of this person, the mother, that for the present it can survive only by physically being with the mother, in a physical unity with her. Such unity, however, does not eliminate the otherness of this being or authorize us to dispute its distinct selfhood. However, to be oneself in this way is to be radically from and through another. Conversely, this being-with compels the being of the other—that is, the mother—to become a being-for, which contradicts her own desire to be an independent self and is thus experienced as the antithesis of her own freedom.[77]

From the very beginning, therefore, the human person is formed by a relationship of interdependence and love, bearing "the memory of its origin from another" and "the intimations of its destiny" for another.[78]

---

75. Ratzinger, *Yes of Jesus Christ*, 100.

76. Ratzinger, *Introduction to Christianity*, 80. In this one may recognize traces of Hans Urs von Balthasar's use of the mother-child relationship as an analogy of the human person's awakening to his or her vocation to love, which Livio Melina interprets as an "anticipatory sign" of divine love. See Balthasar, "Résumé of My Thought," 468–73; Melina, *Sharing in Christ's Virtues*, 41. Balthasar writes: "After a mother has smiled at her child for many days and weeks, she finally receives her child's smile in response. She has awakened love in the heart of her child, and as the child awakens to love, it also awakens to knowledge: the initially empty-sense impressions gather meaningfully around the core of the Thou." Balthasar, *Love Alone is Credible*, 76. He suggests that God awakens love in the human heart through a similar process. "Insofar as we are his creatures, the seed of love lies dormant within us as the image of God (*imago*). But just as no child can be awakened to love without being loved, so too no human heart can come to an understanding of God without the free gift of his grace—in the image of his Son." God "radiates love, which kindles the light of love in the heart of man, and it is precisely this light that allows man to perceive this, the absolute Love." Balthasar, *Love Alone is Credible*, 76. God's love is its own source of recognition. It awakens the human person to his vocation to love.

77. Ratzinger, "Truth and Freedom," 27.

78. López, *Gift and the Unity of Being*, 12.

And as Ratzinger stresses, this form of human interdependence of being-for and being-from continues throughout life: "Human persons are beings of word and of love, beings moving toward Another, oriented to giving themselves to the Other and only truly receiving themselves back in real self-giving."[79] The mother-child relationship thus becomes a paradigm for human nature itself, and an analogy of God's Trinitarian nature according to which we are created: of the Father's "being-for," the Son's "being-from," and Holy Spirit's "being-with."

> Man, for his part, is God's image precisely insofar as the "from," "with," and "for" constitute the fundamental anthropological pattern. Whenever there is an attempt to free ourselves from this pattern, we are not on our way to divinity, but to dehumanization, to the destruction of being itself through the destruction of the truth.[80]

Excluded from this relational concept of human nature is not only every form of individualism, that denies that we come "from" a particular history and nature, but also every attempt at exclusion, that denies that we are "with" and "for" the other. Transhumanism fails on all counts, advocating separation from our origins and denying our common nature with others.

Affirming the Goodness of Creation

The Goodness of the Other

The acknowledgment that love precedes us and affirms our being is the condition of our affirmation of the goodness of the other. I am capable of loving the other because he or she is lovable, declared *good* from the hands of the Creator (see Gen 1:31). Accordingly, the other's dignity does not depend on his or her capacities, nor on my will or magnanimity, but exists simply and objectively in his or her being. As Ratzinger writes, when the real is comprehended as love, "the minimum is a maximum; the smallest thing that can love is one of the biggest things; the particular is more than the universal; the person, the unique and unrepeatable, is at the same time the ultimate and highest thing."[81]

---

79. Ratzinger, *In the Beginning*, 48.
80. Ratzinger, "Truth and Freedom," 28.
81. Ratzinger, *Introduction to Christianity*, 160.

The recognition of the other's intrinsic lovableness is protective against the temptation to objectify the other as a *thing* to be used or as a means to an end. But it is also protective of our own dignity. As Ratzinger writes: "The gaze which I bear toward the other decides my own humanity. I can treat him as a 'thing' only by forgetting his dignity and mine, his being in the image and likeness of God and mine."[82] In this sense, he defines the other as a "guardian" of our dignity, who reminds us of our common origins and the shared promise of a future. From this Ratzinger offers an alternative to Kant's categorical imperative: "We must always see in other human beings persons with whom we shall one day share God's joy."[83]

The Goodness of Nature

This affirmation of the goodness of the individual, while beginning with the particular, has far-reaching consequences. It confirms the goodness of being itself. As Ratzinger writes: "Affirmation of this person would ultimately lose its meaning if being as a whole were not good."[84] And to recognize the goodness of being is to recognize reason in its origin and purpose to its existence. When translated into ethics, it also points to the presence of a moral meaning within being. Philosophically, it is expressed in the notion of a natural law that both affirms an inherent moral reason within nature and the capacity of human reason to engage it.[85]

---

82. Ratzinger, "Human Life," 20.

83. Ratzinger, *In the Beginning*, 49.

84. Ratzinger, *Yes of Jesus Christ*, 92–93. He adds: "The originally limited affirmation of love presupposes the general goodness of being. To put it another way, the 'yes' of my love—it is good that you are—presupposes truth; it presupposes that the being of this man or woman is really good. Included in it is the idea that being of the other stems from a true good, from a true affirmation. Love needs truth. In this sense we can say that without a creator God who vouches for the goodness of what exists, love would lose its justification and become groundless."

85. Fulvio di Blasi writes: "According to Aquinas, the most important philosophical presuppositions of natural law theory are human reason's capacity (1) to grasp the intelligibility of nature, that is, to grasp nature's meaning, order, and laws; (2) to reach the existence of God through the knowledge of nature and, therefore, (3) to refer the existence of nature to the wisdom and will of a Creator, that is, to God's Law; and finally (4) to see the order of nature as important—ethically important!—because thought of and willed by God." Di Blasi, "Role of God," 37.

The concept of natural law has a long genealogy that is not without controversy. In its movement away from the capricious laws of the gods, the Greek Enlightenment began by acknowledging a law derived "from the nature, from the very being, of man himself."[86] As something preexisting, this law is something discovered, not prescribed, and therefore serves as a check to positive law. In its Christian synthesis, with its doctrine of a creating *logos*, there is no conflict between divine and natural law. Rather, the natural law is recognized as a participation in the divine law.[87] However, in later developments, this link was downplayed, influenced by (1) the encounter of cultures beyond the Christian European context that accompanied the age of discovery and colonialization, and (2) the confessional divisions within European Christianity, that having rendered faith and dogma unsustainable bases for the common law, sought a solution in nature and human reason.[88] As a result, the natural law was reduced to the narrow confines of rationalism. In this context, Livio Melina speaks of a juxtaposition within Neo-Scholasticism between the natural law as appealing to "an autonomous reason, based on the ontological structures of creation," and the law of Christ "as a super-added additional element."[89] For his part, Ratzinger has been consistent in his criticism of this strict separation between faith and reason, stemming back to his critique of *Gaudium et spes* in which he recognizes the temptation to treat revelation as a type of "crowning" of a purely rational natural law.[90]

Thus with the sidelining of God, and the abandonment of metaphysics, the modern mind has been rendered deaf to this language of nature, and desensitized to the inherent moral structures in the natural

---

86. Ratzinger, "That Which Holds the World Together," 67.

87. *STh.*, I-II, q. 91, a. 2. Cf. Rhonheimer, "Natural Law as a 'Work of Reason,'" 272–81.

88. Ratzinger, "That Which Holds the World Together," 67–69.

89. Melina, "Pragmatic and Christological Foundations," 301.

90. Ratzinger, "Dignity of the Human Person," 115–63. In his criticism of the anthropology of *Gaudium et spes* Ratzinger writes: "It seemed to many people, especially from German speaking countries, that there was not a radical enough rejection of a doctrine of man divided into philosophy and theology. They were convinced that fundamentally the text was still based on a schematic representation of nature and the supernatural viewed far too much as merely juxtaposed. To their mind it took as its starting point the fiction that it is possible to construct a rational philosophical picture of man intelligible to all and on which all men of goodwill can agree, the actual Christian doctrines being added to this as a sort of crowning conclusion." Quoted in Rowland, "Natural Law," 378.

order.⁹¹ The world has lost its metaphysical and divine transparency.⁹² The so-called "naturalistic fallacy," with its is-ought distinction, denies the validity of extracting moral imperatives from the observation of nature. From within the transhumanist camp, Buchanan speaks of the loss of "normative essentialism."⁹³ For her part, Tracey Rowland associates this loss with postmodern Romanticism and its rejection of the concept of stable essences as a form of "outdated Aristotelianism—something that our knowledge of evolutionary process has rendered redundant."⁹⁴

Indeed, the triumph of an evolutionary philosophy has well and truly severed the link between nature and reason.⁹⁵ Any attempt to define nature in terms other than scientific is rejected as meaningless. As Ratzinger writes: "Theological arguments about the 'nature of humans' or 'natural rights,' resting as they do on the concept of creation, meet a look of blank incomprehension; in fact, they seem nonsensical, the relic of an archaic 'natural philosophy.'"⁹⁶ As a result, Ratzinger has acknowledged on more than one occasion that the natural law has become a "blunt instrument."⁹⁷

---

91. Ratzinger, as Benedict XVI, expressed this eloquently in an address to participants at an International Congress on Natural Law: "The method that permits us to know ever more deeply the rational structures of matter makes us ever less capable of perceiving the source of this rationality, creative Reason. The capacity to see the laws of material being makes us incapable of seeing the ethical message contained in being, a message that tradition calls *lex naturalis*, natural moral law." Benedict XVI, "Address of His Holiness Benedict XVI."

92. "Human reason has lost the capacity to see, in the world and in itself, the transparency of the divine. This a-metaphysical and post-metaphysical reason thus becomes a reason closed in on itself, in which the divine light does not appear." Ratzinger, "Renewal of Moral Theology," 363.

93. Buchanan, *Beyond Humanity?*, 125–26. In support of the claim that human nature is an unreliable source of morality, Buchanan points to its negative elements. The presence of selfishness, excessive partiality, and sin may be explainable in terms of evolutionary advantage, but "there is no reason to assume that all of the human traits that have evolved are good" (136–37).

94. Rowland, "Role of Natural Law," 158.

95. "The idea of the natural law presupposed a concept of nature in which nature and reason overlap, since nature itself is rational. With the victory of the theory of evolution, this view of nature has capsized: nowadays, we think that nature as such is not rational, even if there is rational behavior in nature. This is the diagnosis that is presented to us, and there seem to be few voices today that are raised to contradict it." Ratzinger, "That Which Holds the World Together," 69–70.

96. Ratzinger, *In the Beginning*, 92.

97. Ratzinger, "That Which Holds the World Together," 69.

As evidence, Paolo Flores d'Arcais, in directly engaging Ratzinger on the natural law, deems the concept of moral norms inscribed in being or nature to be "absolutely false and unsustainable."[98] Nature has no message to give; it says nothing.[99] Instead, he recognizes many human laws that, while sharing common features throughout history, nonetheless fail to constitute a universal law. Even with regard to those laws which have the greatest claim to universality (e.g., against murder, incest, or cannibalism), he cites instances of cultures that have not only tolerated such practices, but encouraged them as examples of virtue and religious obligation.[100] In the face of such inconsistencies, he identifies a perennial temptation to judge between cultures: to establish *a priori* that one part of humanity is against nature, while the other exists as the true humanity.[101] In tune with Remotti's criticism against the concept of a stable nature, Flores d'Arcais claims that the notion of a natural law, yielded as a paragon of normality, bears within it the risk of intolerance that threatens contemporary pluralistic societies.[102]

But according to Ratzinger, the fact that humanity has not always and in all places abided by the natural law does not count against it. Rather it demonstrates the fallibility of human beings,[103] who in their freedom are always capable of living contrary to nature.[104] More positively, as evidence of a universal moral law, he cites concepts such as the defense of human dignity and freedom, of obligations toward the poor and needy, as foundational for the moral imperative to do good and avoid evil. While acknowledging that non-believers might be offended by the notion that such values flow from an intrinsic morality within the human person, Ratzinger will not be resigned to the idea that this common movement toward truth and love, and away from evil, counts for nothing.[105]

Thus, Ratzinger's admission of the limitations of the appeal to natural law in contemporary philosophical debate does not equate to its abandonment. Rather he recognizes the need to present the natural

---

98. Ratzinger and Flores d'Arcais, "Controversia su Dio," 127.
99. Ratzinger and Flores d'Arcais, "Controversia su Dio," 144.
100. Ratzinger and Flores d'Arcais, "Controversia su Dio," 128.
101. Ratzinger and Flores d'Arcais, "Controversia su Dio," 128.
102. Ratzinger and Flores d'Arcais, "Controversia su Dio," 127.
103. Ratzinger and Flores d'Arcais, "Controversia su Dio," 131.
104. Ratzinger and Flores d'Arcais, "Controversia su Dio," 141.
105. Ratzinger and Flores d'Arcais, "Controversia su Dio," 108.

law in a context that goes beyond the strict domain of rationalism, and to embrace a broader concept of reason that surpasses the positivistic reduction to what is calculable.[106] This is particularly evident in his treatment of human rights. In defending the universality of the natural law, Ratzinger argues from the basis of the inviolability of certain rights on which the majority opinion cannot decide: rights which the Nuremberg Tribunal, after the horrors of the Holocaust (perpetrated by a democratically elected government) determined were not in the power of any government to discuss,[107] and which the Universal Declaration of Human Rights (1948) recognized as belonging to all human beings by *nature*. Accordingly, a nation which "abrogates to itself the prerogative of defining who is and who is not a subject of rights" not only contradicts democratic principles, but "undermines the basis on which it governs."[108] As Ratzinger recognizes, democracy is more than majority opinion, and positive law always leaves open the question of its ethical foundations.[109] The determination of rights cannot be left to the majority, but is bound by "the common rule of the *nomos*, of what is intrinsically right, that is, to the recognition of values that are an obligatory prerequisite for the majority also."[110]

Ratzinger recognizes the ethical foundation of inviolable rights in creation, from which nature (*physis*) flows.[111] In this context he borrows an expression from Flores d'Arcais, that moral norms could be imagined as being present in the "chromosomes of reality."[112] This does not imply that empirical nature is canonized as the natural law, but that in the order of being there exists a priority of spirit and reason. While modernity wields its charges of "biologism" or "physicalism" as being anti-rational, Ratzinger insists that sensitivity to natural structures in fact engages reason, because creation, as flowing from the mind of God, is inherently

---

106. Ratzinger, *Church, Ecumenism, and Politics*, 205.

107. Ratzinger and Flores d'Arcais, "Controversia su Dio," 130. For, as Ratzinger writes, "majorities, too, can be blind or unjust, as history teaches us very plainly." Ratzinger, "That Which Holds the World Together," 60.

108. Ratzinger, "Human Life," 18.

109. Ratzinger, "That Which Holds the World Together," 60. Cf. Ratzinger, *Turning Point*, 154.

110. Ratzinger, *Church, Ecumenism, and Politics*, 216.

111. Ratzinger and Flores d'Arcais, "Controversia su Dio," 131.

112. Ratzinger and Flores d'Arcais, "Controversia su Dio," 127, 132.

rational.[113] The world is not simply material, objectified by human reason. It is not pre-rational.[114] Creation is intelligible, "saturated" with its own meaning through its participation in the divine *logos*.[115]

But this *logos* within creation is not simply theoretical or speculative. It is not limited to physical laws of nature that can be penetrated by the analytical mind. The language of the *logos* within nature cannot be restricted to the mathematical and mechanical, but is also aesthetic and moral.[116] As Ratzinger writes, creation "teaches us how we can be human in the right way."[117] It offers us "signposts" that give direction for our lives.[118] In this context, Melina makes an important contribution in discerning the natural law as pragmatic. As he writes: "One does not understand which things are moral by means of a law that is given *a priori* to acting."[119] Rather, it is through action, through practical reason, that the moral thing is known. In this Melina notes the significance of Alasdair MacIntyre's seminal work *After Virtue*, which demonstrated "the inadequacy of rationalistic hermeneutics that conceive of the natural law as a series of rational principles that are known beforehand and that would impose themselves extrinsically on action, determining its course in a univocal way."[120]

---

113. Drawing on Ratzinger's thought, David Crawford writes: "Because all of being is created, it bears the impress, the meaning, or logic, or reason, or language, of its Creator. Hence, in this important sense, there is no level of being that does not in some sense express divine reason. There is no level of being lacking an intrinsic intelligibility that is in deep accord with the intelligence of man." Crawford, "Natural Law and the Body," 335.

114. As Crawford writes, nature should "never be understood as simply pre-rational (as not yet participating in, and embodying, *logos*) because its internal order shares in divine reason. Indeed, it is in itself an expression of divine reason." Crawford, "Natural Law and the Body," 347.

115. For Ratzinger, this intelligibility is fully revealed in Christ as the reconciliation of spirit and matter. "Christ is the *Logos* made flesh, that is, the fullness of creative reason itself, who speaks to us and opens our eyes to see anew, even in the darkness of a post-metaphysical era, the presence of a creative truth that lies at the foundation of being and that, with its language, also speaks within being." Ratzinger, "Renewal of Moral Theology," 365.

116. Ratzinger, "Bishops, Theologians, and Morality," 67.

117. Ratzinger, *Turning Point*, 44.

118. Ratzinger, *God and the World*, 164.

119. Melina, "Pragmatic and Christological Foundations," 297.

120. Melina, "Pragmatic and Christological Foundations," 297.

Flores d'Arcais predictably rejects the concept of creation at the foundation of law and rights, claiming it to be a religious principle that cannot be asserted within a pluralistic society.[121] However, while attempting to protect a pluralist society from the dogmatism of creation, Flores d'Arcais has no qualms about being equally "dogmatic" by siding with Monod in asserting the chanced nature of evolution. From this basis he projects the relativist idea that there are no inherent or inviolable human rights, only civil ones that we choose as the foundation of our living together.[122] Brad Gregory highlights the inconsistency of this type of "double speak." Pluralism asserts the truth of relativism and the absence of universal claims, while making an imperative of toleration and diversity.[123] But in the absence of non-subjective moral norms, the determination of what constitutes legitimate diversity, and of what should be tolerated, disintegrates into arbitrariness.

Despite objections against the religious nature of the concept of creation, Ratzinger maintains that the principle that reason precedes matter, and that reason thus exists *within* matter, is within the capacity of every human person to recognize, whether a believer or not. He gives the example of the Stoics, who though having no concept of a Creator or of creation, nonetheless recognized a kind of divine quality within being that was translated as a message for human conduct.[124] He also finds a more contemporary example within ecological movements, whose

---

121. A pluralistic society in which he claims the majority of the population no longer believes in creation. Ratzinger and Flores d'Arcais, "Controversia su Dio," 137.

122. Ratzinger and Flores d'Arcais, "Controversia su Dio," 138.

123. Gregory, *Unintended Reformation*, 19. Ratzinger famously defines such dogmatism as "a dictatorship of relativism that does not recognize anything as definitive and whose ultimate goal consists solely of one's own ego and desires." Ratzinger, "Homily of His Eminence Card. Joseph Ratzinger." He also speaks of "a dogmatism that believes itself in possession of the definitive knowledge of reason and of the right to regard everything else as a mere stage of humanity's development that has been fundamentally superseded and that is best treated as a pure relativity." Ratzinger, "Europe in the Crisis of Cultures," 353.

124. Ratzinger and Flores d'Arcais, "Controversia su Dio," 140. See also Ratzinger, "Renewal of Moral Theology," 363: "Whereas for the Stoics nature pointed to a divine reality of a pantheistic stripe, so that nature, full of gods and divinities, was saturated with signs of the divine will and of the path to divinization, in Christianity, through the concept of creation, nature became transparent to the intentions of the Creator: it expresses the language of the Creator, who lets himself be perceived through creation."

sensitivity to the "message" of nature gives evidence to an inherent morality in being.[125]

The Goodness of Self

Ultimately, Ratzinger insists that one can only love others and the world if one has first learnt to love oneself, since "only someone who has accepted himself can address a real 'yes' to someone else."[126] Indeed, it is only from the height of our end in God that we can learn "to love the human condition."

> Man—every man and woman—is called to salvation. He is willed and loved by God, and his highest task is to respond to this love. He must not hate what God loves. He must not destroy what is destined for eternity. To be called to the love of God is to have a vocation for happiness. To become happy is a "duty" that is just as human and natural as it is supernatural.[127]

The duty to love what God loves begins with oneself. It involves the challenge to love our creatureliness, our dependence, and our limits. Thus, the humility flowing from our origins in the dust of the earth is tempered by the acceptance of our end. Christian humility is therefore hopeful. It is not, as Ratzinger explains, moralistic or denigrating of human nature. Rather, it is "a humility of being": "being as receiving, accepting oneself as created and dependent on 'love.'"[128] He contrasts this Christian humility with its Gnostic distortion in which "nature is undermined for the sake of grace."[129] In this Gnostic detachment from creation, grace no longer fulfills nature. Instead, it overpowers and obliterates it. Human nature is something despised, an obstacle to human transcendence toward union with God. In response, Ratzinger again proposes the Christian doctrine of love. "Christian love presupposes faith in the Creator. It must include acceptance of myself as his creature and love of the Creator's creation in me;

---

125. Ratzinger and Flores d'Arcais, "Controversia su Dio," 140–41.
126. Ratzinger, *Yes of Jesus Christ*, 100. "Those who cannot stand themselves cannot love their neighbor. They cannot accept themselves 'as themselves' because they are against themselves and are bitter as a result and the very foundation of their life makes them incapable of loving" (99).
127. Ratzinger, *Yes of Jesus Christ*, 98.
128. Ratzinger, *In the Beginning*, 99.
129. Ratzinger, *In the Beginning*, 94.

it must lead to the freedom to accept myself as well as any other member of the Body of Christ."[130] The Christian acknowledgment of our human limits, even the limitations of our sinfulness, does not disintegrate into hatred of self. Rather, it finds its response in our *fiat*—our humble "yes" to the givenness of our nature that is open to and orientated toward the healing, elevating and, one could say, *enhancing* effects of divine grace.

Summary

Let us recall once more the fundamental transhumanist question: "Are we good enough?" In the absence of affirmation and love of the human condition, Ratzinger identifies an attitude that "despises existence," especially human existence: "in themselves humans are nothing, naked apes, particularly aggressive rats, though perhaps we can still make something of them."[131] Ratzinger links this attitude to modernity's "opposition between trusting being and doubting being."[132] *Trusting being* flows from the security and dependence of creation, in the assurance that being comes from God and is sustained by God: "for only if it is true that the universe comes from freedom, love, and reason, and that these are the real underlying powers, can we trust one another, go forward into the future, and live as human beings."[133] *Doubting being*, on the other hand (which he also calls "the forgetting of being" or "the refusal of being"), alienates us from all that precedes us. We find ourselves alone, disconnected from God and neighbor, weighed down with the awful responsibility for our own existence and future. As Ratzinger notes, this attitude "manifests itself as the belief in progress, the principle of hope, the principle of class struggle, in other words, creativity as opposed to creation, the production of the world as opposed to the existence of creation."[134]

Can we not hear in this an echo of the transhumanist vision of the human person? Rejection of being, denial of human nature, despair over the current state of our humanity and the hope of making ourselves into something better—all are symptomatic of doubt in the goodness of being and the assurance of a future. The similarity deepens when Ratzinger

130. Ratzinger, *In the Beginning*, 95.
131. Ratzinger, *In the Beginning*, 99.
132. Ratzinger, *In the Beginning*, 100.
133. Ratzinger, *In the Beginning*, 18.
134. Ratzinger, *In the Beginning*, 100.

outlines the hopelessness of the modern project in its stand against creation. One cannot hope to improve creation if there is no foundation to build on, just as one cannot hope to enhance human nature if the concept of human nature is denied. As Ratzinger writes: "Even 'creativity' can only work with the *creatum* of the given creation. Only if the being of creation is good, only if trust in being is fundamentally justified, are humans at all redeemable."[135] Only through "an irrevocable Yes to creation,"[136] through an acceptance and love of our human condition, can we truly hope to enhance the human person.

---

135. Ratzinger, *In the Beginning*, 100.
136. Ratzinger, *In the Beginning*, 99.

Chapter 6

Technology and the Secularization of Hope

IN ADDITION TO THE restrictiveness of positive thought to what is humanly verifiable, this chapter concerns Ratzinger's identification of the dangers inherent in scientific positivism and the technological imperative in their menacing stance over nature. Through drawing on the insights of Romano Guardini, this chapter also includes a reflection on technology's estrangement from humanity, threatening in its power, and dehumanizing in its effects. Applied to transhumanism, such pathologies of reason undermine its excessive confidence in the prospects of science and technology, and reveal the restrictive nature of its hope.

The final section of this chapter considers Ratzinger's claim that modernity's confidence in historical progress has resulted in a secularization of Christian hope. Drawing on Josef Pieper's engagement with Ernst Bloch's "metaphysics of doing" and its rejection of gift and transcendence, Ratzinger exposes an underlying despair in secular concepts of hope, which can be applied to the apparent optimism enshrined within transhumanist thought. In response to this mutation of hope, Ratzinger offers an alternative and richer concept which has its foundation in the human person's nature as a created and transcendent being, who yearns for immortality and the consolation of an enduring love.

The Triumph of the Technological Mindset

The positivistic reduction of human reason is also manifest in transhumanism's embrace of the technological imperative. In its turn toward *techne*, philosophical positivism finds in technology a clear expression of its scientific approach. In the absence of a deeper significance, and the triumph of positivistic knowledge over understanding, technology offers concrete *hope* for the future. When applied to human life, biotechnology advances new possibilities for shaping the course of human history. Transhumanism, with its enthusiastic application of technology to the human body and its refashioning of the human form, embraces these hopes. It finds in technology a means of satisfying the human desire for enhancement which is frustrated by the slowness, inefficiency and unpredictability of both evolution and "low-tech" means of enhancement.[1] Advances in genetic engineering, nanotechnology, cryogenics etc. provide sufficient reason to believe that the transhumanist dream will be realized. As Bostrom and Savulescu write: "These advances will provide the opportunity fundamentally to change the human condition. This presents both great risks and enormous potential benefits. Our fate is, to a greater degree than ever before in human history, in our own hands."[2]

It is typical of the triumph of the technological mindset that the admission of risks and potential abuses of technology does not dampen the transhumanist enthusiasm for pressing forward. Despite acknowledging the possibility that the same technological advances that are the hope of human enhancement could be potentially misused to catastrophic effect,[3] Bostrom seeks solutions in more of the same: better techniques, more effective means, the need for ongoing technological progress unhampered by ideological constraint, and for wide access to enhancements in order to ensure that not only a few benefit from technological advances.[4]

---

1. Bostrom, "Human Genetic Enhancements," 496–97. "There are limits to how much can be achieved by low-tech means such as education, philosophical contemplation, moral self-scrutiny and other such methods proposed by classical philosophers with perfectionist leanings, including Plato, Aristotle, and Nietzsche, or by means of creating a fairer and better society, as envisioned by social reformists such as Marx or Martin Luther King. This is not to denigrate what we can do with the tools we have today. Yet ultimately, transhumanists hope to go further."

2. Savulescu and Bostrom, "Human Enhancement Ethics," 20–21. Or, as Buchanan writes: "Biomedical science is producing new knowledge at an astounding rate—knowledge that will enable us, if we choose, to transform ourselves." Buchanan, *Better than Human*, 4.

3. "While future technological capabilities carry immense potential for beneficial deployments, they also could be misused to cause enormous harm, ranging all the way to the extreme possibility of intelligent life becoming extinct." Bostrom, "Human Genetic Enhancements," 494.

4. Bostrom, "Transhumanist Values," 10–11.

But it begs the question: are such precautions enough to protect against the risks of technology? For a response I turn again to the thought of Ratzinger. Like Bostrom, Ratzinger warmly embraces the value of technology. He acknowledges the benefits of science and upholds its independence.[5] He is honest in his assessment of progress and professes a hope that it may continue into the future. He writes:

> Technology creates new opportunities for humanity. This cannot be disputed. A Christian has no grounds for any kind of resentment of technology. Anyone who grew up in the pre-technical age is unlikely to be tempted to fall for the romanticism of nature. He knows how hard things were in those days, how much inhumanity there could be in the nontechnical world; he knows just how many things have become better and more beautiful and more human now.[6]

But Ratzinger is also painfully aware of the limitations and dangers of science and technology when driven by a positivist mindset. He speaks of "pathological forms of science" that are not at the service of human dignity but of power. He cautions that unrestrained progress threatens humanity and the world, exacerbates existing inequalities among human beings, and places new and unsustainable burdens upon creation. He gives examples of atomic, biological and chemical warfare, and the threats to the environment through the "suffocation" of planning, the pollutions of our activity, the "poisonous breath of our techniques."[7]

While transhumanists clearly advocate these same concerns, they cannot provide an adequate response to the dangers of a disinhibited technology. While they may perceive its dangers, their hopes of finding solutions are ideologically bound to the technological imperative, which ultimately confounds their despair. They are blind to the fact that the pathologies of technology are inherently linked to the positivistic mindset: a mentality that has divorced nature from reason, and alienated morality.

---

5. Ratzinger, *Truth and Tolerance*, 157.
6. Ratzinger, *Faith and the Future*, 94–95.
7. Ratzinger, *Faith and the Future*, 95. Cf. Ratzinger, *Values in a Time of Upheaval*, 26.

Technology in Relation to Nature and Reason

Admittedly, the technological-scientific mindset has a rational basis. As Ratzinger notes, technology flows from the meeting of human reason with the rationality of nature.[8] We learn from the order of the cosmos in order to exert some control over it, thus being liberated from the irrational forces of anxiety and superstition.[9] Ratzinger writes:

> Thus, technology appears as the liberation of man from irrational fear, a fear which technology renders unfounded through a rationally grounded security. Accordingly, one can say that technology originally arose as the means for assuring man's security, that it wanted to be and should be liberation as the guarantee of security: man need no longer fear the cosmos because he knows it, and, in knowing it, he understands how to control it.[10]

This meeting of reasons, in its relation to technology and development, finds resonance in the thought of Romano Guardini (1885–1968). The influence of Guardini on Ratzinger is well documented.[11] In his memoirs, Ratzinger recalls the "hunger for knowledge" of his seminary days: a hunger that in the fields of theology and philosophy was fed by the writings of Guardini (along with Josef Pieper, Theodor Häcker, and Peter Wust).[12] This early fascination continued throughout Ratzinger's career as a theologian. As Emery de Gaál writes, notable themes in the writings of Guardini "reappear" in Ratzinger : "the challenge of modernity, affirmation of the truly real, love, freedom, the creative dimension of God, liturgical renewal as renewal of humankind, and human life becoming meaningful in the encounter with the mystery and person of Jesus Christ."[13] In particular, Ratzinger's *Introduction to Christianity* can be read together with Guardini's *The Essence of Christianity* (*Das Wesen des Christentums*, 1938), united in their presentation of the concrete figure of Christ at the foundation of Christianity.[14] Ratzinger wrote *The Spirit of the Liturgy* in homage to Guardini's book with a similar title (*Vom Geist*

---

8. Ratzinger, "Technological Security," 49.
9. Ratzinger, *In the Beginning*, 46.
10. Ratzinger, "Technological Security," 49.
11. De Gaál, *Theology of Pope Benedict XVI*, 39–43; Rowland, *Benedict XVI*, 17–19; Twomey, *Pope Benedict XVI*, 80; Nichols, *Thought of Pope Benedict XVI*, 153, 203–4.
12. Ratzinger, *Milestones*, 43.
13. De Gaál, *Theology of Pope Benedict XVI*, 39.
14. Rowland, *Benedict XVI*, 18.

der Liturgie, 1918). As Ratzinger confesses, it was among the first books he read after starting his theological studies in 1946.[15] Finally, Ratzinger's trilogy on the life of Jesus may be interpreted in the key of Guardini's seminal work, *The Lord* (*Der Herr*, 1937). In the foreword to *Jesus of Nazareth*, Ratzinger notes the influence of treatises of the life of Jesus from his youth, including that of Guardini: books that were faithful to the Gospel portrayal of Jesus Christ "as a man living on earth who, fully human though he was, at the same time brought God to men, the God with whom as Son he was one."[16]

However, in this context, it is the influence of Guardini on Ratzinger's concept of technology and morality that is significant. Guardini reflects that the process of industrialization has tended to depersonalize human beings; to isolate them from their "Creator and Sustainer."[17] In his *Letters from Lake Como*, written over a period of time in the mid-1920s, Guardini meditates on the changing face of his birthplace through the encroachment of technology from the heavily industrialized north.[18] He contrasts the traditional harmony of human life with nature—the tilled soil, houses with their earthen tones nestling into the hills, the village bell towers mimicking the surrounding mountains—with the jarring intrusion of industrialization and factories which increasingly blight the landscape.[19]

---

15. Ratzinger, *Spirit of the Liturgy*, 7.

16. Ratzinger, *Jesus of Nazareth*, xi. In the face of modernist attempts to demythologize the figure of Christ, both *The Lord* and *Jesus of Nazareth* are attempts to be faithful to the centrality of Jesus in his mystery as the Eternal Word made flesh. Ratzinger writes: "Throughout *The Lord*, Guardini struggled to come to the correct understanding of Jesus: all attempts to 'cleanse' the figure of Jesus of the supernatural result in contradictions and meaningless constructions. One simply cannot strip 'the wholly other,' the mysterious, the divine from this individual. Without this element, the very Person of Jesus himself dissolves. There simply is no psychological portrait of Jesus which can render his different features comprehensible solely from a human perspective." Ratzinger, "Guardini on Christ," 54.

17. Guardini, *Lord*, 373.

18. Though born in Verona in northern Italy, Guardini's parents emigrated to Germany when he was only one year old.

19. "Yet all at once, then, on the singing lines of a small town, I saw the great box of a factory. Look how in a landscape in which all the risings and fallings and measures and proportions came together in one clear melody, along with the lofty bell tower there was suddenly a smokestack, and everything fell apart." Guardini, *Letters from Lake Como*, "First Letter," 6–7.

Guardini's point is not against technology and development. Nor does he foster a romantic notion of pure nature. Rather, he is concerned with the way in which human beings relate to nature. He suggests that, in the past, one could speak of a cultural shaping of nature; of its refashioning by mind and spirit;[20] of inhabited nature as an intimate "continuation and enhancement" of human existence.[21] Indeed, Guardini insists, we cannot relate to pure nature, but only insofar as we dwell within it. He writes:

> In nature "untouched," in the order in which animals live, we have no place. To be human is to have mind and spirit at work. But the human mind or spirit can create only when it has in some way taken over from nature its onward pressing reality, if I might put it thus. The human mind or spirit can create only when the sphere of natural reality has to some extent been released by that of the consciousness, of the ideal, only when it has been challenged and rarefied by this.[22]

This process of human creativity requires some sort of intrusion into nature: its "breaking up," "dissolving," and "dematerializing." This does not signify the negation of nature. Rather, the traditional concept of technology, though a step removed from nature, is yet "so close to it, tied to it so elastically, that it remains natural, and natural juices may flow within it."[23] It is organic, marked by proportion and fittingness.[24] He gives the example of a sailing boat. Though it has no equivalent form in nature, its wood forced into shapes that it does not naturally possess, still its stream-lined figure and its billowing sails "fit" into nature. A harmony exists between it and wind and water. It therefore grieves Guardini to see "these noble creations" encumbered by gasoline motors. They move across the lake oblivious to their surroundings, "so that with upright mast but no sails the vessel clatters through the waves like a ghost of itself."[25]

20. Guardini, *Letters from Lake Como*, "First Letter," 6.
21. Guardini, *Power and Responsibility*, 35–36.
22. Guardini, *Letters from Lake Como*, "Second Letter," 10–11.
23. Guardini, *Letters from Lake Como*, "Second Letter," 11.
24. Guardini, *Power and Responsibility*, 36.
25. Guardini, *Letters from Lake Como*, "Third Letter," 13. Guardini adds: "Go even further and the sailing vessel becomes a steamer, a great ocean liner—culture indeed, a brilliant technological achievement! And yet a colossus of this type presses on through the sea regardless of wind and waves. It is so large that nature no longer has power over it."

It does not embrace nature but overpowers it. It does not proceed from "asceticism" but from power and control.

Guardini explains that these different approaches to nature are significant of two different ways of knowing: one of "sympathising with," penetrating and moving within things; the other of "taking over," tearing apart and subduing. While both forms seek, in some measure, to *possess* nature, the first way does so in order to shape nature to human life: to cultivate a living space within it.[26] However, this form of possession or mastery changes radically in the second way of knowing. With its roots in the Renaissance, in Galileo's attempt to "put nature on the rack by means of experiment and thus extract from nature the secrets that it will not voluntarily reveal,"[27] human beings are no longer content to comprehend nature through their senses, nor to grasp its symbolism. Rather, they desire to know and possess its powers.[28]

Technology and Power

In seeking power over nature, our approach is no longer directed by nature's implicit rationality, but according to human autonomy. Thus severed from the natural order, technology is reduced to a question of power. With the separation of nature and reason, the world is reduced to irrational matter, "raw material," that can be exploited at will.[29] But this separation also means that human beings no longer feel at home within nature. With newer technologies, their connection with nature has become indirect and virtual, abstract and devoid of its former

---

26. "How nature has been possessed and seen and understood here! How it obeys the hand that unconsciously knows it! How the trees grow up in most noble shapes without artificial means! How the landscape follows the will that forms it and commands that more and more of it become a dwelling place, a more vitally flourishing and responsive space for human life! The mastery is gentle. It is irresistibly strong for it courses through the filled nerves of nature, but it is gentle. Its manner, I might almost say, is like that of the soul as it builds up and controls materials and powers for the body." Guardini, *Letters from Lake Como*, "Sixth Letter," 44.

27. Ratzinger, *Yes of Jesus Christ*, 18.

28. "This knowledge does not inspect; it analyzes. It does not construct a picture of the world, but a formula. Its desire is to achieve power so as to bring force to bear on things, a law that can be formulated rationally. Here we have the basis and character of its dominion: compulsion, arbitrary compulsion devoid of all respect." Guardini, *Letters from Lake Como*, "Sixth Letter," 44.

29. Guardini, *End of the Modern World*, 55.

immediateness.[30] As a result, the power of technology has somehow been "let loose." Not knowing how to control it, it threatens human beings and their security. Thus, the fear that was originally banished by technology, in order to make a home for human beings within nature, has returned. As Ratzinger writes:

> What had triumphed over man's primitive fears now let loose a new danger of its own—the danger of the unbridled power of the human spirit that is not ethically formed. The work of man which should protect him now becomes the real danger of both man and world.[31]

Once again, the world becomes an inhospitable place for human beings, this time not due to the rawness of nature, but as the result of their own ingenuity.[32]

Technology and Morality

Ratzinger also acknowledges the danger of technological power wedded to an unformed human ethic. This lack of moral formation may be attributed to the same positivistic mentality that attempts to circumscribe reason. Despite Kant's best attempts to rationalize morality and distinguish between kinds of reason, morality ultimately escapes positivist categories.[33] In effect, this means that morality falls out of consideration

---

30. Guardini, *End of the Modern World*, 69.

31. Ratzinger, "Technological Security," 49. He adds that technology "slips out of the hand of the magician's apprentice, who is unable to find the saving word of ethics that could bring to a halt his own work, once his actions and their unrelenting advance have been set in motion."

32. "Nature is rising up in that very form which subdued the wilderness—in the form of power itself. All the abysses of primeval ages yawn before man, all the wild choking growth of the long-dead forests press forward from this second wilderness, all the monsters of the desert wastes, all the horrors of darkness are once more upon man. He stands again before chaos." Guardini, *End of the Modern World*, 92.

33. Indeed, Ratzinger warns that attempts to circumscribe morality to positive knowledge are threatening to humanity. "Only at the price of ignoring what is precisely human could the question of morality be analyzed in the ordinary way of human knowing. The fact that this is actually being attempted in various quarters today is the great inner threat to mankind today. The tree of knowledge, from which man eats in this case, does not give the knowledge of good and evil, but rather blinds man to discerning the difference between them. Man will not return to paradise through such blindness, because it is not based on a purer humanity but on the rejection of humanity." Ratzinger, "Bishops, Theologians, and Morality," 49.

all together, leaving technology free to do as it wants. The decision to embrace certain technologies is made solely on the basis of feasibility.[34] Pragmatism and power thus define what is ethical.[35] "The only error that it knows is that of incompetence."[36] But Ratzinger warns that whenever science and technology are guided by nothing more than their own capabilities, they become "pathological" and "a threat to life."[37] Whenever "we base ethics on physics, we extinguish what is particularly human, and we no longer liberate the human being but crush him or her."[38]

In response, Ratzinger insists on a return to the original logic of technology that respected nature's rationality. Science and technology are not in themselves liberating or intrinsically ethical. Indeed, the technical view is essentially value free, asking not what we *ought* to do, but what we *can* do in the sense of what is technically possible.[39] Accordingly, science and technology need the guiding wisdom of ethical principles. The technological mindset needs to expand in order to accept a vision of reality that is far broader and richer than it is willing to admit; a vision of reality that is intrinsically ethical. As Pieper writes:

> All obligation is based upon being. Reality is the foundation of ethics. The good is that which is in accord with reality. He who

---

34. Or, as Pastor and García-Cuadrado write: "The adage 'Not everything that can be done should be done' is transmuted into 'Everything that we can do, we should do.'" Pastor and García-Cuadrado, "Modernity and Postmodernity," 344.

35. As evidence, Ratzinger notes that J. Robert Oppenheimer, pioneer of the atomic bomb, recalls that "when the atomic bomb became a possibility, nuclear physicists were fascinated by 'the technically sweet.' The technically possible, the desire to do and the actual doing of what it was possible to do, was like a magnet to which they were involuntarily attracted." Even more chillingly, he adds that "Rudolf Höss, the last commandant of Auschwitz, declared in his diary that the concentration camp was a remarkable technical achievement. If one took into account the pertinent transportation schedules, the capacity of the crematories, and their burning power, seeing how all of these worked together so smoothly, this was clearly a fascinating and well-coordinated programme, and it justified itself." From this, Ratzinger draws the conclusion "that human beings can never retreat into the realm of what they are capable of. In everything that they do, they constitute themselves. Therefore they themselves, and creation with its good and evil, are always present as their standard, and when they reject this standard they deceive themselves. They do not free themselves, but place themselves in opposition to the truth. And that means that they are destroying themselves and the world." Ratzinger, *In the Beginning*, 68–69.

36. Ratzinger, *In the Beginning*, 68.

37. Ratzinger, *Truth and Tolerance*, 158.

38. Ratzinger, *In the Beginning*, 46.

39. Ratzinger, "*Veritatis splendor*," 1.

wishes to know and to do the good must turn his gaze upon the objective world of being. Not upon his own "ideas," not upon his "conscience," not upon "values," not upon arbitrarily established "ideals" and "models." He must turn away from his own act and fix his eyes upon reality.[40]

Perhaps this is what Robert Spaemann means by his call for an "awakening to reality"[41] and which Giuseppe Mazzocato interprets as "returning to the world";[42] or what Guardini seeks in a "wholly new power . . . to see aspects of reality together, to relate to the world in soul as well."[43]

Implications for Hope

This awakening to reality has profound implications for the recognition of genuine hope, just as the restriction of human reality to history and *techne*, to the verifiable and the doable, has profoundly distorted its realization. Bernard Schumacher, an expert on the thought of Pieper, and author of *A Philosophy of Hope: Josef Pieper and the Contemporary Debate on Hope*, writes:

> The world of pure *praxis* maintains that science and the technical power that is tied to work are capable of bringing the human being complete happiness. It rejects any happiness that would be the result of a gift. The object of the principle of hope is reduced to the dimension of that which the human being is capable of achieving through his own efforts. The restriction of happiness, and subsequently of the object of human hope, to a metaphysics of making or doing is inscribed within the current of thought

---

40. Pieper, "Reality and the Good," 111.

41. Spaemann, *Happiness and Benevolence*, 93.

42. Mazzocato, "Inclinazioni naturali del corpo," 138: "Spaemann, infatti, vede la necessità di riformulare l'idea di ragione e propone di pensarla come un profilo dell'esistere umano e precisamente del venire all'esistenza o alla vita, da parte dell'essere umano. Egli usa l'analogia del risveglio dal sonno: avere la ragione significa destarsi alla realtà, percepire e vivere la realtà in un certo modo, il quale non appartiene alle creature che irrazionali. La metafora del destarsi tiene uniti intimamente il darsi della ragione ed il darsi del soggestto stesso. È figura molto vicina a quella della coscienza e al carattere di evento, di meraviglia, di memoria, di relazionalità che essa possiede. Destarsi, infatti, significa anche prendere coscienza, ritornando nel mondo che è di tutti. La ragione è sguardo prima che ragionamento o calcolo."

43. Guardini, *Letters from Lake Como*, "Fifth Letter," 42.

ubiquitous in our century, which politicizes not only happiness, but hope as well.[44]

As Ratzinger confirms, the confidence inspired by positive reason and the human capacity to explore and control the physical processes of life and history became the inspiration for a form of hope that he categorizes as "ideological optimism."[45] As paradigmatic of such optimism, Ratzinger refers to the thought of the German Marxist philosopher Ernst Bloch (1885–1977) as expressed in *The Principle of Hope* (*Das Prinzip Hoffnung*). Through his engagement with Bloch, Ratzinger offers his own understanding of hope, in which his dependence on Pieper is clear. This is particularly evident in the text of a retreat given by Ratzinger at the request of Luigi Giussani to priests of *Comunione e liberazione* in the summer of 1986, the printed edition being dedicated "in gratitude and admiration" to Pieper on the occasion of his eighty-fifth birthday.[46] In it, Ratzinger treats of the theological virtues, using Pieper's philosophical meditations contained in his treatise *Faith, Hope, Love* (*Lieben, Hoffen, Glauben*) as reference and guide.[47] "This explains why," writes Ratzinger in his original Preface, "the basic pattern of my reflections follows Pieper's presentation, to which I also owe a range of excellent quotations and references, especially from Thomas Aquinas."[48] He acknowledges that his own contribution is "to extend Pieper's philosophical presentation, which was devised within the framework of Christianity, into the theological and spiritual spheres."[49]

Ratzinger begins his exploration on hope by acknowledging Bloch's notion that "hope is the ontology of what does not yet exist";[50] what

---

44. Schumacher, *Philosophy of Hope*, 38–39.

45. Ratzinger, *Yes of Jesus Christ*, 45.

46. Originally published as *Aus Christus Schauen: Einübung in Glaube, Hoffnung, Liebe* (Freiburg im Breisgau: Verlag Herder, 1989). First English translation published as *To Look on Christ: Exercises in Faith, Hope, and Love*, trans. R. Nowell, Crossroad, New York 1991. Reprinted with a new title *The Yes of Jesus Christ: Spiritual Exercises in Faith, Hope, and Love*. It is to this reprinting that I refer throughout this work.

47. Ratzinger notes that at the time of receiving Giussani's request, a copy of Pieper's newly compiled treatise of the virtues, originally published as separate editions (1935, 1962, 1971), had just landed on his desk, giving him the inspiration to use it as the basis of his retreat.

48. Ratzinger, *Yes of Jesus Christ*, 133.

49. Ratzinger, *Yes of Jesus Christ*, 133.

50. Ratzinger, *Yes of Jesus Christ*, 41.

TECHNOLOGY AND THE SECULARIZATION OF HOPE

Bloch himself calls "an ontology of the Not-Yet."[51] Human beings are not limited to the prospects of what already exists, but are defined by what is not yet accomplished. They are in a state of "becoming," moving toward their fulfillment, guided by an "anticipatory consciousness" of a better life.[52] Accordingly, hope only becomes real in bidding "farewell to the closed, static concept of being,"[53] recognizing instead the world's latency and tending toward fulfillment.

Bloch's ontology of becoming also finds resonance in the thought of Pieper.[54] Pieper considers it "quite right to listen to what Bloch has to say about the future dimension of the world, about the impossibility of a purely 'static concept of being,' and about the 'ontology of what is not yet in being.'"[55] In admitting this, Pieper does not follow Bloch's premise that there is nothing definitive. (In place of the primacy of being—the truth of all things, as defended by Pieper above—Bloch holds to what might be termed a "primacy of movement"[56]). Rather, Pieper recognizes Bloch's ontology of becoming as a modern expression of a "long-forgotten wisdom" that characterizes human beings as "wayfarers" (*homo viator*); as those who are "on the way," not in a literal sense of movement toward a particular place, but in reference to the "not yet" character of their created and finite being.[57] In this context, hope retains its character as being determined by its object. Individual hopes are differentiated according to what they are directed or moving toward.

However, Pieper departs from Bloch by distinguishing between "ordinary" and "fundamental" hope. In making this distinction he employs the French terms *espoir* and *espérance* which refer to a plurality of hopes or a singular hope respectively. According to Pieper, ordinary hope (plural) is directed toward worldly objects. It possesses an immanent,

---

51. Bloch, *Principle of Hope*, 13.
52. Bloch, *Principle of Hope*, 13.
53. Bloch, *Principle of Hope*, 18.
54. Schumacher notes that "both teach an ontology of becoming, of *not-yet-being*, which they apply to the human being, who is defined by a dynamic state of striving toward the *Totum* or the *summum bonum*, toward full realization. Insofar as he is alive, the human being is constantly moving forward; his condition is that of the *homo viator*." Schumacher, *Philosophy of Hope*, 43.
55. Pieper, *Hope and History*, 79.
56. Schumacher, *Philosophy of Hope*, 45.
57. Pieper, *Faith, Hope, Love*, 93.

"every-day" quality and is restricted to an intra-historical future.[58] In contrast, fundamental hope (singular) has no concrete or specific object in this world. Rather, it seeks transcendence, being directed toward that which is "indefinite," "nebulous," "formless," and "unnameable."[59] Different to the multiplicity of ordinary hopes, the uniqueness of fundamental hope affords it a seriousness and indispensable nature.[60] This differentiation also forms the basis of the distinction between the passion of hope and the theological virtue. It is to this differentiation that I now turn.

Ordinary Hope: Hope as a Passion

In philosophical terms, ordinary or everyday hope assumes the nature of a passion. In his *Treatise on the Passions* within the *Summa Theologiae*, Aquinas lists the passion of hope, along with its opposite despair, among those of the irascible (*irascibilis*) faculty.[61] This irascible faculty is distinguished from the concupiscible (*concupiscibilis*) according to object: not in terms of the material object, but according to the formal or intentional object.[62] As Aquinas writes, while "the object of the concupiscible power is sensible good or evil, simply apprehended as such,

---

58. Pieper, *Hope and History*, 27.

59. Pieper, *Hope and History*, 27–28.

60. Pieper suggests that the distinction between ordinary and fundamental hope becomes even more evident in the absence of hope. "There are thousands of hopes that a person can give up and lose without thereby becoming purely and simply 'hopeless'; it is apparently only one kind of hope, the hope for one sort of thing, whose loss would mean that he had absolutely no more hope and would be purely and simply 'without hope.'" Ibid., 25–26. Furthermore, he contends that the loss of "ordinary" hopes is conditional for the emergence of "fundamental" hope. "The illusion, the perhaps at first totally unavoidable self-deception, consists in our believing that the attainment of certain goods in the objective world, including bodily health, constitutes existential well-being or is at least necessary to it. Disappointment, by contrast, suddenly puts us in the position of experiencing and 'realizing' something that we had perhaps already suspected, namely, that real well-being consists not in some other thing alone but also involves ourselves as hoping for (and having always hoped for) this 'other' from the very depths of our soul, with a much more vital, a truly unconquerable, intensity. Hence, 'disappointment' implies far more here than the correction of an erroneous belief; it implies liberation in a sense extending far beyond the realm of the cognitive." Ibid., 29.

61. *STh.*, I–II, q. 23, a. 1. Cf. *STh.*, I, q. 81, a. 2.

62. Lombardo, *Logic of Desire*, 49.

which causes pleasure or pain,"[63] the object of the irascible faculty is an *arduous* good or evil: a good not easily obtained; an evil difficult to avoid.[64] The irascible faculty acts "in order to remove the obstacles that hinder the concupiscible power from tending toward its object."[65] In its approximation to reason, the irascible faculty may be interpreted as being more perfect than the concupiscible.[66] However, in its dependence on the concupiscible appetite, the irascible faculty remains subordinate.[67] Thus, within the hierarchy of the passions, priority is given to the concupiscible faculty. The irascible passions presuppose the concupiscible; "they are second-order desires and aversions that defend the inclinations of the concupiscible passions and evaporate when the concupiscible power attains its goals."[68]

Along with this priority of the concupiscible faculty over the irascible, there is a hierarchy among the individual passions themselves. Thus, the passion of love (*amor*) is first among the concupiscible powers.[69] Love, indeed, is the primary movement toward a good.[70] Without love there is no apprehension of goods toward which the other passions, both concupiscible and irascible, move. Within this hierarchy, hope is first among the irascible passions,[71] standing nearest to love and bearing "the simplest and most direct relation to the good."[72]

63. *STh.*, I-II, q. 23, a. 1.

64. *STh.*, I-II, q. 23, a. 2. Kevin White explains: "The objects of irascible passions result from complications of the absent good and evil that are objects of desire and aversion. The absence of all these objects is converted into presence when a remote good or evil is united with the subject of appetite to produce delight or pain." White, "Passions of the Soul (Ia IIae, qq. 22–48)," 110.

65. *STh.*, I-II, q. 23, a. 1. Cf. *Summa Theologiae*, I, q. 81, a. 2: "The irascible is, as it were, the champion and defender of the concupiscible when it rises up against what hinders the acquisition of the suitable things which the concupiscible desires, or against what inflicts harm, from which the concupiscible flies. And for this reason all the passions of the irascible appetite rise from the passions of the concupiscible appetite and terminate in them; for instance, anger rises from sadness, and having wrought vengeance, terminates in joy."

66. White, "Passions of the Soul (Ia IIae, qq. 22–48)," 109.

67. *STh.*, I, q. 81, a. 1.

68. Lombardo, *Logic of Desire*, 51. Cf. *STh.*, I-II, q. 25, a. 1; q. 40, a. 1.

69. *STh.*, I-II, q. 25, a. 2.

70. *STh.*, I-II, q. 36, a. 2.

71. *STh.*, I-II, q. 25, a. 3.

72. Miner, *Thomas Aquinas on the Passions*, 216.

As kinds of movement, passions are teleological and admit of contraries.[73] The contrariety of movements constitutes the formal difference between individual passions. Three contraries are identified:

> That between the attractive "pull" of what is good and the repelling "push" of what is evil; that between the calming effect of a present good and the agitating attraction of an absent one; and that between the simple attraction of good as such and the struggle provoked by a great or momentous (*arduum*) good not easily possessed.[74]

Thus, in the case of the concupiscible passions, which concern good and evil absolutely, the contrariety of approach and withdrawal occurs between objects, and not with respect to the same object.[75] On the other hand, the irascible passions also admit of a contrariety with regard to the same object. For example, with regard to the object of a good that is difficult to obtain, two opposing movements or passions are possible: the passion of *hope*, as a tendency toward the arduous good, and the passion of *despair*, that is a turning away from that good which is considered too difficult to obtain.[76]

Like all other passions, the passion of hope (*spes*), is defined by its object. Aquinas identifies this object as "a future good, difficult but possible to obtain."[77] From this definition, four essential characteristics of hope are determined:

- that it is something good. Hope is a striving for goods. It has the good as its object, as opposed to fear whose object is an evil;
- that it is future. Hope is a stretching forward to a good that is not already possessed. In this sense it differs from joy which is the enjoyment of a present good;
- that it must be something arduous[78] and difficult to obtain. It is the arduous nature of the desired good which defines hope as an

---

73. *STh.*, I–II, q. 23, a. 2. The exception is the passion of anger, which according to Aquinas has no contrary. *STh.*, I–II, q. 23, a. 3.

74. White, "Passions of the Soul (Ia IIae, qq. 22–48)," 107.

75. Thus, "every concupiscible passion in respect of good, tends to it, as love, desire and joy; while every concupiscible passion in respect of evil, tends from it, as hatred, avoidance or dislike, and sorrow." *STh.*, I–II, q. 23, a. 2.

76. *STh.*, I–II, q. 23, a. 2.

77. *STh.*, I–II, q. 40, a. 5.

78. Schumacher interprets: "This applies as much to the things the subject is able

irascible passion. In this way it differs from the passion of desire, which, as a concupiscible passion, concerns the future good absolutely; and

- that this difficult thing is something possible to obtain. Hope does not strive for the impossible.[79] A future impossible good is the object of hope's contrary: the passion of despair.[80]

In this architecture of hope, as constitutive of human striving, one recognizes something simple and primordial. As Pieper writes: "In hope, man reaches 'with restless heart,' with confidence and patient expectation, toward the *bonum arduum futurum*, toward the arduous 'not yet' of fulfilment."[81] However, precisely as a *human* passion, hope is also and by necessity bound by reason. The strivings of a restless heart do not coincide with wishful thinking, nor is hope the stuff of dreams.[82] Rather, it is based on reality, and is thus subject to rationality. This does not mean that hope lacks the full character of a passion. Hope always remains an appetitive, and not a cognitive, power.[83] As Robert Miner writes:

> Although hope (like all the passions) requires a logically prior apprehension, it does not consist in this apprehension. Hope is a motion of the appetite, which Thomas describes as a "certain stretching out of the appetite toward the good" (*extensionem quondam appetitus in bonum*).[84]

---

to realize through his own efforts as to the things that do not depend on him, things offered to him as a gift. The difficulty that attends these latter can also become evident in an individual's reservations about receiving the good gratuitously—for example, the reception may require a certain humility." Schumacher, *Philosophy of Hope*, 65.

79. Again Schumacher writes that "the act of hope implies at least some degree of *certainty*, a real possibility, accompanied by a trust that one will obtain one's object. We do not hope for something we know ahead of time we will not be able to possess. Nevertheless, hope also implies a certain leap into the void, insofar as the subject does not know for sure he will really attain the good in question." Schumacher, *Philosophy of Hope*, 75.

80. *STh.*, I-II, q. 40. a. 1.

81. Pieper, *Faith, Hope, Love*, 100. Elsewhere Pieper writes: "Longing, yearning, desiring, wishing, hungering, and thirsting must all play a role in it; otherwise we do not speak of hope. However, I can also long for something and wish to have it while at the same time knowing that I will never get it—something, therefore, that I can hardly be 'hoping' for. Hope, by contrast, includes an element of confidence." Pieper, *Hope and History*, 20–21.

82. Miner notes: "Deprived of rational governance, hope is bound to degenerate into illusion." Miner, *Thomas Aquinas on the Passions*, 230.

83. *STh.*, I-II, q. 40, a. 2.

84. Miner, *Thomas Aquinas on the Passions*, 218; quoting *STh.*, I-II, q. 40, a. 2.

Thus, as opposed to the Stoic solution, which, supposing passions to be irrational, advocates their total suppression,[85] Aquinas proposes passions "moderated by reason" as more fitting to the human good.[86]

In this process of reason-guided striving, one can identify several points at which reason is required in discerning the object of hope: to recognize goods with the aid of prudence, to determine likelihoods and possibilities, and thus to differentiate between true and false hopes. The formation of hope will take into account the means by which a hoped-for good is possible. Aquinas differentiates two ways: by one's own power, or by relying on someone else. As noted to this point, modern hope rests on the first way, trusting only in what one can make oneself. In the second case, one hopes with an expectation of receiving help from another.[87] This idea that one's hope may exist in another has special relevance to the theological virtue of hope to which I now turn, whose object (union with God) is not within the human person's power to achieve, but is realized by the help of divine grace.

Fundamental Hope: Hope as a Theological Virtue

The limitation of ordinary hope to this world and the immanent future is broken open by fundamental hope. Indeed, fundamental hope even goes beyond the large hopes that form part of human history, such as intra-historical aspirations for a better world. It aims, instead, toward something infinite and beyond the human grasp. Such hope emerges before the realization of our limitations; before what Schumacher refers to as "existential limit-situations" that confront us with a choice between hope and despair.[88] This is especially evident before the reality of our mortality and death. In the context of faith, fundamental hope is equated with the theological virtue. Indeed, Pieper writes: "It would never occur to a philosopher, unless he were also a Christian theologian, to describe

---

85. As Pinckaers notes, the Stoics consider "emotions as disorders and propose the ideal of *apatheia*, that is, of the soul as indifferent to emotions." Pinckaers, "Reappropriating Aquinas's Account," 275.

86. *STh.*, I–II, q. 24, a. 3.

87. In this, Aquinas makes a play on words, "as though to await (*exspectare*) implied keeping one's eyes on another (*ex alio spectare*), in so far as the apprehensive power, by going ahead, not only keeps its eye on the good which man intends to get, but also on the thing by whose power he hopes to get it." *STh.*, I–II, q. 40. a. 2.

88. Schumacher, *Philosophy of Hope*, 120.

hope as a virtue. For hope is either a theological virtue or not a virtue at all."[89] Accordingly, it is not a virtue that is natural to the human person, nor nurtured through practice and effort. The virtue of hope can only be received as gift.

In developing a concept of hope as virtue, Aquinas builds on the logic of the passion of hope. It is the same term, *spes*, that is used for both. Both are movements of appetite, the passion of hope belonging to the sensitive appetite, the theological virtue to the intellectual.[90] Both involve cognition, requiring a cognitive discernment of the future good as attainable.[91] Thus, in determining the intentional object of the theological virtue, Aquinas draws a parallel with the movement of the passion of hope toward a good in the future that is difficult, but possible, to obtain.[92] On the basis of this parallel, passion and virtue share the same formal object. However, their material objects differ in infinite proportion. The good to which the virtue aims is not just any good, but the supreme Good, God himself.[93]

The virtue of hope also differs from its namesake in terms of the means by which their respective objects are obtained. While the effort and striving that is intrinsic to the passion moves human beings toward their desired end, they are powerless in their efforts to reach God. Therefore, the virtue of hope achieves its end by "leaning on" God's help. In this way, the end is proportionate to the means, the effect to its cause, for only an infinite power can lead us to an infinite good.[94]

Ratzinger reflects that in the human person's powerlessness to reach the ultimate good unaided, of needing and expecting "more than any

---

89. Pieper, *Faith, Hope, Love*, 99. Pieper further explains: "When we say, then, that hope is a virtue only when it is a theological virtue, we mean that hope is a steadfast turning toward the true fulfilment of man's nature, that is, toward good, only when it has its source in the reality of grace in man and is directed toward supernatural happiness in God" (100).

90. *STh.*, II–II, q. 18, a. 1.

91. Without this cognitive appraisal, Lombardo notes that "the passion of hope would not be elicited, and theological hope could not be sustained." Lombardo, *Logic of Desire*, 154.

92. *STh.*, II–II, q. 17, a. 1.

93. *STh.*, II–II, q. 17, a. 2: "Such a good is eternal life, which consists in the enjoyment of God himself. For we should hope from him for nothing less than himself, since his goodness, whereby he imparts good things to his creature, is no less than his Essence. Therefore the proper and principal object of hope is eternal happiness."

94. *STh.*, II–II, q. 17, a. 2.

present moment will ever be able to give,"⁹⁵ hope must wait for its fulfillment. Thus, the virtue of hope is also characterized by the "not yet." It too is the virtue of the wayfarer, of *homo viatoris*, the one on the way.⁹⁶ However, in its closeness to the virtue of faith, hope rests in the assurance, or anticipation, of its fulfillment. In this sense, Ratzinger asserts that "the 'not yet' is in a certain way already here."⁹⁷ On this point, he admits a divergence from Pieper, who considers all forms of anticipation as being contrary to hope. While acknowledging that some forms of anticipation are contrary to hope (e.g., presumption and despair, to be discussed below), Ratzinger speaks of the "attentive gift" of faith that here and now abides in the expectancy of fulfillment, and without which hope would be impossible.⁹⁸

While the passion of hope and the theological virtue exist as separate entities, with different material objects and ends, both Pieper and Ratzinger point to an intimate connection existing between ordinary and fundamental hope. From Pieper's perspective, fundamental hope "undergirds" all striving after arduous goods, nurturing every aspiration of human hope.⁹⁹ In this regard, Nicholas Lombardo notes an evolution in Aquinas's latter writings, with the recognition of a twofold object of the virtue of hope: of God as one's end and personal fulfillment, and of the particular goods and divine assistance that move us toward that end.¹⁰⁰

---

95. Ratzinger, "On Hope," 306.

96. It is not the virtue of the blessed (who already share in the life of God), nor of the damned (who have no possibility of attaining blessedness). Hope is for the wayfarer, "whether of this life or in purgatory, because in either case they apprehend happiness as a future possible thing." *STh.*, II–II, q. 18, a. 3.

97. Ratzinger, "On Hope," 307. He adds: "This means, on the one hand, that to hope belongs the "dynamism of the provisional," going beyond all human accomplishment. On the other hand, it means that through hope, what is 'not yet' is already realized in our life."

98. Ratzinger, "On Hope," 307n10. This coincides with the foundational theme of the second encyclical of Ratzinger/Benedict XVI, *Spe salvi*. Departing from Saint Paul's assertion that "in hope we were saved" (Rom 8:24), he writes: "Redemption is offered to us in the sense that we have been given hope, trustworthy hope, by virtue of which we can face our present: the present, even if it is arduous, can be lived and accepted if it leads towards a goal, if we can be sure of this goal, and if this goal is great enough to justify the effort of the journey." Benedict XVI, *Spe salvi* n. 1.

99. Schumacher, *Philosophy of Hope*, 123. He continues: "In other words, without fundamental hope, there would be no hope at all; without fundamental hope, we could not speak of hope at all because there would not even be such a thing as despair."

100. Lombardo, *Logic of Desire*, 156. Cf. *STh.*, II–II, q. 17, a. 2 and a. 4.

TECHNOLOGY AND THE SECULARIZATION OF HOPE 163

Thus, temporal goods are recognized in light of the true Good (God) who exists as the object of fundamental hope. As Lombardo adds:

> This account of the object of theological hope strengthens the link with the passion of hope: it means that, in Aquinas's system, theological hope is bound to generate the passion of hope, insofar as any natural good that is helpful for salvation can simultaneously be the object of both virtue and passion, with a consequent mutual strengthening of each.[101]

In these terms, the grace of the virtue invigorates the passion, making its aim more firm and sure. Or, as Pieper contends, supernatural hope rejuvenates and invigorates natural hope, its supernatural vitality "overflowing" into the domain of ordinary hope.[102] Pieper thus speaks of the youthfulness of genuine hope; of that ageless "aspiration that is at once relaxed and disciplined, that adaptability and readiness, that strong-hearted freshness, that resilient joy, that steady perseverance in trust that so distinguish the young and make them lovable."[103] Taking up this theme, Ratzinger gives the example of the youthfulness and energy that characterizes the history of monasticism.[104] In worldly terms, the flight of the monks into the desert was a flight into nothingness, poverty and hopelessness. Yet from the midst of this nothingness, the monks hoped to obtain all things. And the justification of their hope, though resting in a future reality, was also witnessed in the life of the monastery: oases of civilization, of art and culture, and of fraternal love, whose influence spread beyond the monastery walls to renew a crumbling and ancient world. As will be noted in the progression of this present study, this youthful energy, peace and joy that is characteristic of genuine hope stands in stark contrast to the forced and needy optimism that exemplifies its secularized forms.

---

101. Lombardo, *Logic of Desire*, 156.
102. Pieper, *Faith, Hope, Love*, 110.
103. Pieper, *Faith, Hope, Love*, 111.
104. Ratzinger, *Yes of Jesus Christ*, 66.

The Secularization of Hope

Bloch and Hope as an Ontology of "Doing"

While it was noted that Pieper stands in initial agreement with Bloch that hope exists within an ontology of becoming, their ways quickly part concerning the object of hope, the content of humanity's fulfillment, and in how it may be reached. According to Bloch, the object of fundamental hope is an intra-historical reality, a "homeland" toward which human beings press forward by means of their own efforts.[105] Bloch interprets this as revolutionizing hope; of awakening human beings from their ties to the past so as to move forward to a new future. He thus rejects any concept of hope that has its basis in contemplation as opposed to action. Contemplation, he suggests, has its roots in what is closed and past. It turns "Beingness" into "Been-ness."[106] It is thus "helpless against what is present and blind to the future."[107]

In addition to this turning away from the past, Bloch also rejects as fantasy or illusion any concept of hope whose object is beyond time and history.[108] Bloch's hope is firmly founded in the immediacy of praxis, in an objective knowledge that "is actively and partisanly in league with the good which is working its way through."[109] He adds that such knowledge is "the only one which reflects the Real in history: namely the events produced by working people together with the abundant interweaving process-connections between past, present and future."[110] Bloch therefore fixes his hope in the immanent and material; in a dialectical process that propels humanity toward a new world. In its Marxist bent this hope becomes, in the words of Ratzinger, "the virtue of an aggressive ontology, the dynamic force of the march toward utopia."[111] Its goal is the perfect and classless society, the kingdom of man, heaven on earth: "ubi Lenin, ibi Jerusalem."[112]

---

105. Bloch, *Principle of Hope*, 16.
106. Bloch, *Principle of Hope*, 8.
107. Bloch, *Principle of Hope*, 198.
108. As Pieper notes, for Bloch "the range of what can be hoped for is restricted to things realizable within this world; everything else is excluded from consideration on the grounds of being 'illusory.'" Pieper, *Hope and History*, 78.
109. Bloch, *Principle of Hope*, 198.
110. Bloch, *Principle of Hope*, 198.
111. Ratzinger, *Yes of Jesus Christ*, 42.
112. Bloch, *Principle of Hope*, 610.

Accordingly, Bloch's vision has no place for an after-world. Utopia is a constantly evolving reality. He gives the example of Faust, with his constant pressing forward, his "unerring presentiment of the highest moment," and his concept of heaven that "knows only movement and as yet no finite symbol of landing."[113] Instead of a heaven that transcends this reality, Bloch seeks a "transcendence without transcendence,"[114] in which the human person enters "into the Here and Now as himself"; into the fullness of life "without postponement and distance."[115] As Ratzinger interprets, in this pseudo-religious orientation, a secularized optimism becomes the new theological virtue of hope: "the virtue of deified history."[116] In the same breath, pessimism becomes the new despair in its "sin" against the dynamic spirit of progress.[117]

In addition to the Marxist interpretation, Ratzinger notes that ideological optimism also takes a liberal form, marked by an evolutionary inspired confidence in historical development through scientific progress. As discussed above, it is significant of the liberal tradition that hope is reduced to the "anticipation of a rational and human world that would no longer be the result of accident but would be thought out and operated by us human beings and our reason."[118] And while the liberal and Marxist interpretations of hope are distinct, they are united in an optimism that Ratzinger defines as "a secularization of Christian hope," moving from "the transcendent God to the god of 'history.'"[119] From this perspective, hope is the product of human effort and human decision, made manifest through what Ratzinger has termed the human "laboratory of hope."[120]

---

113. Bloch, *Principle of Hope*, 1022. Inez Hedges explains: "There will be no final resting place for Faust, since his 'fair moment' is always just ahead of him—this is the 'forward dreaming' that Bloch sees as humanity's true trajectory." Hedges, *Framing Faust*, 193.

114. Bloch, *Principle of Hope*, 210.

115. Bloch, *Principle of Hope*, 16.

116. Ratzinger, *Yes of Jesus Christ*, 42.

117. Ratzinger, *Yes of Jesus Christ*, 43. Indeed, writes Ratzinger, in the secularization of hope "there is no worse sin against the spirit of the age than to show oneself lacking in optimism."

118. Ratzinger, *Yes of Jesus Christ*, 42.

119. Ratzinger, *Yes of Jesus Christ*, 46.

120. "Its realization is brought to fulfilment in the human 'laboratory of hope.' What one cannot do oneself is very consciously excluded. One could not hope for what one cannot control; there are directives only for what we ourselves can bring about." Ratzinger, "On Hope," 305.

It is no longer an expectant gift from beyond, but "the product of hard work, of planned, calculated, and inventive activity."[121]

Hope within an Ontology of Contingence

In departing ways with Bloch, Pieper bases his conception of hope on a metaphysics that affirms the goodness of being, and situates human beings within the contingency of creation. For Pieper, the *status viatoris* is significant of the human person's creatureliness, of "the 'not-yet-existing-being' of his own existence."[122] However, unlike Bloch, the hope implicit in this "not yet" is not limited to an openness to the future that is in our hands, but is grounded in the gift-nature of being which includes the promise of fulfillment.

From this perspective of contingence and giftedness, hope assumes the character of humility. In humility, we acknowledge our created nature and lack of self-sufficiency. Hope is not found in work, as Bloch would have us think, but in our openness and receptivity that flow from the acceptance of our inadequacy; the willingness to "lean on" the other as Aquinas has suggested. Thus, Ratzinger insists that it is only through a realistic and candid acknowledgment of our limitations that we can discern true hope from the illusion: to resist "the seductive force of the big words for which humanity and its chances are being gambled away."[123] When the ability to do things is the sole guarantor of hope, human beings always seek for more: more power, more intelligence, more capacity, more time in which to "do" things. (One hears clear echoes of the transhumanist project here). In the same way, those who cannot work find themselves without hope. The unproductive, the disempowered, and the dependent, the disabled and the sick, are all essentially "hopeless" and without value.[124] In response, Ratzinger points to the fact that in the ontology of

---

121. Ratzinger, *Faith and the Future*, 92. Cf. Schumacher, *Philosophy of Hope*, 215: "The theory of the continuous progress of humanity toward its complete fulfilment within the temporal and historical dimension alone represents, according to various commentators, a secularization of Christian theology, specifically of its eschatological paradigm, which promises the realization of the new heavens and the new earth."

122. Pieper, *Faith, Hope, Love*, 98.

123. Ratzinger, *Church, Ecumenism, and Politics*, 145.

124. Schumacher adds: "Moreover, the one who exalts work too highly refuses any value to the person except insofar as he is a producer of work, insofar as he is profitable. He thus rejects those who are 'good-for-nothing,' who prevent business from

human striving "doing" and "hoping" are not comparable. While hope inspires and underpins action, action cannot fulfill hope. "If we need hope," Ratzinger writes, "it is because what is done and feasible does not satisfy."[125] Hope extends beyond our grasp; beyond what is doable, what can be produced or obtained by ourselves, or what we can control.[126]

In addition to humility, one might also speak of hope's connection to the virtue of patience. Patience is the antithesis of the positivistic compulsion to "do." As Guardini notes, modernity perceives patience as "something dull and insignificant, a miserable means by which a narrow life seeks to justify its own poverty."[127] Yet in reality it exists as a uniquely personal virtue. Animals, in their instinctive relation to nature's laws, are incapable of patience or impatience. Only those creatures who can rise above what already exists and desire what is not yet realized are so capable.[128] In this one recognizes the link between patience and hope. Patience bears the tension between what we are and what we would like to be; between the "here and now" and the "not yet." It is not simply a matter of waiting, but demands accepting what is given and living with limitations. As Guardini notes, those who are unwilling to make this concession live in a state of constant conflict with their own existence.[129] He gives the example of Goethe's Faust, who rejects reality and spurns his destiny—the same Faust who Bloch presents as a type of hero in his active engagement with the world and his utopian quest.[130] After renouncing hope and faith,

---

optimizing its production through technological and human resources. We may think here of the various 'parasites' on society: the sick, the elderly, contemplatives of all sorts, such as poets, musicians, monks, and even philosophers, whose activities are at bottom useless, representing a 'waste of time.'" Schumacher, *Philosophy of Hope*, 140.

125. Ratzinger, "On Hope," 305.

126. Pieper, *Hope and History*, 23. Pieper adds: "In order to grasp this fact, one need only consider, in a random way, examples from actual linguistic usage: 'I hope that we'll have good weather tomorrow'; 'I hope that the train will come on time'; 'Let's hope that we all stay healthy.' People hope that there might never be another world war; they hope for a good harvest, for the prosperity of their children, for a long life, and so on. What is common to all these everyday expressions is quite clear: what is hoped for is always something over which the one who hopes has no real power—perhaps he can do a little to help things along, but regarding what is decisive he is powerless; he cannot simply cause, generate, manufacture, produce, or create the thing hoped for."

127. Guardini, *Learning the Virtues*, 35.

128. Guardini, *Learning the Virtues*, 39.

129. Guardini, *Learning the Virtues*, 39.

130. Hedges, *Framing Faust*, 198. Hedges writes that, for Bloch, "Faust's best quality is not that he is eternally unsatisfied or endlessly striving—this he regards as a

Faust curses patience as something feeble and cowardly. While for Bloch he exists as a type of "liberated man" who takes his future into his own hands, Guardini suggests that Faust is a slave to fantasy and immaturity. Real maturity involves acceptance of the reality of what is, and it is only with this humble acceptance that we have "the power to change and to reshape it."[131]

Hope Before the "Problem" of Death

The disparity between the conceptions of hope in Bloch and Pieper becomes even more explicit before the problem of death. There is a real sense in which death is an obstacle to the ontology of not-yet-being, an enemy of hope, a "brutal interruption of the human being's ontological striving toward fulfilment."[132] Bloch attempts to get around the problem of death by subordinating it to what Schumacher terms the "supra-individual process" of history's movement toward utopia.[133] The object of human hope is not individual survival, the prospect of "a celestial metaphysics and a Last Judgement in which the righteous receive the reward withheld from them in life."[134] Rather hope is directed toward the attainment of the classless society for which one has lived, worked, and died. The "red hero" of the communist cause dies without pleasure or "pantheism," but in the certainty that eternity is his. He survives death not as an individual ego, but within a collective consciousness, the personal consciousness being so completely "absorbed into a class consciousness that to the person it is not even decisive whether he is remembered or not on the way to victory."[135] For Bloch, this subordination of the individual to class consciousness is the definitive "Novum against death."

But can we really hope for something that we will not personally experience? Is it not rather a personal injustice without hope of restoration? As Ratzinger writes:

'*Schwindel, Hölle*' (swindle, hell); instead, his greatness comes from the circumstance that he has a vision of a better world, but one that remains continually in progress—humanity's unfinished work as a dialectical process." Hedges, *Framing Faust*, 192. Cf. Bloch, *Principle of Hope*, 314, 366.

131. Guardini, *Learning the Virtues*, 40.
132. Schumacher, *Philosophy of Hope*, 154.
133. Schumacher, *Philosophy of Hope*, 177.
134. Bloch, *Principle of Hope*, 1173.
135. Bloch, *Principle of Hope*, 1173.

If only a far distant future will one day bring justice, then all of history's dead prior to that will have been cheated. It does no good to tell them that they have collaborated in the preparation for liberation and in that respect have entered into it. They have not entered into it at all but have exited from history without having received justice. The measure of injustice always remains, then, infinitely greater than the measure of justice.[136]

Further questions arise. For instance, can a "collective consciousness" be the author of hope or is it something restricted to the individual? And once the future, earthly utopia is realized, what new meaning can be given to death? What hope survives the deaths of those who die within it? Ultimately, does not the possibility of complete world destruction (e.g., through nuclear annihilation) turn Bloch's hope of an earthly utopia into despair?

Such questions form the basis of Pieper's response to the problem of death. For Pieper, hope demands personal survival. There is no such thing as collective hope (e.g., of the human species, the universe, or nature), since hope, like death, is a personal act.[137] Furthermore, the prospect of a future utopia cannot be the object of hope if the individual is excluded from sharing in its joys. In saying this, Pieper acknowledges that an individual may speculate on desirable future prospects for humanity,[138] but insists that such prospects, while bearing on his or her curiosity, do not constitute the object of hope. Hope is not speculative but moves toward something concrete, real and good.[139]

Pieper's confidence in this concrete object of human hope beyond death has its foundation, once again, in his recognition of the goodness of being. As Schumacher interprets: "On the basis of God's free and creative love, that is, on the basis of the interrelationship between the metaphysics of love and of creation, Pieper rejects the possibility that things could be reduced back to nothingness through an act of the divine will."[140] Having been created in love, the human person is confident of remaining in that

---

136. Ratzinger, *Church, Ecumenism, and Politics*, 254.

137. Pieper, *Hope and History*, 86–87.

138. In the context of a debate on the possibilities of human enhancement, it is interesting that Pieper includes "interplanetary space flights, electronic information technology, prolongation of the average life span by a decade or perhaps more" among such speculations. Pieper, *Hope and History*, 87.

139. Pieper, *Hope and History*, 88.

140. Schumacher, *Philosophy of Hope*, 160–61.

love. In this sense, Ratzinger confirms that the very idea of God includes human immortality: "For a creature who is looked upon and loved by him who is eternity has thereby a share in eternity."[141]

This accords with Ratzinger's fundamental premise that "the hope which transcends all hopes is the assurance of being showered with the gift of a great love."[142] In this, he reclaims the Christian notion of the kingdom of God, not as an earthly utopia, but as a communion of love between God and the human person.[143] This assurance of love also gives meaning to the singular hopes that mark our lives. In Ratzinger's words, "simple objects become hopes by taking on the coloration of love."[144] Thus love unites small and great hopes: the "pedestrian" and the "eternal,"[145] the passion with the virtue. The particular is not swallowed up by the universal, nor the everyday by the eternal, for Creator and Redeemer are one and the same.[146]

Using the same logic, Ratzinger defines despair as a kind of fear that doubts the goodness of being, that has never been affirmed by love.[147] The great fear—"the fear which transcends all fears"—is therefore the fear of isolation and remaining without love. It is the "fear of an existence in which the little daily disturbances fill everything, without anything large

---

141. Ratzinger, "Beyond Death," 16.

142. Ratzinger, "On Hope," 303. Noting that fundamental hope is the fruit of faith, Ratzinger writes that the "fulfilled totality of being to which faith provides the key is a love without reserve—a love that is an immense affirmation of my existence and that discloses the fullness of all being to me in its breadth and depth. In it the creator of all things says to me: 'All that is mine is yours' (Luke 15:31)." Ratzinger, *Yes of Jesus Christ*, 69. He adds that hope is "the certainty that I shall receive that great love that is indestructible and that I am already loved with this love here and now" (70).

143. Ratzinger, *Yes of Jesus Christ*, 46.

144. Ratzinger, "On Hope," 304.

145. Joseph Godfrey makes a distinction between what he terms "pedestrian," "eternal," and "large" hopes. Godfrey, "Future of Pieper's *Hope and History*," 142.

146. "In redemption he does not take creation back but rather makes it whole and raises it up." Ratzinger, *Yes of Jesus Christ*, 89.

147. "Being is not good, especially if you have not experienced it as welcome, have not had 'Yes' said to you, that is, if you have not been loved." Ratzinger, "On Hope," 303. Elsewhere he writes: "Depression and despair result when the balance of our feelings becomes disordered or even suspended. We no longer see the warmth, the consolation, the goodness, and the salutariness in the world, everything that we can perceive only with our hearts. The world becomes despair in the coldness of knowledge that has lost its roots." Ratzinger, *Images of Hope*, 21–22.

and reassuring coming along to keep the balance."[148] In other words, without the presence of an enduring love that is the source of our hope, the everyday, pedestrian preoccupations (hopes) become insufferable.[149]

In contrast to the promise of an enduring, transcending love, the secular, intra-historical hopes pale into insignificance. Indeed, Ratzinger asserts that there is something profoundly irrational and deceptive in the secularization of Christian hope. The absolutization of historical processes, of human ingenuity and technical power, in which the future depends on our efforts alone, means that there is essentially nothing left to hope for. Ratzinger therefore unveils the pretense of secular hope as "merely the façade of a world without hope that is trying to hide from its own despair with this deceptive sham."[150] In this he echoes the thought of Pieper, who asserts "that the optimism of the philosophy of history or progress is in reality rooted in despair";[151] that it "hides behind a mask of optimism, under the false robes of hope."[152]

Hopelessness

Having touched on the specter of despair, I will proceed to treat of the contraries of hope in more detail. Tradition identifies two types of hopelessness: presumption (*praesumptio*) and despair (*desperatio*). While distinct in their attitude toward the arduous good, Pieper maintains that presumption and despair are united as "perverse anticipations." That is to say, both reject the *status viatoris*, the "not yet" quality of human existence. Presumption takes the form of a perverse anticipation of the fulfillment of hope, in which hope's "not yet" is presumed to be "already." Despair, on the other hands, exists as a perverse anticipation of the non-fulfillment of hope, the "not yet" being reduced to a definite "no."[153]

---

148. Ratzinger, "On Hope," 303.

149. Ratzinger adds: "Then these little fears, if they constitute everything that can be expected of the future, will pass over into the great fear—fear of an unbearable life—because hope no longer dwells in it. In this case, death, which is the end of all hopes, becomes the only hope." Ratzinger, "On Hope," 303.

150. Ratzinger, *Yes of Jesus Christ*, 48.

151. Schumacher, *Philosophy of Hope*, 83. According to Schumacher, Pieper's claim is a little too radical.

152. Schumacher, *Philosophy of Hope*, 82–83.

153. Pieper, *Faith, Hope, Love*, 113; Pieper, *Hope and History*, 31.

Pieper adds that the youthfulness that is characteristic of true hope—the hope of a future that is "not yet"—is destroyed, in different ways, by both forms of anticipation. In the case of despair he speaks of a "senility," a heaviness or forgetfulness, that abandons the arduous good as hopeless. At the other extreme, presumption is associated with an "infantile" anticipation which distorts hope's true character. Accordingly, Pieper classifies presumption as a "fraudulent imitation" (*falsa similitudo*) of hope, while despair exists more correctly as hope's antithesis.[154]

Presumption

Following Pieper, Ratzinger does not dwell extensively on presumption, preferring rather to present two short caricatures of the vice. He first speaks of a "bourgeois liberal Pelagianism"[155] as a form of self-satisfaction that presumes justification by means of underestimating divine justice[156] or by belittling the human capacity for greatness. In this, as will be noted below, it mirrors despair in the lack of greatness of soul that typifies the loss of hope.

Ratzinger identifies the other form of presumption as a "Pelagianism of the pious."[157] In communion with other forms of Pelagianism, it is characterized by an independence from God's gifts and the determination to justify oneself by works.[158] In the realm of piety, such works take the form of scrupulous religious practices—of prayer, fasting, and

---

154. Reprising the analogy of youthfulness Pieper adds: "In much the same way, infantility has a false and merely 'imitative' resemblance to true youthfulness, the proper antitype of which is aging." Pieper, *Faith, Hope, Love*, 124.

155. Ratzinger, *Yes of Jesus Christ*, 81; Pieper, *Faith, Hope, Love*, 126.

156. Aquinas writes: "Just as, through despair, a man despises the Divine mercy, on which hope relies, so, through presumption, he despises the Divine justice, which punishes the sinner." *STh.*, II-II, q. 21, a. 1.

157. Ratzinger, *Yes of Jesus Christ*, 82.

158. The human person presumes on his or her own power, tending toward the good "as though it were possible to him" (*STh.*, II-II, q. 21, a. 1). Such presumption signifies independence from grace, as if humanity could reach the Ultimate Good by its own, unaided efforts. Such presumption, Aquinas adds, is a form of vainglory; a distorted pride: "Man relies on his own power, when he attempts something beyond his power, as though it were possible to him. Such like presumption clearly arises from vainglory; for it is owing to a great desire for glory, that a man attempts things beyond his power, and especially novelties which call for greater admiration." *STh.*, II-II, q. 21, a. 4.

calculated acts of charity—on account of which one presumes to merit beatitude. According to Ratzinger, the pious Pelagian does not seek hope but security. They cannot bear the tension of waiting that is intrinsic to hope, and so attempt to secure a future for themselves. "What they lack," Ratzinger adds, "is the humility essential to any love—the humility to be able to receive what we are given over and above what we have deserved and achieved."[159]

In another context, Ratzinger presents a similar case against Gnosticism, in which the power of knowledge to control one's life and the world is favored over the mystery of divine love.[160] Love is deemed too unpredictable and insecure, a burden of dependence and subjection. It lacks the certainty that comes from verification and knowledge that positivism, as a form of Gnosticism, seeks as an antidote to unpredictability. With words that could easily be applied to the transhumanist project Ratzinger writes that "Gnosticism will not entrust itself to a world already created, but only to a world still to be created."[161] Thus, according to the Gnostic presumption, knowledge and skill are substitutes for trust.

Despair

As noted above, despair exists as "the true antitype of hope,"[162] the etymology of *desperatio* signifying the absence of *spes*.[163] But in the contrariety of movements that constitute the passions, despair is not simply an absence but also a moving away: a withdrawal from the arduous good considered to be unobtainable in an "anticipation of non-fulfilment." Thus, in opposition to the attraction of hope, despair is distinguished by repulsion: "a recoil from the thing desired, by reason of its being esteemed impossible to get."[164]

In constituting despair, Aquinas outlines two ways in which hope might be lacking in a person: "first, through his not deeming it an arduous good; secondly, through his deeming it impossible to obtain either

---

159. Ratzinger, *Yes of Jesus Christ*, 82.
160. Ratzinger, *In the Beginning*, 96.
161. Ratzinger, *In the Beginning*, 97.
162. Pieper, *Faith, Hope, Love*, 124.
163. Miner, *Thomas Aquinas on the Passions*, 219.
164. *STh.*, I–II, q. 40, a. 4.

by himself, or by another."[165] In the first instance, the pursuit of goods is displaced by a preoccupation with sensual pleasures, such that one develops a distaste for the good and places no hope in it.[166] In the second case, hope is lost through sadness of soul, a condition referred to as sloth (*acedia*). Overwhelmed by negative affections, the human person despairs of obtaining the arduous good,[167] and feeling powerless to shift this "oppressive sorrow," resolves to do nothing.[168]

However, drawing on Pieper's interpretation of Aquinas, Ratzinger notes that an alternative translation for *acedia* is *inertia*, that implies something more profound than mere idleness or lack of activity.[169] The concept of inertia constitutes a worldly sorrow or grief that has its roots in the absence of hope and love: "everything one can hope for is known, and all love becomes the disappointment of finiteness in a world whose monstrous surrogates are only a pitiful disguise for profound despair."[170] In the secularization of our age, Ratzinger sees no lack of such worldly sorrow, in which human aspirations for infinity fall short before the oppressive mundaneness of the finite.

Ratzinger goes on to note that such sorrow "stems from a lack of greatness of soul (*magnanimitas*), from an incapability of believing in the greatness of the human vocation that has been destined for us by God."[171] In this he draws on Aquinas's definition of magnanimity as the "stretching forth of the mind to great things."[172] As part of the virtue of fortitude,[173] magnanimity does not shirk from the arduous good, but moves toward

---

165. *STh.*, II–II, q. 20, a. 4.
166. "In this way despair is caused by lust." *STh.*, II–II, q. 20, a. 4.
167. *STh.*, II–II, q. 20, a. 4.
168. *STh.*, II–II, q. 35, a. 1.
169. Ratzinger, *Yes of Jesus Christ*, 71–77.
170. Ratzinger, *Yes of Jesus Christ*, 73.
171. Ratzinger, *Yes of Jesus Christ*, 73. Cf. *STh.*, II–II, q. 129, a. 3: "Magnanimity makes a man deem himself worthy of great things in consideration of the gifts he holds from God: thus if his soul is endowed with great virtue, magnanimity makes him tend to perfect works of virtue; and the same is to be said of the use of any other good, such as science or external fortune." Pieper likewise characterizes *acedia* as meaning "that man denies his effective assent to his true essence, that he closes himself to the demand that arises from his own dignity, that he is not inclined to claim for himself the grandeur that is imposed on him with his essence's God-given nobility of being." Pieper, *Brief Reader on the Virtues*, 51.
172. *STh.*, II–II, q. 129, a. 1.
173. *STh.*, II–II, q. 129, a. 5.

it with confidence.[174] Properly speaking, therefore, magnanimity is the end and perfection of the passion of hope.[175] However, in this confident movement toward the arduous good, hope is once again guided by the virtue of humility: what Pieper describes as "the protective barrier and restraining wall"[176] of human striving. Thus, while magnanimity aims at possible greatness, humility is conscious of "the infinite distance between man and God,"[177] and keeps vigil between sham and true realizations of hope.

In this context, Ratzinger recognizes that *acedia* may exist as a false form of humility: what he calls a "metaphysical inertia" in which human beings lose faith and trust in their divine orientation.[178] This perverted desire to be "more realistic," wedded to the conviction that God is absent from human affairs, transforms the torpor and sluggishness that is typically associated with inertia and sloth into a form of restlessness that aims at compensating for the emptiness caused by oppressive sadness and fear. Accordingly, among the "six daughters" of sloth listed by Saint Gregory in his *Moralia*, and assumed by Saint Thomas in his *Summa*, one finds *evagatio mentis* or a "wandering of the mind after unlawful things."[179] As

---

174. *STh.*, II-II, q. 129, a. 6. "Wherefore, since confidence denotes a certain strength of hope arising from some observation which gives one a strong opinion that one will obtain a certain good, it follows that confidence belongs to magnanimity."

175. *STh.*, II-II, q. 129, a. 2. Cf. Pieper, *Faith, Hope, Love*, 101. Elsewhere Pieper writes: "Magnanimity encompasses an unshakable firmness of hope, a plainly defiant certainty, and the thorough calm of a fearless heart. The magnanimous person submits himself not to the confusion of feelings or to any human being or to fate—but only to God." Pieper, *Brief Reader on the Virtues*, 38.

176. Pieper, *Faith, Hope, Love*, 101.

177. Pieper, *Faith, Hope, Love*, 102.

178. "Man does not trust himself to his own true dimension but wants to be 'more realistic.' Metaphysical inertia would on this account be identical with the false humility that has become so common today: man does not want to believe that God is concerned about him, knows him, loves him, watches over him, is close to him." Ratzinger, *Yes of Jesus Christ*, 73–74.

179. St. Gregory the Great, *Moralia in Iob*, XXXI, 45, 88. The other daughters of sloth are named as malice, spite, faint-heartedness, despair, and sluggishness in regard to the commandments. In expanding on this "wandering of the mind," Aquinas writes: "This tendency to wander, if it reside in the mind itself that is desirous of rushing after various things without rhyme or reason, is called 'uneasiness of the mind' (*importunitas mentis*), but if it pertains to the imaginative power, it is called 'curiosity' (*curiositas*); if it affect the speech it is called 'loquacity' (*verbositas*); and in so far as it affects a body that changes place, it is called 'restlessness of the body' (*inquietudo corporis*), when, to wit, a man shows the unsteadiness of his mind, by the inordinate

Ratzinger notes, in the face of such restlessness *acedia* can "coexist with a great deal of activity and busy-ness,"[180] and despair can wear the mask of purposefulness, self-possession and hope for the future. However, at the root of this self-possession is a profound emptiness: the rejection of one's status as creature,[181] and the subsequent desire to recreate oneself. What begins as a form of self-assertion, of wanting "to be his own creator and to reassemble creation himself with a better form of evolution he had thought out himself,"[182] becomes instead a form of self-negation and self-destruction.

Such despair is not overcome by creating diversions and filling in time, but by an honest and rational acknowledgment of the human condition: of its limitations and its potential; of our status as creatures and our call to divine communion.[183] In response to the extremes of presumption and despair, Ratzinger presents hope as a "middle way"[184] between excess and renunciation, immoderation and discouragement.[185] Navigating between these distortions of human striving, the path of virtue is accompanied by what antiquity called *sophrosyne*—moderation,

---

movements of members of his body; while if it causes the body to move from one place to another, it is called 'instability' (*instabilitas*); or 'instability' may denote changeableness of purpose." *STh.*, II–II, q. 35, a. 4.

180. Ratzinger, *Yes of Jesus Christ*, 75.

181. Ratzinger, *Yes of Jesus Christ*, 75.

182. Ratzinger, *Yes of Jesus Christ*, 74.

183. As Pieper writes: "Despair (except, perhaps, one's awareness of it) is not destroyed by 'work' but only by that clear-sighted magnanimity that courageously expects and has confidence in the greatness of its own nature and by the grace-filled impetus of the hope of eternal life." Pieper, *Faith, Hope, Love*, 122.

184. This middle way (*medietas*) should not be confused with mediocrity (*mediocritas*), since the middle, Ratzinger writes, "can very well be a maximum, a peak, but exactly such a peak as will be found to be that centre of gravity capable of bearing human existence between two abysses." Ratzinger, "Technological Security," 45.

185. "The virtue stands, on the one hand, opposed to *hybris*, immoderation, in which man misses himself: misrepresenting the truth about himself and the truth about reality, he tries to be a god, and failing to respect his own limits and those of others, he becomes the destroyer of being rather that its shepherd. On the other hand, the morality of the Desert Fathers emphasized that the greatest temptation for the monk was *acedia*, discouragement, which trusts itself with nothing and thus leads to inertia, to a deadening of the heart, a renunciation that parades as virtue, confusing itself with humility, but which is in truth a renunciation of existing, a renunciation of morality, and so the real denial of God and man." Ratzinger, "Technological Security," 45–46.

self-control, temperance, prudence—the way of virtue and restraint that recognizes human limits and discerns what is fitting to its nature.[186]

Summary

Building on the identification of its philosophical roots in the positivist reduction, this chapter has situated transhumanism within the secularization of hope to the products of human effort. As noted, Ratzinger rejects this narrowing as a mutation of hope. He does not deny human beings' striving to better themselves and society. Indeed, he acknowledges that such striving is integral to transcendent human nature. However, while harmonizing with and contributing to the ultimate good, human effort cannot bring it to fulfillment. Thus, he contrasts optimism with Christian hope: hope which is made possible through "a gift, the gift of love, which is given us beyond all our activity";[187] "a gift that as something already bestowed we await from him who alone can really give: the God who in the midst of history has already begun his age through Jesus."[188]

As noted, Ratzinger identifies one of the mutations of Christian hope as the absolute belief in progress through science and technology. In the second part of this book, and with the help of practical examples, I intend to show how the transhumanist project fits within this mutation of human hope. In recognizing its origins within the narrow confines of positive thought, it is my intention to show that the transhumanist dream, despite its veneer of hope, is in reality a manifestation of a deep despair for humanity.

---

186. Ratzinger, "Technological Security," 46.
187. Ratzinger, *Yes of Jesus Christ*, 47.
188. Ratzinger, *Yes of Jesus Christ*, 48.

Part II

Practical Applications

Chapter 7

Product or Gift?

The Hope and Despair of Selecting Children

IN THE PREVIOUS SECTION, the positivistic domination of thought was revealed as a pathology of reason, according to which reality is reduced to what is immediate and calculable. It was demonstrated particularly in our dominion over the beginnings of human life. In the current context, I intend to show that this pathology of reason is evident in the prospect of selecting children through genetic engineering.

In addition to a consideration of the science of selection in general, I will particularly focus on Julian Savulescu's principle of procreative beneficence which obliges parents to select the child with the best chance of the best life. This principle will be critiqued according to the nature of this obligation, the possibility of determining "the best life," and its eugenic disposition. Issues of harm and inequality will also be raised, as well as the practical question of its feasibility, which impinges on its prospect of being a legitimate object of hope.

A response to the question of selecting children will attempt to draw together the eugenic mentality against children with disease and disability with the logic of artificial procreation. Accordingly, a significant part of this chapter will attempt to explain the differences in mentality between the artificial reproductive technologies (ARTs) that are foundational for genetic selection and enhancement, and the conjugal act, drawing on the insightful reflections of Martin Rhonheimer in addition to those of Ratzinger. In particular, the lack of contingency that surrounds the beginning of life through ARTs will be shown to be problematic at various levels, transforming the "moral landscape" in terms of responsibility, humility and solidarity (Sandel), distorting the parent-child relationship, and infringing on the child's capacity to emerge as an independent moral subject (Habermas).

On this basis, one can more clearly appreciate Ratzinger's insistence of the "necessity" of the personal nature of sexuality and the conjugal act at the origins of human life. This will be further demonstrated through his distinction between concepts of "reproduction" and "procreation," in which the latter respects the child *not* as an artifact of human engineering, but as a person in the image of God: the fruit of personal love, accepted as gift, and thus a proper object of hope.

Modes of Selection

Through reproductive technologies, the origins of human life, divorced from the loving union of man and woman, become tangled in a web of technology, power and design. Human beings no longer exist as gifts of God or nature, but as products;[1] and like every other product, they are subject to "quality control," to be corrected, manipulated and disposed of at will, and "selected according to requirements that we ourselves stipulate."[2] This is already a reality. In the process of *in vitro* fertilization (IVF) and embryo transfer, the eugenic screening of embryos for various chromosomal disorders and diseases through preimplantation genetic diagnosis (PGD) is now commonplace.[3] Such selection, directed

---

1. Ratzinger, "That Which Holds the World Together," 65.
2. Ratzinger, *Christianity and the Crisis of Cultures*, 26.
3. In its critique of PGD, *Dignitas personae* states: "Unlike other forms of prenatal diagnosis, in which the diagnostic phase is clearly separated from any possible later elimination and which provide therefore a period in which a couple would be free to accept a child with medical problems, in this case, the diagnosis before implantation is immediately followed by the elimination of an embryo suspected of having genetic or chromosomal defects, or not having the sex desired, or having other qualities that are not wanted. Preimplantation diagnosis—connected as it is with artificial fertilization, which is itself always intrinsically illicit—is directed toward the *qualitative selection and consequent destruction of embryos*, which constitutes an act of abortion. Preimplantation diagnosis is therefore the expression of a *eugenic mentality* that 'accepts selective abortion in order to prevent the birth of children affected by various types of anomalies. Such an attitude is shameful and utterly reprehensible, since it presumes to measure the value of a human life only within the parameters of 'normality' and physical well-being, thus opening the way to legitimizing infanticide and euthanasia as well.'" CDF, *Dignitas personae*, n. 22; quoting John Paul II, *Evangelium vitae*, n. 63.

against certain undesirable traits or disabilities, is referred to as *negative selection*.

Selection may be pursued at different stages. Savulescu and Kahane identify three: preconception, preimplantation, and prenatal selection.[4] To date, preconception methods are limited to sex selection by flow cytometric separation of X and Y spermatozoa. Post-conception selection at the stage of preimplantation involves IVF and PGD. Cells removed from an 8-cell stage embryo are screened for chromosomal defects[5] and single gene disorders[6] through a process of Fluorescence In Situ Hybridization (FISH).[7] Prenatal selection, by far the most commonly used form at present, derives genetic information through chorionic villous sampling (CVS) at about eleven weeks gestation or amniocentesis at about fourteen weeks, as well as ultrasound imaging of the fetal anatomy. Maternal serum testing for the presence of fetal cell-free DNA (cfDNA or cffDNA)[8] is a noninvasive method of screening, free of the risks of miscarriage associated with both CVS and amniocentesis.[9] While it has potential to replace invasive methods of prenatal diagnosis, its current application is limited to screening for fetal chromosomal aneuploidies, especially trisomies 21 (Down syndrome) and 18 (Edward's syndrome).[10] On the diagnosis of fetal abnormality, negative selection is achieved through a termination of pregnancy.

---

4. Savulescu and Kahane, "Moral Obligation," 275.

5. E.g., involving chromosomes 13, 16, 18, 21, 22, X and Y.

6. E.g., cystic fibrosis and hemophilia.

7. The authors note that a "newly developed variant of this technique, called preimplantation genetic haplotyping (PGH), takes a single cell and multiplies its genetic complement a millionfold. It may allow testing for a wider range of conditions and will vastly expand the use of genetic selection." Savulescu and Kahane, "Moral Obligation," 275.

8. "CffDNA is a naked molecule and short DNA fragments, 193 base pairs in length, which circulate in the peripheral maternal blood during pregnancy and disappears 2 *hr* after delivery." Keshavarz et al., "Evaluation," 85.

9. The risk of miscarriage through invasive methods of prenatal diagnosis is classically given as between 0.5–2 percent. Along with avoiding the risk of miscarriage, maternal serum testing can provide results at an earlier stage of fetal development (5–7 weeks gestation). Keshavarz et al., "Evaluation," 85.

10. "CfDNA screening has also been proposed as a replacement for first level screening in both high and average risk population for DS (Down syndrome), for some single gene disorders, determination of Rhesus D blood-group status, fetal sex pathologies, sub-chromosomal events, fetal DNA copy number variation, and genome-wide cell-free fetal DNA profiling. Nevertheless, cfDNA screening is not

While negative selection selects against disability and disease states, *positive* selection selects in favor of desirable traits. As noted, it is already possible to select for gender, and the desirability of selecting for intelligence, physical prowess, and other such traits has been advanced. However, with multiple genes and environmental factors involved, such selection is proving more complex, such that positive selection remains at a theoretical stage.

In a bid to relativize the novelty of genetic selection, transhumanists attempt to equate it with various accepted and uncontroversial practices. At a very basic level it is suggested that the selection of a partner based on physical attraction, personality type, and stability of lifestyle, is a form of genetic determination.[11] While Robert Spaemann is willing to admit that "each person owes his genetic makeup to his parents' preference for one another," he nonetheless distinguishes this preference from the "detailed wish lists of individual characteristics of offspring"[12] that is characteristic of genetic engineering.

Transhumanists then suggest that any procreative decision made in view of the good of a future child could be considered selection.

> So, for example, a pregnant woman's avoiding alcohol or drugs that would endanger her fetus, eating a healthy diet, taking folic acid supplements or securing prenatal care are all intended to affect the nature of the child that she will have, and in these examples to help ensure that her child will be born healthy and without serious disability.[13]

In the same vein it is suggested that the timing of conception to coincide with favorable conditions is consistent with selection.[14] Delaying having children until one is financially, materially, or emotionally secure would favor the child's prospects, creating a child with an increased chance for the best outcome. This is particularly evident when a couple decide to avoid conception in circumstances that would threaten the well-being of a future child, such as during a rubella outbreak. The decision to

---

sufficiently sensitive and specific for a diagnostic test and cfDNA screening performance is better documented in trisomies 21 and 18 than for other trisomies." Gekas et al., "Non-invasive Prenatal Testing," 17.

11. Savulescu and Kahane, "Moral Obligation," 276.
12. Spaemann, "Begotten, Not Made," 291–92.
13. Brock, "Is Selection of Children Wrong?," 252.
14. Savulescu and Kahane, "Moral Obligation," 277.

delay conception until the threat has subsided would result in a different child with better prospects for a good life.

Procreative Beneficence

Attempts to justify the selection of children are based on various liberal theories, including procreative autonomy and appeals to the best interest of the child. A variant theory presented by Savulescu and others is the *Principle of Procreative Beneficence*. It is an appeal to a commonsense morality that determines that it is not only morally permissible, but also necessary and expected "of parents to take the means to select future children with greater potential for well-being."[15] The principle simply states:

> Couples (or single reproducers) should select the child, of the possible children they could have, who is expected to have the best life, or at least as good a life as the others, based on the relevant, available information.[16]

Or, in a slightly revised version:

> If couples (or single reproducers) have decided to have a child, and selection is possible, then they have a significant moral reason to select the child, of the possible children they could have, whose life can be expected, in light of the relevant available information, to go best or at least not worse than any of the others.[17]

As noted, the original assertion that parents *should* select the child with the best life expectation is replaced with "have a significant moral reason to" in its revised form. While the language is different, Savulescu is consistent in his thought, explaining in the original context that *should* means "have good reason to." The obligation is therefore conditioned by other reasonable considerations. "In the absence of some other reason for action, a person who has good reason to have the best child is morally required to have the best child."[18]

---

15. Savulescu and Kahane, "Moral Obligation," 277.
16. Savulescu, "Procreative Beneficence," 415.
17. Savulescu and Kahane, "Moral Obligation," 274.
18. Savulescu, "Procreative Beneficence," 415.

The Nature of the Obligation

Savulescu furnishes this relativizing of obligation with a concrete example. While generally admitting that a hearing child has a better life than a non-hearing child, and that parents should therefore choose a hearing child over a non-hearing one, Savulescu acknowledges circumstances in which parents could reasonably select a hearing-impaired child.[19] Hearing-impaired parents may have reason to not view deafness as a disability, but as "defining their cultural identity," enriched by "a sophisticated, unique form of communication" through signing.[20]

Along with these positive reasons, Savulescu suggests that the child is not harmed through being selected for deafness. He argues this on the logic of Parfit's response to the "non-identity problem,"[21] according to which personal harm cannot be attributed to an action which also causes that person to exist. In the context of selection, children are not harmed by the process because they would not have existed otherwise. They could only be harmed if their life was not worth living, which cannot be argued for deafness. Accordingly, Savulescu states the principle: "Because reproductive choices to have a disabled child do not harm the child, couples who select disabled rather than nondisabled offspring should be allowed to make those choices, even though they may be having a child with worse life prospects."[22] However, it would seem that this conditioning of the obligation seems to weaken its moral force, undermining the obligatory nature of the procreative beneficence. Robert Sparrow, for instance, accuses Savulescu of equivocating between reasons and obligations.[23] He suggests that a stricter interpretation of Savulescu's principle would be less flexible: "An obligation to have the best child would require par-

---

19. Savulescu refers to the case of Sharon Duchesneau and Candy McCullough, a deaf lesbian couple in the United States, who deliberately created a deaf child by using the sperm of a deaf friend. Savulescu, "Deaf Lesbians," 771–73; Spriggs, "Lesbian Couple," 283. In spite of this concession, Savulescu risks contradicting himself by maintaining that a deaf child constitutes a "less than best" child, and that "a parent who intentionally inflicted deafness on his or her child, or failed to treat it, would be abusing the child." Savulescu, "In Defence of Procreative Beneficence," 286.

20. Savulescu, "Deaf Lesbians," 771.

21. Parfit, *Reasons and Persons*, 351–80.

22. Savulescu, "Deaf Lesbians," 772.

23. "Savulescu confuses reasons with obligations and moves between the claim that parents have some reason to want the best for their children and the more radical claim that they are morally obligated to attempt to produce the best child possible." Sparrow, "Procreative Beneficence," 44.

ents to do something which is independent of their desire to do it, and would retain its force even in the face of substantial (non-moral) reasons the parents might have to pursue another course of action."[24] In other words, if, as Savulescu suggests, a moral obligation exists to select the child with the best prospects of the best life, this cannot be conditioned by the parents' reasons.[25] It would exist as an imperative, not a reason among others.

The Best Life?

In aiming at the best life, procreative beneficence is not limited to the avoidance of disease states. In relativizing the therapy-enhancement distinction, it is suggested that prospective parents should use genetic testing to select for non-disease states that would enhance the child's chance of a good life. Rather than abandoning the prospects of future children to the chanced nature of the genetic lottery, one is encouraged to positively aim at conceiving enhanced offspring.[26]

While Sparrow objects that the concept of "best" is an absolute, leaving no room for pluralism nor dissent,[27] adherents of procreative beneficence insist that the idea of the "best" life is a comparative concept: the best among the children that a couple (or single reproducer) could possibly have. Reacting against accusations of perfectionism, they deny that it seeks "a child who is 'perfect' or more advantaged or better off than other existing children."[28] Dan Brock similarly insists that "selection need not assume that we know what the perfect child would be, only that we know what would make a given child, or any child, better, what would likely give it a better life."[29]

Procreative beneficence is also open to various interpretations of well-being and the good life, among which Savulescu lists hedonistic, desire-fulfillment, and objective list theories.[30] He claims not to sub-

---

24. Sparrow, "Procreative Beneficence," 46.

25. "An argument for procreative beneficence founded only in the parents' own reasons therefore cannot support any robust generalisations about what they should do." Sparrow, "Procreative Beneficence," 45.

26. Savulescu and Kahane, "Moral Obligation," 276.

27. Sparrow, "Procreative Beneficence," 54.

28. Savulescu and Kahane, "Moral Obligation," 275.

29. Brock, "Is Selection of Children Wrong?," 271.

30. Savulescu, "Procreative Beneficence," 419.

scribe to any particular conception of the good life,³¹ and (with Kahane) insists that within the philosophical disputes which arise in this context, the principle of procreative beneficence takes a neutral stance.³² But in the same breath, they claim that common sense draws a "consensus about the particular traits or states that make life better or worse, a consensus that would rule out many procreative choices as grossly unreasonable."³³ In this, critics discern an inherent contradiction, that while procreative beneficence claims to be philosophically neutral, it in fact offers a clear, "commonsense" concept of the good life.³⁴ As evidence, Savulescu and Kahane speak of a commonsense consensus about certain conditions that make life better (e.g., joy) or worse (e.g., chronic pain).³⁵ Brock similarly acknowledges that, on balance, disease and disability makes life worse, while enhancements of intelligence, memory and powers of concentration generally make life better.³⁶

In their commonsense approach to well-being, Savulescu and Kahane insist that we "apply in our procreative decisions the same concepts we already employ in everyday situations."³⁷ But an objection is again raised: who does this "we" refer to, and in what everyday context?³⁸ Confirming the ambiguity of this approach, Savulescu acknowledges that our conceptions of a good life and disability are partly social constructions and contextually dependent.³⁹ Brock similarly writes that in a pluralistic society judgments are "made relative to particular social, cultural, and economic conditions."⁴⁰ But how far this pluralism should extend, and how elastic out conception of the good life should be, is not determined.⁴¹

31. Savulescu, "In Defence of Procreative Beneficence," 286.
32. Savulescu and Kahane, "Moral Obligation," 279.
33. Savulescu and Kahane, "Moral Obligation," 279.
34. See Sorgner, "Is There a 'Moral Obligation,'" 203–7.
35. Savulescu and Kahane, "Moral Obligation," 279.
36. Brock, "Is Selection of Children Wrong?," 272.
37. Savulescu and Kahane, "Moral Obligation," 279.
38. "Does he refer to the majority of people in Western countries, fellow intellectuals at the University of Oxford, or all strong interest groups in Western countries, like US country folk." Sorgner, "Is There a 'Moral Obligation,'" 204.
39. Savulescu, "In Defence of Procreative Beneficence," 285.
40. Brock, "Is Selection of Children Wrong?," 272.
41. However, in contradiction to the objections by Michael Parker, Savulescu denies that this means that his principle of procreative beneficence is "underdetermining," i.e., that "it is not possible to identify in particular cases which would be the best possible life." Parker, "Best Possible Child," 283.

The Possibility of Harm

In response to the objection that selection of children may cause harm, Peter Singer is left wondering *who* would be thus harmed. He writes: "The parents are not harmed by having the healthier, handsomer and more intelligent children that they want."[42] Nor is it plausible, he suggests, to believe that the children themselves are harmed. Again drawing on Parfit's idea of *possible* persons, Singer insists that the children supposedly harmed by genetic enhancement "could not have existed by any other means."[43]

Savulescu offers a similar response to the question of harm, but in doing so he draws a distinction between selection and genetic manipulation. He builds on a simple case of selection in which Embryo A, with no abnormalities on genetic testing, is preferred to Embryo B, which is found to have a predisposition toward developing asthma.[44] In the eventuality that A develops cancer or severe asthma later in life, A is not harmed by the process of selection, because, as stated above, he or she would not have existed otherwise. But in the situation in which genetic therapy aimed at correcting a predisposition for asthma in A subsequently causes cancer in later life, A has been harmed. "A is worse off in virtue of the genetic manipulation than A would have been if the manipulation had not been performed."[45] Accordingly, selection is differentiated from genetic manipulation.

Confounding Inequality

It is objected that the selection against disability sends a negative message to those living with disability, implying that it is better not to be born than to live with a disability, or that the world would be a better place without disabled persons. Despite the objections of many disabled persons that negative selection is discriminatory, transhumanists like Brock downplay the association.[46] He insists that selection is not responsible for

---

42. Singer, "Parental Choice and Human Improvement," 280.

43. Singer, "Parental Choice and Human Improvement," 280. Cf. Parfit, *Reasons and Persons*, 367.

44. Savulescu, "Procreative Beneficence," 416.

45. Savulescu, "Procreative Beneficence," 422.

46. Brock insists that cases of negative selection "need not imply any message that it would be better if such children never were born, that their lives are not valuable

the harm done to disabled persons, but rather "the prior and underlying value judgements that support and motivate the practice of selection."[47] Furthermore, while the harm done to disabled persons might be real, it needs to be weighed in consequentialist terms against the genuine reasons and wishes of those who chose not to have a disabled child.

Flowing from this, another objection questions the capacity of procreative beneficence to overcome discriminatory attitudes in society. In the affirmation that it is not the presence or absence of disease that is the defining matter for selection, but rather its impact on well-being, Savulescu himself admits certain "counter-intuitive implications" of his principle. He gives the example of a society in which women are discriminated against, treated badly, and enslaved. According to the determinants of well-being, he admits: "Procreative Beneficence implies that couples should test for sex, and should choose males as they are expected to have better lives in this society, even if this reinforces the discrimination against women."[48] However, Savulescu suggests that such action would be self-defeating: that well-being would not be served by a disproportionate ratio of men to women, and that if it were to eventuate, the bias against women would correct itself in time. He also insists that institutional reform, not reproductive interference, is the appropriate response to cases of discrimination. Sparrow, however, is not convinced. While acknowledging that Savulescu's response to the problem of disproportion may work in the case of gender selection, he suggest that it has no force to combat cases of discrimination against race or sexual preference.[49] In following the principle of procreative beneficence, Sparrow suggests that parents would become complicit with the discriminatory attitudes of the society in which they live. "It seems then that an obligation to choose the best child will, if widely realized, inevitably lead to further discrimination against minorities and oppressed groups given that the life prospects of children will be largely determined by existing social relations."[50]

---

to them or to others, of that they have a lesser moral status." Brock, "Is Selection of Children Wrong?," 262.

47. Brock, "Is Selection of Children Wrong?," 265.
48. Savulescu, "Procreative Beneficence," 423–24.
49. Sparrow, "Procreative Beneficence, Obligation, and Eugenics," 51.
50. Sparrow, "Procreative Beneficence, Obligation, and Eugenics," 54.

A New Eugenics?

As noted in chapter 1, Savulescu attempts to draw a distinction between procreative beneficence and the coercive eugenic policies of the past, preferring the language of "moral persuasion" to coercion.[51] He also claims that procreative beneficence does not impose an absolute obligation to choose the better child, but identifies a *significant moral reason* to do so. Accordingly, the "moral obligation" to select against disability[52] and to test for non-disease states[53] is relativized by procreative autonomy and other reasonable considerations. As Savulescu and Kahane write: "The principle states, not what people invariably must do, but what they have significant moral reason to do."[54]

But despite these protestations, both Savulescu and Kahane are not shy of forcefully stating their objective. For instance, they maintain that couples already using IVF "should employ tests to evaluate the genetic potential of their embryos and choose on the basis of it."[55] They also assert that those women at risk of naturally conceiving a child with a condition that compromises well-being, "even if that condition is not a disease,"[56] should be encouraged to "seriously consider" using IVF and genetic testing. Indeed, it is presumed that "there is a moral defect in parents who intend to conceive a child but are indifferent to whether their future child will be born with the potential for a good life."[57] Pressure on prospective parents is amplified when one adopts a minimal threshold

---

51. "If, in the end, couples wish to select a child who will have a lower chance of having the best life, they should be free to make such a choice. That should not prevent doctors from attempting to persuade them to have the best child they can. In some cases, persuasion will not be justified. If self-interest or concern to promote equality motivate a choice to select less than the best, then there may be no overall reason to attempt to dissuade a couple. But in cases in which couples do not want to use or obtain available information about genes which will affect well-being, and their desires are based on irrational fears (e.g., about interfering with nature or playing God), then doctors should try to persuade them to access and use such information in their reproductive decision-making." Savulescu, "Procreative Beneficence," 425–26.

52. Savulescu, "Procreative Beneficence," 51.

53. Savulescu, "Procreative Beneficence," 414.

54. Savulescu and Kahane, "Moral Obligation," 278.

55. Savulescu and Kahane, "Moral Obligation," 281.

56. Savulescu and Kahane, "Moral Obligation," 281. They explain: "This is clearest if natural reproduction is likely to result in a child disposed to, say, clinical depression or autism. But we believe that reproducers also have strong reasons to seek to prevent even an innate tendency to negative affect, or the severe impairment in social skills associated with Asperger's syndrome."

57. Savulescu and Kahane, "Moral Obligation," 276.

of what is acceptable as a good life. According to a Minimal Threshold Constraint, parents should not "bring to life" children who would fall below the threshold, enforceable by law if necessary. As Savulescu and Kahane write: "If reproducers cannot choose a child whose life will be worth living, then they ought not to have a child at all."[58]

However, even in the absence of coercion, the specter of a eugenic mentality remains. As Sparrow notes, the objection to the old eugenics was not simply due to the coercive means used, but more fundamentally concerned its hubris and arrogance in attempting to stand over human lives. As he writes: "There is something fundamentally misguided in the belief that one can determine which are the best human beings."[59] This hubris, this pathology of reason, renders selection suffocatingly oppressive, in spite of the rhetoric of freedom and choice.

A Question of Feasibility

A fundamental objection to the principle of procreative beneficence, of genetically selecting children with the best chance for the best life, regards its practicability. Even without entering into the polemics of what the "best life" consists of,[60] there is a very real and practical objection to the feasibility of genetic manipulation. Drawing on the findings of contemporary genetic science that underline the complexity of gene expression, critics express reasonable doubt over the possibility of achieving transhumanism's hoped for results.[61] In the first place, the massive polygenicity that lies behind individual human traits makes it "nearly impossible" to identity the responsible genes to be manipulated. Second, genetic variance within the population is not sufficiently pronounced as to explain phenotypic diversity. Finally, it seems that phenotype is not only the result of inter-gene interactions, but also of gene-environment interactions (i.e., epigenetics). As Fukuyama explains, "Some genes

---

58. Savulescu and Kahane, "Moral Obligation," 280.

59. Sparrow, "Procreative Beneficence," 55.

60. Sparrow suggests that "the requirements of procreative beneficence, properly understood, are in any case much too demanding, such that very few, if any, parents live up to them. Not only would an obligation to maximise their children's life prospects leave no room for parents' own projects, determining what 'the best life' consists in is extremely difficult and perhaps even impossible." Sparrow, "Procreative Beneficence," 44.

61. Güell Pelayo, "Post-humanist Embryo," 430–31.

control the expression (that is, the activation) of other genes, some interact with the environment in complex ways, some produce two or more effects, and some produce effects that will not be visible until late in the organism's life cycle."[62] While progress has been made in identifying single-gene defects at the basis of such diseases as cystic fibrosis, sickle-cell anemia, Huntingdon's chorea, and Tay-Sachs disease, most diseases follow a more complex genetic basis. When it comes to the positive selection of desirable traits such as intelligence, memory, patience, empathy, or sense of humor,[63] genetic influences seem even more complicated, and our understanding of them further limited.

Another obstacle identified by Francisco Güell Pelayo concerns the safety of ARTs and PGD that are fundamental to the implementation of procreative beneficence. Specifically, Güell Pelayo highlights the risks involved in such reproductive technologies, with research suggesting that the exposure of "gametes or embryos to artificial conditions and PGD may provoke epimutations and alter the imprinting of genes, which may lead to deleterious consequences for development."[64] Along with an increased risk of fetal and perinatal mortality, ARTs and PGD are associated with an increased risk of various disease states: "cancer, malformation, chromosomal anomalies, septal heart defects, esophageal atresia, hypospadias, metabolic disease, imprinting disorders and cerebral palsy."[65] As Güell Pelayo notes, the incidence of such serious risks stand in contradiction to the stated objective of procreative beneficence "to select the child, of the possible children they could have, whose life can be expected, in light of the relevant available information, to go best or at least not worse than any of the others."[66]

Such risks are independent of the potential dangers of genetic manipulation itself, and it would be ingenuous to pretend that such risks

---

62. Fukuyama, *Our Posthuman Future*, 74.

63. Güell Pelayo, "Post-humanist Embryo," 431. Güell Pelayo therefore concludes "that the plan to modify a gene or group of genes in the embryo in order to obtain certain desirable personality traits rests on hypotheses that are no longer supported by developmental biology. The epigenetic dimension, not to mention the complex role of the genes in the context of brain and behavior, exposes the fallacy of trying to correlate single gene modification (or that of a group of genes) in the early embryo with the improvement of traits such as memory, empathy or moral character" (439).

64. Güell Pelayo, "Post-humanist Embryo," 439.

65. Güell Pelayo, "Post-humanist Embryo," 439.

66. Savulescu and Kahane, "Moral Obligation," 274. Cf. Güell Pelayo, "Post-humanist Embryo," 439.

to do not exist. As Stephan Kampowski notes, every intervention on the human organism, even the most simple, is associated with some risk of side effects.[67] It stands to reason that the more radical the intervention, the greater the range and magnitude of the risk. Thus, critics of genetic engineering highlight certain inherent risks associated with manipulation of the human genome. These include the unpredictability of gene expression and the complexity and fragility of the human organism. As members of the President's Council warn: "The human body and mind, highly complex and delicately balanced as a result of eons of gradual and exacting evolution, are almost certainly at risk from any ill-considered attempt at 'improvement.'"[68] This complexity of the human organism is reflected in its integration of systems, such that therapies aimed at a particular system often have universal side effects. Changes at the genetic level would therefore be expected to have widespread and unpredictable effects. In addition to this unpredictability, side effects of genetic manipulation are marked by their irreversibility and potential transferability to future generations.[69]

One's willingness to absorb the risks associated with any intervention will depend on one's current morbidity and probability of improvement.[70] We read in *Dignitas personae*:

> Given that gene therapy can involve significant risks for the patient, the ethical principle must be observed according to which, in order to proceed to a therapeutic intervention, it is necessary to establish beforehand that the person being treated will not be exposed to risks to his health or physical integrity which are excessive or disproportionate to the gravity of the pathology for which a cure is sought.[71]

Accordingly, it might be justifiable to assume risks in the face of grave illness or life-threatening situations that would not be appropriate in less serious cases. In this context, the distinction between therapy and

---

67. Kampowski, *Ricordati della nascita*, 183.

68. President's Council on Bioethics, *Beyond Therapy*, 287. Cf. Kass, "Ageless Bodies, Happy Souls," 18.

69. Baylis and Robert, "Inevitability of Genetic Enhancement Technologies," 7.

70. See Giglio, *Human Enhancement*, 120: "Il bilanciamento fra rischi e benefici in un intervento o una sperimentazione finalizzati alla terapia è valutato in base alla speranza di porre rimedio alla patologia, che di per sé è dannosa per l'integrità fisica dell'individuo."

71. CDF, *Dignitas personae*, n. 26.

enhancement again arises. The acceptance of risks seems more legitimate in attempting to restore someone to health than in subjecting an already healthy person to danger in an attempt to augment certain capabilities.[72]

The Link Between Genetic Engineering and Artificial Procreation

The Child of Desire

While transhumanists equivocate between technologically aided selection and procreative choices that influence the timing of conception, reason would suggest that there is an essential difference between responsible parenting decisions to delay conception for various motives and the direct manipulation of the procreative process. This is illustrated at a basic level in the difference between natural procreation and ARTs. In artificial reproduction, the coming to be of a child is directly dependent upon the will of the parents, which is then executed through the skill of technicians. While there is no guarantee that the action will result in a live birth, the creation of the embryo in the laboratory is the direct result of the parents' decision. As Ratzinger writes: "In separating the origin of new life from the marriage act, artificial procreation tends to regard the child simply as a response to the couple's desire."[73] Or as Martin Rhonheimer adds, the child born of such technology can say: "I exist because you *wanted* me, and only because of this."[74]

It is not the same with a child generated through conjugal love. The child does not exist *because* he or she was wanted. He or she is not dependent on the will of the parents, nor a product of their desire to have a child.[75] Rather, the child is a fruit of the parents' love. Reliance on the conjugal act therefore follows a different logic. According to Livio Melina, even when a couple engage in sexual intercourse with a desire to have a child, there exists a mediate step between their will and the child's being. He writes that the mediation of the body "breaks the direct connection

---

72. Giglio continues: "nel caso dell'*enhancement*, invece, la condizione di partenza è già 'integra,' e quindi ogni rischio per l'integrità stessa appare, in linea di principio, eticamente non giustificabile." Giglio, *Human Enhancement*, 120.

73. Ratzinger, "Bioethics in the Christian Perspective," 14.

74. Rhonheimer, "Instrumentalization of Human Life," 166.

75. Rhonheimer, "Instrumentalization of Human Life," 167.

between the procreative decision and origin of the child's life."⁷⁶ By way of the body, the generation of the child is not the result of the parents' will, but is mediated by processes that exist independently of the couple's decision; by a design to which the couple entrust themselves in their desire for a child, not simply bound by the body's physiology, but by the emotions, the passions, and the interpersonal nature of conjugal union.⁷⁷ As Leon Kass adds, *sexual* reproduction "is established (if that is the right term) not by human decision, culture or tradition, but by nature."⁷⁸

According to this logic, Rhonheimer maintains that the conjugal act "is not truly a 'means' for reaching the goal of 'a child.'"⁷⁹ He justifies this by noting that a couple continue to engage in the conjugal act even when there is little prospect of procreation, for the act retains meaning and purpose in the absence of a procreative result.⁸⁰ However, the same cannot be said of the act of IVF. In cases in which the odds of conceiving a child through IVF are negligible, the couple would normally opt out of the program. In Rhonheimer's mind, this divergence between the conjugal act and IVF confirms that while ARTs directly will the coming to be of a child, the desire of children through the conjugal act is mediated.

Rhonheimer further distinguishes between *desiring* and *intending*, in which the former is directed toward something we cannot achieve by ourselves, while the latter actively seeks means to achieve the desired object. Thus, while the basic desire may be the same in IVF and the conjugal act (i.e., to have a child), IVF forms an intention to generate a child and seeks means that are directly aimed at its fulfillment.⁸¹ The intention of

---

76. "La mediazione corporea interrompe la connessione diretta tra decisione procreative e origine della vita del figlio." Melina, *Corso di Bioetica*, 107.

77. "La disponibilità a procreare si configura piuttosto come consenso ad un progetto che precede quello dell'uomo e della donna: un progetto al quale essi si affidano e nel quale entrano, certo responsabilmente, ma non arbitrariamente." Melina, *Corso di Bioetica*, 107.

78. Kass, *Life, Liberty and the Defense of Dignity*, 153.

79. Rhonheimer, "Instrumentalization of Human Life," 162. He adds: "'The generation of a child' is not therefore in every case an adequate description of what the spouses *do* when they have intercourse; at the most it can be the adequate description of that which (with the consciousness and desire of the spouses) *could occur* at the level of nature, and this *on the occasion of* their union" (163).

80. As Kampowski adds, the conjugal act "is always more than an act of human generation." Kampowski, "Children of Desire," 13.

81. "Or rather, the actions pertaining to IVF are carried out with the intention of fulfilling the desire for a child. The act of procreation, *or better of 'production,' of the child is therefore a function of the fulfilment of the desire. It possesses no other significance.*" Rhonheimer, "Instrumentalization of Human Life," 163.

the conjugal act, on the other hand, is different. It is intended as an act of love; as a mutual giving of one to the other. Accordingly, the child that results from the conjugal act is not directly intended, but comes to be "on the occasion" of the act.[82] The child is "received," not ordained. Even in their desire for a child, the couple who engage in the conjugal act are open to both the fulfillment and the non-fulfillment of their desire. The logic of desire of those open to the conjugal act is therefore different from those who engage IVF. As Rhonheimer writes: "The legitimate desire to have a child can only be simply a *hope* for the coming about of a new human life."[83]

This has implications for the recognition of the goodness of the child conceived. As the fruit of the parents' will, the *goodness* of the child conceived through IVF is made dependent "on its 'being desired,' on the *recognition* or acceptance given by others."[84] The child is thus instrumentalized or exploited as the means of satisfying the parents' desire. The good sought is not the being of the child itself, but the satisfaction of the desire. As Rhonheimer writes: "A 'wanted child' in *this* sense would amount to a degradation of human life, because it implies an acceptance or recognition by the parents of this life that is *conditioned*."[85]

In this conditional acceptance of the "wanted child," a continuum exists between artificial reproduction and the selection / genetic enhancement of children. Drawing on the thought of Marcel Gauchet, who discerns an intimate connection between the "child of desire" and the child *as* I desire him or her,[86] Kampowski predicts that the child who exists solely on the basis of parental desire "will logically turn out to be a designer baby."[87] Kass makes a similar point in relation to cloning. Despite a majority opposition to human cloning, he suggests that cloned children would *fit perfectly* within the logic of the child of desire.

---

82. "Said otherwise, the child *arises from this act*, which is, in its personal structure, not an act or a means for the generation of a child, but an act of love, that is, an act in which two persons who love one another in their bodily-spiritual totality mutually give themselves, joining themselves the one to the other." Rhonheimer, "Instrumentalization of Human Life," 164.

83. Rhonheimer, "Instrumentalization of Human Life," 158.

84. Rhonheimer, "Instrumentalization of Human Life," 156.

85. Rhonheimer, "Instrumentalization of Human Life," 158–59.

86. "Dal figlio del desiderio al figlio così come io lo desidero, la strada è una." Gauchet, *Il figlio del desiderio*, 87.

87. Kampowski, "Children of Desire," 16.

"Thanks to our belief that all children should be *wanted* children[88] (the more high-minded principle we use to justify contraception and abortion), sooner or later only those children who fulfil our wants will be fully acceptable."[89]

The Burden of Responsibility

Highlighting the awful responsibility of being directly responsible for willing a child's life through artificial procreation, Robert Spaemann ponders what response parents could give to their unhappy child who asks why they brought him or her into being. While parents who conceive through the conjugal act might speak of the child's origin in their love, those who make a child "by hand" must justify themselves. But who, asks Spaemann, can give a justification for the life or death of another human being?[90] This burden of responsibility is increased exponentially by the prospect of genetic engineering. Parents would not simply be responsible for the existence of the child, but for his or her characteristics and talents. Again Spaemann questions who can give a justification for the existence of a human being who has been willed or designed according to one's own private taste.[91] In this context, Michael Hanby speaks of the "excruciating burden" of being the artisans of our children, given power to make "intolerable choices" that go beyond our capacity.[92] For his part, Michael Sandel here identifies a paradox. While it is often objected that genetic enhancement undermines personal responsibility, effort, and striving, in reality there is an "explosion" of responsibility. "As humility gives way, responsibility expands to daunting proportions. We attribute

---

88. Kampowski similarly argues that "every child a wanted child"—Margaret Sanger's campaign slogan for legal contraception and abortion—also forms the logic of artificial reproductive technologies. Kampowski, "Children of Desire," 11.

89. Kass, *Life, Liberty and the Defense of Dignity*, 144.

90. Spaemann, "Wozu der Aufwand?," 409: "Von einem unglücklichen Kind gefragt, warum er und seine Frau es ins Dasein gesetzt haben, kann ein Vater mit Gottfried Benn antworten: 'Glaubt doch nicht, daß ich an euch dachte, als ich mit eurer Mutter ging. Ihre Augen wurden so schön bei der Liebe.' Wer das Kind von Hand gemacht hat, müßte sich rechtfertigen. Aber wer kann sich rechtfertigen für den Tod oder das Leben eines anderen Menschen?" Cf. Melina, *Corso di Bioetica*, 106–7.

91. "Und wer kann sich rechtfertigen für dessen Sosein, das er seinem privaten Geschmack entsprechend entworfen hat?" Spaemann, "Wozu der Aufwand?," 409.

92. Hanby, "When Art Replaces Nature," 23.

less to chance and more to choice. Parents become responsible for choosing, or failing to choose, the right traits for their children."[93]

Giftedness

According to Sandel, this burgeoning of responsibility constitutes just one of the transformations in the "moral landscape" as a result of genetic engineering. Humility and a sense of solidarity also fall victim to its influence.[94] In Sandel's interpretation, humility in parenting is tied to the notion of giftedness; of what William F. May calls an "openness to the unbidden."[95] According to Sandel, such openness "invites us to abide the unexpected, to live with dissonance, to reign in the impulse to control."[96]

Contra Sandel, transhumanists question the virtue of such openness. They ask whether it is not irresponsible to leave our children at the mercy of nature. As Bostrom objects, the alternative to parental choice is the abandonment of our children's welfare to blind chance and the caprices of nature, adding: "Had Mother Nature been a real parent, she would have been in jail for child abuse and murder."[97] In response, Kampowski argues that respect for the unbidden does not aim at "sacralising nature," but at upholding *contingency* in preference to parental programming. It aims at welcoming the being of each person with unconditional respect that is foundational for human equality.[98] In the midst of a world that seeks mastery and control, the openness of parents to the unbidden teaches us the virtue of humility. But such openness is threatened by the prospect of genetic engineering, in which indebtedness and giftedness give way to ownership and personal responsibility. As Erik Parens comments, when we neglect the gifted nature of life, we lose our

---

93. Sandel, *Case Against Perfection*, 87.
94. Sandel, *Case Against Perfection*, 86.
95. Quoted in Sandel, *Case Against Perfection*, 45.
96. Sandel, *Case Against Perfection*, 86.
97. Bostrom, "In Defense of Posthuman Dignity," 211.
98. "Indeed one can make the case that *our contingent beginning is the ground of our equality and that a being who is worthy of unconditional respect must never be brought into being conditionally* which is precisely the case when the principle origin of its coming to be is its parents' desires." Kampowski, "Children of Desire," 12.

grip on reality; we "make a mistake about the sort of creatures we really are and the way the world really is."[99]

In Sandel's analysis, our sense of solidarity with those less fortunate suffers in proportion to our increasing responsibility for our fate. Expressed otherwise: "The more alive we are to the chanced nature of our lot, the more reason we have to share our fate with others."[100] He gives the example of insurance. Before the risks and uncertainties of life, people cooperate in sharing their lot in order to insure against unforeseen disasters. But this only works if individuals do not have control over their future. If genetic engineering advanced to a stage of ensuring good health or long life, enhanced individuals would opt out of insurance policies, with the result that premiums for the unenhanced would increase dramatically, and the sense of social solidarity weakened.

In response, Sandel again admonishes an acknowledgment of giftedness as the means of maintaining a sense of solidarity: of recognizing talents as flowing from nature, from the "genetic lottery," as opposed to personal design and manipulation. This acknowledgment of giftedness protects against claiming gifts as one's own, and thus encourages sharing and solidarity. As Sandel writes:

> A lively sense of the contingency of our gifts—an awareness that none of us is wholly responsible for his or her success—saves a meritocratic society from sliding into the smug assumption that success is the crown of virtue, that the rich are rich because they are more deserving than the poor.[101]

The acceptance of children "as they come"[102] is foundational to this sense of contingency, and thus to a sense of humility and solidarity between individuals.

Habermas's Objection to Genetic Enhancement

Jürgen Habermas develops the case for contingency even further, suggesting that it not only upholds the sense of life's giftedness, but is essential

---

99. Parens, "Toward a More Fruitful Debate," 188.

100. Sandel, *Case Against Perfection*, 89.

101. Sandel, *Case Against Perfection*, 91.

102. "To appreciate children as gifts is to accept them as they come, not as objects of our design, or products of our will, or instruments of our ambition." Sandel, *Case Against Perfection*, 45.

for "being oneself" and for assuming ownership of one's life. Arguing within the context of a communicative concept of morality,[103] he worries that the prospect of parents genetically enhancing their children would introduce an inequality into the relationship that would diminish the child's autonomy, self-understanding, and dignity, would compromise their moral subjectivity, and adversely affect their ability to take possession of their lives and to own their choices and actions.[104]

The Imperative of Contingency

According to Habermas, before the advent of ARTs human procreation was characterized by a certain uncontrollability and contingency that was protective of human equality.[105] While from the perspective of parental choice and responsibility such contingency might appear as a limitation and obstacle, Habermas insists that "this rather ordinary contingency proves to be—in the very moment we can master it—a necessary presupposition for being-able-to-be-oneself and for the fundamentally egalitarian nature of our interpersonal relationships."[106] Only the chanced and contingent nature of one's origins, free from the manipulation of design and control, can provide the space for an open relation with oneself and others.[107]

Spaemann makes a similar point. While human beings are temporal, they also possess a "temporal shape" (*Zeitgestalt*) which respects human

103. As Kampowski explains: "For Habermas the individual becomes a moral subject by entering into a communicative context with others. It is through the medium of language and thus intersubjectively that the persons come to themselves, that they develop self-consciousness and become actors." Kampowski, *Greater Freedom*, 136–37.

104. Habermas, *Future of Human Nature*, 63.

105. As Kass elaborates, by the natural and chanced nature of our genetic makeup, each individual "is at once equally human, equally enmeshed in a particular familial nexus of origin, and equally individuated in our trajectory from birth to death." Kass, *Life, Liberty and the Defense of Dignity*, 153.

106. Habermas, *Future of Human Nature*, 13.

107. As Kampowski interprets: "It is Habermas's provocative suggestion that we can be free in the realm of human affairs only if we have a place to stand that is withdrawn from direct human intervention. Such a place is provided by our contingent beginning, expressed in our untampered bodily existence. When we genetically manipulate individuals or use other, already available eugenic methods, it is as if we were to remove the sure ground from under their feet, the ground on which they can stand to actualize their freedom." Kampowski, *Greater Freedom*, 155.

transcendence and represents the Absolute. According to Spaemann, this temporal shape requires that one's "beginning and end are not the result of intentional making by other human beings."[108] At the end of life, this signifies that life should not be extended indefinitely or artificially, nor ended precipitously or violently. At the beginning of life, respect for the human person's temporal shape demands that he or she is not the product of a human intention. "Only in this way can a human being come to life in his own right, 'by nature,' as a creature of God, or a least of nature, yet not of his parents."[109]

Distortion of the Parent-Child Relationship

With the loss of contingency at the beginning of life, it is Habermas's conviction that the relationship between parent and child is distorted. He argues thus against the prospect of genetic programming in which the parents stand over the child and the direction of his or her life, signifying an inequality and lack of reciprocity that should be part of any proper relationship. It is not simply a matter of parental expectations for the child, but that in the case of genetic engineering such expectations are "one-sided" and "unchallengeable." They are fixed, inscribed into the core of the child's being.

While proponents of eugenic enhancements insist that there is no substantial difference between genetic enhancement and enhancements through socialization,[110] the differences appear to be real and troubling. As Habermas writes, unlike the overbearing attitudes of parents who attempt to control their child's environment, the child who is the product of genetic programming is denied "an opportunity to take a *revisionist* stand."[111] Unlike the effects of a controlling parent or a "pathogenic

---

108. Spaemann, *Love and the Dignity of Human Life*, 39.

109. Spaemann, *Love and the Dignity of Human Life*, 39.

110. For example, Bostrom cites the hypothetical case of enhancing musical talent in children by playing Mozart to pregnant mothers. "Nobody," he claims, "would argue for a ban on Mozart-in-the-womb on grounds that we cannot rule out that some psychological woe might befall the child once she discovers that her facility with the violin had been prenatally 'programmed' by her parents. Yet when, for example, it comes to genetic enhancements, eminent bioconservative writers often put forward arguments that are not so very different from this parody as weighty, if not conclusive, objections. To transhumanists, this looks like doublethink." Bostrom, "In Defense of Posthuman Dignity," 212.

111. Habermas, *Future of Human Nature*, 51.

socialization process," the once-for-all nature of genetic manipulation cannot "be revised by 'critical appraisal.'"[112] The child who is the product of genetic engineering cannot undo what has been done. "The genetic program is a mute and, in a sense, unanswerable fact."[113]

Contrary to objections by transhumanists, this does not signify a belief in genetic determinism that overrides the effects of environment and choice.[114] Drawing on the thought of Hans Jonas in addition to Habermas, Kampowski writes:

> Neither Habermas nor Jonas claim that genetically engineered human beings would have *no* choice over their life at all. What they affirm is rather that the knowledge of owing part of one's very identity to the arbitrary decisions of peers would be a liability in the task of making one's life completely one's own because one could always blame or would always have to credit others for characteristic marks that form part of who one is without ever being able to make these characteristics really one's own.[115]

In his concern for the psychological impact of knowing that one has been genetically engineered, Habermas's argument is not dependent on phenotypic evidence of genetic change. Even in the absence of phenotypic expression, Habermas suggests that "*post factum* knowledge of this circumstance may intervene in the self-relation of the person, the relation to her bodily or mental existence."[116] This signifies that the parents' choice creates its own environment which profoundly affects the child's ability to make his or her own choices in the future and to be the subject of his or her existence.

Habermas also suggests that the knowledge of being genetically determined affects that child's ability to be "at home" in his or her body,

---

112. Habermas, *Future of Human Nature*, 62.

113. Habermas, *Future of Human Nature*, 62.

114. Brock, "Is Selection of Children Wrong?," 254–55; Tamburrini and Tännsjö, "Enhanced Bodies," 278: "However, even if genetic engineering might predispose an individual to develop certain traits and skills, she might still retain the capacity of making her own choices. The deterministic picture presupposed in the present objection is simply not true. Whether or not a child develops certain (genetically conditioned) traits depends to a great degree on environmental and social factors as well."

115. Kampowski, *Greater Freedom*, 154.

116. Habermas, *Future of Human Nature*, 53. Or as Kampowski again writes: "Independent of the effects of the genotype on the phenotype, they are, in their bodies, confronted with the expectations of others for their lives." Kampowski, *Greater Freedom*, 152–53.

which is essential in order to be able to differentiate between oneself and others, and to assume responsibility for one's actions. He insists that in order for people to identify themselves with their body, the body should be perceived as something natural: "as a continuation of the organic, self-regenerative life from which the person was born."[117] While genetically engineered individuals would experience their bodies as the only ones they had ever known, and in that sense would perceive them to be "natural," nonetheless the knowledge that it existed as the result of the deliberate design and intention of another would be more likely to render their body the continuation of an alien intention, rather than as something organically their own.

An Oppressive Paternalism

Habermas suggests that the knowledge of having been genetically engineered by one's parents would be similar to the experience of a clone, "who, by being modelled on the person and the life history of a 'twin' chronologically out of phase, is deprived of an unobstructed future of his own."[118] This echoes Jonas's concern that cloning obstructs the "right to ignorance," or what Joel Feinberg calls "a right to an open future."[119] Like the cloned child, the genetically engineered individual would feel restricted in his or her choices and future possibilities, limited by parental hopes and expectations, and by an exaggerated and crippling relationship of dependence. Against this charge of a compromised autonomy, Bostrom claims that certain enhancements could provide not less, but significantly *more* choice and autonomy. He suggests that "being healthy, smarter, having a wide range of talents, or possessing greater powers of self-control are blessings that tend to open more life paths than they block."[120] But as Habermas continues, autonomy is not simply an instrumental faculty but also demands mutuality and symmetry, which is in turn dependent on "reversibility" within interpersonal relationships. But it is precisely this reversibility that is lacking in cases of genetic

---

117. Habermas, *Future of Human Nature*, 58.
118. Habermas, *Future of Human Nature*, 62–63.
119. National Bioethics Advisory Commission, "Cloning Human Beings," 51. Citing Jonas, *Philosophical Essays*; Feinberg, "Child's Right."
120. Bostrom, "In Defense of Posthuman Dignity," 212.

engineering. The relationship between parent and child is asymmetrical, forming what Habermas calls "a specific type of paternalism."[121]

Here it should be noted that with genetic interventions into the germline,[122] this paternalism extends beyond one's immediate offspring, with the genetic changes being transmitted through future generations. The result is a form of dependence in which future generations are irreversibly effected by the decisions of the current generation. As C. S. Lewis recognizes, future generations would exist as "patients of that power" yielded by the current generation.[123] Despite enhanced capacities that are the fruit of genetic engineering, future generations are rendered weaker, not stronger, "for though we may have put wonderful machines in their hands we have pre-ordained how they are to use them."[124]

Limitations of Habermas's Argument

Despite the coherence of Habermas's argument against genetic manipulation, it nonetheless lacks binding force. This can be explained by his avoidance of metaphysical claims,[125] and his distinction between morality and ethics.[126] According to this distinction, ethics draws on metaphysical or religious concepts to answer questions about the "good life," which in a postmodern, pluralistic culture cannot be universalized.[127]

---

121. Habermas, *Future of Human Nature*, 64.

122. "*Germ line cell therapy* aims instead at correcting genetic defects present in germ line cells with the purpose of transmitting the therapeutic effects to the offspring of the individual." CDF, *Dignitas personae*, n. 25.

123. "In reality, of course, if any one age really attains, by eugenics and scientific education, the power to make its descendants what it pleases, all men who live after it are the patients of that power." Lewis, *Abolition of Man*, 58.

124. Lewis, *Abolition of Man*, 58.

125. Habermas readily admits that his argument "doesn't proceed on the assumption that the technicization of 'inner nature' constitutes something like a transgression of natural boundaries"; that it is independent "of the idea of a 'natural' or even 'holy' order, which can be sacrilegiously 'overstepped.'" Habermas, *Future of Human Nature*, 87.

126. See Brino, "Bioetica e 'metafisica,'" 745–46; Kampowski, *Greater Freedom*, 137–39.

127. "Cultural forms of life are bound up with systems of interpretations that explain the position of humanity in the universe and provide the 'thick' anthropological context in which the prevailing moral code is embedded. In pluralistic societies, these metaphysical or religious interpretations of the self and the world are, for good reasons, subordinated to the moral foundations of the constitutional state, which is neutral

By contrast, morality, with its concern for questions of justice, imposes universal obligations. According to this reasoning, there is a "primacy of the just (in the deontological sense) over the good."[128] Consistent with his noted openness to the insights of religious claims, this priority of morality is not exclusive of ethical considerations.[129] However, it is the only means of assuring a definitive foundation for universal moral norms. In line with this distinction, Habermas's argument against genetic enhancement is not based on morality and justice. Rather, he relies on ethical considerations drawn from "emotions roused by moral sentiments" and current convictions,[130] both of which cannot be universalized or held to with certainty. But as Kampowski laments: "If the threat is rightly diagnosed as the abolition of the human person as a moral being, then, in the face of the danger's magnitude, this conclusion is rather weak."[131]

While welcoming Habermas's contribution, Spaemann expresses a similar concern over his methodology. He suggests that what Habermas objects to as "metaphysics" is in reality nothing other than an attempt to take seriously the way in which we envisage our lives.[132] In other words, one cannot have a normative sense of morality without a concept of the good life for human beings, and thus of a definitive account of human nature.[133] It is fundamentally in this sense that the means of human generation has moral significance. Accordingly, Spaemann contends that Habermas's imperative of contingency is not merely an ethical argument against cases of genetic manipulation, but touches on the very morality of the means by which a human being comes to be. He therefore insists that

---

with respect to competing worldviews and committed to their peaceful coexistence. Under the condition of postmetaphysical thought, the ethical self-understanding of the species, which is inscribed in specific traditions and forms of life, no longer provides the arguments for overruling the claims of a morality presumed to be universally accepted." Habermas, *Future of Human Nature*, 40.

128. Habermas, *Justification and Application*, vii.

129. Habermas thus recognizes that ethics and morality meet in dialogue; that "metaphysical doctrines and humanistic traditions also provide contexts in which the 'overall structure of our moral experience' is embedded." Habermas, *Future of Human Nature*, 40.

130. Habermas, *Future of Human Nature*, 73.

131. Kampowski, *Greater Freedom*, 140.

132. Spaemann, "Habermas über Bioethik," 107: "Was Habermas Metaphysik nennt, ist nichts anderes als das Ernstnehmen eines Phänomens, das Ernstnehmen der Weise, wie wir uns selbst erleben."

133. See Brino, "Bioetica e 'metafisica,'" 746.

the argument logically extends to all methods of artificial reproduction, before which, as noted above, a justification for the existence of the child can be demanded.¹³⁴

The "Necessity" of the Conjugal Act in the Thought of Ratzinger

In this context, one perceives Ratzinger taking Habermas's argument a step further in speaking of the "necessity" of the child's coming to be through the sexual union of his or her parents. He admits that, with the advent of ARTs, sexual union is no longer a *technical* necessity for reproduction, and that before this reality, one is left pondering (in Hegelian style) if the affective and psychological attraction between the sexes, and the personal dimension of conjugal love, are not merely "tricks of nature."¹³⁵ In forming a response, Ratzinger refers to the difference between the scientific conception of *reproduction*, which explains the origins of life in its mechanical process, and the richer concept of *procreation* in which the "biological process of 'reproduction' is enveloped in a personal process of the body-soul self-giving of two human beings."¹³⁶

The Reproductive Mentality

Recalling the divergence between positivistic and creation-based accounts of the human person, Ratzinger contends that the differences between concepts of reproduction and procreation constitute two different modes of contemplating reality.¹³⁷ The idea of reproduction flows from the positivism of knowing and making, epitomized in Goethe's *Faust* in which the scientist Wagner succeeds in creating a human being in a test tube. Reading Goethe in the light of contemporary challenges, Ratzinger identifies two characteristics of the reproductive mentality: (1) a demys-

---

134. Spaemann, "Habermas über Bioethik," 107: "Unter dem Aspekt der nachträglichen Zustimmung des Betroffenen wäre übrigens auch die Herstellung von Menschen *in vitro* neu zu bedenken. Wo Menschen nicht naturwüchsig als Nebenfolge sexuellen Umgangs entstehen, sondern willentlich von Hand gemacht werden, werden die Hersteller rechenschaftspflichtig für die Existenz ihrer Nachkommen. Dieser Rechenschaftpflicht aber kann niemand genügen."
135. Ratzinger, "Man between Reproduction and Creation," 72.
136. Ratzinger, "Man between Reproduction and Creation," 72.
137. Ratzinger, "Man between Reproduction and Creation," 71.

tification of nature in favor of a bland rationalism; and (2) a "despising" of the given in search of rationally guided objectives.

In the first instance, Ratzinger speaks of "the desire to unveil mysteries, to see through the world and reduce it to a flat rationalism, which attempts to prove itself through its capacity to make something."[138] In this reduction of reality to what is *made*, artificial reproduction treats human beings as a product of human ingenuity, "dethroned" from their glory as an image of God and reduced instead to "the image of man."[139] This is further intensified in the context of genetic engineering. With the de-mystification of the human person to physical laws, to a mere combination of information, technology moves beyond reproduction "in search of new combinations";[140] of new ways of making human beings. Thus, while acknowledging the real opportunities for healing offered by genetic science when exercised "with due reverence for creation,"[141] Ratzinger cautions against the perils of assuming the attitude of an "engineer" who dominates over human life.[142]

> With this kind of manipulation, man makes other men his own artifacts. Man no longer originates in the mystery of love, by means of the process of conception and birth, which remains in the end mysterious, but is produced industrially, like any other product. He is made by other men. He is robbed thereby of his proper status and of his true splendor as a created being.[143]

At the root of this pathology is an important distinction between an "artifact" and a "natural thing." As Hanby writes, according to Aristotle a natural thing "is characterized by *entelechia*, by having, or rather *being*, its own end, its own project."[144] In bearing this characteristic it demands

---

138. Ratzinger, "Man between Reproduction and Creation," 75.
139. Ratzinger, *Christianity and the Crisis of Cultures*, 26.
140. Ratzinger, "Man between Reproduction and Creation," 81.
141. Ratzinger, *God and the World*, 132.
142. "It is important to be completely clear about this: great reverence toward those things we should not touch must become a fundamental rule of all human conduct. We must be quite aware that man cannot and must not be seen as being secondary to our projects for genetic development. We must realize quite clearly that even the beginning of genetic manipulation is liable to develop into an assumption of domination over the world, which will then carry within it the seeds of destruction." Ratzinger, *God and the World*, 132.
143. Ratzinger, *God and the World*, 134.
144. Hanby, "When Art Replaces Nature," 22.

a certain respect. An artifact, on the other hand, is not an end in itself, but receives its end from outside, projected forward by its maker. Thus, in reducing human persons to artifacts of reproduction, we fail to respect them as ends in themselves, violating not only Kant's categorical imperative, but their inherent dignity as human subjects. As Hanby adds, this power exercised over human life as a product of our engineering is "*essentially* despotic";[145] "profoundly dehumanizing" in the words of Kass. "As with any product of our making, no matter how excellent, the artificer stands above it, not as an equal but as a superior, transcending it by his will and creative prowess."[146]

The second characteristic of the reproductive mentality identified by Ratzinger is what he describes as "a despising of 'nature' and its mysterious higher reasonableness, in favor of a calculating, goal-determined rationalism."[147] This despising of nature is revealed in the rejection of what is *given*, attempting to improve what nature has ordained. In the context of human procreation, nature's way is not good enough; it is unpredictable and risky. It needs to be augmented, manipulated, or even altogether replaced by human ingenuity and technology. This rejection of the given is further aggravated through attempts to enhance or change human nature, treating the human person as an experiment. The link between artificial reproduction and enhancement is thus also evident here. Kass perceives it clearly:

> Make no mistake: the price to be paid for producing optimum or even only genetically sound babies will be the transfer of procreation from the home to the laboratory. Increasing control over the product can only be purchased by the increasing depersonalization of the entire process and its coincident transformation into manufacture. Such an arrangement will be profoundly dehumanizing, no matter how genetically good or healthy the resultant children.[148]

---

145. Hanby, "When Art Replaces Nature," 23.

146. Kass, *Life, Liberty and the Defense of Dignity*, 160.

147. Ratzinger, "Man between Reproduction and Creation," 75.

148. Kass, *Life, Liberty and the Defense of Dignity*, 131. Further on he adds: "To achieve the requisite quality control over new human life, human conception and gestation will need to be brought fully into the bright light of the laboratory, beneath which the child-to-be can be fertilized, nourished, pruned, weeded, watched, inspected, prodded, pinched, cajoled, injected, tested, rated, graded, approved, stamped, wrapped, sealed and delivered. There is no other way to produce the perfect baby." Kass, *Life, Liberty and the Defense of Dignity*, 165.

Earnestly resisting the constrictions of a calculating reason, which he refers to as "the positivistic hemming in of thought" and its rejection of nature's *mysterious higher reasonableness*, Ratzinger seeks a deeper meaning of human procreation. Indeed, he insists "that man denies himself, and so denies incontrovertible reality, if he refuses to go beyond the laboratory in his thinking."[149]

The Logic of Procreation

In going *beyond the laboratory*, Ratzinger offers the biblical notion of procreation, with its broadened sense of reality, as a challenge to the positivistic reduction. Compared to the restrictive impersonalism of reproduction, procreation presumes a participation in God's creativity—a creative process in which, from the biblical accounts, God is actively involved, forming the human person with his own hands from the dust of the earth (see Gen 2:7), and according to his image and likeness (see Gen 1:26–27). As Ratzinger notes, in this personal dimension of God's creativity, the human person does not exist "merely as one specimen in a class of beings, but as a new being in each case, in whom more appears than reproduction."[150]

Human procreation corresponds to this personal creativity of God. As Rhonheimer relates, the conjugal act is primarily not an act of *producing* but of *doing* (*praxis*). It is God alone who is "productive" of human life. "The conjugal act of the parents gives 'space' and occasion to this divine creative act; as such it is truly a 'service of life,' but not a 'dominion over life.'"[151] This accords with the idea of human procreation as envisaged in *Donum vitae*:

> The human person must be accepted in his parents' act of union and love; the generation of a child must therefore be the fruit of that mutual giving which is realized in the conjugal act wherein the spouses cooperate as servants and not as masters in the work of the Creator who is Love.[152]

Ratzinger further notes that the uniqueness of human beings created in the divine image is essentially linked to their creation as man and

---

149. Ratzinger, "Man between Reproduction and Creation," 80.
150. Ratzinger, "Man between Reproduction and Creation," 77–78.
151. Rhonheimer, "Instrumentalization of Human Life," 166.
152. CDF, *Donum vitae*, II, B, 4, c.

woman: "in the image of God he created him; male and female he created them" (Gen 1:27). This is further highlighted in God's command to multiply and fill the earth (see Gen 1:28), in which, unlike the command to the plants and wild animals, the blessing of human fruitfulness is not simply *imposed* but is bound to sexual difference and complementarity. As Ratzinger interprets: "The emphasis of the text on God's being Creator does not make human orientation to one another superfluous, but rather gives it its unique quality."[153] This reality is poetically expressed in the biblical image of man and woman forming "one flesh" (see Gen 2:24), as well as in the description of sexual union as a form of *knowing*: "Adam *knew* Eve his wife, and she conceived" (Gen 4:1). In this context, Ratzinger draws out the deeper meaning of procreation. Citing Claus Westermann,[154] he notes that the Hebrew word *yada'*, to know, has a significance beyond objective knowledge.[155] In its personal dimension, such knowledge, which becomes fruitful through the procreation of a child, allows man and woman to escape the solitude of self-reference.[156]

The body, as the expression of sexual difference and complementarity, is therefore essential to our creation in the divine image and constitutive of our sharing in God's creativity. Melina thus recognizes that when the symbolic mediation of the body is replaced by technical processes of reproduction, not only is human parentage deformed, but the originality of God's paternity is obscured.[157] By contrast, the wonder of human procreation demands a spirit of adoration, as expressed in the Letter to the Ephesians: "For this reason I bow my knees before the Father, from whom every family in heaven and on earth is named" (Eph 3:14–15). Indeed, Ratzinger confirms that in their sexual difference, human beings are "brought into the closest proximity with the Creator."[158] It involves "an intermingling of divine creativity and human fruitfulness," in which

153. Ratzinger, "Man between Reproduction and Creation," 78.
154. Westermann, *Genesis I–II*.
155. Ratzinger, "Man between Reproduction and Creation," 79.
156. Kass expresses this same reality in the following words: "To be male or to be female derives its deepest meaning only in relation to the other, and therewith in the gender-mated prospects for generation through union. Our separated embodiment prevents us as lovers from attaining that complete fusion of souls that we as lovers seek; but the complementarity of gender provides a bodily means for transcending separateness through the children born of sexual union." Kass, *Life, Liberty and the Defense of Dignity*, 101.
157. Melina, *Corso di Bioetica*, 111.
158. Ratzinger, *God and the World*, 427.

the child conceived both "belongs to us and yet does not belong, who comes from us and yet not from us."[159]

Thus, while again conceding that the affective gift of self might not be *technically* necessary for the transmission of human life, Ratzinger speaks of "another kind of necessity," "a higher kind of necessity," and "the ethical necessity which bears the obligation of freedom."[160] It is the necessity that recognizes human beings as something more than the result of mechanical processes; that insists that humanity is demeaned and denied when only physical laws are recognized as necessary; that acknowledges that human beings are created *through* and *for* a communion of love.[161] Ultimately, Ratzinger upholds the necessity of the conjugal act for procreation as reinforcing "the personal as the really real, the stronger and higher form of reality, which does not reduce the biological and mechanical to mere appearance, but draws them into itself and thus opens them up to a new dimension."[162]

Pathologies of Reducing Procreation to Reproduction

Loss of the Sense of Gratitude

In the reduction of the mystery of procreation to production, technological process replaces the act of love. The child does not come forth as the fruit of the parents' mutual gift, but as the result of a preconceived arrangement with technicians. In this arrangement, the parents' relationship with the child is changed. One cannot be grateful for something that is ordained toward satisfying specific expectations. As Romano Guardini notes, one does not give thanks on receiving something that one has ordered and to which one has a rightful claim. Instead, one asks for

---

159. Ratzinger, *God and the World*, 427.

160. Ratzinger, "Man between Reproduction and Creation," 73. Rhonheimer writes: "The link between procreation and sexual union is a necessary, even though insufficient, human condition for the transmission of life." Rhonheimer, "Instrumentalization of Human Life," 171.

161. Arguing within the context of cloning, Kass again draws out this necessity, maintaining that it is "grossly distorting to view the wondrous mysteries of birth, renewal and individuality, and the deep meaning of parent-child relations, largely through the lens of our reductive science and its potent technologies." Kass, *Life, Liberty and the Defense of Dignity*, 152.

162. Ratzinger, "Man between Reproduction and Creation," 82.

a receipt.[163] By engaging the services of ARTs and embryo selection, a couple make certain demands of the technicians whose services they employ, in the anticipation that the resulting child will correspond to their expectations.[164] And while this attitude already exists within reproductive technologies, it would be heightened in situations of genetic engineering and selection for certain traits. Gratitude is replaced by expectation, bestowing and grateful receiving by duties, rights, and the demand for appropriate functioning.[165]

A sense of gratitude is further obviated by an inequality within the relationship between the parents and the child, similar to that noted by Habermas above. Again citing Guardini, gratitude requires reverence and mutual respect on the part of the giver. In the absence of reverence, there exists an imbalance of power in which the gift becomes a burden to the recipient and wounds his or her self-respect.[166] As has been already noted, the child conceived through reproductive technologies receives his or her life as the fruit of the parents' will: "You exist because we wanted it so." In this situation, Rhonheimer suggests that the child's relationship with his parents is not founded on gratitude, but on "an *existential obligation to give account of himself*,"[167] and to avoid frustrating his parents' desires.[168] However, this level of existential dependence on one's parents

---

163. Guardini, *Learning the Virtues That Lead You to God*, 144. According to Guardini, genuine gratitude is dependent on three conditions: that it is a personal virtue, existing between an "I" and a "thou"; that it exists in the sphere of freedom; and that it demands reverence and mutual respect.

164. "In effetti quando il bambino è esito di un *facere* e non di un *agire*, di uno produzione tecnica e non di un gesto umano di donazione, si nega la sua condizione di pari dignità rispetto ai genitori e ai medici. Come 'prodotto' egli deve corrispondere alle richieste che ne hanno comandato la programmazione. Egli rientra in un piano, che ne verifica e controlla la qualità. I fenomeni di rifiuto di bambini nati mediante fecondazioni artificiali con malattie o handicap non sono appena spiacevoli episodi, ma conseguenze coerenti di una logica che in partenza non riconosce la piena dignità di persona del figlio. Per non parlare della selezione degli embrioni e dei feti abortiti, di cui non si danno notizie e per i quali non si fa problema. In tali condizioni il figlio non è voluto 'per se stesso,' ma solo in quanto soddisfa un'esigenza di paternità dei genitori. La 'qualità della sua vita,' così come il suo stesso, certe caratteristiche fisiche o addirittura mentali, possono essere poste come condizioni della sua accoglienza." Melina, *Corso di Bioetica*, 109–10.

165. Guardini, *Learning the Virtues*, 142.

166. Guardini, *Learning the Virtues*, 144.

167. Rhonheimer, "Instrumentalization of Human Life," 167.

168. Rhonheimer, "Instrumentalization of Human Life," 171.

is an obstacle to the child's sense of self and freedom, and an exaggeration of parental providence on a divine scale; for as Rhonheimer continues: "Only before God is such a dependence tenable, becoming, indeed, the *foundation* of one's freedom."[169]

To this, Ratzinger adds the temptation of parents to surreptitiously live their lives through their children; "to achieve whatever they failed to do in their own lives—in order to make a second attempt at their lives and thereby validate themselves."[170] And while admittedly parents can and do attempt to do the same through "traditional" means,[171] genetic engineering will take this to a wholly new and irreversible level. As noted, Sandel insists on accepting children "as they come, not as objects of our design or products of our will or instruments of our ambition."[172] While it may be appropriate that we select friends and spouses according to their qualities, we should not do so with our children.

A Conditional Love

The implication of Sandel's objection is that genetic selection undermines parents' unconditional acceptance of their children, a claim that transhumanists reject as unsubstantiated.[173] They deny that parental love would necessarily be compromised by the choice for enhancement. In this context, Jonathan Glover, though seemingly cautious of "choosing children,"[174] distinguishes parental love from the means and motives for

---

169. Rhonheimer, "Instrumentalization of Human Life," 168.

170. Ratzinger, *God and the World*, 137.

171. "Much mischief is already done by parents who try to live vicariously through their children. Children are sometimes pushed to fulfil the broken dreams of unhappy parents. Many parents already treat their children as projects, compelling them to master this or excel at that, so that the parents may bask in the reflected glory of their 'product.'" Kass, *Life, Liberty and the Defense of Dignity*, 161.

172. Sandel, "Case Against Perfection," 79.

173. "There is, however, currently no clear evidence for the hypothesis that parents making use of enhancement options in procreation would become incapable of accepting and loving their children. When in vitro fertilization was first introduced, bioconservative critics predicted similar psychological harms which, fortunately, did not materialize." Bostrom and Sandberg, "Cognitive Enhancement," 325.

174. Glover writes: "There is a case against placing additional moral burdens on people having children, a case for simply welcoming whatever children are born. We may lose something if we substitute the mindset of quality control for the cheerful moral anarchy of the free-range approach." Glover, *Choosing Children*, 54.

having children. While there are many reasons why a couple choose to have a child,[175] Glover suggests that the determination of whether or not a child is treated merely as a means is dependent upon the degree of the parents' love and care for them.[176] Bostrom goes further, speculating that selection could in fact *help* parents to love their children, suggesting that parents "might find it easier to love a child who, thanks to enhancements, is bright, beautiful, healthy, and happy."[177]

But both these objections seem at odds with the definition of love proposed by Ratzinger. As noted previously, he defines love as "an act of fundamental assent to another, a 'yes' to the person towards whom the love is directed."[178] In this, he assumes Pieper's definition that love means "it is good that you exist."[179] This affirmation of the goodness of the beloved is unconditional, independent of "this or that quality." The beloved is loved for him- or herself; "and though the person is revealed in his or her qualities, that person is more than the sum of them."[180]

A Distortion of Hope

As Ratzinger continues, this unconditional "yes" to the other, the delight in his or her existence, is not only independent of the other's qualities, but also precedes any consciousness of self, personal desire or expectation. Writing specifically within the context of human generation, Rhonheimer echoes these sentiments:

> The human dignity of the generated life must be acknowledged in a way that allows one to say to another: "It is a good thing that you exist, *because you exist,*" and not "It is a good thing that you exist, and you in fact exist *because and in the measure in which I have considered it good that you exist,* that is, in the measure in which *I have wanted* your existence."[181]

---

175. E.g., "We hoped having children would save our marriage"; or, "We thought it would be nice for Fred to have a brother or sister."

176. Glover, *Choosing Children*, 65.

177. Bostrom, "Human Genetic Enhancements," 498.

178. Ratzinger, *Yes of Jesus Christ*, 89.

179. Pieper, *Faith, Hope, Love*, 188: "It's good that you are; it's wonderful that you exist."

180. Ratzinger, *Yes of Jesus Christ*, 93.

181. Rhonheimer, "Instrumentalization of Human Life," 171–72.

One might reflect that this difference in attitude toward "the good," between the goodness of the child's existence and the good of having one's desire for a child fulfilled, is not only significant of a distortion of the concept of love, but also of the object of hope. As we recall, Aquinas defines the object of hope as a future good, difficult, but possible, to obtain.[182] The question of feasibility has already been discussed above. From a purely practical perspective, the obstacles outlined by Güell Pelayo suggest that one would be "hoping" for the impossible in aiming for genetically enhanced children. However, the real question seems to be whether the desire to create genetically enhanced children constitutes a "good," and therefore whether or not it exists as a worthy object of hope. It would seem that in hoping to have a child, the good sought should be the child itself, in the goodness of his or her existence. But once we start qualifying what *kind* of child, it appears that the object of our desire is not the good itself, but something extraneous to it.

In this context, one can agree with Steven Jensen that there is a sense in which "the good of the child must be discovered."[183] Or as Melina writes, the dignity of the child is respected, not when it is treated as our own creation, but when it is recognized as a gift received with gratitude and surprise.[184] But when this sense of wonder and gratitude is replaced by manipulation and control, the unconditional nature of acceptance and love is undermined, and a fear simultaneously arises of not being able to accept anything less. Thus, while the principle of procreative beneficence and the transhumanist appeal to genetic enhancement is always couched in positive terms of the best possible life for the child, there exists an underlying recoil from the good itself; a despair of not being able to love the child as he or she is.[185] In cases of selection the child is not willed *for itself*, but only insofar as he or she satisfies the needs of the parents. The presence or absence of certain characteristics become the terms of condition of the child's acceptance.[186] In Jensen's more stark words, these con-

---

182. *STh.*, I–II, q. 40. a. 1.

183. Jensen, "Roots of Transhumanism," 520.

184. "Si può dare la vita degnamente ad un figlio non come si decide di creare qualcosa di nostro, ma come si accetta di trasmettere un dono, dal quale per primi siamo stati gratificati e sorpresi." Melina, *Corso di Bioetica*, 111.

185. Remembering that Aquinas defines despair as "not only privation of hope, but also a recoil from the thing desired, by reason of its being esteemed impossible to get." *STh.* I–II, q. 40, a. 4.

186. Melina, *Corso di Bioetica*, 109–10.

ditions quickly turn into a form of loathing toward the less-than-perfect, in which those who do not fit the ideal are eliminated "to make way for the 'satisfactory' child."[187] In this he discerns a parallel with the whole transhumanist project, whose aspirations for enhancement conceal "a hatred of the species as it is now realized."[188]

Summary

As outlined in this chapter, objections to the principle of procreative beneficence, and to the genetic engineering of children in general, are concerned with the presence of internal contradictions over the determination of the "best" life, its eugenic mentality, its exacerbation of inequalities, and the question of its feasibility.

However, of greater interest in the current context, genetic selection is also found lacking in its hopes and aspirations. While the selection of children confidently aims at the "best" that we can offer our children, this confidence betrays an underlying hopelessness or despair, evident in the willful need to control, to deny contingence, and to avoid the uncertainties of an open future. But far from bringing out the best in human beings, this domineering attitude dehumanizes us. In particular it distorts the parent-child relationship, exaggerating parental responsibility and inhibiting the emergence of the child as an independent moral subject. It is suggested that this attitude, already present in methods of artificial reproduction, would be amplified by the possibility of genetic manipulation and enhancement.

While hope for our children is undermined by the burden of responsibility and the oppressive paternalism of standing over the origins of human life, Ratzinger teaches us that hope is respected and sustained by a magnanimous appreciation of our participation in God's creation, accompanied by a humble reverence for the gift of life. The logic of procreation, therefore, in recognizing the gifted nature of new life, preserves the contingency of our beginnings that needs no justification by being wanted or desired.[189] It is only when human beings have their origins in freedom and love that we can fully appreciate the goodness of our existence.

187. Jensen, "Roots of Transhumanism," 520.
188. Jensen, "Roots of Transhumanism," 520.
189. Rhonheimer, "Instrumentalization of Human Life," 168.

Chapter 8

The Case for Moral Enhancement

Unfit for the Future or Called to Love?

IN THIS CHAPTER, THE prospect of moral bioenhancement is presented as a further mutation of human hope, exposing the pessimism and despair that is present in Persson and Savulescu's support for technological moral enhancement. Rooted in a materialistic reduction of human nature, transhumanists perceive morality to be restricted by evolutionary biases and biological limitations. The human spirit, bound by these shortcomings, finds difficulty in surpassing its inherent moral limitations, even when cognitively aware of them. Thus, moral development lags behind cognitive enhancement, with the danger that technological power is increasingly placed in the hands of morally inept human beings.

In again highlighting the fiction of the positivistic attenuation of the human spirit, Ratzinger offers a more hopeful account of the human potential for morality. He insists that the human capacity for love offers real hope for moral enhancement. Love affirms both the goodness of the other and of creation, moving from the particular toward the universal, and allowing human beings to go beyond spatial and temporal biases and limitations.

In placing love at its foundation, Ratzinger highlights the relational nature of morality. In the absence of such love, he identifies an emerging hatred for humanity, born of despair and a lack of trust in the human potential for goodness. Ultimately, in the affirmation of love, morality exists within the horizon of humanity's communion with God. Offering a distinctively Christian take on moral development, Ratzinger recognizes human beings' dependence on divine grace toward enhancement, acknowledging that, in contrast to the secularization of hope through human activity, the human person never acts alone in history.

Unfit for the Future: The Case for Moral Enhancement

Persson and Savulescu's case for biotechnological moral enhancement rests on the premise that moral development has been unable to keep pace with the rapid changes in human society through advancements in science and technology, such that human beings lack the moral and psychological capacity to adequately respond to the challenges that these advances create.[1] According to their thesis, human morality and psychology evolved within small and close-knit communities, responding to issues affecting their immediate environment.[2] Human morality therefore has a bias toward short-term and close-range issues. However, within the contemporary context, the horizon of moral responsibility has expanded. With scientific and technological advancements, human beings now have the power to affect global changes, but their capacity to reason globally has not advanced alongside it. There is, therefore, an urgent need to bridge the gap between power and responsibility, "to prevent the powerful output of technological progress being misused with catastrophic results."[3]

Persson and Savulescu identify two areas in which the disparity between technological power and morality has reached crisis point: (1) the threat of weapons of mass destruction, especially if they were to fall into the hands of terrorist groups; and (2) the threat of climate change and environmental degradation. In order to respond properly to these challenges, it is suggested that some radical changes are necessary in the way we live our lives. To combat the threat of terrorism, increased surveillance would mean encroachments on personal privacy. To tackle the problem of environmental change, we need to seriously curb our use of the world's resources, seek alternative means of energy, implement policies that are more altruistic and with an eye to the future.

The authors propose two possible solutions to the impending threats to human existence: (1) increased surveillance by external authority; and (2) moral enhancement through biotechnology.

1. Persson and Savulescu, *Unfit for the Future*, 1.
2. Persson and Savulescu, *Unfit for the Future*, 1.
3. Persson and Savulescu, "Getting Moral Enhancement Right," 130.

Increased Restrictions

Persson and Savulescu acknowledge that security restrictions and reductions in energy consumption will be felt most keenly in affluent, liberal societies which advocate personal rights and opportunities for advancement. In order to effectively respond to the current threats, governments will need to become much more directive, abrogating personal privacies in order to ensure security, and imposing the necessary restrictions on energy consummation that human beings, limited by close-range biases and lacking in altruism, find difficult to make by themselves.[4] They suggest that providing information about what needs to be done is not enough, but in light of our malleability to social norms are hopeful that appropriate coercion can bring about change.[5] However, they concede that modern liberal democracies, founded upon prosperity and self-interest,[6] are ill-equipped to apply such coercion, caught in a vicious cycle in which those responsible for realizing policies are themselves lacking in the necessary motivation, and perceiving their role to be the guardians of negative rights rather than promoters of altruism. Limited by short-sightedness and self-preservation, politicians are therefore reluctant to implement unpopular policies.

Accordingly, Persson and Savulescu suggest that, in order to achieve the desired results, "liberal democracies will have to become less liberal."[7] In this context, they note that totalitarian regimes are more successful in changing behavior through the imposition of unpopular decisions. For instance, they praise the foresightedness of Communist China's imposition of the one-child policy as a way of curbing population growth,

---

4. The authors list several energy-saving behavioral changes which should be promoted: favoring a vegetarian diet, since grazing animals take up a disproportionate amount of food-producing land, their methane gas emissions add to global warming, and the farming of animals consumes vast amounts of water; restricting car and air travel in order to reduce carbon dioxide emissions; and restricting reproduction to reduce the problems of overpopulation. Persson and Savulescu, *Unfit for the Future*, 77–79.

5. Persson and Savulescu, *Unfit for the Future*, 102.

6. "This restraint of self-interest is the very opposite of the unrestrained satisfaction of it made possible by industrialization and its profusion of material goods, which brought liberal democracy into existence. Liberal democracy has so far been a politics of prosperity, and this induces doubt whether it could turn into a politics of parsimony, voluntary restraint, and decreasing welfare." Persson and Savulescu, *Unfit for the Future*, 84.

7. Persson and Savulescu, *Unfit for the Future*, 1.

while lamenting that the more liberal-minded India was unable to do the same.[8] Hans Jonas, amid his critique of Marxist utopianism, makes a similar observation. He suggests that the equality of a classless society encourages willingness to make sacrifices, protecting "the renunciations that have to be imposed from the suspicion of being exacted in the interest of a privileged class."[9] In the end, however, both Jonas, and Persson and Savulescu, do not find Marxist totalitarianism to be a viable alternative to the democratic state.

Bioenhancement

In face of the practical and ideological limitations of external coercion to change behavior, Persson and Savulescu perceive an urgent need to target the moral development of individuals. While acknowledging the place of "traditional" methods in shaping morality—education, laws, religion and ethics—they claim that they are insufficient to face the challenge of contemporary threats.[10] The long history of moral education has not dented xenophobic sentiments that obstruct efforts toward ensuring peace between nations. It has not been able to overcome the narrowness of immediate concerns that hamper attempts to change behavior in light of serious environmental threats. Even though traditional means of moral education can boast of awakening humanity to the recognition of equal rights, it is not reflected in reality, with economic inequalities between nations, and inequalities of opportunity, being "arguably greater today than it was before this egalitarian creed conquered the world."[11] It is in the light of such challenges that the prospect of moral enhancement is proposed as a way of improving our motivations toward positive action and cooperation.

---

8. Persson and Savulescu, *Unfit for the Future*, 86–87.

9. Jonas, *Imperative of Responsibility*, 150.

10. Reflecting their loss of confidence in the power of traditional methods of moral formation, Persson and Savulescu highlight that "the degree of moral improvements in the 2,500 years that have elapsed since the first great teachers of morality appeared is nowhere near matching the degree of technological progress during the same period." Persson and Savulescu, *Unfit for the Future*, 106. This includes an implicit dismissal of the power of Christian revelation to profoundly change human behavior.

11. Persson and Savulescu, "Turn for Ultimate Harm," 443.

The Limitations of Human Morality

At this point, I turn once more to the thought of German-born philosopher Hans Jonas (1903–1993). In highlighting the shortcomings of traditional morality to give an adequate response to the threat of modern technology, Jonas's "ethics of responsibility," as presented in *The Imperative of Responsibility* (*Das Prinzip Verantwortung*), treads a path between the *status quo* of traditional ethics and transhumanist projections. This path is followed by Ratzinger, who adopts Jonas's call to responsibility[12] and consistently laments that advancements in science and technology are "not matched by an equal development of our moral energy."[13]

Jonas notes a significant limitation of traditional morality in its exclusion of nature and the cosmic order from human responsibility, the sphere of morality being restricted to interpersonal relations. Jonas summarizes traditional morality according to four characteristics:[14] (1) human interaction with the nonhuman world was considered ethically neutral. This included the realm of *techne*, limited to this earthly reality and thus incapable of impinging on humanity's real and ultimate vocation; (2) human morality was *anthropocentric*, concerned with dealings between human beings and with the individual's treatment of him- or herself; (3) human nature was deemed to be constant and unchangeable, and therefore was not subject to the redefining potential of *techne*; and (4) the effects of good and evil were proximate to the act, both physically and temporally. As Jonas writes:

> The effective range of action was small, the time span of foresight, goal-setting, and accountability was short, control of circumstances limited. Proper conduct had its immediate criteria and almost immediate consummation. The long run of consequences beyond was left to chance, fate, or providence. Ethics accordingly was of the here and now, of occasions as they arise between men, or the recurrent, typical situations of private and public life.[15]

While not dismissing the ongoing relevance of such "neighbor" ethics, Jonas suggests that something more is needed. In light of technology's

---

12. Ratzinger, "Truth and Freedom," 30.
13. Ratzinger, *Christianity and the Crisis of Cultures*, 27.
14. Jonas, *Imperative of Responsibility*, 4.
15. Jonas, *Imperative of Responsibility*, 5.

growing power over nature, a new and more universal morality of responsibility is required.

Explanation from Evolution

The limitations of traditional ethics, as outlined by Jonas, in its anthropocentricism and restrictive concepts of space and time, find a particular explanation in the thesis of Persson and Savulescu, and of the transhumanist movement in general, in presuming an evolutionary and biological foundation for morality. According to Persson and Savulescu, the *core* of our moral motivation is shared "with non-human animals from which we have evolved."[16] They argue this on the basis of observations of animal behavior, especially of higher primates, in their display of "tit-for-tat" justice, gratitude and fairness, which they suggest form the rudimentary structure of human morality.[17] In this perspective, it is presumed that the current limitations to human morality are explicable as features of the evolutionary fight for existence. In the drive toward survival and reproduction, in the midst of an unpredictable and often hostile world, a bias toward immediate relations and associates, and for temporally proximate concerns (as opposed to those in the future), was deemed to be evolutionary advantageous.[18] A bias toward one's children, parents and siblings (*kin altruism*) was strategic for ensuring genetic continuity.[19] While such altruism was sometimes extended to include regular and intimate contacts, it was never offered indiscriminately to foreigners and strangers.[20] Rather, fear toward strangers and violence in response to external threats were protective of one's immediate environment. It is therefore supposed that an inclination toward homicide and genocide is actually part of human nature, forged through this struggle for survival in the competition for scarce resources.[21]

---

16. Persson and Savulescu, "Perils of Cognitive Enhancement," 168.

17. Persson and Savulescu, *Unfit for the Future*, 497.

18. As Persson and Savulescu explain, "We are personally and temporally 'myopic,' disposed to care more about what happens in the near future to ourselves and some individuals who are near and dear to us than about what happens to ourselves in the more remote future and to strangers." Persson and Savulescu, *Unfit for the Future*, 4.

19. Persson and Savulescu, "Unfit for the Future?," 487.

20. Persson and Savulescu, *Unfit for the Future*, 32–33.

21. Persson and Savulescu, "Moral Transhumanism," 662.

The current context, however, is very different, in which "recalcitrant drives" toward self-preservation, reproduction, and protection of one's own group is no longer considered to be advantageous.[22] Rather, this personal and temporal "myopia" is deemed to be damaging to interpersonal relations. For example, kin altruism, as a "hangover" from our evolutionary past, is offered by Buchanan as an explanation for why stepfathers have a tendency to abuse their stepchildren more than their genetic offspring.[23] Persson and Savulescu add that suspicion of strangers in our evolutionary past explains the existence of widespread *xenophobia* and racist attitudes.[24]

Our evolutionary past is also proposed as an explanation for our moral "numbness" to the sufferings of those removed from us by space and time, and it is suggested that such moral shortcomings are amplified in the face of contemporary challenges. For example, our "close-range" altruism means that "our inhibitions to use weapons of mass destruction are likely to be disproportionately weak in comparison to our inhibitions to kill single individuals with 'in-fight' weapons like machetes and axes, which cannot be used without close-up confrontations with blood and guts."[25] The limitations of close-range altruism are even more pronounced in response to the environmental crisis. While the cumulative effects of human action to protect the environment are significant, individual efforts are negligible. A sense of personal responsibility and the motivation to change behavior is therefore lacking. One's willingness to make altruistic sacrifices is further limited by a strong sense of individualism, compounded by the anonymity associated with large populations living together,[26] and by the need to consider the future, since most of the sacrifices that are required today will not benefit the current context, but are aimed toward the welfare of future generations.

---

22. Persson and Savulescu, *Unfit for the Future*, 101.

23. "From the standpoint of what Richard Dawkins calls the 'selfish gene,' this shameful behavior makes perfectly good sense: Why would one expect an organism, hovering on the edge of subsistence a hundred thousand years ago, to waste resources on sustaining some other guy's gene line? If there's competition for survival within the species, one would expect not only neglect but abuse, and unfortunately that's what we sometimes see." Buchanan, *Better than Human*, 35–36.

24. Persson and Savulescu, *Unfit for the Future*, 38.

25. Persson and Savulescu, *Unfit for the Future*, 47.

26. Persson and Savulescu, *Unfit for the Future*, 73.

The Relative Ease of Doing Harm over Good

According to Persson and Savulescu, these moral shortcomings are intensified by additional considerations. In the first place, they assert that in general it is easier to do harm than to do good.[27] They give the following example: "It is quite easy for virtually anyone to do serious harm, say, to take a car and run down a number of people in a few seconds, but very few are ordinarily capable of saving as many lives in the same period of time."[28] On the basis of this premise, it is acknowledged that the facility with which we do harm is amplified by the destructive potential of technological advances. While technology admittedly brings many benefits, and offers the potential for saving many lives, its destructive capacities far outweigh the benefits. Indeed, technology has already reached the point where it can cause *Ultimate Harm*, that is, harm "which consists in making worthwhile life *forever* impossible on this planet."[29]

It is also claimed that the comparative ease of harming over doing good explains the predominance, both in incidence and intensity, of the negative emotion of fear over hope, of anger over gratitude.[30] This phenomena, too, is claimed to have an evolutionary origin.

> In a world in which most of the time we risk losing more than we could reasonably hope to gain, and in which we compete with each other over scarce resources, it has survival value that the negative reaction of anger be more widespread and stronger than its positive counterpart of gratitude, since it will be more important to scare off attackers than to return favors done by do-gooders.[31]

Accordingly, our moral response is conditioned to be fearful, distrusting and self-preserving, since altruism and gratitude do not produce the same intensity of emotion as do fear and threats.

Another claim is that the relative ease of doing harm biases morality toward concern for the causes of harm over and against the obligation to do good, toward what should be avoided rather than positively done.[32]

27. Persson and Savulescu, *Unfit for the Future*, 12.
28. Persson and Savulescu, *Unfit for the Future*, 46.
29. Persson and Savulescu, *Unfit for the Future*, 46. The authors further define this as the point at which the development of scientific technology "turned from being for the better all things considered to being for the worse all things considered" (127).
30. Persson and Savulescu, *Unfit for the Future*, 18.
31. Persson and Savulescu, *Unfit for the Future*, 18.
32. "This implies that we intuitively feel, for example, that we are more responsible

According to Persson and Savulescu, this bias also finds expression in a *doctrine of negative rights*, which protects us from outside interference.[33]

"Commonsense" Morality

The above-mentioned phenomena—the comparative ease of causing harm over doing good, the predominance of fear over hope, and the focus on causation over responsibility—signify what Persson and Savulescu identify as a "common-sense morality." By commonsense they mean a morality that is common to humanity, having been forged through the process of evolution. It could therefore be called a "natural law," but without the normative, universally binding or unchangeable values that are traditionally associated with the term.[34] Indeed, their point is that this natural morality needs to be enhanced; that "its deficiencies, and the deficiencies of the related psychological dispositions, make us ill-equipped to cope with the moral problems generated by the advanced scientific technology, over-population, and the globalization of the modern world."[35] All in all, it is a seemingly negative conception of human nature and morality, offering a bleak prospect with regard the human person's capacity to change.

A Critique of the Relationship between Technology and Morality

Before entering into a critique of the proposal for moral bioenhancement and its foundation in evolutionary theory, I would like to draw out

---

for the harm we cause than for the benefits we fail to cause and, thus, have moral duties or obligations not to harm, but not to benefit." Persson and Savulescu, *Unfit for the Future*, 4. Included in our failure to benefit are those "things that we let happen by our omissions to prevent them" (22).

33. Persson and Savulescu, *Unfit for the Future*, 19.

34. "By 'common-sense morality' we mean a set of moral attitudes that is a common denominator of the diversely specified moralities of human societies over the world. We take it that the explanation of why there is a set of moral attitudes that is a common feature of culturally diverse moralities is that it has its origin in our evolutionary history. However, it should not be thought that we regard common-sense morality to be sacrosanct and beyond criticism." Persson and Savulescu, *Unfit for the Future*, 12.

35. Persson and Savulescu, *Unfit for the Future*, 12.

what is positive in Persson and Savulescu's identification of the disproportion between technological and moral development. In recognizing the implicit dangers of technological advances unhinged from morality, Persson and Savulescu attempt to distance themselves from modernity's exaggerated confidence in progress. The idea that human history is necessarily moving toward its utopia, ushered in by technological advances, has been seriously shaken by the prospect of total destruction.[36]

This acknowledgment of the fallacy of historical and technological progress creates a space for dialogue with other philosophers of a more conservative bent. Jonas, for example, agrees that with the possibility of world annihilation, the progress of history can no longer be trusted.

> It now has a direction which, instead of a fulfilment, *could* lead to a universal disaster, and a tempo whose frightening exponential acceleration is apt to escape every control. Thus threatened by catastrophe from the very progress of history itself, we surely can no longer trust in an immanent "reason in history."[37]

Similarly, Pieper suggests that the legacy of Hiroshima undermines Bloch's hope of utopia within human history.[38] Guardini interprets the shift from the supreme optimism that marked the modern era to the contemporary acknowledgment of the limits of progress as evidence of the abandonment of modernity's striving for the infinite.[39] Human beings have been "sobered," he suggests; their optimism tempered.[40] Finally, Ratzinger himself offers a sober account of the prospects of history, suggesting that we must bid farewell to the "mirage" of a future better world, to "the myth of innerworldly eschatologies."[41] Since morality flows from

---

36. "We believe that a turning point at which technological and scientific progress changed from being to the overall advantage to being to the overall disadvantage of humanity was passed when, in the middle of the last century, humans acquired the means of forever destroying life on Earth." Persson and Savulescu, *Unfit for the Future*, 10.

37. Jonas, *Imperative of Responsibility*, 128.

38. "Confronted with the antihope and the anti-utopia that Hiroshima represents, this death on a global scale, which seems inevitable to some and which cannot be transcended within the horizons of time and history by a collective consciousness, we could ask if there is any room left for a glimmer of hope, or if, on the contrary, all that is left is a vision of despair, nothingness, and annihilation." Schumacher, *Philosophy of Hope*, 205.

39. Guardini, *End of the Modern World*, 53.

40. Guardini, *Power and Responsibility*, xii–xiii.

41. Ratzinger, *Turning Point*, 141.

human freedom, the future remains open, "and therefore always has the possibility of failure."[42]

Seizing "Power" over Technology

This sensitivity provokes an awakening to moral responsibility. Humanity recognizes the need to confront the nameless forces of technology, or, borrowing a phrase from Guardini, to take "power over power."[43] Jonas adopts the same phrase in response to the threat of world destruction through technology.[44] In order to confront the asymmetry of power, "which now has power over nature in general and over human nature in particular, we need a new ethics, an ethics of responsibility for the future of human nature, which for the first time in our history has become vulnerable."[45]

As was noted in chapter 6, Ratzinger follows Guardini in interpreting the problem of technology in the key of power and morality. "Man today holds power over things, but we can assert confidently that he does not yet have power over his own power."[46] Essentially, what Guardini outlines here is the current crisis that confronts us. Human beings have power over nature through their knowledge of its structures and its manipulation through technology, but they fail to comprehend their power, and as a result it turns threatening. As Ratzinger adds, "Being able to do and make is of no use if we do not know what it is for, if we no longer

---

42. Ratzinger, *Turning Point*, 140.
43. Guardini, *End of the Modern World*, 94.
44. "Power over power is required now before the halt is called by catastrophe itself—the power to overcome that impotence over against the self-feeding compulsion of power to its progressive exercise." Jonas, *Imperative of Responsibility*, 141.
45. Kampowski, *Greater Freedom*, 68.
46. Guardini, *End of the Modern World*, 90. Ratzinger expresses the same reality in these words: "When the first man set foot on the moon, no one was able to avoid feeling pride and joy and enthusiasm over man's colossal achievement. The event was felt, not as a victory over a nation, but as a victory for mankind. But this moment of joy had its mixture of sadness, for no one could escape the thought that this same man, who is capable of such marvellous things, is unable to prevent millions of men dying of hunger every year, has to allow millions to live without human dignity, is unable to put a stop to war or to stem the rising tide of crime. The road to the moon is easier to find than the road to man himself. Technical 'know-how' is not necessarily human 'know-how.' Quite obviously knowledge of how to deal with himself lies on a totally different plane from technical accomplishment." Ratzinger, *Faith and the Future*, 94.

ask who we are and what the truth of things is."[47] Human beings are free to use or misuse this power, for good and for evil, and nothing can guarantee that they will use it wisely.[48] Echoing the concerns of Persson and Savulescu, the presence of such power in the hands of imperfect human beings harbors ill for the future of humanity.

In order to regain proper power, Guardini highlights the necessity of certain virtues, among them the virtues of *earnestness* and *gravity*. As he explains, both are rooted in truth. Earnestness is needed in order to honestly confront the deceptions surrounding humanity's hope in technology, to "brush aside empty rhetoric extolling progress or the conquest of nature" and to "face heroically the duties forced upon man by his new situation."[49] Gravity, on the other hand, must take the form of a "personal courage" in confronting the source of the problem. It is not simply the courage to face external dangers and change structures of power. Guardini writes: "This gravity or courage must be purer and stronger even than the courage man needs to face either atom bombs or bacteriological warfare, because it must restrain the chaos rising out of the very works of man."[50]

Guardini offers a third and final virtue: the virtue of *asceticism*. Man seizes "power over power," becomes a true master, not primarily through knowledge and mastery of the processes of nature, but more fundamentally through self-mastery, "by conquering and by humbling himself."[51] In contrast to the optimism that characterizes secular ideologies, such asceticism might be interpreted as "faint-hearted pragmatism," a "renunciation of moral passion." But, as Ratzinger suggests, morality does not exist in a hubristic presumption "which tries to mind God's business," but in honesty, "which accepts man's limits and does man's work within them."[52] And an elemental part of this honesty is the acknowledgment of the origins of human power in its likeness to God. Dominion is given to human beings as something essential to their created human nature.[53]

47. Ratzinger, *Yes of Jesus Christ*, 18.
48. Guardini, *End of the Modern World*, 78.
49. Guardini, *End of the Modern World*, 93; Guardini, *Power and Responsibility*, 14–15.
50. Guardini, *End of the Modern World*, 93.
51. Guardini, *End of the Modern World*, 93.
52. Ratzinger, *Church, Ecumenism, and Politics*, 145.
53. Guardini, *Power and Responsibility*, 14. Adriano Pessina writes that power (*potere*) is inscribed in the ontological structure of human beings, not only manifest in

But the created nature of human dominion relativizes the use of this power. As Guardini attests:

> If human power and the lordship which stems from it are rooted in man's likeness to God, then power is not man's in his own right, autonomously, but only as a loan, in fief. Man is lord by the grace of God, and he must exercise his dominion responsibly, for he is answerable for it to him who is Lord by essence. Thus sovereignty becomes obedience, service.[54]

This humble obedience rests on human beings' acceptance of their limitations, on a concept of giftedness, and the recognition that their power exists at the service of a given purpose or plan for humanity. "Man's sovereignty is not meant to establish an independent world of man, but to complete the world of God as a free, human world in accordance with God's will."[55]

Furthermore, Guardini reflects that humility is not a denial of human power, but an expression of it. He acknowledges that in the course of the modern age, humility has been misrepresented as "weakness," "paltriness," "cowardice" and "low-mindedness"; of what Nietzsche deplored as "decadence" and a "slave morality."[56] While acknowledging such decadence in certain conceptions and practices of humility throughout Christian history that would justify Nietzsche's lament, Guardini insists that they exist as aberrations of true humility. "True Christian humility," he insists, "is a virtue of strength, not of weakness. In the original sense of the word, it is the strong, high-minded, and bold, who dare to be humble."[57] This form of humility does not debase human beings but

---

power over things through technology, but also in one's capacity for self-dominion as foundational for one's freedom. Pessina, "L'uomo e la tecnica," 11.

54. Guardini, *Power and Responsibility*, 15.

55. Guardini, *Power and Responsibility*, 16. Guardini adds: "The serpent, a symbolical figure for Satan, confuses man by misrepresenting the fundamental facts of human existence: the essential difference between Creator and created; between Archetype and image; between self-realization through truth and through usurpation; between sovereignty in service and independent sovereignty" (18–19).

56. Guardini, *Power and Responsibility*, 24.

57. Guardini, *Power and Responsibility*, 24. Guardini adds that this true form of humility is first revealed in God himself. "The act by which this took place was the Incarnation of the Logos. St. Paul says in his letter to the Philippians that Christ 'being in the form of God, thought it not robbery [i.e., something which one does not possess by right and thus, out of weakness, clings to with anxiety] to be equal with God: But emptied himself, taking the form of a servant, being made in the likeness of men, and

empowers them. It strengthens them to take control of their lives and not be a victim of circumstances; to take "power over power."

Subjection to Technology

On the other hand, an alternative temptation always remains. It is the temptation, already outlined in the discussion on the secularization of hope, of abdicating moral responsibility and placing confidence in historical processes and the positive assurance of science and technology—the very means that threaten our future. Francesca Giglio labels this attitude as a form of "holism" (*olismo*) that concedes to science total responsibility for human enhancement and relegates morality to the private sector.[58]

Persson and Savulescu appear to be aware of this danger. They attempt to distance themselves from excessive confidence in the possibilities of technology, calling it "wishful thinking" to believe that the challenges that face us could be resolved by technological solutions alone.[59] They also deny that progress equates with moral enhancement, proclaiming it to be "a naïve illusion to think that we could eventually rid ourselves of the necessity of having to make morally hard decisions with respect to science because it will in the future enable us to do everything we want."[60] Instead, our moral responsibility increases with the power that scientific progress and technological advancement affords us.[61] Therefore, it is all the more necessary that science and technology, like political institutions, be controlled by morally responsible people.[62] It is therefore somewhat contradictory that, in response to the moral "crisis" that confronts us, Persson and Savulescu seemingly revert to both a technological solution through moral bioenhancement and institutional intervention through

---

in habit formed as a man. He humbled himself, becoming obedient unto death, even to the death of the cross' (Phil 2:6–8)" (25).

58. "La scienza, quindi, assume man mano sempre di più il ruolo ufficiale di strumento per il miglioramento nel comportamento sociale, nell'intelligenza e nella concentrazione, o in attività, capacità e attributi specifici, promettendo un miglioramento della condizione umana globalmente intesa, mentre la crescita morale e spirituale viene relegata alla sfera privata dei singoli." Giglio, *Human Enhancement*, 15.

59. Persson and Savulescu, *Unfit for the Future*, 103.
60. Persson and Savulescu, *Unfit for the Future*, 131.
61. Persson and Savulescu, *Unfit for the Future*, 130.
62. Persson and Savulescu, *Unfit for the Future*, 121–22.

increased restrictions. What began as an awakening of the moral subject ends with an abandonment of moral responsibility in favor of institution and *techne*.

Their justification for this reversion is as follows: moral enhancement by traditional means is too uncertain, while unfettered cognitive enhancement will surely place greater and more destructive power into human hands. The uncertainty of moral education is said to be intensified by the fact that every generation must start again. As Persson and Savulescu write:

> Theoretical knowledge can be imparted from one generation to the next; thus, it will gradually accumulate over generations, making scientific and technological progress possible. But when people undergo great moral development in the course of their lives, their moral competence will largely die with them. It cannot be transmitted to the next generation as easily as, say, mathematical competence.[63]

Ratzinger agrees that the moral project must begin anew in each generation: indeed, in each person. He notes that in the attempt to politicize hope, moral responsibility is transferred from the individual person to the State. The good does not depend on personal striving, but is conferred by the corporate structures of society.[64] Indeed, it is not the individual human acts that are good or evil, but the structures themselves. But Ratzinger insists that this "unburdening"[65] of personal responsibility cannot hold. Human beings are not saved by renouncing responsibility and freedom, but are diminished by it. He therefore insists that there is no substitute for "individual moral conscience and personal decision."[66] In the political sphere this signifies that society is never complete, but must be built anew again and again.[67] For human moral formation it means that humanity "begins anew in every single individual,"[68] always in need

---

63. Persson and Savulescu, *Unfit for the Future*, 117–18.
64. Ratzinger, *Church, Ecumenism, and Politics*, 196.
65. Or "liberation" as it is called in theories of liberation theology.
66. Ratzinger, "Technological Security," 50.
67. Ratzinger, *Church, Ecumenism, and Politics*, 205.
68. Ratzinger, *Values in a Time of Upheaval*, 25.

of redemption.[69] The development of our ethical nature is not linear but circular, troubled by the vicissitudes of history and temptations to sin.[70]

He makes the same point in distinguishing technological progress from human progress. Technology is capable of creating better living conditions for humanity, but it has not power to "bring forth the new man or the new society."[71] In other words, technology does not equate with salvation.[72] Human progress, on the other hand, flows from freedom; and in freedom, human beings must struggle to form themselves and their society ever anew in accord with justice. Thus, in contrast to the utopian hope of a flattened but contented future humanity, Jonas speaks of the need to preserve a genuine humanity: "*Hope* we should, quite contrary to the utopian hope, that in future, too, every contentment will breed its discontent, every having its desire, every resting its unrest, every liberty its temptation—even every happiness its unhappiness."[73]

Moral competence is therefore likened to artistic proficiency, in which the human potential for morality needs to be drawn out and nurtured. This accords with Alasdair MacIntyre's determination that there is a difference between "human-nature-as-it-happens-to-be" and

---

69. Guardini, *Power and Responsibility*, 44. Guardini uses this as an apology against the claim that Christianity has added nothing to the progress of human moral formation. He writes: "Salvation does not mean that the arrangements of the world have been changed once and for all, but that a new beginning of existence has been set by God. This beginning remains as a permanent possibility" (29).

70. Ratzinger, "Truth and Freedom," 35.

71. Ratzinger, *Values in a Time of Upheaval*, 25. Elsewhere he writes: "Man's progress lies not in having more, but in being more; progress that leads only to having more is not progress at all. Progress should never be understood simply in the sense of a material 'more,' nor in the sense of ethical independence. It must be understood in the sense of greater service among men, of deeper communication, and of liberation for what is real." Ratzinger, "Technological Security," 51.

72. In this context, Ratzinger finds fault with a tendency within the thought of Teilhard de Chardin to conflate his theory of "hominization" or "christification" of the human person with technological progress, and thus to confuse the technological utopia with the Christian hope for the kingdom of God. Ratzinger, *Theological Highlights of Vatican II*, 226. He is similarly critical of such influences within *Gaudium et spes*. "Thus, for example, statements about Christian expectation of the world to come were here and there mixed up with technological hopes. Most important, the schema as a whole tended, in its definition of the relationship between the Christian and the technological world, to see the real meaning of the christological in the sacred aura it confers upon technological achievement, rather than developing the christological on the very different plane of the passion of human life and human love" (228).

73. Jonas, *Imperative of Responsibility*, 201.

"human-nature-as-it-could-be-if-it-realized-its-*telos*," in which human nature in its actual *untutored* state, "discrepant and discordant with the precepts of ethics,"[74] requires the transforming influence of practical reason and the virtues in order "to realize our true nature and to reach our true end."[75] But while Ratzinger interprets the process positively, as a reflection of human beings' personal and creative response toward the fulfillment of their nature, Persson and Savulescu regard it as a burden and obstacle to moral enhancement. In light of the gravity of the problems that confront the future of humanity, and the difficult decisions that have to be made now, the time needed to morally form a generation is a luxury that we cannot afford. Thus, they clutch at moral bioenhancement in a desperate attempt to find a solution.

> The development and application of such techniques is no doubt a risky course to take—it is after all humans in their current morally inept state that must apply them—but we think that our present situation is so desperate that this is a course of action that must be investigated and, depending upon the outcome of that investigation, perhaps deployed.[76]

This desperate grasping at solutions in the context of little "realistic hope,"[77] and the need for some concrete reassurance, is consistent with what Ratzinger identifies as positivism's inability to live with uncertainty and doubt; "the inability to be reconciled with the imperfection of human affairs."[78] Essentially, it reflects an unwillingness to live within the tension of the "not yet" of human hope. It is characterized by fear and the need to replace anxiety with certainty.

It can also be argued that in being willing to take the risk on moral enhancement, Persson and Savulescu gamble too much. In weighing the stakes, Jonas suggests that in small matters we may risk many misses, but "we may allow but few where greater things are concerned. And in the really great, irreversible ones, which go to the roots of the whole human

---

74. MacIntyre, *After Virtue*, 53.

75. MacIntyre, *After Virtue*, 52.

76. Persson and Savulescu, *Unfit for the Future*, 9.

77. "We think that the enormity of the moral problems that face us makes it reasonable to explore the possibility of such techniques, though their discovery may turn out to lie too far into the future for such techniques to offer any realistic hope of helping us with the overwhelming moral problems that we have reviewed." Persson and Savulescu, "Moral Transhumanism," 667.

78. Ratzinger, *Church, Ecumenism, and Politics*, 195.

enterprise, we really must allow none."⁷⁹ He argues from the logic of evolution, which proceeds by slow and small steps, never gambling everything, and therefore capable of absorbing "innumerable 'mistakes' in its single moves."⁸⁰ Modern technology, by contrast, especially through genetic manipulation, is able to reduce these many small steps into single large ones. As a result, the risks increase exponentially.

> It is therefore far from true that "taking his own evolution in hand"—that is, replacing blind and slow-working chance with conscious and fast-working planning—would give man a surer prospect of evolutionary success. On the contrary, it would inject entirely new elements of insecurity and hazard, which rise in proportion as the stakes are raised and the times are shortened in which the inevitable (and no longer small) mistakes can be corrected.⁸¹

While Persson and Savulescu are legitimately concerned with the future of human life, they fail to recognize that interfering with the human organism, especially at the genetic level, could threaten human nature itself. As Jonas insists, it is not just a case of preserving human existence but of keeping intact human nature as it is given to us, with its unique capacity, "(albeit fallible), for truth, valuation, and freedom."⁸² It was noted in the previous chapter that both Jonas and Habermas fear that genetic manipulation could limit the human capacity for autonomy and benevolence, and thus to assume moral subjectivity. The loss of such human qualities would be of infinite proportion, and therefore should not be risked at any cost. The incommensurability between the risk of "infinite loss" and the chance of "finite gain" demands caution and sobriety. "No gain is worth this price, no hope of gain justifies this risk."⁸³

Admittedly, Jonas concedes an exception that when "under the threat of a terrible future," it is possible to take greater risks in order to prevent a "supreme evil."⁸⁴ While Persson and Savulescu might claim that the current situation fits such a description, Jonas conditions his exception with the prohibition "to incur the risk of nothingness."⁸⁵

79. Jonas, *Imperative of Responsibility*, 31.
80. Jonas, *Imperative of Responsibility*, 31.
81. Jonas, *Imperative of Responsibility*, 31.
82. Jonas, *Imperative of Responsibility*, 33.
83. Jonas, *Imperative of Responsibility*, 33.
84. Jonas, *Imperative of Responsibility*, 36.
85. Jonas, *Imperative of Responsibility*, 38. As Kampowski interprets: "Given our

In this context, Jonas proposes his "imperative of responsibility":

> "Act so that the effects of your action are compatible with the permanence of genuine human life"; or expressed negatively: "Act so that the effects of your action are not destructive of the future possibility of such life"; or simply: "Do not compromise the conditions for an indefinite continuation of humanity on earth"; or, again turned positive: "In your present choices, include the future wholeness of Man among the objects of your will."[86]

In safeguarding the future of humanity, he offers a *primitive* rule "that the prophecy of doom is to be given greater heed than the prophecy of bliss."[87] In the context of transhumanism, this means that the risks to humanity through biotechnical enhancement should weigh heavier in our considerations than the possible benefits. But in their gamble with moral enhancement, Persson and Savulescu do the exact opposite.

Love and Morality

In the context of this discussion surrounding risk and reassurance, the concept of hope arises once more. In response to the craving for certainty, Ratzinger proposes the intimate connection between hope and love. He explains that love offers its own kind of certainty: not the certainty of positive knowledge, but a "certainty of dialogue,"[88] of confidence and patient expectation.[89] He then situates fear within this context: not the fear of lacking control, but "the fear of hurting the beloved";[90] of injuring love. He claims that when this fundamental fear is lacking,[91] a myriad

---

new power to extinguish the human race or to render miserable the conditions of its existence, the continued presence of authentic human life in the world has itself become a matter of human obligation." Kampowski, *Greater Freedom*, 69.

86. Jonas, *Imperative of Responsibility*, 11.
87. Jonas, *Imperative of Responsibility*, 31.
88. Ratzinger, *Yes of Jesus Christ*, 83.
89. Pieper, *Faith, Hope, Love*, 100.
90. Ratzinger, *Yes of Jesus Christ*, 83.
91. Ratzinger claims that the overcoming of fundamental fear, which is precisely the "fear of the Lord" (Ps 111:10), was at the heart of the project of Modernity. "Liberalism and the Enlightenment want to talk us into accepting a world without fear: they promise the complete elimination of every kind of fear. They would like to get rid of every 'not yet,' every reliance on other people and their inner tension, even though

of other forms take its place: "fear of the scourge of the major illnesses that destroy people; anxiety about the consequences of our technological power; anxiety about the emptiness and meaninglessness of existence."[92] He gives the example of the "overexcited reactions" that followed the nuclear disaster at Chernobyl in 1986, as symptomatic of the fear evoked by human finiteness, and of doubt cast on the "dogma of progress."[93]

The anxieties listed by Ratzinger are symptomatic of the transhumanist preoccupation for moral enhancement, just as the inability to entrust oneself to another is symptomatic of positivism's need for control: exorcising fear by trusting only in what one can achieve for oneself,[94] and reducing all reality to categories of calculation and to "the realm of 'exact' knowledge."[95] Lacking in a transhumanist account of moral enhancement is an acknowledgment of the human capacity to love that stands at the heart of morality. In its place, they attempt to rationalize morality according to a materialistic reduction, seeking "the genetic and neurobiological bases of our behavior."[96] In other words, their approach to morality is underpinned by what Ratzinger has already diagnosed as a reduction of spirit to matter, signifying "that mind or spirit is not the origin of matter but only a product of material developments."[97]

Accordingly, the idea that morality could have its foundations in the physical process of evolution is alien to Ratzinger. In the first place he describes an evolutionary ethic, based on natural selection and survival of the fittest, as "bloodthirsty" and "of very little use for an ethic of universal peace, of practical love of one's neighbor, and of the necessary overcoming of oneself, which is what we need."[98] More fundamentally, he maintains that a morality that does not have its origins in reason is without foundation. Here again he finds agreement with Jonas, who (as Christoph

---

this is something that belongs essentially to hope and love. Anyone who liberates man from fear in this way liberates him from hope and love too." Ratzinger, *Yes of Jesus Christ*, 83–84.

92. Ratzinger, *Yes of Jesus Christ*, 85.
93. Ratzinger, *Yes of Jesus Christ*, 48.
94. "From this point of view fear must be exorcized independently of the others through what is at my own disposal—through what I do myself, through my own work." Ratzinger, *Yes of Jesus Christ*, 83.
95. Ratzinger, *Church, Ecumenism, and Politics*, 197.
96. Persson and Savulescu, *Unfit for the Future*, 107.
97. Ratzinger, *Church, Ecumenism, and Politics*, 196.
98. Ratzinger, *Truth and Tolerance*, 182–83.

Schönborn relates) at the time of writing *The Imperative of Responsibility* was awakened to the conviction that it is not genes, but living people, who can be held responsible for their actions; that one cannot found ethics in biology, but in mind, soul, reason and free will.[99] It has already been noted that Ratzinger insists that the spirit cannot originate from matter, or as Aidan Nichols interprets, "the quantification of the physical world is not a proper analogue for the 'measuring' of the human spirit."[100] One cannot define human morality on the basis of evolutionary biology, on MacIntyre's concept of "untutored" human nature, but on its teleological fulfillment. Morality goes beyond instinct. As Robert Spaemann writes, finite beings transcend the demands of self-preservation, discovering infinite possibilities for beneficence.[101] Thus, the bid to explain human morality in evolutionary terms represents yet another attempt to make the theory of evolution into a *philosophia universalis*, placing limits on the human spirit and thus alienating human beings from the truth of their created nature.

The Dialogical Nature of Morality

As noted in Ratzinger's concept of anthropology, the emergence of the human spirit coincides with the realization of a Thou, with the idea of God. In this context, morality does not emerge as a commentary on human behavior. Nor is it a consequence of the human person's will to survive. Rather, it exists from the beginning as a response to the Other.[102] Ratzinger gives the example of the Ten Commandments, foundational for Christian morality. As he notes, their significance does not lie in their distinction from other moralities, since the confluence with Egyptian

---

99. Schönborn notes this in the context of the choice between reason and irrationality that stands at the center of the philosophical debate over evolution—a theme central to Ratzinger's argument, as already noted in this work. Schönborn, *Chance or Purpose?*, 121.

100. Nichols, *Thought of Pope Benedict XVI*, 115.

101. Spaemann, *Happiness and Benevolence*, 106.

102. "Christian moral theology is never simply an ethics of the law, it surpasses even the realm of an ethics of virtue: it is a dialogical ethics, because the moral human action develops out of the person's encounter with God, therefore it is never an activity in itself, self-sufficient and autonomous, pure human achievement, but a response to the gift of love and thus a being drawn into the dynamic of love—of God himself—who first of all truly frees the person and brings him to his true high dignity." Ratzinger, "Current Doctrinal Relevance," 6.

THE CASE FOR MORAL ENHANCEMENT 239

and Babylonian traditions must be admitted. He adds: "Even the introductory formula 'I am the Lord your God' is not entirely new."[103] Rather, their significance lies in the context of the Lord introducing himself as the One who hears the complaint of his people and comes to liberate them. The commandments are thus firmly established in the context of the covenant between God and Israel. They are the practical expression of what it means to believe in God and to belong to him who took the initiative to save Israel from bondage. "They are not supplementary to faith, to the Covenant; they show who this God is, with whom Israel stands in a covenant relationship."[104]

The Ordo Amoris

In this relational context, morality can be more clearly conceived as a response to love. As already noted, Ratzinger defines love's essential nature as a "yes" to the being of the other, and the presence of love affirms not only the goodness of the other but the whole of creation. Accordingly, Ratzinger recognizes "that every love bears within itself a universal tendency."[105] While it is admittedly impossible to love a nameless multitude, love for the individual person opens us to a new reality. Here again we touch on the distinction between the universal demands of benevolence, the finiteness of the individual, and the particularity of action that constitutes the *ordo amoris*.[106] As Spaemann writes, in their finiteness benevolent beings "have to establish commensurability and relativize that which they encounter."[107] Action is always selective. Recognition of our human limitations involves the acknowledgment that

---

103. Ratzinger, "Church's Teaching," 55.

104. Ratzinger, "Church's Teaching," 56.

105. Ratzinger, *Yes of Jesus Christ*, 91. He continues: "The world to which this beloved belongs seems different once I start to love. The lover would as it were like to embrace the whole world in and with his beloved. The encounter with the one person restores the whole to me afresh. Of course, love is a choice: it is directed not at millions but at precisely this person. But precisely in this choice, in this one person, reality as a whole appears in a new light to me" (91–92).

106. Spaemann explains: "For the finite being benevolence in its universality has to organize itself into a structure which corresponds both to the finitude of its perspective as well as the finitude of the objects of benevolence. In other words there exists what Augustine called the *ordo amoris*. Everyone has their own place in the *ordo amoris* of the other." Spaemann, *Happiness and Benevolence*, 109.

107. Spaemann, *Happiness and Benevolence*, 106.

our responsibility is not universal. Stated otherwise, the only universal responsibility toward *every* human being is negative: "to avoid and to renounce influencing them in such a way that does not respect them as persons."[108] While love has a universal orientation, individual acts cannot take all consequences into account. Indeed, any attempt to universalize positive duties would paralyze action.[109]

With the exception of ritual and forms of worship, God cannot be the object of our action. We can only direct our actions toward other finite beings, and in our own finiteness as agents, we cannot order our actions toward everyone. Similarly, love or benevolence cannot be directed toward something abstract like "humanity" in general but only toward individuals.[110] This is so because in love the other becomes as real to us as we are to ourselves.[111] The beloved is addressed as a "Thou," while the multitudes can only be addressed in concepts and generalizations. As Spaemann writes:

> Not around everyone can be that glow that is around those we love. Most people I will perceive only under certain aspects and concepts. Nobody can do justice to the uniqueness of each human person, except God. "Only for God is everyone irreplaceable,"[112] says Dávila. Only for God does the individual not disappear in the great number. To become real as this non-interchangeable unique individual—this is possible for me only in the exclusive forms of friendship and love.[113]

In the unequal distribution of love, there is a hierarchical order of preference toward family, friends and close acquaintances. What evolutionary ethicists interpret as close-range biases are in fact rationally justifiable according to the finiteness of human beings. This natural "creaturely relation of nearness and distance" is not invalidated by the

---

108. Spaemann, *Happiness and Benevolence*, 182. Commenting on this universality of negative duties, Kampowski writes: "In this negative sense, all of the biosphere along with future human generations can become the object of my responsibility to the extent—and only to the extent—that I am able to abstain from certain compromising actions." Kampowski, *Greater Freedom*, 126.

109. Spaemann, *Happiness and Benevolence*, 182.

110. Spaemann, *Happiness and Benevolence*, 107.

111. Spaemann, *Love and the Dignity of Human Life*, 19.

112. "Tan sólo para Dios somos irreemplazables." Dávila *Escolios a un texto implícito*, 113.

113. Spaemann, *Love and the Dignity of Human Life*, 20.

universal commandment to love one's neighbor.[114] Rather, it is the other way around. The reality of the beloved awakens us to the other's claim to be recognized as real.[115] In the context of responding to the plight of human suffering, Spaemann writes: "What counts is not so much diffuse universal information about human suffering, which tends to render it unreal, but that we allow some small part of that which we know to become real to ourselves."[116] In this sense, following the example of the Good Samaritan, "anyone at any time can become our 'neighbor.'"[117] The other, the stranger, is someone real to me. Thus, there exists "an inner connection, rather than a mutually exclusive relationship, between the experience of a unique and particular love and the universality of benevolence."[118] The human capacity for love, inscribed in our very nature, opens a path toward the multitude and enables us to look upon the world and the stranger with new eyes of compassion and responsibility.[119] However, contrary to transhumanist claims, such a response cannot be manipulated or engineered through technology and science. It can only come from the one who freely chooses to love, who responds with his or her free and personal "I" to the "thou" of the other.

The Concrete Imperative of Christ's Love

In the Christian context, this universality of benevolence finds its inspiration and source in the particularity of the person of Jesus Christ. "Christianity is not an intellectual system, a collection of dogmas, or moralism," writes Ratzinger. "Christianity is instead an encounter, a love story; it is an event."[120] Here too one discerns the influence of Guardini. As Rat-

---

114. Spaemann, *Love and the Dignity of Human Life*, 18.

115. Spaemann, *Love and the Dignity of Human Life*, 21.

116. Spaemann, *Happiness and Benevolence*, 112. Following Aquinas he adds that love as benevolence is "the becoming real of the real for us" (113).

117. Spaemann, *Happiness and Benevolence*, 111.

118. Spaemann, *Happiness and Benevolence*, 108.

119. This connection between love and responsibility may go toward answering Jonas's bewilderment that responsibility has been seemingly absent from traditional ethics. As Kampowski writes: "The response would simply be that responsibility *has* actually always been at the centre of morality, only that previously it has gone by a different name, and that is: love or benevolence." Kampowski, *Greater Freedom*, 124. Cf. Jonas, *Imperative of Responsibility*, 87.

120. Ratzinger, "Funeral Homily for Msgr. Luigi Giussani," 685. This corresponds with Ratzinger's interpretation of the renewal of moral theology envisaged at the

inger himself writes, Guardini teaches us that "the essence of Christianity is not an idea, not a system of thought, not a plan of action. The essence of Christianity is a person: Jesus Christ himself."[121] It is from him that we learn what it means to be truly human. John Paul II expresses something similar in *Veritatis splendor*, writing that morality essentially "involves *holding fast to the very person of Jesus*, partaking of his life and his destiny, sharing in his free and loving obedience to the will of the Father."[122] Christian morality therefore takes the form of imitation of Christ: "*to follow him and to imitate him along the path of love, a love which gives itself completely to the brethren out of love for God.*"[123] This finds expression in Christ's new commandment that fulfills all others: "that you love one another as I have loved you" (John 15:12).[124]

Christian morality as imitation of Christ is also echoed in the thought of Ratzinger's friend Hans Urs von Balthasar and his identification of Christ as the "concrete categorical imperative."

> Christ's concrete existence—his life, suffering, death and ultimate bodily resurrection—surpass all other systems of ethical norms. In the final analysis it is to this norm alone, which is itself the prototype of perfect obedience to God the Father, that the moral conduct of Christians has to answer.[125]

Vatican Council II: "To return to a substantially biblical and christological ethics, inspired by the encounter with Christ, and ethics conceived not as a series of precepts but as the event of an encounter, of a love that then also knows how to create corresponding actions. If this happens—a living encounter with a living person who is Christ—and this encounter stirs up love, it is from love that everything else flows." Ratzinger, "Renewal of Moral Theology," 358–59.

121. Ratzinger, "Guardini on Christ in Our Century," 55. Ratzinger expresses the same sentiments in his first encyclical as Pope Benedict XVI: "Being Christian is not the result of an ethical choice or a lofty idea, but the encounter with an event, a person, which gives life a new horizon and a decisive direction." Benedict XVI, *Deus caritas est*, n. 1.

122. John Paul II, *Veritatis splendor*, n. 19.

123. John Paul II, *Veritatis splendor*, n. 20.

124. John Paul adds: "The word 'as' requires imitation of Jesus and of his love, of which the washing of feet is a sign: 'If I then, your Lord and Teacher, have washed your feet, you also ought to wash one another's feet. For I have given you an example, that you should do as I have done to you' (John 13:14–15). Jesus' way of acting and his words, his deeds and his precepts constitute the moral rule of Christian life." John Paul II, *Veritatis splendor*, n. 20.

125. Balthasar, "Nine Propositions on Christian Ethics," 82.

As prototype, this perfect obedience of Christ is "eschatological" and "unsurpassable," and as such "universally normative."[126] But more than a mere model or paradigm for imitation, Christ is also a *personal* norm, "who, in virtue of his suffering for us and his eucharistic surrender of his life for us (which imparts it to us—*per ipsum et in ipso*), empowers us inwardly to do the Father's will together with him (*cum ipso*)."[127] He is himself the means of overcoming the distance between the particular and the universal, the personal and the "other." Through our communion with him, we take on the Christ-form of filial obedience; we love with his own love.

Balthasar cautions that our participation in the action of Christ can only be carried out in "infinite reverence," since God's love that is the force of the moral life "towers infinitely above us—in the *maior dissimilitudo*."[128] He thus underlines the inseparable link between the cult of worship (*leiturgia*) and ethical conduct.[129] Ratzinger agrees that this dissimilitude relativizes our conception of moral autonomy. As created beings, we are contingent and finite. It is not within our competence to determine the nature of the world and our own, to decide what the world should be and how we should act in it. We live in a relationship of dependence on God as Creator.

However, according to God's nature as love, this relationship of dependence is not slavish, but truly a form of participation: "a union of love in love."[130] In our communion with Christ through the action of the Holy Spirit, we are made participants in the love of God. In a very real sense we become "lovers" like God, and are enabled to fulfill his command to love as he himself loves. Thus, we are reassured that dependence does not undermine human subjectivity; that configuration to the moral norm of Christ through the internal working of the grace of the Holy Spirit does

---

126. Balthasar, "Nine Propositions on Christian Ethics," 83.

127. Balthasar, "Nine Propositions on Christian Ethics," 79.

128. Balthasar, "Nine Propositions on Christian Ethics," 80.

129. In *Deus caritas est*, Benedict XVI explains that this liturgical, and especially Eucharistic, orientation moves us further beyond the conception of morality as obedience to norms that "could exist apart from and alongside faith in Christ and its sacramental re-actualization." Worship and ethics are united in Eucharistic communion which includes both the vertical realization of being loved and the horizontal call to love others in return. "Faith, worship and *ethos* are interwoven as a single reality which takes shape in our encounter with God's *agape*." Benedict XVI, *Deus caritas est*, n. 14.

130. Ratzinger, "Renewal of Moral Theology," 366.

not negate moral autonomy. Rather, in our relationship with God we find our true identity.[131]

The Realism of Love

In setting morality within the key of love, Ratzinger maintains its inner connection to truth. Love is not blind. It is not indulgent toward the beloved, but includes an honest acknowledgment of failure and sin. In this context, the capacity for forgiveness flows directly from love, but so does justice, the divine "wrath," which seeks restitution and conversion.[132] Thus, relevant to the moral problems that threaten contemporary society, love does not weaken the demands of moral conversion. It does not turn a blind eye to the wrongs of the world and the human faults that lie at the heart of the current crisis. Instead, love demands action and justice.

At the same time, love always remains hopeful. It sees the goodness that lies at the heart of being and draws it forth. Love does not despair at the failures of human beings, but believes in their capacity for change and conversion. While recognizing the dark side of human nature and its capacity for evil, Ratzinger remains hopeful that, in a "world created and willed on the risk of freedom and love," the redemption of human nature is always possible. "As the arena of love it is also the playground of freedom and also incurs the risk of evil. It accepts the mystery of darkness for the sake of the greater light constituted by freedom and love."[133]

---

131. Ratzinger, "Renewal of Moral Theology," 366: "St. Augustine teaches us that God is *intimior intimo meo*, and that thus, obeying and uniting myself to God and to Christ, I do not leave myself to enter into heteronomy and an unacceptable dependence, a sort of slavery. To the contrary, precisely in this way I find my interiority and my identity, which until this moment remained locked up in sin. Through communion with Christ, I can find myself again and, entering into myself, I can find God and my *theosis*, my true essence, my true autonomy." Again, this corresponds with Benedict's sentiments in *Deus caritas est*: "The love-story between God and man consists in the very fact that this communion of will increases in a communion of thought and sentiment, and thus our will and God's will increasingly coincide: God's will is no longer for me an alien will, something imposed on me from without by the commandments, but it is now my own will, based on the realization that God is in fact more deeply present to me than I am to myself." Benedict XVI, *Deus caritas est*, n. 17. Cf. Saint Augustine, *Confessions*, III, 6, 11.

132. Ratzinger, *Yes of Jesus Christ*, 94.

133. Ratzinger, *Introduction to Christianity*, 160.

The Absence of Love

As noted previously, the diminishment of love in the context of human action is connected with a lack of trust in humanity and the desire to be "more realistic" concerning human potential. However, as Ratzinger notes, this lack of magnanimity, which is essentially a lack of love for humanity,[134] inevitably turns to hatred.[135] A new attitude arises: "an attitude that looks upon the human being as a disturber of the peace, as the one who wrecks everything, as the real parasite and disease of nature."[136] This is evident in the dilemmas that moral enhancement seeks to address: in the threat of world destruction through terrorism and climate change. As an example, Ratzinger suggests that the "monstrous and enormous hatred that seethes in many terrorist organizations today"[137] is explicable only in light of the rejection of the greatness of the human vocation to love, that wants to destroy every semblance of the divine image in the human person, and that is blind to the *theosis* between God and humanity. He notes a similar turning against humankind in response to the problems of environmental destruction:

> Today there is a remarkable hatred among people for their own real greatness. Man sees himself as the enemy of life, of the balance of creation, as the great disturber of the peace of nature (which would be better off if he did not exist), as the creature that went wrong.[138]

With their destructive capacity, heightened by their development of technology, human beings are seen as "diseased" and threatening to the rest of nature, disturbing its beauty and balance.[139] To restore balance, the human significance and distinction must be neutralized: "humans

---

134. He deems that "the person who refuses his or her metaphysical greatness is an apostate with regard to the divine vocation of being human." Ratzinger, *Yes of Jesus Christ*, 80.

135. "Man despises himself; he is no longer in accord with God, who found his human creation to be 'something very good' (Gen 1:31). On the contrary, man today sees himself as the destroyer of the world, an unhappy product of evolution. In reality, man, who no longer has access to the infinite, to God, is a contradictory being, a failed product." Ratzinger, "Problem of Threats to Human Life," 390–91.

136. Ratzinger, *In the Beginning*, 38.

137. Ratzinger, *Yes of Jesus Christ*, 80.

138. Ratzinger, *Yes of Jesus Christ*, 74.

139. Ratzinger, *In the Beginning*, 93.

must be healed of being human."¹⁴⁰ This is particularly evident in certain environmental movements and extreme forms of animal liberation. But it is also evident in the transhumanist project, built on the premise that humanity in its given form is not good enough. To find its place within the world it must radically change. There is little within the human person that can respond to this need to change, and therefore it must be imposed from outside, whether that be through external structures or biotechnological enhancement.

In his analysis of the tension between technology and power, Guardini recognizes two options open to human beings: either "to match the greatness of his power with the strength of his humanity, or to surrender his humanity to power and perish."¹⁴¹ In their denial of human goodness transhumanists choose the latter course. They surrender humanity to the whims of technology that is incapable of bringing healing but only destruction. While they plead for the chance to explore the possibilities of human enhancement, it would seem unwise to allow life-changing technology to be wielded by those who possess such a negative conception of human nature. This is Jonas's point. In responding to the charge of pessimism over his preference for the "prophecy of doom," he suggests that "the greater pessimism is on the side of those who consider the given to be so bad or worthless that every gamble for its possible improvement is defensible."¹⁴² In other words, those who consider the human condition so lightly as to risk everything should not be trusted with its future. Transhumanists, with their negative attitude toward the given, should be the last to offer counsel on what is good for the future of humanity. Only those who are truly human, who love and appreciate the giftedness of human life, can be trusted to use technology in a way that fosters integral human development.

The Hope for Human Morality

Accordingly, the proper response to the distortions of human nature is not its denial, but the recognition of its dignity and the hopeful expectation of its fulfillment. The solution does not lie in overcoming human nature through a process of "re-creation," but in the acceptance of human limitations as the path toward transcendence. As Ratzinger writes:

140. Ratzinger, *In the Beginning*, 94.
141. Guardini, *Power and Responsibility*, xiii.
142. Jonas, *Imperative of Responsibility*, 34.

Humans are dependent—that is the primary truth about them. And because it is, only love can redeem them, for only love transforms dependence into freedom. Thus human beings will only succeed in destroying their own redemption, destroying themselves, if they eliminate love "to be on the safe side."[143]

In recognizing dependence as the fruit of the goodness and love that stands at the origins of human creation, Ratzinger offers a more positive and hopeful reading of the human person. He has faith in humanity's potential. He believes that the human person is intrinsically ordered toward a moral life, and is capable of living it. While acknowledging the obvious failures and ever-present dangers posed by humanity, he maintains that hope placed in humankind is not deceptive. He argues this on the basis of a historical precedent: that it is precisely through the humanity assumed by the Son of God that humankind is saved.[144] As noted above, the goodness and trustworthiness of Christ is not extrinsic to us. In communion with him, human beings are capable of great things. To Ratzinger's mind, this is evident in two ways, which also provide the "only really effective apologia for Christianity":[145] the *saints* that the Christian faith has produced, and the beauty in *art* that it has inspired.[146] Both reveal the capacity of human beings to transcend themselves. The lives of the saints give witness to a human love that becomes universal in its configuration to Christ. The beauty of art in all its forms reveals the depths of human ingenuity, taking intellect and talent beyond the narrow confines of calculation and manipulation toward a true participation in divine creativity.

This stands in stark contrast to Bostrom's reductive explanation for the emergence of these human qualities. While he acknowledges that such characteristics as leisure, humor, love, art, philosophy and friendship have meaning in themselves for the enjoyment they provide, he ultimately interprets them as evolutionary adaptive signs of physical and

---

143. Ratzinger, *In the Beginning*, 98–99.

144. "That faith can well and truly place its hope in man is because, for faith, man is no longer an unpredictable being—as he is progressively coming to know himself—but in the end is Jesus Christ. In him, for the first time definitively, is man the hope of humanity." Ratzinger, *Faith and the Future*, 98.

145. Ratzinger and Messori, *Ratzinger Report*, 129.

146. "Nothing can bring us into close contact with the beauty of Christ himself other than the world of beauty created by faith, and light that shines out from the faces of the saints, through whom his own light becomes visible." Ratzinger, "Feeling of Things."

mental strength, social status, and fitness for survival.[147] In Ratzinger's analysis, this diminishment of reality to the mechanisms of nature's laws is ignorant of what is truly human, dismissing "all that is personal, all love and self-giving, as mere appearance, which, though psychologically useful, is ultimately unreal and untenable."[148] Such qualities are not deemed to be essential to the human person, nor do they possess any intrinsic value. As evidence, Bostrom envisages that in moving toward a posthuman state, communication could be achieved without the need for such symbols, and that with the advent of asexual means of technologically assisted reproduction, displays of physical fitness, and love itself, become unnecessary.[149] However, this flattening of human behavior to the mechanistic and functional is essentially reductive, and incapable of capturing the transcendence of the human spirit. In the words of Ratzinger is constitutes "the denial of humanity."[150]

The Human Person Is Not the Only Actor in History

For Ratzinger, human beings' participation in the life (goodness, love, and beauty) of Christ underscores the relational nature of morality. Again, as created beings they are dependent and limited. In this sense, Ratzinger could agree with Persson and Savulescu that, unaided, human beings are "unfit for the future," but would deny that this "unfitness" is the result of a failure to enhance by whatever means. Rather, it is rooted in their existential inability to save themselves. Technology, social structures, and historical processes exist as products of humanity. They do not have the power to make us fit. Rather, "fitness" for the future comes as gift. Its origins lie in the bestowal of love. Human beings must therefore look beyond themselves in order to grow morally.

This dependence accords with Ratzinger's insistence that the human person is not the only actor in history. While it is right that human beings should take responsibility for the future, their efforts can never exhaust hope. As already stressed, there is something greater than our finite reality. Faith in God assures us of the divine presence in history, guiding it to its fulfillment. Thus, writes Ratzinger, "despite all the horrors human history will not be drowned in the night of self-destruction; God will

---

147. Bostrom, "Future of Human Evolution," 6, 8.
148. Ratzinger, "Man between Reproduction and Creation," 82.
149. Bostrom, "Future of Human Evolution," 9.
150. Ratzinger, "Man between Reproduction and Creation," 82.

not let it be torn from his hands."[151] According to Guardini, the presence of God in human history contextualizes human reality and configures human hope. It cuts between what he terms the "natural-optimistic" (or presumptive) and the "cultural-pessimistic" (or despairing) interpretations of history,[152] which both limit history to human action. When human beings acknowledge a *presence* that is more permanent than their contingence—a *reason* greater than their own, a *love* purer than anything they could muster—they can freely accept the limitations of their human nature, and look expectantly and hopefully toward God as the source of their fulfillment. This saves humanity from assuming the awful responsibility of being solely responsible for the future, and from the frenetic grasping at "solutions" to the problems that threaten our peace. As Ratzinger writes: "only the courage to rediscover and accept the divine dimension of our being can give our souls and our society a new inner stability once again."[153]

Conscience

In the context of a relational concept of morality, Ratzinger presents a particular reading of moral conscience that is essential to moral formation.[154] In doing so, he builds on the medieval recognition of two levels of conscience, drawing particularly on the Thomistic distinction between concepts of *synderesis* and *conscientia*. In the *Summa Theologiae*, this distinction is made in the context of his treatment of the intellectual powers, following a distinction between the speculative and practical intellect.[155] As Servais Pinckaers explains, *synderesis* and *conscientia* are interpreted as sources of practical reason, "from above" and "from below" respectively.[156]

151. Ratzinger, *Yes of Jesus Christ*, 55. He adds: "Even 'after Auschwitz,' even after the most tragic catastrophe of history, God remains God: he remains good with an indestructible goodness. He remains the redeemer in whose hands man's destructive and cruel activity is transformed by his love. Man is not the only actor on the stage of history, and that is why death does not have the last word in it. The fact that there is this other person who is active is alone the firm and certain anchor of a hope that is stronger and more real than all the frightfulness of the world" (55–56).

152. Guardini, *Power and Responsibility*, 21.
153. Ratzinger, *Yes of Jesus Christ*, 78.
154. Ratzinger, "Conscience and Truth," 534.
155. *STh.*, I, q. 79, a. 12 and 13.
156. Pinckaers, "Conscience and Christian Tradition," 330.

Synderesis/Anamnesis

Considered "from above," *synderesis* is that inner consciousness of the law that Saint Paul speaks of in his Letter to the Romans;[157] "the original moral light in the depths of the human mind and heart."[158] For Aquinas it is a natural habit that "incites to good" and "murmurs at evil";[159] an expression of our creation in the image of God, with the freedom, intellect and will to know good and evil.[160] However, in adopting this concept of a form of conscience from above, Ratzinger avoids the term *synderesis*, preferring the Platonic notion of *anamnesis* as a type of "remembering."[161] In this, one notes a continuity with his concept of human thought as a rethinking of divine reason. Thus, this level of conscience originates in our creation,[162] as a participation in the divine *logos*: the Pauline law written on the heart, or, in the words of Saint Basil, a "spark of divine love" that makes us capable of observing God's law.[163]

In drawing out what he means by conscience as *anamnesis*, Ratzinger writes:

---

157. "When Gentiles who have not the law do by nature what the law requires, they are a law to themselves, even though they do not have the law. They show that what the law requires is written on their hearts, while their conscience also bears witness" (Rom 2:14-15).

158. Pinckaers, "Conscience and Christian Tradition," 330.

159. *STh.*, I, q. 79, a. 12.

160. In the Prologue to the *Seconda Pars*, Aquinas writes: "Since, as Damascene states (*De Fide Orth.* ii, 12), man is said to be made in God's image, in so far as the image implies 'an intelligent being endowed with free-will and self-movement': now that we have treated of the exemplar, i.e. God, and of those things which came forth from the power of God in accordance with his will; it remains for us to treat of his image, i.e. man, inasmuch as he too is the principle of his actions, as having free-will and control of his actions." Referred to in Pinckaers, "Conscience and Christian Tradition," 331.

161. Ratzinger's reasoning is twofold: first, he acknowledges the problematic use of the term *synderesis* in tradition, in which its meaning was often unclear "and for this reason became a hindrance to a careful development of this essential aspect of the whole question of conscience"; secondly, because the concept of *anamnesis* "harmonizes with key motifs of biblical thought and the anthropology derived from it." Ratzinger, "Conscience and Truth," 534.

162. David Crawford writes: "We might put it this way: the first principle of practical reason—*bonum est faciendum et prosequendum et malum vitandum*—looks not only forward to the fulfilment of human aspiration, but also, so to speak, 'backward' to origins and their deep structures in order to see the inherent order and meaning of those aspirations." Crawford, "Natural Law and the Body," 331.

163. Ratzinger, "Conscience and Truth," 534.

This means that the first so-called ontological level of the phenomenon of conscience consists in the fact that something like an original memory of the good and true (the two are identical) has been implanted in us, that there is an inner ontological tendency within man, who is created in the likeness of God, toward the divine. From its origin, man's being resonates with some things and clashes with others. This *anamnesis* of the origin, which results from the godlike constitution of our being, is not a conceptually articulated knowing, a store of retrievable contents. It is so to speak an inner sense, a capacity to recall, so that the one whom it addresses, if he is not turned in on himself, hears its echo from within. He sees: "That's it! That is what my nature points to and seeks."[164]

Of note in this definition, Ratzinger does not reduce moral subjectivity to the discovery of "retrievable contents," according to a strict application of the speculative reason. Morality is not a theoretical but an applied science, the domain of practical reason, which is guided by conscience as a memory of "a kind of irreducible 'knowledge' that conditions ethical reasoning from its beginning."[165]

One also notes Ratzinger's affirmation of the moral conscience as "an inner ontological tendency." As he indicates elsewhere, morality forms part of our "spiritual makeup" through "a basic capacity to choose between good and evil."[166] However, he does not simply reduce conscience to the subjective level, of one "turned in on himself." Conscience speaks to the perfection of one's nature which has objective content. In this context, the remembering associated with *anamnesis* is not simply a personal recalling but has a universal character. Thus, Ratzinger writes that this "anamnesis instilled in our beings needs, one might say, assistance from without so that it can become aware of itself."[167] In the context of faith, Ratzinger speaks of such assistance "from without" in terms of "the sureness of the Christian memory,"[168] that through our incorporation into the body of Christ makes us sharers in "the anamnesis of the new 'we.'"[169]

164. Ratzinger, "Conscience and Truth," 535.

165. Crawford, "Natural Law and the Body," 330. In this sense, Crawford speaks of conscience (anamnesis) as an intersection between speculative and practical reason.

166. Ratzinger, *God and the World*, 91.

167. Ratzinger, "Conscience and Truth," 536.

168. Ratzinger, "Conscience and Truth," 537.

169. Ratzinger, "Conscience and Truth," 536. Ratzinger explains: "The original encounter with Jesus gave the disciples what all generations thereafter receive in their

Conscientia

The second level of conscience, which might be considered "from below," is concerned with judgment and decision, applying the recalled knowledge of good and evil to particular situations. According to Aquinas it is not a power but an act.[170] To this faculty tradition has given the term *conscientia*. In this orientation toward judgment and decision we more clearly recognize the practical nature of conscience and of morality in general.[171] Citing Saint Thomas, Ratzinger writes "that conscience is not a *habitus*, that is, a lasting ontic quality of man, but *actus*, an event in execution."[172]

In the Thomistic schema, this faculty of the practical reason is formed and perfected by the virtues, among which the virtue of prudence is foremost.[173] In this context too, therefore, one can recognize the formation of conscience from "within" and from "without." As Pinckaers writes:

> The proper action of prudence is a clear, active discernment of the conditions for action and of oneself, a discernment gained by personal experience and by the kind of reflection that knows how to profit by the opinions and experience of others as well.[174]

From the perspective of faith, such profit comes from the accumulated wisdom of the church and the example of its saints,[175] which give witness to a form of Christian prudence illuminated by faith, strengthened by charity, and guided by the gifts of counsel, understanding, and wisdom.[176]

---

foundational encounter with the Lord in Baptism and the Eucharist, namely, the new *anamnesis* of faith which unfolds, similarly to the *anamnesis* of creation, in constant dialogue between within and without."

170. *STh.*, I, q. 79, a. 13.

171. Following Aquinas, Ratzinger underlines the practical reasoning the lies behind the act of conscience by noting that the conclusions reached "do not come from mere knowing or thinking." Ratzinger, "Conscience and Truth," 538.

172. Ratzinger, "Conscience and Truth," 537.

173. Pinckaers, "Conscience and Christian Tradition," 331. Pinckaers adds that, for Aquinas, prudence "occupies almost the same position that the modern manuals give to the treatise on conscience."

174. Pinckaers, "Conscience and Christian Tradition," 332.

175. Ratzinger, "Bishops, Theologians, and Morality," 56.

176. Pinckaers, "Conscience and Christian Tradition," 332.

Morality, Autonomy, and Freedom

This leads to further important considerations for human morality: our conceptions of autonomy and freedom as moral subjects. In this regard, it has already been noted that critics of moral enhancement express concern that human autonomy would be compromised through biotechnology. We recall John Harris's insistence that moral freedom must include the "freedom to fall," and that moral virtue can only grow within freedom's space between knowing and doing.

For his part, Ratzinger insists that a freedom that is imposed on humanity is no freedom at all.[177] Writing in the context of a critique of utopian conceptions of a perfect society, he explains that external structures cannot make human beings moral. In fact, a society which presumes absolute moral responsibility destroys human freedom,[178] and prevents human beings from acting as moral subjects. He writes: "One cannot free man from his freedom by lining with concrete the channels along which it [the human spirit] must move."[179] In placing freedom at the heart of moral subjectivity, Ratzinger's emphasis is rather different. For him it is not the freedom to fall that is important, but freedom bound to truth. In this, Ratzinger differentiates between negative and positive freedom.

Negative Freedom

Negative freedom is freedom from constraint and obligation: "Every obligation appears as a fetter that restricts freedom; every obligation one eliminates means progress in freedom."[180] Ratzinger highlights various manifestations of this concept of freedom. In the first place there is the demand of the unconstrained right to do whatever one desires. In this context, he quotes Marx's ideal of freedom in the future Communist society: "to do one thing today and another tomorrow; to hunt in the

---

177. Ratzinger, *Church, Ecumenism, and Politics*, 241.

178. As Ratzinger explains, such a society proceeds "from the assumption that it is not man who determines the structures, but the structures that determine man, and that he must necessarily act well if the structures are right. His freedom then consists in the necessity of not being able to do otherwise. Happiness is imposed on him from without. Such a definitively liberated society would therefore be definitive slavery." Ratzinger, *Church, Ecumenism, and Politics*, 253.

179. Ratzinger, *Turning Point*, 91.

180. Ratzinger, *Church, Ecumenism, and Politics*, 243. He adds: "It is clear that in such a view, family, Church, morals, and God must appear as antitheses of freedom."

morning, fish in the afternoon, breed cattle in the evening and criticize after dinner, just as I please."[181] But as Ratzinger objects, a freedom that is concerned only with satisfying need and desire is more akin to animal freedom than it is to human freedom.[182] Furthermore, in being reduced to doing whatever and only what one wants, freedom becomes arbitrariness.[183]

In the Marxist interpretation, anything which constrains upon freedom is to be rejected. As a practical example, Marx cautions against looking backward to our human origins so as not to be bound to the idea of a Creating Mind. Instead, he fixes his gaze on the future, denying the creation of human beings in favor of looking toward what they can create of themselves.[184] In another example, Marxism is suspicious of education as restricting freedom in the hands of authority and tradition. As Ratzinger writes, in the Marxist ideal education is restricted to a pedagogy of freedom: "education to rebel against all preconceived values, the unlimited liberation of the human being, who is himself the first to design himself 'creatively.'"[185]

There is also the existentialist concept of freedom as proposed by Sartre. In this interpretation human beings are condemned to be free. They have no nature to restrain them, being pure existence and without essence.[186] Freedom is therefore independent of any truth claims about what is good, which in any case lie beyond human comprehension. Instead, since human beings can only conceive of their own personal good, freedom consists in "an emancipation from all conditions which prevent each one from following his own reason."[187] In this sense, negative freedom is also referred to as the *freedom of indifference.*

---

181. Ratzinger, "Truth and Freedom," 17.
182. Ratzinger, *Values in a Time of Upheaval*, 48.
183. Ratzinger, *Church, Ecumenism, and Politics*, 242.
184. Ratzinger, *In the Beginning*, 36.
185. Ratzinger, *Church, Ecumenism, and Politics*, 181.
186. Ratzinger, *Church, Ecumenism, and Politics*, 182. He adds: "What he is and what he ought to be are not determined. One must define humanity anew out of the nothingness of an empty freedom. The idea of freedom here has been taken to its most radical extreme: no longer mere emancipation from tradition and authority, but now emancipation from the idea of 'man' as a creature, emancipation from one's own nature, complete indeterminacy that is open to everything. But this very freedom appears simultaneously to be hell; to be free means to be damned."
187. Ratzinger, "Problem of Threats to Human Life," 382.

Finally, there is the positive reduction in which "know-how" becomes the measure of action. As Ratzinger interprets: "If we know how to do it, we are allowed to do it. There is no longer any such thing as knowing how to do something without being allowed to do it—such a situation would be contrary to freedom, which is the supreme, absolute value."[188]

Positive Freedom

Alternatively, Ratzinger speaks of *positive* freedom as respecting and in dialogue with the truth: the truth about God and the human person.[189] Positive freedom is not the freedom to do whatever one wants, but the freedom to know and pursue what is fitting to our human nature as created in the image and likeness of God.

At the heart of concepts of negative freedom, Ratzinger recognizes a theological program: a distorted image of God as "boundlessly free and unrestricted by any limit," and the human desire to become "like" this God.[190] But Ratzinger insists that this desire to be completely free, without ties to nature, history, and others, does not flow from an image of God, but from an idol, the devil. As noted already, the real God, as revealed by Christ, is a God of relation. Accordingly, freedom must be interpreted in the light of Christ's filial obedience, with human freedom "read from within the christological vision of man, who is free not when he defends himself against God, but when he accepts the union with God offered to him in Christ."[191] In imaging God, human freedom "is a freedom in the coexistence of freedoms,"[192] who exists "for," "from," and "with" the other. To use our freedom rightly requires respect for this given nature; "to live our being as an answer—as a response to what we are in truth."[193]

In referring to the work of Jonas, Ratzinger also insists that freedom must be understood in terms of responsibility.[194] Freedom does not only

---

188. Ratzinger, "Europe in the Crisis of Cultures," 352.

189. Ratzinger writes: "If there is no truth about man, man also has no freedom. Only the truth makes us free." Ratzinger, "Truth and Freedom," 35.

190. Ratzinger, *Church, Ecumenism, and Politics*, 243.

191. Ratzinger, "Renewal of Moral Theology," 366–67.

192. Ratzinger, "Truth and Freedom," 32.

193. Ratzinger, "Truth and Freedom," 32.

194. Ratzinger, "Truth and Freedom," 30.

concern individual rights, but a sense of responsibility which recognizes the claims of others, extending beyond the immediate environment and becoming more universal both in space and time. Freedom with responsibility implies "acceptance of the ever greater bonds required both by the claims of humanity's shared existence and by conformity to man's essence."[195] Similarly, freedom with responsibility relativizes the technological imperative that equates knowing how to do something with being allowed to do it. Instead, Ratzinger speaks of an imperative toward recognition of the moral sphere; toward the admission that human action is not only limited by physical laws, but equally by moral principles. The human person is free "when he not only bows to the law of necessity but also acknowledges the law of freedom as the sphere that determines him."[196]

Summary

In presenting the very real problem of the disjunction between technological development and moral progress, and the subsequent threats that face humanity, Savulescu and Persson admit to having painted a "rather gloomy" picture.[197] Yet it appears that the despair goes much deeper than doubts over the prospect of finding a solution to the crises that threaten us. As noted, there is despair over the goodness of human nature itself, formed through the evolutionary fight for survival, tainted by self-interest and immediate concerns, conditioned by fear, and limited in altruism. There is despair over the limitations of culture to be morally informative, with traditional forms of education, laws, religion, and ethics deemed incapable of providing reliable and lasting moral formation. Ultimately, there is despair over the ability to break free from the constraints of the positivistic categories of calculation and control, as witnessed in Persson and Savulescu's reversion to technological solutions, despite an "awakening" to the deceptive hopes of technological progress.

In contrast, Ratzinger presents a truly hopeful account of human morality, building on an anthropology that has its roots in the goodness and rationality of creation. From the beginning, human morality is formed by relationality—by the encounter with another—not in a crude

---

195. Ratzinger, "Truth and Freedom," 30.
196. Ratzinger, *Turning Point*, 175.
197. Persson and Savulescu, "Perils of Cognitive Enhancement," 173.

fight for survival, but in the acknowledgment of communion and dependence. This is the basis of a morality rooted in love, in which the goodness of the other is affirmed. This capacity for love allows human beings to surpass the limitations of their biases and moral myopia, moving from the particularity of love toward the universal horizon of concern. Thus, morality has a truly personal character. It cannot be institutionalized or replaced by technology. In the face of the crises that threaten humanity today, only a truly human response will suffice. As Guardini writes: "We have to become lords of the unleashed forces and shape them into a new order that relates to humanity. In the last resort only living people and not the tackling of technological problems themselves can do this."[198]

In the end, the transhumanist solution of moral bioenhancement will not only prove to be ineffective, failing to engage the core of human morality, but it will also dehumanize us by rejecting that which is most personal to our nature. The prospect of moral bioenhancement is thus most disturbing in subverting human beings' identity as acting persons and moral subjects—substituting impersonal technology in the place of individual conscience, personal authenticity, and the realization of the vocation to love.

---

198. Guardini, *Letters from Lake Como*, "Ninth Letter," 82–83.

Chapter 9

Should We Live Forever?

The Transhumanist Quest for Immortality versus Ratzinger's Hopeful Eschatology

As noted in chapter 6, the authenticity of hope faces its greatest challenge before the reality of death. Utopianism in its various forms attempts to deny this reality, but in the end they are revealed as forms of despair. In this final chapter, it is my intention to show that the transhumanist quest for age extension is in keeping with the utopian despair over the contingency of our human lot. Indeed, I suggest that it is in its quest for immortality that transhumanism's despair, and its rejection of the human condition, is most pronounced.

I begin this chapter with a presentation of the transhumanist case against aging and death, metaphorically portrayed in Bostrom's *Fable of the Dragon Tyrant*. In it Bostrom outlines the badness of aging and its overshadowing of life. He challenges the rhetoric of those who preach caution, admonishes against acceptance of the *status quo*, and invokes a moral imperative to find a cure for aging. Since he is confident that science can indeed find such a cure, a brief look at the science of age-retardation and lifespan extension follows.

A response to the quest to extend the human lifespan is in two parts. An initial response draws together the main points against the transhumanist case, as primarily expressed in the criticism of Leon Kass and Gilbert Meilaender and their work together on the President's Council. Noting a connection between the determination of the badness of aging and the quest for immortality, these critics defend the blessing of finitude: the condition for our appreciation of the goods of human life, for taking life seriously, for appreciating beauty and practicing virtue. Before the prospect of an indefinite extension of the lifespan, concern is also raised over its effect on intergenerational relations, on our appreciation of the cycle of life, and the meaning of generativity. In this context, death is presented as a necessary aspect of our contingency, and as giving meaning to our desire for transcendence.

A proper interpretation of our desire for transcendence forms the second part of the response to the prospect of lifespan extension, in which I draw exclusively on the wisdom of Ratzinger. In light of the human capacity for transcendence, he speaks pointedly against the insufficiency of "more of this life" to satisfy our aspirations. Indeed, he considers the quest for an earthly utopia as a mutilation of our human nature, a denial of our greatness and as robbing us of real hope. The mystery of life and death cannot be reduced to empirical concepts but requires a more profound understanding that only faith can provide: a faith that promises a future and recasts the concepts of life and death in terms of a communion of love. As Ratzinger suggests, this has practical implications for living, in which we even now have a foretaste of the fullness of life in our experiences of love and our communion with God. In this context, the transhumanist quest for lifespan extension is not only revealed as a misinterpretation of our hope for the future, but as a dehumanization of our lives here and now.

The Fable of the Dragon Tyrant

The Fable

In *The Fable of the Dragon Tyrant*, Bostrom recounts the mythical story of a kingdom tormented by a tyrannical dragon, afflicting suffering and death on human beings, demanding thousands[1] of souls every day in order to satiate its horrendous appetite. After various unsuccessful attempts to overthrow the dragon, the majority of the citizens resolve themselves to its presence and to their fate. Life in the kingdom is conformed to this reality. The selection and transportation of victims for the dragon

---

1. Ten thousand per day originally, rising to one hundred thousand by the end of the fable.

requires a systematic organization, which together with compensation owed to the families of victims, poses a significant economic burden on the State. In the uncertainty of their future, people tend to have more children, beginning from a younger age. In light of their inevitable fate as dragon fodder, people seek consolation in the thought of a life after death. They attempt to justify the dragon's existence as part of the natural order, or as a means of preventing over-population.[2]

But despite such concessions, and notwithstanding the disillusionment of previous failures to kill the dragon, a handful of hopeful scientists continue in the search for means to overcome the tyrant. Through their perseverance they succeed in producing a composite material capable of penetrating the dragon's "impenetrable" scales. If fashioned into a projectile, and launched with sufficient force, it is hoped that it might succeed in killing the dragon. However, its production will be expensive.

A request for public funding is rejected because of more immediate concerns within the kingdom: the threat of a menacing tiger, an infestation of rattlesnakes, the costs of new infrastructure to meet the increasing demands of the dragon. Notwithstanding, a public meeting is held to openly debate the merits of the plan to kill the dragon. A leading scientist presents the "antidragonist" proposal. In response, the king's chief advisor for morality speaks of the willfulness and presumptuousness of the proposal, asserting its threat to human dignity and espousing the blessing of human finitude.[3] In a moment of silence between speakers, a young boy from the audience cries out: "The dragon is bad!" Indeed, the child's

---

[2]. "Spiritual men sought to comfort those who were afraid of being eaten by the dragon (which included almost everyone, although many denied it in public) by promising another life after death, a life that would be free from the dragon scourge. Other orators argued that the dragon had its place in the natural order and a moral right to be fed. They said it was part of the very meaning of being human to end up in the dragon's stomach. Others still maintained that the dragon was good for the human species because it kept the population size down." Bostrom, "Fable of the Dragon Tyrant," 273.

[3]. "The finitude of human life is a blessing for every individual, whether he knows it or not. Getting rid of the dragon, which might seem like such a convenient thing to do, would undermine our human dignity. The preoccupation with killing the dragon will deflect us from realising more fully the aspirations to which our lives naturally point, from living well rather than merely staying alive. It is debasing, yes debasing, for a person to want to continue his or her mediocre life for as long as possible without worrying about some of the higher questions about what life is to be used for." Bostrom, "Fable of the Dragon Tyrant," 275.

SHOULD WE LIVE FOREVER?

grandmother had recently been taken away as food for the dragon. "The dragon is bad and it eats people," he repeated. "I want my Granny back!"[4]

In the midst of the debate, the child's simple words "punctured the rhetorical balloon" of the opposition argument.[5] The dragon had terrorized the kingdom for too long and they would make every effort to overcome it. However, despite the simplicity of the concept, the realization of the antidragon missile proved expensive, time consuming, and risky.[6] Yet in the end, skill and perseverance was rewarded with the production of the projectile.

On the day agreed for its launch, an expectant crowd assembles. As the projectile is launched, all follow its path: a "white flame, shooting into the dark, embodying the human spirit, its fear and its hope . . . striking at the heart of evil."[7] As the missile hits its tyrannical target, the people as one rejoice, overcome by the realization that their lives would be forever changed. "We did it!" they cried. But amid the rejoicing, the King was subdued. "Yes, we did it, we killed the dragon today. But damn, why did we start so late? This could have been done five, maybe ten years ago! Millions of people wouldn't have had to die."[8]

The Moral

The dragon in the fable is an allegory for aging (senescence) and for the suffering and death that accompany it. In the past, in the face of the inevitability of death, approaches to aging encouraged "graceful accommodation" and "resignation," accompanied by "an effort to achieve closure in practical affairs and personal relationships."[9] Faced with no other alternative, such advice made sense. But Bostrom insists that the current situation is different. While science and technology have not yet succeeded in slowing the aging process, he is confident that success is foreseeable.[10] In

---

4. Bostrom, "Fable of the Dragon Tyrant," 275.
5. Bostrom, "Fable of the Dragon Tyrant," 275.
6. "In one tragic accident, a wayward missile landed on a hospital and killed several hundred patients and staff. Now, however, there was a real seriousness of purpose, and the tests continued even as the corpses were being dug out from the debris." Bostrom, "Fable of the Dragon Tyrant," 275.
7. Bostrom, "Fable of the Dragon Tyrant," 276.
8. Bostrom, "Fable of the Dragon Tyrant," 276.
9. Bostrom, "Fable of the Dragon Tyrant," 276.
10. "Many distinguished technologists and scientists tell us that it will become

the light of such hope, acceptance of the *status quo* is intolerable. He is insistent: "'Deathist' stories and ideologies, which counsel passive acceptance, are no longer harmless sources of consolation. They are reckless and dangerous barriers to urgently needed action."[11]

In this context, the rhetoric of the king's morality advisor, who spoke eloquently against the plan to slay the dragon, is intended as a caricature of the voices raised against the prospect of human enhancement through age extension.[12] In contrast, like the boy's impassioned cry, Bostrom means to cut through the rhetoric by asserting that "aging is bad." Human senescence destroys people; it is "the principal cause of an unfathomable amount of human suffering and death."[13] Just as there were urgent and compelling reasons to destroy the dragon, so there exist important motives to overcome the aging process. As Bostrom writes: "Searching for a cure for aging is not just a nice thing that we should perhaps one day get around to. It is an urgent, screaming moral imperative."[14]

Does Overcoming Aging Constitute a Human Good?

From the perspective of our finitude, we admittedly cling to life and are attracted to the promise of more.[15] Transhumanists, like Bostrom, interpret these impulses as justifying the pursuit of age extension. Like the attempt to relativize the term "enhancement" to include any improvement

---

possible to retard, and eventually to halt and reverse, human senescence." Bostrom, "Fable of the Dragon Tyrant," 276.

11. Bostrom, "Fable of the Dragon Tyrant," 276.

12. Bostrom cites Leon Kass's case against enhancement in "Ageless Bodies, Happy Souls." The role of the "king's morality advisor" is no doubt intended as a pun on Kass's position as chairman of the President's Council on Bioethics which he held at the time of the publication of *Beyond Therapy*, but also includes other council members who have individually expressed concern over the prospect of life extension, such as Gilbert Meilaender, Francis Fukuyama, and Michael Sandel.

13. Bostrom, "Fable of the Dragon Tyrant," 277. Elsewhere he writes: "In the developed world, aging is currently the number one killer. Aging is also the biggest cause of illness, disability and dementia." Bostrom, "Transhumanist Values," 13.

14. Bostrom, "Fable of the Dragon Tyrant," 277.

15. For example, Kass writes: "The case for ageless bodies seems at first glance to look pretty good. The prevention of decay, decline, and disability, the avoidance of blindness, deafness, and debility, the elimination of feebleness, frailty, and fatigue, all seem to be conducive to living fully as a human being at the top of one's powers—of having, as they say, a 'good quality of life' from beginning to end." Kass, "Ageless Bodies, Happy Souls," 24.

or development, so he attempts to relativize the terms of lifespan extension by suggesting that we all implicitly seek to extend our lifespan. He suggests that our everyday behavior reflects this desire for more life: we go to the doctor when sick, install airbags in cars, pay higher salaries to those who engage in physically risky work, and give money for medical research.[16]

This clinging to life does not necessarily correspond to a desire for immortality. According to Bostrom's fable, it is aging that is bad, not death. However, in treating aging as a kind of disorder, "as a disease to be cured, we are, in principle, and at least tacitly, expressing a desire never to grow old and die, or, in a word, a desire to live forever."[17] This is compounded by the fact that age-retardation has no definable end point.[18] Thus, despite objections to the contrary, the pursuit of life extension becomes synonymous with the quest for immortality.[19]

As briefly noted in chapter 2, an adequate response to the question of life extension cannot be limited to feasibility. A more fundamental question concerns the goodness of the object of the transhumanist hope to overcome aging and death.[20] Indeed, Meilaender insists that even if the quest for immortality turns out in the end to be no more than a "pipe dream," the fact that it is even proposed as the object of hope demands a response, since our hopes define us.[21] Similarly, he suggests that "there is no metaphysically neutral ground from which to discuss whether an immortal life could be satisfying,"[22] since satisfaction depends on a determination of what a human being is and a concept of human flourishing.[23]

---

16. Bostrom, "Why I Want to Be a Posthuman," 33.
17. President's Council on Bioethics, *Beyond Therapy*, 186.
18. President's Council on Bioethics, *Beyond Therapy*, 162.

19. As Kass explains: "For truth to tell, victory over mortality is the unstated but implicit goal of modern medical science, indeed of the entire modern scientific project, to which mankind was summoned almost four hundred years ago by Francis Bacon and René Descartes. They quite consciously trumpeted the conquest of nature for the relief of man's estate, and they founded a science whose explicit purpose was to reverse the curse laid on Adam and Eve, and especially to restore the tree of life, by means of the tree of (scientific) knowledge." Kass, "L'Chaim and Its Limits," 18–19.

20. Kass writes: "The core question is this: Is it really true that longer life for individuals is an unqualified good?" "L'Chaim and Its Limits," 19.

21. "What we hope for tells us a great deal about who we are." Meilaender, *Should We Live Forever?*, 23.

22. Meilaender, *Should We Live Forever?*, 42.

23. "In order to know how best to characterize a complete human life, we have to know what sort of being a human being is." Meilaender, *Should We Live Forever?*, 96.

In the same spirit, Hans Jonas ponders how desirable an indefinite extension of lifespan would be for the individual and for the species. "These questions," he suggests, "involve the very meaning of our finitude, the attitude toward death, and the general biological significance of the balance of death and procreation."[24]

The Blessing of Mortality

On the basis of this clarification, critics object that an immortal life would not be human.[25] Kass writes:

> For to argue that human life would be better without death is, I submit, to argue that human life would be better being something other than human. To be immortal would not be just to continue life as we mortals now know it, only forever. The new immortals, in the decisive sense, would not be like us at all.[26]

In defense of a truly human life, Kass posits the necessity of death. He speaks of "the virtues of mortality"[27] and "the blessings of finitude,"[28] echoing Jonas's concept of the "blessing" of mortality.[29] He draws out certain human goods that would be threatened by immortality: "goods that are inseparable from our aging bodies, from our living in time, and from the natural human life cycle by which each generation gives way to the one that follows it."[30] Such goods include the capacity for seriousness, for seeking meaning, for the appreciation of beauty and the possibility of virtue, as well as the goods associated with the ties between generations. They exist in proportion to our consciousness of our finitude and would be threatened by a life that extends indefinitely into the future. Accordingly, Kass asks:

> Could life be serious or meaningful without the limit of mortality? Is not the limit on our time the ground of our taking life

---

24. Jonas, *Imperative of Responsibility*, 18.

25. As Bellver Capella writes: "The human immortality project is nothing more than the door leading to the post-human world." Bellver Capella, "Ethics and Policies," 498.

26. Kass, "L'Chaim and Its Limits," 20.

27. Kass, "L'Chaim and Its Limits," 20.

28. Kass, "Ageless Bodies, Happy Souls," 25.

29. Jonas, "Burden and Blessing of Mortality."

30. Kass, "Ageless Bodies, Happy Souls," 25.

seriously and living it passionately? To know and to feel that one goes around only once, and that the deadline is not out of sight, is for many people the necessary spur to the pursuit of something worthwhile. "Teach us to number our days," says the Psalmist, "that we may get a heart of wisdom."[31]

Jonas underlines the importance of mortality in teaching us wisdom, as a necessary "incentive to number our days and make them count."[32] Robert Spaemann similarly speaks of human significance as "meaning 'toughened' by the consciousness of finitude—by which is understood that it asserts itself in the face of death."[33] Meilaender too warns that lives extending indefinitely into the future would lose their sense of meaning; that without an end, the steps along the way would lack significance.[34] Mortality therefore exists as something essential to our human reality. It makes living possible, bestows meaning on our lives, and shows forth it value.[35] Stephan Kampowski adds: "In short, the temporality of our earthly existence, its unfolding from a beginning to an end, appears to be a condition by which we hold on to life as something precious."[36]

In keeping with this awakening to life's preciousness, Kass makes a connection between mortality, our appreciation of beauty, and our capacity to love. He offers several explanations for this connection. In

---

31. Kass, "L'Chaim and Its Limits," 21. The President's Council writes: "Many of our greatest accomplishments are pushed along, if only subtly and implicitly, by the spur of our finitude and the sense of having only a limited time. A far more distant horizon, a sense of essentially limitless time, might leave us less inclined to act with urgency. Why not leave for tomorrow what you might do today, if there are endless tomorrows before you?" President's Council on Bioethics, *Beyond Therapy*, 188.

32. Jonas, *Imperative of Responsibility*, 19.

33. Spaemann, *Persons*, 119.

34. "But for these steps to have meaning, for them to give our lives significance, there must be more to them than the overcoming of old limits. They must go somewhere, have some end, find their place in a story whose overall shape makes and gives sense." Meilaender, *Should We Live Forever?*, 85.

35. "The reason that living things *are* emphatically, i.e., the reason that they show concern for their being and value it, is precisely because of death, because they are constantly pitted against non-being, so that, in a somewhat paradoxical way, death turns out to be one of the very conditions of the possibility of life as concerned existence, that is, an existence that affirms and treasures itself." Kampowski, *Greater Freedom*, 52–53.

36. "In breve, la temporalità della nostra esistenza terrena, il suo svolgersi da un inizio ad un termine, sembra essere una condizione per cui teniamo alla vita come a qualcosa di prezioso." Kampowski, *Ricordati della nascita*, 194.

the first place, our fascination for the beautiful, and our desire to surround ourselves with objects of beauty, may be provoked by our awareness of our mortality "and the transience and vulnerability of all natural things."[37] Objects of beauty are therefore created as an immunization against death.[38] Alternatively, he speaks of the connection between death and the fragile beauty of nature, suggesting that its beauty depends on its ephemeral quality.[39] In similar fashion, Kass wonders whether love is inspired by the impermanence of our being; that our appreciation of the other, like the appreciation of the passing glory of the things of nature, is enhanced by their transience. He therefore wonders: "How deeply could one deathless 'human' being love another?"[40]

Finally, a connection is made between mortality and one's capacity for *virtue and moral excellence*; the possibility of giving one's life for another. Only mortal beings are so capable.[41] Fukuyama reiterates the point by asking some probing questions:

> Will people still be willing to sacrifice their lives for others, when their lives could potentially stretch out ahead of them indefinitely, or condone the sacrifice of the lives of others? Will they cling desperately to the life that biotechnology offers? Or might the prospect of an unending empty life appear simply unbearable?[42]

Intergenerational Relations and the Meaning of a Generative Life

As noted above, Jonas implies that the question of mortality touches on the biological significance of the balance of death and procreation.

---

37. Kass, "L'Chaim and Its Limits," 21.

38. Kass suggests that "only a mortal being, aware of his mortality and the transience and vulnerability of all natural things, is moved to make beautiful artifacts, objects that will last, objects whose order will be immune to decay as their maker is not." Kass, "L'Chaim and Its Limits," 21.

39. "Could the beauty of flowers depend on the fact that they will soon wither? Does the beauty of spring warblers depend upon the fall drabness that precedes and follows? What about the fading, late afternoon winter light or the spreading sunset? Is the beautiful necessarily fleeting, a peak that cannot be sustained?" Kass, "L'Chaim and Its Limits," 21.

40. Kass, "L'Chaim and Its Limits," 21.

41. "To be mortal means that it is possible to give one's life, not only in one moment, say, on the field of battle, but also in the many other ways in which we are able in action to rise above attachment to survival." Kass, "L'Chaim and Its Limits," 21–22.

42. Fukuyama, *Our Posthuman Future*, 71.

"Having to die is bound up with having been born: mortality is but the other side of the perennial spring of 'natality' (to use Hannah Arendt's term)."[43] The link between mortality and generativity has biological and evolutionary indicators. It has already been noted that nature seems to "abandon" us once we have passed reproductive age. It is also noteworthy that one of the side effects of caloric restriction, which significantly increases one's life span, is reduced fertility.[44]

While the quest for immortality ignores this biological fact, of greater significance is its confusion of the meaning of generativity and the relations between generations. This is of particular concern for Meilaender, who maintains that in the absence of aging, intergenerational relations would be rendered meaningless.[45] In the natural process of aging, one generation makes way for another in a "cycle of succession" in which the vitality of youth, in whom "aspiration, hope, freshness, boldness, and openness spring anew,"[46] proceeds from and is complimented by the stability and wisdom of the aged.[47] The cyclical nature of life is marked by different stages and associated with different levels of dependence: "birth and initiation into life; developing personal life projects and taking on responsibilities; and outcome, generally preceded by a gradual decline of physical and cognitive faculties."[48] Life is more than a progression of individual moments.[49] Looked at from the perspective of the generations,

---

43. Jonas, *Imperative of Responsibility*, 19. Cf. Arendt, *Human Condition*, 247: "The miracle that saves the world, the realm of human affairs, from its normal, 'natural' ruin is ultimately the fact of natality, in which the faculty of action is ontologically rooted. It is, in other words, the birth of new men and the new beginning, the action they are capable of by virtue of being born."

44. Meilaender, *Should We Live Forever?*, 58.

45. "Once we begin to attend to the parent-child bond, or more generally to the relations between generations, we have begun to think not just of life but of a 'complete life'—a life marked in some way by stages and movement, a life that has shape and not just duration, a life whose moments are not identical but take their specific character from their place in the whole. Moreover, it is difficult to imagine a 'relation between the generations' that does not include aging—coming into being and going out of being." Meilaender, *Should We Live Forever?*, 15.

46. Kass, "L'Chaim and Its Limits," 23–24.

47. "The cycle of succession proceeds, and the world is made fresh with a new generation, but is kept firmly rooted by the experience and hard-earned wisdom of the old." President's Council on Bioethics, *Beyond Therapy*, 194.

48. Bellver Capella, "Ethics and Policies," 500.

49. Meilaender, *Should We Live Forever?*, 31. Kass adds: "Those who propose adding years to the human lifespan regard time abstractly, as physicists do, as a

and acknowledging its social, psychological and spiritual dimensions, life has "a narrative shape."[50] In this richer context, aging is much more than a biological process. It is an essential experience that affords meaning to the whole biography of one's life.

The quest for age extension denies the cycle to life and the importance of intergenerational relations. Should we be successful in significantly prolonging life its narrative shape would be lost.[51] With an indeterminate extension of the stage of function and independence, the perceived need to pass on to the next generation would be blurred. "The succession of generations could be obstructed by a glut of the able. The old might think less of preparing their replacements, and the young could see before them only layers of their elders blocking the path, and no great reason to hurry in building families or careers."[52] "Unhinged" from the life cycle, one is in danger of losing one's place within the generations; of losing a sense of time, age and change.[53] From the point of view of the younger generations, there is the risk of perpetual immaturity: of "remaining functionally immature 'young adults' for decades, neither willing nor able to step into the shoes of their mothers and fathers."[54] From the perspective of the perpetually mature generations, there is the risk of self-centeredness and an unwillingness to "make way" for others. As Meilaender writes, "A simple thirst for more (and more) life might seem to carry an unmistakable whiff of narcissism,[55] for it is hard to imagine

---

homogeneous and continuous dimension, each part exactly like any other, and the whole lacking shape or pattern. Yet, the 'lived time' of our natural lives has a trajectory and a shape, its meaning derived in part from the fact that we live as links in the chain of generations." Kass, "Ageless Bodies," 26.

50. Meilaender, *Should We Live Forever?*, 31–32.
51. Bellver Capella, "Ethics and Policies," 500.
52. President's Council on Bioethics, *Beyond Therapy*, 194–95.
53. President's Council on Bioethics, *Beyond Therapy*, 192.
54. President's Council on Bioethics, *Beyond Therapy*, 194–95.

55. Kass writes: "For the desire to prolong youthfulness is not only a childish desire to eat one's life and keep it; it is also an expression of a childish and narcissistic wish incompatible with devotion to posterity. It seeks an endless present, isolated from anything truly eternal, and severed from any true continuity with past and future. It is in principle hostile to children, because children, those who come after, are those who will take one's place; *they* are life's answer to mortality, and their presence in one's house is a constant reminder that one no longer belongs to the frontier generation. One cannot pursue agelessness for oneself and remain faithful to the spirit and meaning of perpetuation." Kass, "L'Chaim and Its Limits," 23.

how we can act responsibly toward the generations that succeed us if we cling firmly (and desperately?) to our own continued youthfulness."[56]

Related to the distortion of intergenerational relations, an indefinite extension of life also risks a loss of meaning and significance. While transhumanists perceive boundless opportunities for pursuing life-enriching experiences that the limitations of our current lifespan curtail, lifespan extension bears with it the danger of "horrifying" boredom[57] at the interminable monotony of "more of the same."[58] As Kass writes: "After a while, no matter how healthy we are, no matter how respected and well placed we are socially, most of us cease to look upon the world with fresh eyes. Little surprises us, nothing shocks us, righteous indignation at injustice dies out. We have seen it all already, seen it all."[59]

A Further Imperative of Contingency

In *The Immortalization Commission* John Gray writes: "The pursuit of immortality through science is only incidentally a project to defeat death. At bottom it is an attempt to escape contingency and mystery."[60] The pursuit of life extension is therefore another manifestation of transhumanism's

---

56. Meilaender, *Should We Live Forever?*, 15–16.

57. At the prospect of an indefinite extension of life as it is, though free from pain and suffering and enriched by intelligence and benevolence, Bellver Capella objects: "This utopia is both boring and horrifying at the same time. Human existence consists of confronting challenges, in which success or failure does not depend entirely one [sic] oneself. If (post)human existence came to consist of the inexorable realization of one's own desires by means of an intelligence of cosmic proportions it might be unbearably boring." Bellver Capella, "Ethics and Policies," 498.

58. "Our spirits are kept alive by new discoveries, by hopes yet unfulfilled but worth striving for, by experiences had for the first time. Now it is the fate of the earthly immortals that they no longer have the experience of the new." Kampowski, *Greater Freedom*, 57.

59. Kass, "L'Chaim and Its Limits," 23. The President's Council echoes these concerns: "Familiarity and routine blunt awareness. Fewer things shock or surprise. Disappointed hopes and broken dreams, accumulated mistakes and misfortunes, and the struggle to meet the economic and emotional demands of daily life can take their toll in diminished ambition, insensitivity, fatigue, and cynicism—not in everyone, to be sure, but in many people growing older. As a general matter, a society's aspiration, hope, freshness, boldness, and openness depend for their continual renewal on the spirit of youth, of those to whom the world itself is new and full of promise." President's Council on Bioethics, *Beyond Therapy*, 195–96.

60. Gray, *Immortalization Commission*, 213. Gray is cited both in Bellver Capella, "Ethics and Policies," 498 and Meilaender, *Should We Live Forever?*, 28.

desire to overcome the unpredictability of the human condition, to assume control over every aspect of our lives, to leave nothing to the unbidden. As Meilaender writes:

> Not to be in control, to suffer the limits of a fate we have not chosen—that is the enemy. The goal of indefinite life-extension is not so much in service of particular loves or projects as it is in service of one indefinitely expansive desire—to become agents who are not at the mercy of forces beyond our own control, in particular, the forces of decline and decay that are built into the very nature of organic life.[61]

But in the effort to overcome contingency, we find ourselves at odds with our nature as dependent beings. As Meilaender wisely explains: "Our agency is not mastery but participation in a power greater than our own."[62] In attempting to assume ever more control and responsibility for our lives we risk losing what Sandel identifies as the "blessing" that "we are not wholly responsible for the way we are."[63] As created beings, therefore, we cannot negate our contingency. As already noted by Spaemann in chapter 7, death and birth, coming in and going out of live, are equally marked by contingence. Thus, in response to attempts to extend life toward immortality, we can also speak of an "imperative of contingency" which recognizes the necessity of death.

Yearning for Immortality as a Sign of Transcendence

Positing the blessings of mortality does not negate the authenticity of the human desire for immortality. It is simply that transhumanism, with its pursuit of more of this life, misinterprets a fundamental human aspiration. As Kass explains, in the face of mortality the natural desire for more life simply points to the fact that there is something more to the human person than this temporal existence.

---

61. Meilaender, *Should We Live Forever?*, 28.
62. Meilaender, *Should We Live Forever?*, 83.
63. Sandel, *Case Against Perfection*, 87: "One of the blessings of seeing ourselves as creatures of nature, God, or fortune is that we are not wholly responsible for the way we are. The more we become masters of our genetic endowments, the greater the burden we bear for the talents we have and the way we perform. Today when a basketball player misses a rebound, his coach can blame him for being out of position. Tomorrow the coach may blame him for being too short."

> The promise of immortality and eternity answers rather to a deep truth about the human soul: the human soul yearns for, longs for, aspires to some condition, some state, some goal toward which our earthly activities are directed but which cannot be attained in earthly life. Our soul's reach exceeds our grasp; it seeks more than continuance; it reaches for something beyond us, something that for the most part eludes us. Our distress with mortality is the derivative manifestation of the conflict between the transcendent longings of the soul and the all-too-finite powers and fleshly concerns of the body.[64]

As Kass notes, the interpretation of this "something more" varies between cultures and times: the naturalistic desire to survive through another; the classical Greek notion of attaining wisdom; the Christian concept of the beatific vision. But despite these variations in aspiration, he underlines a common denominator: not a yearning for "deathlessness," but for "wholeness, wisdom, goodness, and godliness"[65] that signify more than length of days. In other words, "mere continuance" of more of the same cannot satisfy the human aspiration for immortality.

Meilaender is even more explicit in this regard.

> The restless heart longs to live forever because it longs for God—not vice versa. To live an indefinitely prolonged life but never to see God, to be always on the way but with no *telos* that gives a point to the journey, might be pleasant in many ways, but it could not satisfy the heart's deepest desire.[66]

Here again we are faced with the reality that transcendence, the "freedom to step beyond nature's limits,"[67] is integral to human fulfillment and cannot be substituted by a mere increase of this life, however long. Our restlessness for something more is significant of our teleological nature; that "we are always incomplete, always *in viatoribus*, always on the way."[68] To settle for more of the same is a refutation of our human greatness, a denial of our capacity for God. Indeed, an indefinite extension of our present reality can only seem attractive when "the human eros for God" is suppressed.[69]

64. Kass, "L'Chaim and Its Limits," 22.
65. Kass, "L'Chaim and Its Limits," 22.
66. Meilaender, *Should We Live Forever?*, 51.
67. Meilaender, *Should We Live Forever?*, 18–19.
68. Meilaender, *Should We Live Forever?*, 36.
69. Meilaender, *Should We Live Forever?*, 36. Kass writes: "It is probably no

It is precisely here that hope enters in.[70] In this context, Meilaender discerns a significant difference between transhumanism's optimism and the virtue of hope. Borrowing a term from David Kelsey,[71] Meilaender speaks of the "eccentric" nature of hope that, in seeking fulfillment, looks "not to the natural course of life, nor to the achievements of human progress or history, but to the genuinely creative and re-creative power that is God's."[72] Hope draws us "out of ourselves" toward something definitive and incorruptible. At this point, Meilaender significantly quotes an Easter homily of Benedict XVI in which he insists that a "cure for death" cannot exist in an indefinite prolongation of life as we know it, but must "transform our lives from within," making us "fit for eternity."[73]

The Significance of Life and Death according to Ratzinger

In the same homily, Benedict sums up much of what has been discussed to date regarding the prospect of overcoming death:

> Modern medical science strives, if not exactly to exclude death, at least to eliminate as many as possible of its causes, to postpone it further and further, to prolong life more and more. But let us reflect for a moment: what would it really be like if we were to succeed, perhaps not in excluding death totally, but in postponing it indefinitely, in reaching an age of several hundred years?

---

accident that it is a generation whose intelligentsia proclaim the death of God and the meaninglessness of life that embarks on life's indefinite prolongation and that seeks to cure the emptiness of life by extending it forever." Kass, "L'Chaim and Its Limits," 23.

70. "Hope is the virtue that sustains us on the way toward the divine beauty and goodness—protecting us against a presumption which supposes that any of us could here and now become a *comprehensor*, as if an indefinitely extended earthly life, whether organic or virtual, could quench our longing. And protecting us also against despair, against the temptation to make of our vulnerability a virtue." Meilaender, *Should We Live Forever?*, 36.

71. Kelsey, *Eccentric Existence*.

72. Meilaender, *Should We Live Forever?*, 34. In this context Meilaender also draws on Aquinas's distinction between a *comprehensor* and a *viator*. "A *comprehensor* possesses—and cannot lose—the happiness he desires. A *viator*, by contrast, is always and only on the way to that desired end. Hence, we can hope only for what is not yet a permanent and present condition. Hope is possible only for those for whom life, however long, always seems less than complete—'those who are still en route' (*in viatoribus*)." Ibid., 36. Cf. *STh.*, II–II, q. 18, a. 3.

73. Meilaender, *Should We Live Forever?*, 106.

Would that be a good thing? Humanity would become extraordinarily old, there would be no more room for youth. Capacity for innovation would die, and endless life would be no paradise, if anything a condemnation. The true cure for death must be different. It cannot lead simply to an indefinite prolongation of this current life. It would have to transform our lives from within. It would need to create a new life within us, truly fit for eternity: it would need to transform us in such a way as not to come to an end with death, but only then to begin in fullness.[74]

As noted, he questions the goodness of the object of an indefinite extension of our current lives, the effect on relations between old and young, and diminishment of things innovative and new. In other words, his concern is for human fulfillment and for the maintenance of authentic hope.

The Absurdity of Lifespan Extension

Here, one can identify themes present in Ratzinger's writings before assuming the chair of Peter. In the first place, he is insistent that more of this life cannot satisfy the yearnings of the human spirit, since in their teleological nature human beings are oriented beyond themselves. In this, Ratzinger echoes the thought of Aquinas: "If a thing be ordained to another as to its end, its last end cannot consist in the preservation of its being."[75] Or as Pieper translates: "The allaying of the thirst cannot consist simply in the mere continued existence of the thirster."[76] Accordingly, Ratzinger considers an eternal recurrence of the same a form of damnation, an absurdity,[77] a "nightmare."[78] While the temporal framework of

---

74. Benedict XVI, "Homily," Holy Saturday, April 3, 2010.

75. *STh.*, I–II, q. 2, a. 5.

76. Pieper, *Happiness and Contemplation*, 36. He adds: "Man as he is constituted, endowed as he is with a thirst for happiness, cannot have his thirst quenched in the finite realm; and if he thinks or behaves as if that were possible, he is misunderstanding himself, he is acting contrary to his own nature. The whole world would not suffice this 'natural' nature of man. If the whole world were given to him, he would have to say, and would say: It is too little. Too little, that is, to 'gratify entirely the power of desire,' or in other words, too little to make him happy" (38–39). Cf. *STh.*, I–II, q. 2, a. 8.

77. Ratzinger, *Images of Hope*, 105.

78. "No one can wish for himself that things will continue endlessly in this way; the endlessness of our everyday life is not a worthwhile goal, and therefore a medically induced immortality for man and mankind can only be a nightmare after all. Man is

our current life enables us to "get through it," he insists that "we could not bear it for eternity."[79] Instead, we are created for transcendence. We seek to escape the immanent and the temporal. We yearn for something more.[80]

According to Ratzinger, this human "longing for the infinite" should not be denied.[81] The fact that it often is signifies a mutilation of human beings, robbing them of their greatness, their sense of magnanimity, and distorting their hopes. Without a sense of transcendence they grasp for novel solutions, "flights into utopia."[82] As evidence, he notes that Marx rejected transcendence in order to "heal" humanity of false consolations and move toward building the perfect world. Marx feared that the projection of human hope beyond this world would distract us from the task of overcoming the inequalities and injustices that confront human beings here and now. However, Ratzinger rejects the notion that the hope of transcending our current reality signifies an escape from this world and its sufferings. "It is precisely when a man possesses an eternal future, which determines his present, that this present acquires an unheard-of, almost unbearable, significance."[83] Furthermore, in light of the dehumanizing influences of Marxist-inspired systems in their pursuit of an earthly utopia, Ratzinger insists that our hopes must go beyond this world. "Today we know that man needs transcendence so that he can

---

not psychologically equipped for the immortality of the body, and humanity would necessarily break into pieces from the internal tensions caused by the coexistence of generations that were speeding away from each other, not to mention the economic problems that would arise in such a world full of elderly people." Ratzinger, "What Comes After Death?," 256.

79. Ratzinger, *Images of Hope*, 105. Reinforcing the insufficiency of our temporal lives, Ratzinger writes: "Day-to-day living is for the most part merely a shadow existence, a form of Hades, in which we have only the most occasional inkling of what life should truly be. This is why, in general, people have no immediate desire for immortality. The continuance *ad infinitum* of life as it is cannot appear desirable to anybody." Ratzinger, *Eschatology*, 94.

80. Ratzinger, *Turning Point*, 45: "Man needs transcendence. Immanence alone is too narrow for him. He is created for more."

81. Ratzinger, *Images of Hope*, 36.

82. Ratzinger, *Church, Ecumenism, and Politics*, 199.

83. Ratzinger, *Faith and the Future*, 54. Elsewhere Ratzinger writes: "There is no antithesis between hope for heaven and loyalty to the earth, since this hope is also hope for the earth. While we hope for something greater and definitive, we Christians may and must bring hope into that which is transitory, into the world of our states." Ratzinger, *Values in a Time of Upheaval*, 72.

shape his ever-imperfect world in such a way that one can live in it with human dignity."[84]

Here, a parallel may be drawn between Marxism's forgetfulness of death in its march toward the perfect society[85] and the transhumanist project in its pursuit of immortality through curing aging. Both attempt to forge the "new man" through human ingenuity and effort. As Ratzinger puts it, they are attempts to generate an immortal life out of our "own stuff"; to become god-like through our autonomy, independence and self-sufficiency.[86] But he warns that every attempt to create ourselves anew must fail in the end. "No revolution can create a new man,"[87] he insists. Rather, the authentic hope of the "new man" comes from elsewhere. It is not within the power of human beings to achieve. It is not the work of human hands but a gift that is received.[88] Only God is capable of creating us anew, from within.[89]

For this reason, Ratzinger insists that the Christian faith does not recognize a utopia within history. In this he makes a distinction between "utopia" as a political philosophy and "eschatology" as a statement of faith.[90] While admitting of chiliastic attempts to marry the two in the expectation of an intra-historical restoration,[91] Ratzinger insists that "the

---

84. Ratzinger, *Church, Ecumenism, and Politics*, 199.

85. Ratzinger, *Yes of Jesus Christ*, 49.

86. Ratzinger, *Eschatology*, 156.

87. Ratzinger, *Church, Ecumenism, and Politics*, 254.

88. Ratzinger, *Eschatology*, 66.

89. Ratzinger, *Church, Ecumenism, and Politics*, 254. Brice de Malherbe critiques the transhumanist project precisely from this perspective, that human enhancement cannot come through a change of external form, but through an internal transformation through the love of the Holy Spirit: "Pour la tradition chrétienne, l'exaltation de l'homme n'est pas à chercher dans un changement d'espèce, mais dans la transformation interne de tout homme par l'Esprit de Dieu qui repose sur le Christ, un Esprit d'amour." Malherbe, "Créer ou revêtir l'homme nouveau," 39.

90. Ratzinger, "Eschatology and Utopia," 12.

91. Chiliasm has its origins in chapter 20 of the book of Revelation, in which Christ is expected to reign on earth for a thousand years before the end of the world. As a particular expression of chiliastic hope, Ratzinger notes the historicization of utopian expectations in the theologized history of Joachim of Fiore "who deduced a threefold periodization of history from faith in the triune God. The age of the Father, the Old Testament, and the age of the Son, the church as found hitherto, would be followed by an age of the Holy Spirit, characterized by a church living in spontaneous fulfilment of the Sermon on the Mount, through the universally efficacious activity of the Holy Spirit." Ratzinger, *Eschatology*, 13. This in turn opened the way for the "messianic"

idea of history's being brought to its consummation within history forms no part of the eschatological expectation."[92] He argues this not only from the content of faith—of the promise of a resurrection of the dead, a final Judgment, and the coming of the kingdom of God[93]—but claims that it is "rationally intelligible" that the expectation of an intra-historical resolution "is irreconcilable with the perpetual openness and the perpetually peccable freedom of man."[94]

The Limitations of Science before the Problem of Death

In the absence of a proper appreciation of human transcendence, death is incomprehensible. And without a human conception of death, our understanding of life is distorted, for as Ratzinger writes: "Attitudes to dying determine attitudes to living."[95] And again: "Only the one who can see hope in death can also lead a life of hope."[96] As noted above, when death is deemed to be the enemy, a disorder, an obstacle to be overcome, it is reduced to the level of biology. Life and death, health and sickness, are demystified, rationalized, reduced to positivist categories. But in the process, life and death, and human beings themselves, are dehumanized.[97] This reduction of the human person to positivist categories does not throw light on the mystery of life and death but rather confounds their incomprehensibility.[98] As was the case in Ratzinger's critique of the positivist distortion of knowledge, so too a penetrative understanding of the mystery of life and death requires a broader appreciation of human

---

utopias of Hegel and Marx, in which history becomes "a forward-thrusting process, in which man actively works at his salvation, which cannot be known through the bare logic of the present but is guaranteed by the logic of history." Ratzinger, "Eschatology and Utopia," 23.

92. Ratzinger, "Eschatology and Utopia," 19.
93. Ratzinger, *Church, Ecumenism, and Politics*, 253.
94. Ratzinger, "Eschatology and Utopia," 19.
95. Ratzinger, *Eschatology*, 72.
96. Ratzinger, *Images of Hope*, 105.
97. Ratzinger, *Eschatology*, 72.
98. Ratzinger writes: "Since positivist and materialist answers leave us finally perplexed at this crucial juncture, it should be clear that the issues of life and death are not among those which progress in the exact sciences can clarify." Ratzinger, *Eschatology*, 72.

beings, moving beyond a materialist reduction in order to embrace their spiritual natures.

The Meaning of Death in the Light of Faith

Accordingly, Ratzinger returns to the necessity of faith in order to move beyond the measurable and the calculable, and broaden our understanding of the human reality of death. The example has already been given of Abraham, who in response to God's word, "let go of what was safe, comprehensible, calculable, for the sake of what was unknown."[99] In the current context, Abraham's faith becomes a paradigm for the one facing death. His trust "signifies the certainty that it is God who guarantees man his future," breaking free from the limitations of the everyday in order "to make contact with what is eternal."[100] This broadened horizon of faith means that our human existence cannot be confined to this temporal reality. Faith offers a perspective that goes beyond the false sense of security within "what is 'small but my own,' thus depriving him of true greatness."[101] Before the smallness of this life, faith perceives death as a passage toward a greater, transcendent reality.

According to Ratzinger, Abraham's faith in a God-given future is consistent with faith in the promise of the risen Christ.[102] But in Christ, the promise of a future and homeland is radically transformed. As Ratzinger writes, the focus of Christian hope "is not space and time, the question of 'Where?' and 'When?,' but relationship with Christ's person and longing for him to come close."[103] Immortal life does not consist in an extension of the experiences of this life, but in a personal communion of love with God in Jesus Christ.

Through an encounter with Christ we discover what true life is (see John 14:6), and our yearning for eternity is awakened. Thus, as Ratzinger asserts: "The desire for immortality does not arise from the fundamentally unsatisfying enclosed existence of the isolated self, but from the experience of love, of communion, of the Thou."[104] In other words, it is

---

99. Ratzinger, *Faith and the Future*, 40.
100. Ratzinger, *Faith and the Future*, 42.
101. Ratzinger, *Faith and the Future*, 53.
102. Ratzinger, *Faith and the Future*, 49.
103. Ratzinger, *Eschatology*, 8.
104. Ratzinger, *Eschatology*, 94.

not the frustration of a life cut short that sets us yearning for more, but rather the foretaste of a love that promises eternity.[105] This corresponds to what Ratzinger has already asserted, that "the hope which transcends all hopes" is the assurance of a love without end.[106] "Thus all our hopes are at bottom hope in the great and boundless love: they are hope in paradise, the kingdom of God, being with God and like God, sharing his nature (2 Pet 1:4)."[107]

Life in Christ answers both the human yearning for a life after death, as well as the understanding that one cannot survive death alone: what Ratzinger refers to as "man's conviction that he has no permanence on his own and hence can live on only if he lives in another."[108] Throughout human history, this awareness has been expressed through hopes of surviving through others, whether that be through one's offspring, memory, fame, or even the Marxist concept of the perfect society. But as Ratzinger points out, in the end such hopes are unsustainable. Their objects lack permanence for they themselves will pass away. Our hope of living on in another can only be assured if God remembers us.

> Only *he* remains; only *his* thought is reality. And this is precisely the hopeful certainty that biblical faith intends to offer: the Eternal One remembers man; man lives in God's remembering and, thus, lives truly as himself, for God's remembrance is not a shadow but reality.[109]

With immortal life recast in terms of relationship with God through Christ, the Christian perspective of life and death is transformed. In the first place, Ratzinger recognizes different levels of meaning of life. At the basic level, life is biological. Organisms are defined by their capacity for reproduction and self-contained functioning, from the simplicity of single-cell organisms through to higher and more complicated forms of life, "becoming ever more wonderful, richer, and more mysterious."[110] According to Ratzinger's hierarchy of life, the emergence of human beings

---

105. "If isolation is deadly even in this earthly life and if only being-in-relation, love, sustains us, then eternal life only make sense in a quite new totality of love that surpasses all temporality." Ratzinger, *Images of Hope*, 105.

106. Ratzinger, "On Hope," 303.

107. Ratzinger, *Yes of Jesus Christ*, 68.

108. Ratzinger, "What Comes After Death?," 258.

109. Ratzinger, "What Comes After Death?," 258.

110. Ratzinger, *God and the World*, 277.

constitutes a new level. This new level is characterized by the appearance of spirit, "which lives and is itself life,"[111] and when incarnate in biological existence gives rise to a new dimension to life. According to Ratzinger, the potential of our spiritual nature for transcendence reaches its end through encounter with Christ, thus moving us to yet another level of being. "[Life] reaches its highest level when it becomes life with God. It is in this that the whole thrill of the human adventure resides."[112]

If the fullness of life is found in communion with Christ, and "the human capacity for truth and for love is the place where eternal life can break forth,"[113] it follows that one can experience something of eternity here and now. Wherever one experiences the love of Christ, "eternal life" becomes real and present. Accordingly, the "new man" is not a utopian figure of the future. He already exists. And the object of his hope is not a far distant reality, but is in some sense already realized. In this context, Ratzinger draws on Saint Augustine's notion of the "here-and-now quality of Christian hope," elaborating on the Pauline doctrine: "In this hope we are saved" (Rom 8:24).[114] According to Augustine, Ratzinger suggests, "Paul is teaching not that salvation will be granted us but that we *are* saved. Of course we do not yet see what we hope for. But we are already the body of the head in whom everything is already present that we are hoping for."[115]

Accordingly, the enormity of the problem of death is relativized, but not denied. Indeed, Ratzinger insists that Christian realism appreciates the "frightful negation" of death.[116] It is not deceived by the seductive voices of a Platonic-like idealism that proclaims death to be a liberation of the soul from the prison of the body.[117] But neither is it content with the materialist reduction that asserts the end of the individual with the death of the body.[118] A Christian fear of death does not flow from a belief in annihilation, but precisely from the belief that we are incomplete

---

111. Ratzinger, *God and the World*, 277.
112. Ratzinger, *God and the World*, 278.
113. Ratzinger, *Eschatology*, 157.
114. Ratzinger, *Yes of Jesus Christ*, 64.
115. Ratzinger, *Yes of Jesus Christ*, 64. As Benedict XVI, Ratzinger develops this concept of the immanence of the fulfillment of hope in *Spe salvi*, drawing on the same Pauline text with which the encyclical begins. Benedict XVI, *Spe salvi*, n. 1.
116. Ratzinger, "On the Theology of Death," 249.
117. Ratzinger, "On the Theology of Death," 244–47.
118. Ratzinger, "On the Theology of Death," 247.

and yearn for something more. We cannot bear the idea of not having a future.[119] We have tasted immortality through our experiences of love and communion and will not be satisfied with anything less. "We rebel against death because we simply cannot believe that so many great and meaningful things that occur in a life should suddenly fall into oblivion. We resist death because love demands eternity and because we cannot accept the destruction of love that death brings with it."[120]

Thus, the Christian realism of the awfulness of death is tempered by hope,[121] not glossing over the shadows that darken our lives in this world, but interpreting them in consideration of "the great light that casts them."[122] According to Christian hope, death cannot separate us from communion with God, because the darkest moment in human history, the Good Friday of Christ's death, becomes the source of light and life. His cross shatters the monotony of our finite lives, breaking open "the eternal, futile circling around what is always the same, the vain circular motion of endless repetition."[123] It becomes "the fishhook of God, with which he reels up the entire world to his height."[124] This irruption of God into human history thus gives new direction to our lives. While the "inescapable linearity of our path towards death"[125] remains, it is transformed,

---

119. "Nothing is so unbearable for man as to have no future." Ratzinger, *Faith and the Future*, 50.

120. Ratzinger, *Images of Hope*, 104.

121. "But we must add: hope does not simply cancel sadness. Faith is human, and it is honest. It gives us a new horizon, the larger and comforting view into the expanse of eternal life. But it lets us at the same time remain in the place where we are. We do not have to suppress mourning; we accept it, and through the view into the expanse, mourning is slowly transformed and thereby purifies us, makes us more keen-sighted for today and tomorrow. It was very human that the funeral liturgy earlier omitted the alleluia and so gave clear room for mourning. We cannot simply jump over the Now of our lives. Only in accepting mourning can we learn to discover hope in darkness." Ratzinger, *Images of Hope*, 99–100.

122. "The Christian does not gloss over and deny the deep shadows that fall upon man's existence in this world. And yet these very shadows are also signs of hope for him, because he believes and, in believing, knows that they are shadows, which would not be there without the great light that casts them. And if the present belongs to the shadows, then the future is that much more in the possession of the light." Ratzinger, "On the Theology of Death," 254.

123. Ratzinger, *Images of Hope*, 76.

124. Ratzinger, *Images of Hope*, 76.

125. Ratzinger, *Yes of Jesus Christ*, 58.

receiving a new destination, going forth "with Christ to the hands of God."[126]

This new direction of our lives in Christ transforms our hope. As Ratzinger writes, "hope is now personalized."[127] According to Christian tradition, this transformation of our hope in Christ finds expression in prayer. Citing Aquinas, Ratzinger calls prayer the "interpretation" and the "language" of hope;[128] as "hope in execution."[129] The traditional orientation of liturgical prayer toward the east, in expectation of the risen Lord "who comes to meet us,"[130] is expressive of our hope that Christ will return to lead us to our end. Our communion with the saints in prayer is a window through which we "look into God's eternity."[131] Living communion with Christ is therefore more powerful than death. It is "true reality, and by comparison with it everything, no matter how massively it asserts itself, is a phantom, a nothing."[132] Thus, with the apostle we can say: "Whether we live or whether we die, we are the Lord's" (Rom 14:8).

---

126. Ratzinger, *Images of Hope*, 76.

127. Ratzinger, *Eschatology*, 8.

128. Ratzinger, *Yes of Jesus Christ*, 66. Cf. *STh.*, II–II, q. 17, a. 4.

129. Ratzinger, *Yes of Jesus Christ*, 67. Following the same logic Ratzinger adds: "Those who despair do not pray any more because they no longer hope: those who are sure of themselves and their own power do not pray because they rely only on themselves. Those who pray hope in a goodness and in a power that transcends their own capabilities."

130. Ratzinger, *Spirit of the Liturgy*, 80. Reflecting on this liturgical expression of Christian hope in the writings of Ratzinger, Emery de Gaál writes: "Orienting Eucharistic prayer toward the Risen Christ symbolizes the people of God's openness toward the eternity that only God can grant as a personal gift." De Gaál, *Theology of Pope Benedict XVI*, 264.

131. Ratzinger, "Sermon on the Feast of Saint Augustine," 362. Ratzinger adds: "In the world of the saints, with which we come in contact during the liturgical year, the simple, invisible light of God is refracted, as it were, through the prism of our human history so that we can encounter the eternal glory and light of God right here in our human world and in our human brothers and sisters. The saints are, so to speak, our older brothers and sisters in the family of God. They want to take us by the hand and lead us, and their lives tell us: 'If this person or that could do it, why can't I?'"

132. Ratzinger, *Eschatology*, 89. To reinforce the point, Ratzinger adds: "Communication with God *is* reality. It is true reality, the really real, more real, even, than death itself."

Implications for Life

Ratzinger takes his reflection a step further. If life and death are defined respectively in terms of the presence or absence of loving communion, death cannot be merely equated with the end of biological existence. Rather, death is recognized in whatever frustrates communion, "ever present in the inauthenticity, closedness and emptiness of our everyday life."[133] Just as we can experience something of eternity here and now through our relationships of love, so too death is present "in all the breakdowns of our lives."[134] However, Ratzinger also insists that these moments of death can purify us; "they are ultimately God's action upon us, through which he tears away from us our selfish, self-seeking, egotistical existence so as to reshape us according to his image."[135]

In this context, Ratzinger insists that the physical pain and disease associated with death are less threatening to life than are the failures to enter into our true selves and find our vocation in loving communion. For it is this latter, more dangerous failure "which allows the promise of life to evaporate, leaving only banalities and leading to final emptiness."[136] While acknowledging the paralyzing potential of pain and disease, Ratzinger maintains that suffering offers a unique opportunity. In the "flesh and blood" reality of our sufferings, we are invited to face the fact of our dependence and contingency, to acknowledge that our existence is not at our disposal, that our lives are not our own. In accepting our mortality, and the ever-present reality of death, we are being prepared for eternal life.

However, before the reality of our finitude, there is always the possibility to "snap back defiantly,"[137] refusing to accept our limitations and attempting to assume power over our lives. But in making this choice,

---

133. Ratzinger, *Eschatology*, 95.

134. Ratzinger, "On the Theology of Death," 250.

135. Ratzinger, "On the Theology of Death," 250. He adds: "In practice this means: Death, as a movement that leaves its mark on human existence, must not be regarded by man himself as something merely biological or external but, rather, must be assimilated spiritually and humanly so as to come to the fruition that this event can and should have in us. This means, therefore, that for the human being everything depends on correctly grasping the dying movement in this life, starting from the little humiliation and onward to the major failures (of health, of physical or mental abilities: the death of loved ones is a part of a person's own death, and so on)."

136. Ratzinger, *Eschatology*, 95.

137. Ratzinger, *Eschatology*, 96.

suggests Ratzinger, our basic attitude toward life is characterized by "a desperate anger"—a desperation which we might deem to be consistent with transhumanism's "Baconian project" of aggressively pursuing science and technology in order "to relieve and benefit the condition of man."[138] In this sense Ratzinger likens the quest for immortality to justification by works, in which "man wants to construct a little immortality of his own," fashioning his life as "a self-sufficient totality."[139] Consistent with the positivist reduction of knowledge to the verifiable and practical, the future depends on human action.[140] But Ratzinger insists that such attempts to make human beings self-sufficient are an illusion and a denial of our relational nature.

> Such self-assertion is at root a refusal of communication, which issues in a misjudgment about reality at large and the truth of man's existence in particular. For man's own truth is that he passes away, having no abiding existence in his own right. The more he takes a stand on himself, the more he finds himself suspended over nothing. He falls a prey to that nothingness which, taken by himself, he will assuredly enter everlastingly.[141]

In contrast, the way of acceptance is the way of trust, allowing oneself "to be led, unafraid, by the hand, without *Angst*-ridden concern."[142] According to Ratzinger, this way is consistent with love, not seeking to escape but to enter more deeply into communion. For unlike the attitude of power, love cannot be forced or taken into our own hands. Instead, it emerges through patient endurance and open trust. This choice before the reality of suffering and death therefore constitutes a basic attitude toward life: "to accept either the pattern of love, or the pattern of power."[143] In choosing the pattern of power, the transhumanist attempt to assume control over life runs up against a fundamental truth of our human nature: we cannot give ourselves immortality, and we are not enhanced by always grasping for more. Rather, we are fulfilled by a love that is bestowed upon us, transforming us and enabling us to love in return.[144]

138. McKenny, *To Relieve the Human Condition*, 18.

139. Ratzinger, *Eschatology*, 99.

140. Ratzinger, "What Comes After Death?," 258: "For contemporary man, who accepts only verifiable, praxis-oriented knowledge, this seems to be the only way."

141. Ratzinger, *Eschatology*, 99.

142. Ratzinger, *Eschatology*, 96.

143. Ratzinger, *Eschatology*, 96.

144. As Ratzinger writes, the human person is thus "obliged to expect less of his

Summary

Ratzinger's richer conception of life and death, essentially cast in terms of a communion of love, both gives depth to the human goods contingent on mortality and exposes the hollowness of the transhumanist pursuit of lifespan extension. Love is the end of every human good: of life, beauty, virtue, and our human relations. It sustains our present and gives hope to our future. As Ratzinger describes, it constitutes a moment "that should never pass away."[145] There is an immortality in love that is incomprehensible to the scientific mentality that can only think in linear terms of "more of the same." Positivist categories cannot plumb the depths of life's goodness and meaning. They are unequal to the task of determining the contours of a fulfilled life and of answering the aspirations of the human heart.

In this regard, one might call the pursuit of a cure against aging both a "distraction" from the content and source of human fulfillment, and a "deformation" of human nature and hope.[146] It distracts us from the task of living, of taking life seriously, and of pursuing our vocation to love. It deforms and dehumanizes by alienating us from our relations of dependence. This corresponds to Ratzinger's identification of the mutilating effects of the quest for the "self-made man": a fiction which overlies despair for our finitude and contingency. Thus, the quest for "more of this life" threatens human happiness, not only in averting our gaze from the ultimate object of authentic hope, but also in living here and now as those already saved *in* hope, experiencing and developing our communion of love with God and our neighbor.

---

own *power* and more of *love*, which he can now receive only as a gift." Ratzinger, "What Comes After Death?," 259.

145. Ratzinger, *Eschatology*, 94.

146. Kass, "Ageless Bodies, Happy Souls," 28.

Conclusion

HUMAN BEINGS CANNOT LIVE without hope. It is fundamental for human aspiration, striving, and action. But as noted in this study, through an engagement with the penetrative thought of Joseph Ratzinger, purpose and busyness are not guarantors of the presence of hope. They may instead mask an underlying despair: a despair without sense of human existence, that has lost trust in the goodness of life, that despises contingency and dependence; a fear that craves control and is frantically active in an attempt to appear meaningful.

It is my thesis that this sketch of a hidden despair characterizes the transhumanist project for human enhancement, especially as presented by individuals of the "Oxford School." At the beginning of this study, Nick Bostrom and Julian Savulescu posed a significant question: Are we good enough? And if not, what measures can we take to improve ourselves? As has been noted, the transhumanist project offers us one way of improving the human condition, using biotechnology to "relieve" it of its limitations; to enhance cognition, physical capacities, mood and mores, and to extend the healthy human lifespan.

But to ask "Are we good enough?" presumes a prior comprehension of what constitutes the human good. It requires an answer to some fundamental anthropological questions: What are human beings? What is the meaning of their lives? What is their nature? From whence do they come, and to what end are they moving? Accordingly, before the prospect of human enhancement, it is not primarily a question of "What can we do?" but "Who are we?" and therefore "What *should* we do" in order to be true to ourselves, to our nature, and to our end. I have suggested that transhumanists cannot give an adequate response to these questions, their worldview being constricted to positivistic categories of knowledge and a technological mindset. With Ratzinger's help we have traced the origins of this worldview to a rejection of "being" in favor of "doing," first through a limitation of reality to the *factum*, or the thing made, followed by a further reduction to the *faciendum*, the process of making in which reality becomes movement, action and process.

Ratzinger calls into question this absolutization of positive reason; the imposition of a scientific rationality with its narrow conception of reality, its reduction of meaning to calculation and praxis, and its limitation of hope to what human beings can produce. He maintains that while positive reason is adequate to the technological sphere, if generalized it becomes the "mutilation of man." He characterizes it as a shriveling of human reason that seeks knowledge without understanding, and leaves no room for the question of God and the enlightenment of faith. He presents it as a pathology that becomes manifest in the unleased powers of a technology void of moral content, with morality itself falling victim to positive categories in which nothing is good or evil in itself, but determined by one's own calculations, subject to practicability and the consequences of actions. This is particularly evident in science's domineering stance over the beginnings of human life, in which the ability to make human beings in the laboratory, and to construct their genetic identity according to design, is interpreted as a practical imperative. With the demystification of human life manufactured in a test tube, new life is no longer perceived as a gift, but as the product of human engineering; the "image of man" in place of the "image of God."

The transhumanist project emerges from this reimaging of reality, with its embrace of historical process, its limitation of knowledge to experiment and verification, its embrace of technological progress, and its striving toward an intra-historical utopia that is the product of human effort. In the first place, transhumanists unquestionably embrace evolutionary theory as a *philosophia universalis*. Human beings emerge as chanced products of genetic mutation, within a hostile environment where only the fittest survive due to their ability to change and adapt. Not only our bodies, but also our morality and emotions evolve through this process, suited to the "Environment of Evolutionary Adaptedness," but often found wanting in our current context. Responding to this "evolutionary lag" and conflict of values, transhumanists seek to continue moving along the trajectory of change and adaptation allowing human beings to continue to evolve, even to move beyond humanity toward a transhuman or posthuman existence, substituting biotechnology for natural selection. This is particularly evident in the transhumanist concept of the plasticity of the human body, both in its genetic manipulability, and its potential for morphological change: for hybridization with other species and synchronization with artificial intelligences. It also explains their fluid concept of human nature, denying both a metaphysical basis for human dignity and the human significance according to species. Indeed, no imperative exists to remain human; no reason why we should preserve human nature in its current form or prevent it from "evolving" into something else.

But as Ratzinger eloquently points out, there are aspects of the human person that cannot be explained by evolution. Materialism cannot give rise to the human spirit, and the human capacity to reason cannot originate in unreason. In this context, Ratzinger offers an alternative anthropology that places Reason at the origins of human existence: a personal Reason that ensures that human beings do not emerge as products of chance, but as persons who are willed and loved; a Love that renders every individual important and necessary. From this solid foundation, human beings can move toward their end with hope and confidence. Their life constitutes a project, and their potential for enhancement is built into their very nature. This stands in stark contrast to the vagaries of the transhumanist concept of well-being and enhancement, which, without a rational foundation rooted in human nature, is plagued by relativism and void of objective content. With no end in sight, its projections forward become meaningless, without aim or limit, and enhancement is reduced to an arbitrary seeking for "more": more intelligence, more strength, more life.

The contrast between Ratzinger's hopeful ontology and transhumanist despair is further manifest as a difference between doubt and trust. Rooted in faith and trust, Ratzinger envisages creation as flowing from freedom, from the firm foundation of reason, and the assurance of God's love. This not only offers human beings the hope of a sustaining providence, of the ability to move forward with confidence, but also the capacity to live with others here and now with trust, knowing that human nature is good and rooted in rationality. On the other hand, transhumanism's doubt over the goodness of human origins drives a wedge between us and God and others. It isolates us, weighs us down with the awful responsibility for our own existence and future. This was particularly noted in the transhumanist concept of human morality, as a morality of self-interest forged by the processes of evolution. It was also evident in its secularization of hope in progress and technological skill, in which creativity replaces creation, doing replaces being. But Ratzinger insists that creativity necessarily flows from creation, and that enhancement can only proceed from a prior acceptance of creation's goodness. Enhancement is not served by transhumanism's "not good enough," but only by saying "yes" to what has been given on trust.

Thus, in the distraction of the transhumanist project, it was suggested that we lose sight of our true nature, of our potential for greatness, and of the source of our enhancement. While Ratzinger stresses that we are creatures made for communion, created for love and relationship, existing as beings "from," "with," and "for" others, the attempt of the transhumanist project to re-create ourselves is a denial of our humanity, makes us forgetful of others, and abandons us to a life of solitude. This was revealed in the proposal to enhance human morality through bioenhancement, forgetful that morality is a relational concept, that our incompleteness is a sign of our contingence, and that morality is a process of always beginning anew. It was also manifest in the proposal to select children through genetic manipulation, not arising from love but willed as artifacts of our making. Finally, the negation of our identity as creatures was reflected in attempts to extend the human lifespan indefinitely, neglectful not only of the blessing of intergenerational relations and the meaning of the life cycle, but ultimately forgetful of our end as a communion love.

The connection between hope and love is significant in the context of a response to the transhumanist project. Ratzinger does not only place love as the object of our great hope, and therefore as the only legitimate end toward which human being should strive, but also presents the human capacity to love as offering hope for human beings in their limitations and dependence. Our capacity for love is the means of our "enhancement." It is through love that we fulfill our potential. It is love, not technology, that assures our children a future, providing them a secure space in which they can grow and develop in a human way. In being loved, we are enabled to love in return, giving us hope that we can transcend our moral limitations. It is hope of an enduring love that sustains us in our sufferings and old age, and assures us of a future beyond death. Love transcends the categories of positive knowledge. Despite transhumanist attempts, it cannot be reduced to neuronal pathways or manufactured by potions. Love is revealed in relations, in persons, in events. Ultimately, for Ratzinger, it is revealed in the person of Christ, in the event of his self-offering. In this context he offers an apology for the relevance of Christian faith as the remembrance of Christ's look of love toward us: a look that confirms our goodness, calls us forward, and offers us hope for the future.

In asking "Are we good enough?" the transhumanist project recognizes a valid human experience: the sense of dissatisfaction with our current lives and a desire to transcend our limitations. However, through its distortion of human nature and human flourishing, its restricted worldview, its philosophy that has lost faith in being and limits reality to what can be produced, transhumanism misinterprets this primordial human experience. In its denial of the "given"—its negation of human limitation and dependence as things to be overcome at all costs—it offers solutions that not only fail to satisfy, but ultimately dehumanize and mutate hope.

Ratzinger offers another way. Our striving for transcendence is not satisfied by denying our limitations, but by embracing them: acknowledging our imperfections and accepting our finitude; saying "yes" to our insufficiency, our neediness, and our status as creatures. Dependence, humility, and the acceptance of limits, are the condition of human freedom and transcendence. Acceptance of our finiteness is the way toward infinity. In recognizing the goodness of our origin in God's love, we hope for something more than a continuation of this current life, and will not be satisfied with anything less than communion with him.

Bibliography

Aquinas, Thomas. *Quaestiones disputatae de veritate.* Translated by R. W. Mulligan. Chicago: Regnery, 1952.
———. *Summa Theologiae.* Translated by the Fathers of the English Dominican Province. New York: Benziger, 1947.
Arendt, Hannah. *The Human Condition.* 2nd ed. Chicago: University of Chicago Press, 1998.
Austriaco, Nicanor Pier Giorgio. *Biomedicine and Beatitude: An Introduction to Catholic Bioethics.* Washington, DC: Catholic University of America Press, 2012.
Ayer, A. J. *Language, Truth and Logic.* London: Penguin, 1946.
Balthasar, Hans Urs von. *Love Alone Is Credible.* Translated by D. C. Schindler. San Francisco: Ignatius, 2004.
———. "Nine Propositions on Christian Ethics." Translated by Graham Harrison. In *Principles of Christian Morality*, by Heinz Schürmann, Joseph Ratzinger, and Hans Urs von Balthasar, 77–104. San Francisco: Ignatius, 1986.
———. "A Résumé of My Thought." Translated by Kelly Hamilton. *Communio* 15 (1988) 468–73.
Barazzetti, Gaia. "Looking for the Fountain of Youth: Scientific, Ethical, and Social Issues in the Extension of Human Lifespan." In *Enhancing Human Capacities*, edited by Julian Savulescu et al., 335–48. Chichester, UK: Wiley-Blackwell, 2011.
Barazzetti, Gaia, and Massimo Reichlin. "Life Extension and Personal Identity." In *Enhancing Human Capacities*, edited by Julian Savulescu et al., 398–408. Chichester, UK: Wiley-Blackwell, 2011.
Baylis, Francoise, and Jason Scott Robert. "The Inevitability of Genetic Enhancement Technologies." *Bioethics* 18 (2004) 1–26.
Bellver Capella, Vicente. "Ethics and Policies in the Face of Research into Extending Human Life." *Cuadernos de Bioética* 25 (2014) 493–506.
Benedict XVI. "Address of His Holiness Benedict XVI to the Participants in the International Congress on Natural Moral Law." February 12, 2007. http://w2.vatican.va/content/benedict-xvi/en/speeches/2007/february/documents/hf_ben-xvi_spe_20070212_pul.html.
———. *Deus caritas est.* Encyclical letter. December 25, 2005. *AAS* 98 (2006) 217–52.
———. "Faith, Reason and the University: Memories and Reflections." Lecture at the Aula Magna of the University of Regensburg, September 12, 2006. http://w2.vatican.va/content/benedict-xvi/en/speeches/2006/september/documents/hf_ben-xvi_spe_20060912_university-regensburg.html.

———. "Homily of His Holiness Benedict XVI." Holy Saturday, April 3, 2010. http://w2.vatican.va/content/benedict-xvi/en/homilies/2010/documents/hf_ben-xvi_hom_20100403_veglia-pasquale.html.

———. *Spe salvi*. Encyclical letter. November 30, 2007. *AAS* 99 (2007) 985–1027.

Berghmans, Ron, et al. "Scientific, Ethical, and Social Issues in Mood Enhancement." In *Enhancing Human Capacities*, edited by Julian Savulescu et al., 153–65. Chichester, UK: Wiley-Blackwell, 2011.

Berkman, John, and Craig Steven Titus, eds. *The Pinckaers Reader: Renewing Thomistic Moral Theology*. Washington, DC: Catholic University of America Press, 2005.

Berkman, John, and William C. Mattison III, eds. *Searching for a Universal Ethic: Multidisciplinary, Ecumenical, and Interfaith Responses to the Catholic Natural Law Tradition*. Grand Rapids: Eerdmans, 2014.

Bioviva USA Inc. "First Gene Therapy Successful against Human Aging: American Woman Gets Biologically Younger after Gene Therapies." April 21, 2016. http://bioviva-science.com/2016/04/21/first-gene-therapy-successful-against-human-aging/.

Bloch, Ernst. *The Principle of Hope*. 3 vols. Translated by Neville Plaice et al. Cambridge: MIT Press, 1986.

Bond, John. "Enhancing Human Aging: The Cultural and Psychosocial Context of Lifespan Extension." In *Enhancing Human Capacities*, edited by Julian Savulescu et al., 435–52. Chichester, UK: Wiley-Blackwell, 2011.

Bostrom, Nick. "Dignity and Enhancement." In *Human Dignity and Bioethics: Essays Commissioned by the President's Council on Bioethics*, 173–206. Washington, DC: President's Council on Bioethics, 2008.

———. "The Fable of the Dragon Tyrant." *Journal of Medical Ethics* 31 (2005) 273–77.

———. "The Future of Human Evolution." http://www.nickbostrom.com/fut/evolution.pdf.

———. "The Future of Humanity." *Geopolitics, History, and International Relations* 1 (2009) 41–78.

———. "A History of Transhumanist Thought." *Journal of Evolution and Technology* 14 (2005) 1–25.

———. "Human Genetic Enhancements: A Transhumanist Perspective." *The Journal of Value Inquiry* 37 (2003) 493–506.

———. "In Defense of Posthuman Dignity." *Bioethics* 19 (2005) 202–14.

———. "Transhumanist Values." *Journal of Philosophical Research* 30, supplement (2005) 3–14.

———. "Why I Want to Be a Posthuman When I Grow Up." In *The Transhumanist Reader: Classical and Contemporary Essays on the Science, Technology, and Philosophy of the Human Future*, edited by Max More and Natasha Vita-More, 28–53. Chichester, UK: Wiley-Blackwell, 2013.

Bostrom, Nick, and Toby Ord. "The Reversal Test: Eliminating Status Quo Bias in Applied Ethics." *Ethics* 116 (2006) 656–79.

Bostrom, Nick, and Rebecca Roache. "Ethical Issues in Human Enhancement." In *New Waves in Applied Ethics*, edited by Jesper Ryberg et al., 120–52. Basingstoke, UK: Pelgrave Macmillan, 2007.

———. "Smart Policy: Collective Enhancement and the Public Interest." In *Enhancing Human Capacities*, edited by Julian Savulescu et al., 138–48. Chichester, UK: Wiley-Blackwell, 2011.

Bostrom, Nick, and Anders Sandberg. "Cognitive Enhancement: Methods, Ethics, Regulatory Challenges." *Science and Engineering Ethics* 15 (2009) 311–41.

———. "The Wisdom of Nature: An Evolutionary Heuristic for Human Enhancement." In *Human Enhancement*, edited by Julian Savulescu and Nick Bostrom, 375–416. Oxford: Oxford University Press, 2009.

Bourne, Hannah, et al. "Procreative Beneficence and *in vitro* Gametogenesis." *Monash Bioethics Review* 30 (2012) 29–48.

Brino, Omar. "Bioetica e 'metafisica': Sul dibattito tra Habermas, Siep e Spaemann in merito a 'Il futuro della natura umana.'" *Humanitas* 59 (2004) 744–51.

Brock, Dan W. "Is Selection of Children Wrong?" In *Human Enhancement*, edited by Julian Savulescu and Nick Bostrom, 251–76. Oxford: Oxford University Press, 2009.

Buchanan, Allen. *Better than Human: The Promise and Perils of Enhancing Ourselves.* New York: Oxford University Press, 2011.

———. *Beyond Humanity? The Ethics of Biomedical Enhancement.* Oxford: Oxford University Press, 2011.

Buchanan, Allen, et al. *From Chance to Choice: Genetics and Justice.* Cambridge: Cambridge University Press, 2000.

Coady, C. A. J. "Playing God." In *Human Enhancement*, edited by Julian Savulescu and Nick Bostrom, 155–80. Oxford: Oxford University Press, 2009.

Colombetti, Elena. "Contemporary Post-Humanism: Technological and Human Singularity." *Cuadernos de Bioética* 25 (2014) 367–77.

Conger, Krista. "Telomere Extension Turns Back Aging Clock in Cultured Human Cells." *Stanford Medicine*, January 23, 2015. https://med.stanford.edu/news/all-news/2015/01/telomere-extension-turns-back-aging-clock-in-cultured-cells.html.

Congregation for the Doctrine of the Faith. *Dignitas personae*. Instruction on Certain Bioethical Questions. September 8, 2008. *AAS* 100 (2008) 858–87.

———. *Donum vitae*. Instruction on Respect for Human Life in Its Origin and on the Dignity of Procreation. February 2, 1987. *AAS* 80 (1988) 70–102.

Conrad, Peter, and Deborah Potter. "From Hyperactive Children to ADHD Adults: Observations on the Expansion of Medical Categories." *Social Problems* 47 (2000) 559–82.

Crawford, David S. "Natural Law and the Body: Between Deductivism and Parallelism." *Communio* 35 (2008) 327–53.

Darwall, Stephen L. "Two Kinds of Respect." *Ethics* 88 (1977) 36–49.

Dávila, Nicolás Gómez. *Escolios a un texto implícito: Selección*. Bogotá: Villegas Editores, 2001.

De Gaál, Emery. *The Theology of Pope Benedict XVI: The Christocentric Shift.* New York: Palgrave MacMillan, 2010.

Descartes, René. *Meditations on First Philosophy: With Selections from the Objections and Replies.* 2nd ed. Translated and edited by John Cottingham. Cambridge: Cambridge University Press, 2017.

Di Blasi, Fulvio. "The Role of God in the New Natural Law Theory." *National Catholic Bioethics Quarterly* 13 (2013) 35–45.

Di Pietro, Luisa Maria, and Elio Sgreccia, eds. *Biotecnologie e futuro dell'uomo*. Milan: Vita e Pensiero, 2003.

Ditzen, Beate, et al. "Intranasal Oxytocin Increases Positive Communication and Reduces Cortisol Levels during Couple Conflict." *Biological Psychiatry* 65 (2009) 728–31.

Domes, Gregor, et al. "Oxytocin Improves 'Mind-Reading' in Humans." *Biological Psychiatry* 61 (2007) 731–33.

Douglas, Thomas. "Human Enhancement and Supra-personal Moral Status." *Philosophical Studies* 162 (2013) 473–97.

———. "Moral Enhancement." *Journal of Applied Philosophy* 25 (2008) 228–45.

———. "Moral Enhancement via Direct Emotion Modulation: A Reply to John Harris." *Bioethics* 27 (2013) 160–68.

Dupré, Louis. *Passage to Modernity: An Essay in the Hermeneutics of Nature and Culture*. New Haven, CT: Yale University Press, 1993.

Earp, Brian D. "Love and Other Drugs." *Philosophy Now* 91 (2012) 14–17.

Earp, Brian D., et al. "Brave New Love: The Threat of High-Tech 'Conversion' Therapy and the Bio-Oppression of Sexual Minorities." *AJOB Neuroscience* 5 (2014) 4–12.

———. "If I Could Just Stop Loving You: Anti-Love Biotechnology and the Ethics of a Chemical Breakup." *American Journal of Bioethics* 13 (2013) 3–17.

———. "The Medicalization of Love." *Cambridge Quarterly of Healthcare Ethics* 24 (2015) 323–36.

———. "Natural Selection, Childrearing, and the Ethics of Marriage (and Divorce): Building a Case for the Neuroenhancement of Human Relationships." *Philosophical Technology* 25 (2012) 561–87.

———. "When Is Diminishment a Form of Enhancement? Rethinking the Enhancement Debate in Biomedical Ethics." *Frontiers in Systems Neuroscience* 8 (2014) 1–8.

Ehninger, Dan, et al. "Longevity, Aging and Rapamycin." *Cellular and Molecular Life Sciences* 71 (2014) 4325–46.

Faggioni, Maurizio P. "La natura fluida: le sfide dell'ibridazione, della transgenesi, del transumanesimo." *Studia Moralia* 47 (2009) 387–436.

Fahy, Gregory M., et al., eds. *The Future of Aging: Pathways to Human Life Extension*. Dordrecht: Springer, 2010.

Feinberg, Joel. "The Child's Right to an Open Future." In *Whose Child? Children's Rights, Parental Authority, and State Power*, edited by William Aiken and Hugh LaFollette, 125–53. Totowa, NJ: Rowman and Littlefield, 1980.

Fenton, Elizabeth. "The Perils of Failing to Enhance: A Response to Persson and Savulescu." *Journal of Medical Ethics* 36 (2010) 148–51.

Flores D'Arcais, Paolo. *La sfida oscurantista di Joseph Ratzinger*. Milan: Adriano Salani, 2010.

Foddy, Bennett. "Enhancing Skill." In *Enhancing Human Capacities*, edited by Julian Savulescu et al., 313–25. Chichester, UK: Wiley-Blackwell, 2011.

Fukuyama, Francis. *Our Posthuman Future*. New York: St. Martin's, 2002.

———. "Transhumanism." *Foreign Policy* 144 (2004) 42–43.

Gauchet, Marcel. *Il figlio del desiderio: Una rivoluzione antropologica*. Milan: Vita e Pensiero, 2009.

Gekas, Jean, et al. "Non-invasive Prenatal Testing for Fetal Chromosome Abnormalities: Review of Clinical and Ethical Issues." *Application of Clinical Genetics* 9 (2016) 15–26.

Giglio, Francesca. "*Enhancement*: definizione e questioni aperte." In *Migliorare l'uomo? La sfida etica dell'enhancement*, edited by Stephan Kampowski and Dino Moltisanti, 15–34. Siena: Cantagalli, 2011.

———. *Human Enhancement: Status quaestionis, implicazioni etiche e dignità della persona*. Portogruaro: Edizioni Meudon, 2014.

Glover, Jonathan. *Choosing Children: Genes, Disability, and Design*. Oxford: Oxford University Press, 2008.

Godfrey, Joseph J. "The Future of Pieper's *Hope and History*." In *A Cosmopolitan Hermit: Modernity and Tradition in the Philosophy of Joseph Pieper*, edited by Bernard N. Schumacher, 141–70. Washington, DC: Catholic University of America Press, 2009.

Gray, John. *The Immortalization Commission: Science and the Strange Quest to Cheat Death*. New York: Farrar, Straus and Giroux, 2011.

Gregory, Brad S. *The Unintended Reformation: How a Religious Revolution Secularized Society*. Cambridge: Harvard University Press, 2012.

Grens, Kerry. "First Data from Anti-Aging Gene Therapy." *Scientist*, April 25, 2016. http://www.the-scientist.com/?articles.view/articleNo/45947/title/First-Data-from-Anti-Aging-Gene-Therapy/.

Guardini, Romano. *The End of the Modern World*. Translated by Joseph T. Theman and Herbert Burke, 1956. Wilmington, DE: ISI, 2001.

———. *Learning the Virtues That Lead You to God*. Translated by Stella Lange, 1967. Manchester, NH: Sophia Institute Press, 1998.

———. *Letters from Lake Como: Explorations in Technology and the Human Race*. Translated by Geoffrey W. Bromiley. Grand Rapids: Eerdmans, 1994.

———. *The Lord*. Translated by Elinor C. Briefs. Washington, DC: Regnery, 1982.

———. *Power and Responsibility: A Course of Action for the New Age*. Translated by Elinor C. Briefs. Chicago: Regnery, 1961.

Güell Pelayo, Francisco. "The Post-humanist Embryo: Genetic Manipulation, Assisted Reproductive Technologies and the Principle of Procreative Beneficence." *Cuadernos de Bioética* 25 (2014) 427–43.

Habermas, Jürgen. *The Future of Human Nature*. Translated by William Rehg et al. Cambridge: Polity, 2003.

———. *Justification and Application: Remarks on Discourse Ethics*. Translated by Ciaran P. Cronin. Cambridge: MIT Press, 1993.

———. "Pre-political Foundations of the Democratic Constitutional State?" Translated by Brian McNeil. In *The Dialectics of Secularization: On Reason and Religion*, edited by Florian Schuller, 19–52. San Francisco: Ignatius, 2006.

Haisma, Hidde J. "Physical Enhancement." In *Enhancing Human Capacities*, edited by Julian Savulescu et al., 259–65. Chichester, UK: Wiley-Blackwell, 2011.

Hanby, Michael. "When Art Replaces Nature." *Humanum* 2 (2014) 22–25. http://www.humanumreview.com/uploads/pdfs/ART-Conference_Whole.pdf.

Harris, John. *Enhancing Evolution: The Ethical Case for Making Better People*. Princeton: Princeton University Press, 2010.

———. "Intimations of Immortality." *Science* 288 (2000) 59.

———. "Moral Enhancement and Freedom." *Bioethics* 25 (2011) 102–11.

Hedges, Inez. *Framing Faust: Twentieth-Century Cultural Struggles*. Carbondale: Southern Illinois University Press, 2005.

Hildt, Elisabeth. "Living Longer: Age Retardation and Autonomy." *Medicine, Health Care and Philosophy* 12 (2009) 179–85.
Horn, Stephan O., and Siegfried Wiedenhofer, eds. *Creation and Evolution: A Conference with Pope Benedict XVI in Castel Gandolfo*. Translated by Michael J. Miller. San Francisco: Ignatius, 2008.
Horrobin, Steven. "The Value of Life Extension to Persons as Conatively Driven Processes." In *Enhancing Human Capacities*, edited by Julian Savulescu et al., 421–34. Chichester, UK: Wiley-Blackwell, 2011.
Housden, Charlotte R., et al. "Cognitive Enhancing Drugs: Neuroscience and Society." In *Enhancing Human Capacities*, edited by Julian Savulescu et al., 113–25. Chichester, UK: Wiley-Blackwell, 2011.
Huxley, Julian. *New Bottles for New Wine*. London: Chatto & Windus, 1957.
Jefferson, Will, et al. "Enhancement and Civic Virtue." *Social Theory and Practice* 40 (2014) 499–527.
Jensen, Steven J. "The Roots of Transhumanism." *Nova et Vetera*, English ed., 12 (2014) 515–41.
John Paul II. *Evangelium vitae*. Encyclical letter. March, 25 1995. AAS 87 (1995) 401–522.
———. *Fides et ratio*. Encyclical letter. September 14, 1998. AAS 91 (1999) 5–88.
———. *Veritatis splendor*. Encyclical letter. August 6, 1993. AAS 85 (1993) 1133–228.
Jonas, Hans. "The Burden and Blessing of Mortality." *Hastings Center Report* 22 (1992) 34–40.
———. *The Imperative of Responsibility: In Search of an Ethic for the Technological Age*. Translated by Hans Jonas and David Herr. Chicago: University of Chicago Press, 1985.
———. *The Phenomenon of Life: Towards a Philosophical Biology*. Evanston, IL: Northwestern University Press, 2001.
———. *Philosophical Essays: From Ancient Creed to Technological Man*. Englewood Cliffs, NJ: Prentice-Hall, 1974.
Kahane, Guy. "Reasons to Feel, Reasons to Take Pills." In *Enhancing Human Capacities*, edited by Julian Savulescu et al., 166–78. Chichester, UK: Wiley-Blackwell, 2011.
Kampowski, Stephan. "Children of Desire: The Technological Control of Fertility and the Fundamental Logic of ARTs." *Humanum* 2 (2014) 11–17. http://www.humanumreview.com/uploads/pdfs/ART-Conference_Whole.pdf.
———. *A Greater Freedom: Biotechnology, Love, and Human Dignity; In Dialogue with Hans Jonas and Jürgen Habermas*. Eugene, OR: Pickwick, 2013.
Kampowski, Stephan, ed. *Neuroscienze, amore e libertà*. Siena: Cantagalli, 2012.
———. *Ricordati della nascita: l'uomo in ricerca di un fondamento*. Siena: Cantagalli, 2013.
———. "Technology, Virtue, and the Brave New World." *Nova et Vetera*, English ed., 12 (2014) 543–63.
Kampowski, Stephan, and Dino Moltisanti, eds. *Migliorare l'uomo? La sfida etica dell'enhancement*. Siena: Cantagalli, 2011.
Kant, Immanuel. *Critique of Practical Reason*. Translated by Werner S. Pluhar. Indianapolis: Hackett, 2002.
Kass, Leon. "Ageless Bodies, Happy Souls: Biotechnology and the Pursuit of Perfection." *New Atlantis* 1 (2003) 9–28.

―――. "L'Chaim and Its Limits: Why Not Immortality?" *First Things* 113 (2001) 17–24.

―――. *Life, Liberty and the Defense of Dignity: The Challenge for Bioethics*. San Francisco: Encounter, 2002.

―――. *Toward a More Natural Science: Biology and Human Affairs*. New York: Free Press, 1985.

Kelsey, David H. *Eccentric Existence: A Theological Anthropology*. Louisville: Westminster John Knox, 2009.

Keshavarz, Zeinab, et al. "Evaluation of a Modified DNA Extraction Method for Isolation of Cell-Free Fetal DNA from Maternal Serum." *Avicenna Journal of Medical Biotechnology* 7 (2015) 85–88.

Kolnai, Aurel. "Dignity." *Philosophy* 51 (1976) 251–71.

Knapton, Sarah. "World's First Anti-Ageing Drug Could See Humans Live to 120." *Telegraph*, November 29, 2015. http://www.telegraph.co.uk/science/2016/03/12/worlds-first-anti-ageing-drug-could-see-humans-live-to-120/.

Kraj, Tomasz. "The Magisterium and Modern Genetics." *National Catholic Bioethics Quarterly* 2 (2002) 617–34.

―――. "The Role of Virtue Ethics in Determining Acceptable Limits to Genetic Enhancement." *Theological Research* 1 (2013) 109–16.

Kramer, Peter D. *Listening to Prozac*. New York: Viking, 1993.

Kurzweil, Ray, and Terry Grossman. "Bridges to Life." In *The Future of Aging: Pathways to Human Life Extension*, edited by Gregory M. Fahy et al., 3–22. Dordrecht: Springer, 2010.

Landeweerd, Laurens. "Asperger's Syndrome, Bipolar Disorder and the Relation between Mood, Cognition, and Well-Being." In *Enhancing Human Capacities*, edited by Julian Savulescu et al., 207–17. Chichester, UK: Wiley-Blackwell, 2011.

Lewis, C. S. *The Abolition of Man*. New York: HarperCollins, 2009.

Liao, S. Matthew, et al. "The Ashley Treatment: Best Interests, Convenience, and Parental Decision-Making." *Hastings Center Report* 37 (2007) 16–20.

Liao, S. Matthew, and Rebecca Roache. "After Prozac." In *Enhancing Human Capacities*, edited by Julian Savulescu et al., 245–56. Chichester, UK: Wiley-Blackwell, 2011.

Lomanno, Matthew P. "The Possibilities and Problems of Transhumanism." *National Catholic Bioethics Quarterly* 8 (2008) 57–66.

Lombardo, Nicholas E. *The Logic of Desire: Aquinas on Emotion*. Washington, DC: Catholic University of America Press, 2011.

López, Antonio. *Gift and the Unity of Being*. Eugene, OR: Cascade, 2014.

Lubac, Henri de. *The Drama of Atheist Humanism*. Translated by Edith M. Riley et al. San Francisco: Ignatius, 1995.

MacIntyre, Alisdair. *After Virtue: A Study in Moral Theology*. 2nd ed. London: Duckworth, 1985.

Malherbe, Brice de. "Créer ou revêtir l'homme nouveau?" *Connaître* 35 (2011) 25–40.

―――. "L'homme nouveau, utopie de la bioéthique." *Revue Théologique des Bernardins* 2 (2011) 33–57.

Marchesini, Roberto. "Ruolo delle alterità nella definizione dei predicati umani." In *Apocalisse e post-umano: Il crepuscolo della modernità*, edited by Pietro Barcellona et al., 33–56. Bari, Italy: Dedalo, 2007.

Maslen, Hannah, et al. "Pharmacological Cognitive Enhancement: How Neuroscientific Research Could Advance Ethical Debate." *Frontiers in Systems Neuroscience* 8 (2014) 1–12.

Mazzocato, Giuseppe. "Inclinazioni naturali del corpo e destino della persona." In *La soggettività morale del corpo (VS 48)*, edited by Livio Melina and Juan José Pérez-Soba, 129–72. Siena: Cantagalli, 2012.

McKenny, Gerald P. *To Relieve the Human Condition: Bioethics, Technology, and the Body*. Albany: State University of New York Press, 1997.

McMahan, Jeff. *The Ethics of Killing: Problems at the Margins of Life*. Oxford: Oxford University Press, 2002.

Meilaender, Gilbert. *Should We Live Forever? The Ethical Ambiguities of Aging*. Grand Rapids: Eerdmans, 2013.

Melina, Livio. *Corso di bioetica: il Vangelo della vita*. Casale Monferrato, Italy: Piemme, 1996.

———. *La conoscenza morale: Linee di riflessione sul comment di San Tommaso all'Etica Nicomachea*. Rome: Città Nuova Editrice, 1987.

———. "Pragmatic and Christological Foundations of Natural Law." In *Searching for a Universal Ethic: Multidisciplinary, Ecumenical, and Interfaith Responses to the Catholic Natural Law Tradition*, edited by John Berkman and William C. Mattison III, 293–303. Grand Rapids: Eerdmans, 2014.

———. *Sharing in Christ's Virtues: For a Renewal of Moral Theology in Light of Veritatis Splendor*. Translated by William E. May. Washington, DC: Catholic University of America Press, 2001.

Melina, Livio, and Juan José Pérez-Soba, eds. *La soggettività morale del corpo (VS 48)*. Siena: Cantagalli, 2012.

Miah, Andy. "Physical Enhancement: The State of the Art." In *Enhancing Human Capacities*, edited by Julian Savulescu et al., 266–73. Chichester, UK: Wiley-Blackwell, 2011.

Milbank, John. *Beyond Secular Order: The Representation of Being and the Representation of the People*. Chichester, UK: Wiley-Blackwell, 2013.

Miller, Michael J., ed. *Dogma and Preaching: Applying Christian Doctrine to Daily Life*. San Francisco: Ignatius, 2011.

Miner, Robert. *Thomas Aquinas on the Passions: A Study of Summa Theologiae 1a2ae 22–48*. Cambridge: Cambridge University Press, 2010.

Moltisanti, Dino, and Elena Postigo Solana. "Transumanesimo: un'analisi antropologica ed etica." In *Migliorare l'uomo? La sfida etica dell'enhancement*, edited by Stephan Kampowski and Dino Moltisanti, 201–25. Siena: Cantagalli, 2011.

Monod, Jacques. *Le hasard et la nécessité: essai sur la philosophie naturelle de la biologie moderne*. Paris: Ed. du Seuil, 1970.

More, Max. "The Philosophy of Transhumanism." In *The Transhumanist Reader: Classical and Contemporary Essays on the Science, Technology, and Philosophy of the Human Future*, edited by Max More and Natasha Vita-More, 3–17. Chichester, UK: Wiley-Blackwell, 2013.

More, Max, and Natasha Vita-More, eds. *The Transhumanist Reader: Classical and Contemporary Essays on the Science, Technology, and Philosophy of the Human Future*. Chichester, UK: Wiley-Blackwell, 2013.

Murillo, José Ignacio. "Does Post-Humanism Still Need Ethics? The Normativity of an Open Nature." *Cuadernos de Bioética* 25 (2014) 469–79.

Murphy, William F., Jr., ed. *Ethics of Procreation and the Defense of Human Life: Contraception, Artificial Fertilization and Abortion*. Washington, DC: Catholic University of America Press, 2010.
National Bioethics Advisory Commission. "Cloning Human Beings." In *Flesh of My Flesh: The Ethics of Cloning Humans*, edited by Gregory E. Pence, 45–66. Lanham, MD: Rowman and Littlefield, 1998.
Nebel, Almut, and Thomas C. G. Bosch. "Evolution of Human Longevity: Lessons from Hydra." *Aging* 4 (2012) 730–31.
Nichols, Aidan. *The Thought of Pope Benedict XVI: An Introduction to the Theology of Joseph Ratzinger*. 2nd ed. London: Burns and Oates, 2007.
Nietzsche, Friedrich. *The Gay Science*. Edited by Bernard Williams. Translated by Josefine Nauckhoff and Adrian Del Caro. Cambridge: Cambridge University Press, 2001.
———. *Thus Spoke Zarathustra*. Edited by Robert Pippin. Translated by Adrian Del Caro. Cambridge: Cambridge University Press, 2006.
Nikolich-Zuglich, Janko, and Ilhem Messaoudi. "Mice and Flies and Monkeys Too: Caloric Restriction Rejuvenates the Aging Immune System of Non-Human Primates." *Experimental Gerontology* 40 (2005) 884–93.
Overall, Christine. "Lifespan Extension: Metaphysical Basis and Ethical Outcomes." In *Enhancing Human Capacities*, edited by Julian Savulescu et al., 386–97. Chichester, UK: Wiley-Blackwell, 2011.
Parens, Erik. "Toward a More Fruitful Debate about Enhancement." In *Human Enhancement*, edited by Julian Savulescu and Nick Bostrom, 181–97. Oxford: Oxford University Press, 2009.
Parfit, Derek. *Reasons and Persons*. Oxford: Oxford University Press, 1984.
Parker, Michael. "The Best Possible Child." *Journal of Medical Ethics* 33 (2007) 279–83.
Pastor, Luis Miguel, and José Ángel García-Cuadrado. "Modernity and Postmodernity in the Genesis of Transhumanism-Posthumanism." *Cuadernos de Bioética* 25 (2014) 335–50.
Pepperell, Robert. "Posthumans and Extended Experience." *Journal of Evolution and Technology* 14 (2005) 27–41.
Persson, Ingmar, and Julian Savulescu. "Getting Moral Enhancement Right: The Desirability of Moral Bioenhancement." *Bioethics* 27 (2013) 124–31.
———. "Moral Enhancement, Freedom, and the God Machine." *Monist* 95 (2012) 399–421.
———. "Moral Transhumanism." *Journal of Medicine and Philosophy* 35 (2010) 656–69.
———. "The Perils of Cognitive Enhancement and the Urgent Imperative to Enhance the Moral Character of Humanity." *Journal of Applied Philosophy* 25 (2008) 162–77.
———. "The Turn for Ultimate Harm: A Reply to Fenton." *Journal of Medical Ethics* 37 (2011) 441–44.
———. "Unfit for the Future? Human Nature, Scientific Progress, and the Need for Moral Enhancement." In *Enhancing Human Capacities*, edited by Julian Savulescu et al., 486–99. Chichester, UK: Wiley-Blackwell, 2011.
———. *Unfit for the Future: A Need for Moral Enhancement*. Oxford: Oxford University Press, 2012.

Pessina, Adriano. "L'uomo e la tecnica: annotazioni filosofiche." In *Biotecnologie e futuro dell'uomo*, edited by Luisa Maria Di Pietro and Elio Sgreccia, 3–16. Milan: Vita e Pensiero, 2003.

Pieper, Josef. *A Brief Reader on the Virtues of the Human Heart*. Translated by Paul C. Duggan. San Francisco: Ignatius, 1991.

———. *The End of Time: A Meditation on the Philosophy of History*. Translated by Michael Bullock. San Francisco: Ignatius, 1999.

———. *Faith, Hope, Love*. Translated by Richard Winston et al. San Francisco: Ignatius, 1997.

———. *Happiness and Contemplation*. Translated by Richard and Clara Winston. South Bend, IN: St. Augustine, 1998.

———. *Hope and History*. Translated by David Kipp. San Francisco: Ignatius, 1994.

———. *Living the Truth*. San Francisco: Ignatius, 1989.

———. "Reality and the Good." In *Living the Truth*, translated by Stella Lange, 107–77. San Francisco: Ignatius, 1989.

———. *Tradition: Concept and Claim*. Translated by E. Christian Kopff. Wilmington, DE: ISI, 2008.

———. "The Truth of All Things: An Inquiry into the Anthropology of the High Middle Ages." In *Living the Truth*, translated by Lothar Krauth, 9–105. San Francisco: Ignatius, 1989.

Pinckaers, Servais. "Conscience and Christian Tradition." Translated by Mary Thomas Noble. In *The Pinckaers Reader, Renewing Thomistic Moral Theology*, edited by John Berkman and Craig Steven Titus, 321–41. Washington, DC: Catholic University of America Press, 2005.

———. "Reappropriating Aquinas's Account of the Passions." Translated by Craig Steven Titus. In *The Pinckaers Reader: Renewing Thomistic Moral Theology*, edited by John Berkman and Craig Steven Titus, 273–87. Washington, DC: Catholic University of America Press, 2005.

Pope, Stephen J., ed. *The Ethics of Aquinas*. Washington, DC: Georgetown University Press, 2002.

Postigo Solana, Elena. "Transumanesimo e postumano: principi teorici e implicazioni bioetiche." *Medicina e Morale* 59 (2009) 271–87.

Powell, Russell, and Allen Buchanan. "Breaking Evolution's Chains: The Prospect of Deliberate Genetic Modification in Humans." *Journal of Medicine and Philosophy* 36 (2011) 6–27.

President's Council on Bioethics. *Beyond Therapy: Biotechnology and the Pursuit of Happiness*. Washington, DC: President's Council on Bioethics, 2003.

———. *Human Dignity and Bioethics: Essays Commissioned by the President's Council on Bioethics*. Washington, DC: President's Council on Bioethics, 2008.

Ratzinger, Joseph. *Auferstehung und ewiges Leben: Beiträge zur Eschatologie und zur Theologie der Hoffnung*. Gesammelte Schriften: Band 10. Freiburg: Herder, 2012.

———. "Belief in Creation and the Theory of Evolution." Translated by Michael J. Miller. In *Dogma and Preaching: Applying Christian Doctrine to Daily Life*, edited by Michael J. Miller, 131–42. San Francisco: Ignatius, 2011.

———. "Beyond Death." Translated by W. J. O'Hara. In *Joseph Ratzinger in Communio*, vol. 2: *Anthropology and Culture*, edited by David L. Schindler and Nicholas J. Healy, 1–16. Grand Rapids: Eerdmans, 2013.

———. "Bioethics in the Christian Perspective." *Dolentium Hominum* 18 (1991) 10–15.

———. "Bishops, Theologians, and Morality." In *On Conscience*, 43–75. San Francisco: Ignatius, 2007.

———. *Christianity and the Crisis of Cultures*. Translated by Brian McNeil. San Francisco: Ignatius, 2006.

———. *Church, Ecumenism, and Politics: New Endeavors in Ecclesiology*. Translated by Michael J. Miller et al. San Francisco: Ignatius, 2008.

———. "The Church's Teaching Authority—Faith—Morals." Translated by Graham Harrison. In *Principles of Christian Morality*, 45–73. San Francisco: Ignatius, 1986.

———. "Concerning the Notion of Person in Theology." Translated by Michael Waldstein. *Communio* 17 (1990) 439–54.

———. "Conscience and Truth." *Communio* 37 (2010) 529–38.

———. "The Current Doctrinal Relevance of the *CCC*." *L'Osservatore Romano* (weekly edition in English), November 20, 2002, 6–8.

———. "The Dignity of the Human Person." In *Commentary on the Documents of Vatican II*, vol. 5, edited by Herbert Vorgrimler. London: Burns & Oates, 1969.

———. *Einführung in das Christentum: Bekenntnis—Taufe—Nachfolge*. Gesammelte Schriften: Band 4. Freiburg: Herder, 2014.

———. "Eschatology and Utopia." Translated by James M. Quigley. In *Joseph Ratzinger in Communio*, vol. 1, *The Unity of the Church*, edited by David L. Schindler, 10–25. Grand Rapids: Eerdmans, 2010.

———. *Eschatology: Death and Eternal Life*. 2nd ed. Translated by Michael Waldstein and Aidan Nichols. Washington, DC: Catholic University of America Press, 1988.

———. "Europe in the Crisis of Cultures." *Communio* 32 (2005) 345–56.

———. "*Evangelium vitae*." *L'Osservatore Romano* (weekly edition in English), April 5, 1995, 1–2.

———. *Faith and the Future*. San Francisco: Ignatius, 2009.

———. "The Feeling of Things, the Contemplation of Beauty." Message to the Communion and Liberation (CL) meeting at Rimini, August 24–30, 2002. http://www.vatican.va/roman_curia/congregations/cfaith/documents/rc_con_cfaith_doc_20020824_ratzinger-cl-rimini_en.html.

———. "Funeral Homily for Msgr. Luigi Giussani." *Communio* 31 (2004) 685–87.

———. *God and the World: Believing and Living in Our Time: A Conversation with Peter Seewald*. Translated by Henry Taylor. San Francisco: Ignatius, 2002.

———. "Guardini on Christ in our Century." Translated by John M. Haas. In *The Essential Pope Benedict XVI: His Central Writings and Speeches*, edited by John F. Thornton and Susan B. Varenne, 53–55. New York: HarperCollins, 2007.

———. "Homily of His Eminence Card. Joseph Ratzinger." Mass *Pro Eligendo Romano Pontifice*. April 18, 2005. http://www.vatican.va/gpII/documents/homily-pro-eligendo-pontifice_20050418_en.html.

———. "Human Life: A Fundamental Value and an Inviolable Human Right." In *Medicine and Law: For or Against Life?*, edited by Elio Sgreccia et al., 16–21. Vatican City: Libreria Editrice Vaticana, 1999.

———. *Images of Hope: Meditations on Major Feasts*. Translated by John Rock. San Francisco: Ignatius, 2006.

———. *In the Beginning: A Catholic Understanding of the Story of Creation and the Fall*. Translated by Boniface Ramsey. Grand Rapids: Eerdmans, 1995.

———. *Introduction to Christianity*. Translated by J. R. Foster and Michael J. Miller. San Francisco: Ignatius, 2004.

———. *Jesus of Nazareth: From the Baptism in the Jordan to the Transfiguration*. Translated by Adrian J. Walker. London: Bloomsbury, 2007.

———. "Man between Reproduction and Creation: Theological Questions on the Origin of Human Life." Translated by Thomas A. Caldwell. In *Joseph Ratzinger in Communio*, vol. 2, *Anthropology and Culture*, edited by David L. Schindler and Nicholas J. Healy, 70–83. Grand Rapids: Eerdmans, 2013.

———. *Milestones: Memoirs 1927–1977*. Translated by Erasmo Leiva-Merikakis. San Francisco: Ignatius, 1998.

———. *On Conscience*. San Francisco: Ignatius, 2007.

———. "On Hope." Translated by Esther Tillman. *Communio* 35 (2008) 301–15.

———. "On the Theology of Death." Translated by Michael J. Miller. In *Dogma and Preaching: Applying Christian Doctrine to Daily Life*, edited by Michael J. Miller, 243–54. San Francisco: Ignatius, 2011.

———. Preface to *Evolutionismus und Christentum*, edited by Robert Spaemann et al. Weinheim: Acta Humaniora VCH, 1986.

———. *Principles of Catholic Theology: Building Stones for a Fundamental Theology*. Translated by Mary Frances McCarthy. San Francisco: Ignatius, 1987.

———. "The Problem of Threats to Human Life." In *The Essential Pope Benedict XVI: His Central Writings and Speeches*, edited by John F. Thornton and Susan B. Varenne, 381–92. New York: HarperCollins, 2007.

———. "The Renewal of Moral Theology: Perspectives of Vatican II and *Veritatis splendor*." *Communio* 32 (2005) 357–68.

———. *Salt of the Earth: The Church at the End of the Millennium; An Interview with Peter Seewald*. Translated by Adrian Walker. San Francisco: Ignatius, 1997.

———. "Sermon on the Feast of Saint Augustine." Translated by Matthew J. O'Connell. In *Dogma and Preaching: Applying Christian Doctrine to Daily Life*, edited by Michael J. Miller, 362–68. San Francisco: Ignatius, 2011.

———. *The Spirit of the Liturgy*. Translated by John Saward. San Francisco: Ignatius, 2000.

———. "Technological Security as a Problem of Social Ethics." Translated by Peter Verhalen. In *Joseph Ratzinger in Communio*, vol. 2, *Anthropology and Culture*, edited by David L. Schindler and Nicholas J. Healy, 42–51. Grand Rapids: Eerdmans, 2013.

———. "That Which Holds the World Together: The Pre-political Moral Foundations of a Free State." Translated by Brian McNeil. In *The Dialectics of Secularization: On Reason and Religion*, edited by Florian Schuller, 53–80. San Francisco: Ignatius, 2006.

———. *Theological Highlights of Vatican II*. Translated by Henry Traub et al. New York: Paulist Press, 1966.

———. *The Theology of History in St. Bonaventure*. Translated by Zachary Hayes. Chicago: Franciscan Herald, 1989.

———. "Truth and Freedom." Translated by Adrian Walker. *Communio* 23 (1996) 16–35.

———. *Truth and Tolerance: Christian Belief and World Religions*. Translated by Henry Taylor. San Francisco: Ignatius, 2004.

———. *A Turning Point for Europe? The Church in the Modern World: Assessment and Forecast*. 2nd ed. Translated by Brian McNeil. San Francisco: Ignatius, 2010.

———. *Values in a Time of Upheaval*. Translated by Brian McNeil. San Francisco: Ignatius, 2006.

———. "Veritatis splendor." *L'Osservatore Romano* (weekly edition in English), October 6, 1993, 1–2.

———. "What Comes After Death." Translated by Michael J. Miller. In *Dogma and Preaching: Applying Christian Doctrine to Daily Life*, edited by Michael J. Miller, 255–59. San Francisco: Ignatius, 2011.

———. *The Yes of Jesus Christ: Spiritual Exercises in Faith, Hope and Love*. Translated by Robert Nowell. New York: Crossroad, 1991.

Ratzinger, Joseph, et al. *Principles of Christian Morality*. San Francisco: Ignatius, 1986.

Ratzinger, Joseph, and Paolo Flores D'Arcais. "Controversia su Dio." In *La sfida oscurantista di Joseph Ratzinger*, 95–146. Milan: Adriano Salani, 2010.

Ratzinger, Joseph, and Vittorio Messori. *The Ratzinger Report: An Exclusive Interview on the State of the Church*. Translated by Salvator Attanasio and Graham Harrison. San Francisco: Ignatius, 1985.

Reddy, Sumathi. "Scientists' New Goal: Growing Old Without Disease." *Wall Street Journal*, March 16, 2015. https://www.wsj.com/articles/scientists-new-goal-growing-old-without-disease-1426542180.

Remotti, Francesco. *Contra natura: una lettera al papa*. Rome: Laterza, 2008.

Rhonheimer, Martin. "The Instrumentalization of Human Life." In *Ethics of Procreation and the Defense of Human Life: Contraception, Artificial Fertilization and Abortion*, edited by William F. Murphy Jr., 153–78. Washington, DC: Catholic University of America Press, 2010.

———. "Natural Law as a 'Work of Reason': Understanding the Metaphysics of Participated Theonomy." In *Searching for a Universal Ethic: Multidisciplinary, Ecumenical, and Interfaith Responses to the Catholic Natural Law Tradition*, edited by John Berkman and William C. Mattison III, 272–81. Grand Rapids: Eerdmans, 2014.

Rich, Nathaniel. "Can a Jellyfish Unlock the Secret of Immortality?" *New York Times Magazine*, November 28, 2012. http://www.nytimes.com/2012/12/02/magazine/can-a-jellyfish-unlock-the-secret-of-immortality.html.

Rimmele, Ulrike, et al. "Oxytocin Makes a Face in Memory Familiar." *Journal of Neuroscience* 29 (2009) 38–42.

Rowland, Tracey. *Benedict XVI: A Guide for the Perplexed*. London: T. & T. Clark, 2010.

———. "Natural Law: From Neo-Thomism to Nuptial Mysticism." *Communio* 35 (2008) 374–96.

———. *Ratzinger's Faith: The Theology of Pope Benedict XVI*. Oxford: Oxford University Press, 2008.

———. "The Role of Natural Law and Natural Right in the Search for a Universal Ethic." In *Searching for a Universal Ethic: Multidisciplinary, Ecumenical, and Interfaith Responses to the Catholic Natural Law Tradition*, edited by John Berkman and William C. Mattison III, 156–66. Grand Rapids: Eerdmans, 2014.

———. "Variations on the Theme of Christian Hope in the Work of Joseph Ratzinger-Benedict XVI." *Communio* 35 (2008) 200–220.

Rubin, Charles. "Commentary on Bostrom." In *Human Dignity and Bioethics: Essays Commissioned by the President's Council on Bioethics*, 207–11. Washington, DC: President's Council on Bioethics, 2008.

Russo, Maria Teresa, and Nicola Di Stefano. "Post-Human Body and Beauty." *Cuadernos de Bioética* 25 (2014) 457–66.

Ryberg, Jesper, et al., eds. *New Waves in Applied Ethics*. Basingstoke, UK: Pelgrave Macmillan, 2007.

Sandberg, Anders. "Cognition Enhancement: Upgrading the Brain." In *Enhancing Human Capacities*, edited by Julian Savulescu et al., 71–91. Chichester, UK: Wiley-Blackwell, 2011.

———. "Morphological Freedom: Why We Not Just Want It, but Need It." In *The Transhumanist Reader: Classical and Contemporary Essays on the Science, Technology, and Philosophy of the Human Future*, edited by Max More and Natasha Vita-More, 56–64. Chichester, UK: Wiley-Blackwell, 2013.

Sandberg, Anders, and Julian Savulescu. "Neuroenhancement of Love and Marriage: The Chemicals Between Us." *Neuroethics* 1 (2008) 31–44.

———. "The Social and Economic Impacts of Cognitive Enhancement." In *Enhancing Human Capacities*, edited by Julian Savulescu et al., 92–112. Chichester, UK: Wiley-Blackwell, 2011.

Sandel, Michael J. "The Case Against Perfection: What's Wrong with Designer Children, Bionic Athletes, and Genetic Engineering." In *Human Enhancement*, edited by Julian Savulescu and Nick Bostrom, 71–89. Oxford: Oxford University Press, 2009.

———. *The Case against Perfection*. Cambridge: Harvard University Press, 2009.

Savulescu, Julian. "Deaf Lesbians, 'Designer Disability,' and the Future of Medicine." *British Medical Journal* 325 (2002) 771–73.

———. "The Human Prejudice and the Moral Status of Enhanced Beings: What Do We Owe the Gods?" In *Human Enhancement*, edited by Julian Savulescu and Nick Bostrom, 211–47. Oxford: Oxford University Press, 2009.

———. "In Defence of Procreative Beneficence." *Journal of Medical Ethics* 33 (2007) 284–88.

———. "Justice, Fairness, and Enhancement." *Annals of the New York Academy of Sciences* 1093 (2006) 321–38.

———. "Procreative Beneficence: Reasons to Not Have Disabled Children." In *The Sorting Society: The Ethics of Genetic Screening and Therapy*, edited by Loane Skene and Janna Thompson, 51–68. Cambridge: Cambridge University Press, 2008.

———. "Procreative Beneficence: Why We Should Select the Best Children." *Bioethics* 15 (2001) 413–26.

Savulescu, Julian, et al., eds. *Enhancing Human Capacities*. Chichester, UK: Wiley-Blackwell, 2011.

———. "Well-Being and Enhancement." In *Enhancing Human Capacities*, edited by Julian Savulescu et al., 3–18. Chichester, UK: Wiley-Blackwell, 2011.

———. "Why We Should Allow Performance Enhancing Drugs in Sport." *British Journal of Sports Medicine* 38 (2004) 666–70.

Savulescu, Julian, and Nick Bostrom, eds. *Human Enhancement*. Oxford: Oxford University Press, 2009.

———. "Human Enhancement Ethics: The State of the Debate." In *Human Enhancement*, edited by Julian Savulescu and Nick Bostrom, 1–22. Oxford: Oxford University Press, 2009.

Savulescu, Julian, and Bennett Foddy. "Le Tour and Failure of Zero Tolerance: Time to Relax Doping Controls." In *Enhancing Human Capacities*, edited by Julian Savulescu et al, 304–12. Chichester, UK: Wiley-Blackwell, 2011.

Savulescu, Julian, and Guy Kahane. "Disability: A Welfarist Approach." *Clinical Ethics* 6 (2011) 45–51.

———. "The Moral Obligation to Create Children with the Best Chance of the Best Life." *Bioethics* 23 (2009) 274–90.

Schermer, Maartje, and Ineke Bolt. "What's in a Name? ADHD and the Gray Area between Treatment and Enhancement." In *Enhancing Human Capacities*, edited by Julian Savulescu et al., 179–93. Chichester, UK: Wiley-Blackwell, 2011.

Schindler, David L., ed. *The Unity of the Church*. Vol. 1 of *Joseph Ratzinger in Communio*. Grand Rapids: Eerdmans, 2010.

Schindler, David L., and Nicholas J. Healy, eds. *Anthropology and Culture*. Vol. 2 of *Joseph Ratzinger in Communio*. Grand Rapids: Eerdmans, 2013.

Schönborn, Christoph. *Chance or Purpose? Creation, Evolution, and a Rational Faith*. Translated by Henry Taylor. San Francisco: Ignatius, 2007.

———. Foreword to *Creation and Evolution: A Conference with Pope Benedict XVI in Castel Gandolfo*, edited by Stephan O. Horn and Siegfried Wiedenhofer, 7–23. San Francisco: Ignatius, 2008.

Schuller, Florian, ed. *The Dialectics of Secularization: On Reason and Religion*. San Francisco: Ignatius, 2006.

Schumacher, Bernard N., ed. *A Cosmopolitan Hermit: Modernity and Tradition in the Philosophy of Joseph Pieper*. Washington, DC: Catholic University of America Press, 2009.

———. *A Philosophy of Hope: Josef Pieper and the Contemporary Debate on Hope*. Translated by D. C. Schindler. New York: Fordham University Press, 2003.

Scola, Angelo, ed. *Quale vita? La bioetica in questione*. Milan: Mondadori, 1998.

Sgreccia, Elio. *Manuale di bioetica*. Vol. 1, *Fondamenti ed etica biomedica*. Milan: Vita e Pensiero, 1999.

———. *Personalist Bioethics: Foundations and Applications*. Translated by John A. Di Camillo and Michael J. Miller. Philadephia: National Catholic Bioethics Center, 2012.

Shulman, Carl, and Nick Bostrom. "Embryo Selection for Cognitive Enhancement: Curiosity or Game-Changer?" *Global Policy* 5 (2014) 85–92.

Silver, Lee M. *Remaking Eden: Cloning and Beyond in a Brave New World*. New York: Avon, 1998.

Singer, Peter. "Parental Choice and Human Improvement." In *Human Enhancement*, edited by Julian Savulescu and Nick Bostrom, 277–89. Oxford: Oxford University Press, 2009.

———. *Practical Ethics*. 2nd ed. Cambridge: Cambridge University Press, 1993.

———. "Speciesism and Moral Status." *Metaphilosophy* 40 (2009) 567–81.

Skene, Loane, and Janna Thompson, eds. *The Sorting Society: The Ethics of Genetic Screening and Therapy*. Cambridge: Cambridge University Press, 2008.

Sorgner, Stefan Lorenz. "Is There a 'Moral Obligation to Create Children with the Best Chance of the Best Life'?" *Humana.Mente Journal of Philosophical Studies* 26 (2014) 199–212.
Spaemann, Robert. "Begotten, Not Made." Translated by Michelle K. Borras. *Communio* 33 (2006) 290–97.
———. "Habermas über Bioethik." *Deutsche Zeitschrift für Philosophie* 50 (2002) 105–9.
———. *Happiness and Benevolence*. Translated by Jeremiah Alberg. Edingburgh: T. & T. Clark, 2000.
———. *Love and the Dignity of Human Life: On Nature and Natural Law*. Grand Rapids: Eerdmans, 2012.
———. *Persons: The Difference between "Someone" and "Something."* Translated by Oliver O'Donovan. Oxford: Oxford University Press, 2006.
———. "Wozu der Aufwand? Sloterdijk fehlt das Rüstzeug." In *Grenzen: Zur ethischen Dimension des Handelns*, 406–10. Stuttgart: Klett-Cotta Verlag, 2001.
Sparrow, Robert. "Procreative Beneficence, Obligation, and Eugenics." *Genomics, Society and Policy* 3 (2007) 43–59.
Spriggs, M. "Lesbian Couple Create a Child Who Is Deaf Like Them." *Journal of Medical Ethics* 28 (2002) 283.
Tamburrini, Claudio, and Torbjörn Tännsjö. "Enhanced Bodies." In *Enhancing Human Capacities*, edited by Julian Savulescu et al., 274–90. Chichester, UK: Wiley-Blackwell, 2011.
Temkin, Larry. "Is Living Longer Living Better?" In *Enhancing Human Capacities*, edited by Julian Savulescu et al., 350–67. Chichester, UK: Wiley-Blackwell, 2011.
Thornton, John F., and Susan B. Varenne, eds. *The Essential Pope Benedict XVI: His Central Writings and Speeches*. New York: HarperCollins, 2007.
Tintino, Giorgio. "From Darwinian to Technological Evolution: Forgetting the Human Lottery." *Cuadernos de Bioética* 25 (2014) 387–95.
Tooley, Michael. *Abortion and Infanticide*. Oxford: Clarendon, 1983.
Transhumanist FAQ 3.0. http://humanityplus.org/philosophy/transhumanist-faq/.
Twomey, D. Vincent. Introduction to *The Essential Pope Benedict XVI: His Central Writings and Speeches*, edited by John F. Thornton and Susan B. Varenne, xiii–xxxiv. New York: HarperCollins, 2007.
———. *Pope Benedict XVI: The Conscience of Our Age: A Theological Portrait*. San Francisco: Ignatius, 2007.
Valera, Luca. "Posthumanism: Beyond Humanism?" *Cuadernos de Bioética* 25 (2014) 481–91.
Valera, Luca, and Vittoradolfo Tambone. "The Goldfish Syndrome: Human Nature and the Posthuman Myth." *Cuadernos de Bioética* 25 (2014) 353–66.
Vatican Council II. *Gaudium et spes*. Pastoral constitution. December 7, 1965.
Voegelin, Eric. *The New Science of Politics: An Introduction*. Chicago: University of Chicago Press, 1987.
Westermann, Claus. *Genesis I–II: A Continental Commentary*. Translated by John J. Scullion. Minneapolis: Augsburg Fortress, 1984.
White, Kevin. "The Passions of the Soul (Ia IIae, qq. 22–48)." In *The Ethics of Aquinas*, edited by Stephen J. Pope, 103–15. Washington, DC: Georgetown University Press, 2002.

Williams, Bernard. "The Human Prejudice." In *Philosophy as a Humanistic Discipline*, 135–54. Princeton: Princeton University Press, 2006.

Wudarczyk, Olga A., et al. "Could Intranasal Oxytocin Be Used to Enhance Relationships? Research Imperatives, Clinical Policy, and Ethical Considerations." *Current Opinion in Psychiatry* 26 (2013) 474–84.

Zak, P. J., et al. "Oxytocin Increases Generosity in Humans." *Public Library of Science* 2 (2007) 1–5.

———. "Oxytocin Is Associated with Human Trustworthiness." *Hormones and Behavior* 48 (2005) 522–27.

Index

A

Abraham, 110, 277
acedia, 174–76
Attention Deficit Hyperactivity Disorder (ADHD), 31, 46, 68
adrenaline, 50
agency, moral, 57, 270
aging, 60–64, 70, 258, 261–63, 264, 267, 268, 275, 284
agnosticism, 103, 104, 105
alterity, 72
altruism, 23, 50, 55, 56, 59, 219, 220, 225, 256
   close-range, 220, 224
   kin, 223, 224
amniocentesis, 183
androgen, blockers, 52
anthropogenesis, 124
anthropology, 4, 22, 71, 99, 125, 135, 238, 250, 256, 287
   transhumanist anthropology, xviii, 21, 27, 66–87, 88, 91
Aquinas, Thomas. *See* Thomas Aquinas, Saint
Arendt, Hanna, 267, 291
art, 247
artefact, xx, 44, 72, 182, 208, 209, 266, 288,
Artificial Reproductive Technologies (ARTs), 131, 181, 193, 195, 196, 198, 213
asceticism, as virtue, 150, 229
atheism, 101, 103, 104, 119

Augustine, Saint, xiii, xiv, 93, 239, 244, 279, 281
authenticity, 35–37, 43, 44, 47, 57, 236, 257, 258, 270, 273, 275, 284
   inauthenticity, 12, 35, 58, 282
autonomy, 6, 35, 43, 53, 57, 59, 76, 90, 106, 107, 150, 201, 204, 235, 243, 244, 253, 275
   procreative, 185, 191
Ayer, A. J., 98, 291

B

Bacon, Francis, 89, 90, 263
Baconian project, 90, 283
Balthasar, Hans Urs von, xiv, 132, 242–43, 291
Barazzetti, Gaia, 59–60, 62–63, 291
Basil, Saint, 250
beauty, xx, 81, 85, 111, 120, 245, 247, 248, 259, 264–266, 272, 284
being, xix, 25, 87, 88, 92–98, 101–2, 104, 108–10, 117, 121, 129, 132–43, 152–53, 155, 164, 166, 169, 170, 244, 279, 286, 288, 289
Bellver Capella, Vicente, 264, 267–69, 291
Benedict XVI. *See* Ratzinger, Joseph
benevolence, 80, 235, 239–41, 269
Berghmans, Ron, 44–46, 48, 292
bias, xiii, xx, 13, 22, 54, 55, 190, 218–20, 223, 225–26, 240, 257
biologism, 138

INDEX

Biomedical Enhancement Exceptionalism, 11
biotechnology. *See* technology, biotechnology
Bloch, Ernst, 144, 154–55, 164–69, 227, 292
Body, 6, 10, 12, 13, 17, 23, 40, 44, 47, 51, 61, 63, 64, 65, 72, 73–75, 125–26, 131, 145, 150, 175, 176, 194, 195–96, 203–4, 207, 211, 271, 274, 279, 287
Body of Christ, 142, 251
Bolt, Ineke, 46, 305
Bonaventure, Saint, xiii, xiv, 101, 119
Bond, John, 59–61, 292
boredom, 269
Bostrom, Nick, xi–xii, xx, 3, 5–13, 18, 20, 22–25, 27, 29–35, 37–38, 43, 45–47, 60–62, 66–71, 75, 82–85, 89, 92, 102–3, 108, 115–16, 122, 145–46, 199, 202, 204, 214–15, 247–48, 258–63, 285, 292–93, 299, 304–5
Brain-computer interfaces, 10, 30, 33, 34
breath, 146
  of God, 118, 125–28
Brock, Dan, 184, 187–90, 203, 293
Buchanan, Allen, xiii, 9–11, 13–14, 17–19, 23, 54, 65, 69–71, 86, 103, 108, 116, 122–23, 136, 145, 224, 293, 300

C

calculation, 99, 111, 237, 247, 256, 286
caloric restriction, 62, 64, 267
chance, xiv, 26, 61, 104, 115–21, 140, 187, 199, 200, 201, 222, 286, 287
changed trade-offs, 67–68
charity, 173, 254
cheating, 27
  death, 10
  and enhancement, 37–38
"child of desire," 195–98
choice, 19, 81, 90, 91, 103, 106, 118, 160, 192, 214, 236, 238, 242, 282
  and burden, 198–99

and love, 239, 282
  and moral agency, 57, 59, 201, 203–4
  reproductive, 24, 186, 188, 189, 191, 195
Chorionic Villous Sampling (CVS), 183
Christ. *See* Jesus Christ
Christianity, 92, 101, 105–6, 135, 140, 147, 154, 233, 241–42, 247
church, xv, xvii, 20, 104, 106, 252, 253, 275
climate change, 23, 57, 219, 245
cloning, 63, 197, 204, 212
coercion
  and enhancement, 43
  and eugenics, 24–25, 191–92
  political, 220, 221
cognitive enhancement. *See* enhancement, types
collective consciousness, 168, 169, 227
Colombetti, Elena, 12, 65, 74, 92, 293
commonsense, morality, 185, 188, 226
communion, of love, with God, xx, 127, 129, 130, 170, 176, 212, 218, 243, 244, 247, 257, 259, 277, 279–83, 284, 288, 289
Comte, Auguste, 95, 98–100
Congregation for the Doctrine of the Faith, xiii, 112, 126, 293. *See also* *Donum vitae, Dignitas personae*
conjugal act/love, xix, 181–82, 195–98, 207, 210–12
Conrad, Peter, 46, 293
contemplation, xv, 5, 145, 164
contingence, contingency, xix, xx, 102, 116, 121, 166, 181, 199–202, 206, 217, 249, 258, 259, 269–70, 282, 284, 285, 288
  imperative of, xix, 201, 206, 269–70
control, xi, xvi, xix, 8, 10, 13, 33, 36, 61, 72, 90, 131, 147, 150–151, 154, 165, 167, 173, 182, 193, 199–202, 204, 209, 213, 214, 216, 217, 222, 227, 231, 236–37, 250, 256, 270, 283, 285
  impulse control, 23, 59
  self-control, 8–9, 13, 56, 84, 177
conscience, 25, 106, 153, 232, 249–52, 257

anamnesis, 250–52
conscientia, 249, 252
synderesis, 249–50
cosmetic surgery, 11, 35
courage, xv, 176, 229, 249
Crawford, David S., 139, 250–251, 293
creation, creator, xx, 26, 93–94, 95, 101, 102, 104, 114, 116–18, 120–121, 123–31, 133–43, 147–49, 152, 169, 170, 176, 208, 210–11, 217, 218, 230, 239, 243, 244, 245, 247, 252, 254, 256, 287–88
cross, 231, 280
cryogenics, 145

D

Darwall, Stephen L., 84, 293
Darwin, Charles, 95, 103, 116
Dávila, Nicolás Gómez, 240, 293
death, xx, 10, 16, 21, 42, 62, 70, 76, 91, 125, 127, 160, 168–69, 171, 198, 201, 227, 231, 242, 249, 258–66, 269–73, 275–84, 288
Deep Brain Stimulation (DBS), 45
dehumanization, xii, 12, 35, 36, 58, 133, 144, 209, 217, 257, 259, 274, 276, 284, 289
democracy/democratic, 86, 105–7, 138
  liberal, 220–21
dependence, 11, 42, 52, 84, 96, 100, 106, 128–31, 141–42, 154, 157, 173, 204–5, 213–14, 219, 243–44, 247–48, 257, 267, 282, 284, 285, 288–89
Descartes, René, 90, 94, 96, 263, 293
despair, xviii–xx, 28, 48, 52, 116, 120, 142, 144, 146, 156, 158–60, 162, 165, 169–77, 181, 216–18, 227, 244, 249, 256, 258, 272, 281, 284, 285, 287
Di Blasi, Fulvio, 134, 293
Dignitas personae, xvii, 20, 21, 22, 23, 24, 112, 113, 127, 128, 182, 194, 205, 293
Dignity
  of effort, 43–44

human, ix, xvii, 6, 24, 74, 76, 81–86, 107, 113, 122, 126–27, 133–34, 137, 146, 174, 201, 209, 215–16, 228, 238, 246, 260, 275, 287
  as quality, 82–86
disability, 15, 17, 181, 184, 186, 188, 189, 191, 262, 295, 304, 305
Di Stefano, Nicola, 74–75, 304
DNA, 41, 61, 63, 122, 125, 183–184, 297,
doing, metaphysics/ontology of, 144, 153, 164, 167, 286, 288
dominion, xix, 25, 114, 150, 181, 210, 229–30
Donum vitae, 112, 113, 126, 210, 293
dopamine, 50, 51, 52
doubt, 94, 103, 104, 113, 119, 142, 192, 234
Douglas, Thomas, xiii, 53, 55, 56, 294
dualism, 74
Dupré, Louis, 102, 294

E

earnestness, 229
Earp, Brian, 14, 45, 50–53, 68–69, 294
embryo, 10, 11, 41, 85, 112, 189, 191, 193, 195
  screening, 10, 182, 183
  selection, 9, 213
  transfer, 182
embryonic stem cells, 63
enhancement
  types
    cognitive, xii, xviii, 9, 10, 18, 29–38, 40, 43, 53, 54–57, 218, 232
    mood, xi, xviii, 11, 13, 29, 44–53, 54, 56, 69, 285
    moral, xii, xviii, xix–xx, 9, 23, 25, 29, 53–59, 218–19, 221, 231–32, 234, 236–37, 245, 253
    physical, xviii, 29, 39–44
    lifespan extension, xviii, xix, 29, 59–65, 258–59, 263–64, 267, 269, 273, 284, 285, 288
  modes
    internal versus external, 29–31, 33
(continued on next page)

enhancement (continued)
  functional versus human, 12–16, 20, 22
  models
    ideological, 16–17, 122
    sociological pragmatic, 16
    therapy-enhancement, xviii, 16–18, 21, 46, 187, 194–95
    welfarist, xviii, 12–21, 28
enlightenment, xvi, xix, 88–91, 95, 104–6, 120, 135, 236
Environment of Evolutionary Adaptedness (EEA), 67, 286
equality, 20, 43, 81, 83, 85, 125, 128, 191, 199, 201, 221
eschatology, 102, 258, 275
estrogen, 14, 50, 62
erythropoietin (EPO), 40, 42
eternity, 130, 168, 170, 271–74, 277–82
eugenics, 9, 23–25, 72, 181, 182, 191–92, 202, 205, 217
evil, 120, 137, 151, 152, 156–58, 222, 229, 232, 235, 244, 250, 251, 252, 261, 286
evolution, xviii, xx, 4, 11, 24–25, 33, 50, 55, 58, 59, 61, 66–72, 78, 86, 88–90, 95, 97, 99, 115–116, 118–20, 123–25, 129, 136, 140, 145, 162, 165, 176, 194, 218, 223–26, 235, 237–38, 240, 245, 247, 256, 267, 286–87
evolution heuristic, 67–71, 86, 115
evolutionary lag, 70–71, 286
evolutionary restrictions, 67, 71–71
existentialism, 90, 91, 110, 122, 156, 160, 213, 248, 254

F

"Fable of the Dragon Tyrant," xx, 258, 259–62, 263, 292
faciendum, xix, 98, 108, 109, 250, 286
factum, xix, 94, 95, 98, 286,
Faggioni, Maurizio, 7, 27, 71, 294
faith, xv, xvi, xix, xx, 26, 88, 93–95, 101–11, 116, 118–23, 135, 141, 154, 160, 162, 167, 170, 175, 239, 243, 247, 248, 251, 252, 259, 275, 276, 277–81, 286–89
Faust, 165, 167–68, 207
fear, 35, 47, 50, 103, 105, 120, 147, 151, 158, 170–71, 175, 191, 216, 223, 225, 226, 234, 235, 236–37, 256, 261, 274, 279, 285,
Feinberg, Joel, 204, 294
Fenton, Elizabeth, 56–57, 294, 299
fertility, 23, 69, 267
fetal cell-free DNA (cfDNA, cffDNA), 183
finitude, 111, 128, 239, 260, 262, 264, 265, 282, 284, 289; (blessing of): xx, 259, 260, 264
Flores d'Arcais, Paolo, 104–7, 137–38, 140, 294, 303
Fluorescence In Situ Hybridization (FISH), 183
Foddy, Bennett, 39–41, 294, 305
forgiveness, 81, 244
freedom, xx, 20, 53, 54, 85, 87, 90, 106, 107, 116, 120, 121, 122, 129, 132, 137, 142, 147, 192, 201, 212, 213, 214, 217, 228, 230, 232, 233, 235, 244, 247, 250, 253, 271, 276, 287, 289
  negative, 253–55
  positive, 255–56
  reproductive, 25
  "of indifference," 254
  "to fall," 58–59, 253
Fukuyama, Francis, 18, 56, 58, 71, 81–82, 192–93, 262, 266, 294

G

García-Cuadrado, José Ángel, 90–91, 152, 299
Gauchet, Marcel, 197, 294
Gaudium et spes, 109, 127, 135, 233, 306
Gekas, Jean, 184, 294
gene doping, 41, 43
genetic engineering/enhancement/manipulation, xvii, xix, 10, 21, 24–25, 30, 32–33, 37, 42–43, 55, 62–63, 71, 92, 145, 181, 184, 189,

192–194, 195, 197–206, 208, 213–14, 216–17, 235, 287–88
geneceuticals, 45
gift/giftedness
    as received, xix, xx, 25–27, 121–123, 144, 153, 159, 161–62, 166, 170, 172, 174, 177, 181–82, 199–200, 213, 216–17, 230, 238, 246, 248, 275, 281, 284, 286
    as grace, 132, 252
    as given, 212
Giglio, Francesca, 9, 20, 21, 22, 194, 195, 231, 295
globalization, 23, 226
Glover, Jonathan, xiii, 214, 215, 295
Gnosticism, 100–101, 141, 173
God, xv, xvi–xvii, xx, 20, 26, 58, 81, 88, 91, 93–96, 101–8, 110–14, 116, 118, 120–21, 124–30, 132–35, 138, 141–42, 147–48, 160–63, 165, 169–70, 172, 174–77, 182, 191, 202, 208, 210–11, 214, 217–18, 229–30, 233, 238–40, 242–45, 247–51, 253, 255, 259, 270–72, 275–82, 284, 286–87, 289
gods, 18, 73, 120, 135, 140, 165, 176
Godfrey, Joseph J., 170, 295
goodness, 78, 111, 263, 271, 273, 284
    of human life, xii, xviii, xx, 15, 19, 20, 112, 114, 127, 133–34, 141–42, 197, 215–16, 217, 218, 239, 246, 256, 257, 285, 287, 289
    of being, 25, 134–41, 142, 166, 169, 170, 244, 256, 288
    of God, 161, 247, 248, 249, 272, 281
goods, 220
    human, 16, 19–20, 156, 157, 158, 160, 162, 163, 174, 259, 264, 284
    social, 24
    positional versus intrinsic, 38, 43
grace, xx, 95, 132, 141, 142, 160, 161, 163, 172, 176, 219, 230, 243
gratitude, 121, 212–14, 216, 223, 225
gravity, (virtue of), 229
Gray, John, 269, 295
Gregory, Brad, 86, 91, 92, 102, 119, 140, 295

Guardini, Romano, xiv, 95, 96, 144, 147–53, 167–68, 212–13, 227–31, 233, 241–42, 246, 249, 257, 295
Güell Pelayo, Francisco, 24, 192–93, 216, 295

H

Habermas, Jürgen, 19, 25, 54–55, 106–8, 182, 200–207, 213, 235, 293, 295, 296, 306
Haisma, Hidde J., 41–43, 295
Hanby, Michael, 198, 208–9, 295
harm, 15, 52, 53, 56, 157
    of technology, 145, 225
    of selecting children, 181, 186, 189–90, 214
    ease of, 225–226
    ultimate, 225
Harris, John, 10, 54, 57–58, 63, 86, 253, 294, 295
hate/hatred, 127, 141, 142, 158, 217, 218, 245
Hedges, Inez, 165, 167–68, 295
Hegel, Georg Wilhelm Friedrich, 95, 96, 102, 207, 276
Heidegger, Martin, 108, 111
historicism/Historicization, 95, 275
Homo orans, 124
Homo viator(is), 155, 162
hope, xii, xvi–xx, 3–6, 10, 21–23, 27–28, 29, 32–33, 44–45, 51, 55, 57, 60–62, 65, 89, 93, 103, 121, 123, 125, 129–31, 142–43, 144–46, 153–55, 181–82, 192, 197, 204, 215–17, 218, 220, 225–27, 229, 232–37, 244, 246–49, 256, 258–63, 267, 269, 272–81, 284, 285–89
    ordinary/passion, 155–60
    fundamental/virtue, 155–56, 160–63, 166–71, 177
    secularization of, xix, 144, 164–66, 171, 177, 219, 231, 287
Housden, Charlotte R., 29–32, 296
hubris, 112, 192, 229
human
    being, xi–xii, xvii, xix–xx, 4, 6–8, 10,
    (continued on next page)

human being (continued)
13–14, 21–22, 36, 44, 48, 54–55, 57, 62, 64–65, 66–68, 70–72, 74–82, 84, 86, 88, 90–92, 96, 100, 104, 108–9, 111–13, 115, 117–18, 120–31, 134, 137–38, 142, 146, 148–53, 155, 161, 164–66, 168, 175, 177, 182, 192, 198, 201–4, 206–8, 210–12, 217–20, 222, 227–30, 232–34, 238, 240, 244–49, 253–54, 257, 259, 262–63, 266, 273–76, 278, 282–83, 285–88

person, xviii–xix, 17, 21–22, 66, 71–72, 74–76, 78–79, 81, 85, 88, 90, 94, 96–97, 110, 112–15, 118, 122–28, 130–33, 135, 137, 140, 142–44, 160–61, 165–66, 169–70, 172, 174, 202, 206–10, 219, 226, 233, 238, 240, 245–48, 255–56, 270, 276, 283, 287

nature, xx, 21, 81, 112, 132–33, 144, 155, 161, 166, 170, 176, 202, 208, 210–12, 229–30, 238, 240, 243, 248, 250–51, 254, 255, 270, 274, 275, 288–89

Human Growth Hormone (HGH), 39, 40, 42
human prejudice, 77–81
humility, 25, 26, 105, 125, 129, 141, 142, 159, 166, 167, 168, 173, 175, 176, 182, 198, 199, 200, 217, 230, 231, 289
Huxley, Aldous, xvi
Huxley, Julian, 4–6, 296
hybridization, 72, 287

I

image of God/*imago Dei*, xvii, xx, 104, 107, 112, 125–28, 130, 132, 133, 134, 182, 208, 210–11, 245, 250, 255, 282, 286
immaturity, 168, 268
immortality, xix, xx, 21, 60, 62–63, 70, 96, 144, 170, 258–59, 263–64, 267, 269–71, 273–75, 277, 280, 283, 284,
imperative

of benevolence, 80
categorical, 134, 209
concrete, 241–44
of contingency, xix, 201–7, 269–70
for enhancement, 3, 287
for life, 112
moral, 86, 136, 137, 256, 258, 262
procreative benevolence, 187, 286
of responsibility, 97, 221, 222, 227, 228, 233, 235, 236, 238, 246, 264, 265, 267, 296
technological, xix, 144, 146, 256
toleration, 140
Incarnation, 95, 112, 127, 230
independence, 82, 90, 119, 146, 172, 233, 268, 275
individualism, 133, 224
inequality, 181, 189–90, 201, 202, 213
inertia, 174–76
infinite, 21, 80, 111, 129, 160, 161, 169, 175, 227, 238, 245, 274
loss, 35
reverence, 243
injustice, 11, 168–69, 269, 274
insulin-like growth factor 1 (IGF-1), 39–40, 41, 62
interdependence, 132–33
intergenerational relations, xx, 21, 259, 266–69, 288
intrinsic goods, 14, 38, 43
Introduction to Christianity, 92–95, 98, 103–4, 108–11, 114, 117, 121, 130, 132–33, 147, 244, 302
in vitro fertilization (IVF), 10, 182–83, 191, 196–97, 207, 214

J

Jensen, Steven, 91, 216–17, 296
Jesus Christ, xv, 96, 121, 127, 139, 147–148, 177, 230, 241–44, 247–48, 251, 255, 275, 277–81, 288
Joachim of Fiore, 101, 275
John Duns Scotus, 102
John Paul II, xiii, xv, 182, 242, 296
Jonas, Hans, xiv, 21, 75–76, 97, 203, 204, 221, 222–23, 227–28, 233–37, 241, 246, 255, 264–67, 296

justice, 43, 69, 85, 104, 169, 172, 206, 223, 233, 240, 244

K

Kahane, Guy, xiii, 12, 15, 19, 46, 48–49, 183–85, 187–88, 191–93, 296, 305
Kampowski, Stephan, ix, 21, 35–36, 38, 97, 109, 194, 196–99, 201, 203, 205–6, 228, 235–36, 240–41, 265, 269, 295, 296, 298
Kant, Immanuel, 89, 94, 96, 102, 111, 134, 151, 209, 296
Kass, Leon, xii, 12, 14, 26–27, 37, 47, 57–58, 87, 131, 196–98, 201, 209, 211–12, 214, 258, 262–72, 284, 296–97
Kelsey, David H., 272, 297
Keshavarz, Zeinab, 183, 297
kingdom, 259–61
    of God, 170, 233, 276
    of man), 164
knowledge, 19, 33, 78, 119, 132, 134, 136, 147, 203, 232
    divine/participatory, 93–94, 105, 251–52
    empirical/positive, xv, xix, 4–5, 42, 51, 54–55, 65, 88–89, 95, 98–99, 100–102, 107–8, 140, 145, 150, 151, 164, 173, 228–29, 236–37, 263, 276, 283, 285, 286, 288
    versus understanding, 108–13, 115, 123, 170, 211, 286
Kolnai, Aurel, 83–84, 297
Kraj, Tomasz, xviii, 127, 297
Kramer, Peter, 44–45, 47, 297

L

Letters from Lake Como, 148–50, 153, 257, 295
Lewis, C. S., 72–73, 205, 297
Liao, Matthew, 14, 44–45, 48–50, 297
lifespan extension. *See* enhancement, types
limit/limitation, human, xi, xviii, xx, 4, 6, 7, 8, 16, 21–22, 28, 36, 55, 60, 65–66, 68, 80, 91, 115, 125, 128–29, 141–42, 155, 160, 166–67, 176–77, 222–23, 229–30, 239, 246, 248–49, 257, 264, 265, 269, 270, 282, 285, 288–89
Local Optimality Traps, 70–71
logos, xv, 94, 97, 115, 117, 120–21, 135, 139, 230, 250
Lomanno, Matthew P., 16, 297
Lombardo, Nicholas, 156–57, 161–63, 297
love, 20, 58, 147, 157–58, 163, 174, 214–15, 216, 244, 245–46, 248, 270
    human capacity for, xx, 104, 110–11, 129–34, 137, 141, 142–43, 170, 173, 212, 218, 233, 235, 236–37, 239–41, 247, 257, 265–66, 279, 283, 284, 288
    conjugal, xix, 195, 197–98, 207–8, 210, 211, 212
    diminishment of, 52–53
    divine, xx, 120–21, 127, 128, 129–30, 131–32, 133, 141, 142, 169–71, 173, 175, 177, 182, 210, 238, 241–43, 244, 247, 248–49, 250, 259, 275, 277–80, 282, 283, 284, 287–89
    enhancement of, 22, 48, 49–52, 69
    as "yes," 131–32, 134, 141, 170, 215, 239
"Love drugs," 51–52
Lubac, Henri de, xiv, 98, 99, 109, 297

M

MacIntyre, Alasdair, 139, 233–34, 238, 297
macro-/microevolution, 119
magnanimity, 133, 174–76, 217, 245, 274
Malherbe, Brice de, 102, 275, 297
Marchesini, Roberto, 72, 297
Marx, Karl, 95, 97, 98, 102, 123, 145, 253, 254, 274, 276
Marxism, xvi, 97, 100, 123, 154, 164–65, 221, 254, 274–75, 278
materialism, 75–76, 100, 129, 287
May, William F., 199
Mazzocato, Giuseppe, 153, 298

McKenny, Gerald P., 89–90, 283, 298
McMahan, Jeff, 76, 298
Meilaender, Gilbert, 61, 64, 258, 262–63, 265, 267–72, 298
Melina, Livio, ix, 125–27, 132, 135, 139, 195–96, 198, 211, 213, 216, 298
metaphysics, xviii, xix, 16, 19, 77, 79, 81, 86, 90–92, 94, 96, 99–100, 106, 108–9, 112, 122, 135–36, 139, 144, 153, 166, 168–69, 175, 205–6, 245, 263, 287
Miah, Andy, 39–40, 42, 298
Milbank, John, 102, 298
Miner, Robert, 157, 159, 173, 298
Minimal Threshold Constraint, 191–92
modernity, 75, 88, 90–91, 101, 138, 142, 144, 147, 167, 227, 236
Moltisanti, Dino, 4, 7, 21–22, 62, 74, 76, 86, 89, 295, 296, 298
Monod, Jacques, 116, 140, 298
mood enhancement. *See* enhancement, types
moral enhancement. *See* enhancement, types
More, Max, 6, 74, 75, 86, 103, 292, 298, 304
mortality, 58, 59–60, 64, 89, 125, 160, 193, 263, 264, 266–68, 270–71, 282, 284
　blessing of), 264–66, 270
morphological freedom, 6, 25, 73–75, 122, 131, 287
Murillo, José Ignacio, 74–75, 87, 91–92, 298
Mutilation
　of hope, xx, 259
　of human beings, 113, 259, 274, 284, 286
Mystery
　of being, 110, 208–10, 244, 269, 278
　of God, 96, 108, 127, 147–48, 173
　of human life, xx, 101–2, 112, 127, 208, 212, 259, 276

N

naltrexone, 52
nanotechnology, 5, 10, 145
natality, 267
nature. *See* human, nature
natural law, 134–39, 226
natural selection, 66, 69, 71, 116, 237, 286
naturalistic fallacy, 136
necessity, 102, 153, 159, 229, 231, 253, 256
　of death, 270
　of faith, 277
　of the conjugal act for procreation, xix, 182, 207, 212
　versus chance, 116–17
Neo-Scholasticism. 93, 135
neuroceuticals, 45
"new man," 233, 275, 279
Newman, John Henry, xiv
Nichols, Aidan, 147, 238, 299, 301
Nietzsche, Friedrich, 91–92, 145, 230, 299
"not yet," 154–55, 159, 162, 166–68, 171–72, 234, 236

O

obedience, 230, 242–43, 255
obligation, 80–81, 137, 152, 181, 185, 186–87, 190, 191, 192, 206, 212, 213, 225, 226, 236, 253
ontology, 21, 73, 74, 76, 93, 95–96, 154–55, 164, 166, 168, 287
optimism, xvii, xviii, xix, 19, 23, 144, 154, 163, 165, 171, 177, 227, 229, 272
ordo amoris, 80, 239
Overall, Christine, 60, 299
"Oxford School," xii, xvii, xviii, 3–4, 29, 65, 285
oxytocin, 50–52, 56

P

Parens, Erik, 199–200, 299
Parent-child relationship, xix, 182, 202, 212, 217, 267
Parfit, Derek, 186, 189, 299
Parker, Michael, 48, 188, 299
Pastor, Luis Miguel, 90–91, 152, 299

paternalism, 204–5, 217
patience, 19, 167–68, 193
Paul, Saint, 162, 230, 250, 279
Pelagianism, 172–73
Pepperell, Robert, 72, 299
perfectionism, 22–23, 25–26, 145, 187
person. *See* human, person
personism, 78–79
Persson, Ingmar, xiii, xx, 53–56, 59, 78, 218–21, 223–27, 229, 231–32, 234–37, 256, 294, 299
pessimism, xx, 23, 165, 218, 246, 249
Pessina, Adriano, 229–30, 300
philosophia universalis, 119, 238, 286
philosophy, xiii, xvi, 91, 95, 101, 107, 119, 135, 147, 171, 247, 275
  evolutionary, 119, 136
  positivist, 98–99, 113, 122
  transhumanist, 103, 289
physical enhancement. *See* enhancement, physical
physicalism, 138
Pieper, Josef, xiv, 92–95, 108, 118, 129, 144, 147, 152–56, 159–64, 166–76, 215, 227, 236, 273, 295, 300, 305
Pinckaers, Servais, 160, 249–50, 252, 292, 300
pluralism, 140, 187, 188
polygenicity, 192
positional goods, 38, 43
positivism, xv, xix, 88, 92, 98–104, 108–13, 138, 144–46, 151, 167, 173, 177, 181, 207, 210, 218, 234, 237, 256, 276, 283–85
posthuman, xi, 6–8, 16, 27, 56, 72–73, 78, 91, 248, 264, 286
Postigo Solana, Elena, 4, 7, 21–22, 62, 74, 76, 86, 89, 298, 300
postmodernity, xix, 8, 72, 74, 89–91, 105, 122, 136, 205
power
  human, xv, xx, 9, 12, 13, 26, 39, 42–43, 52, 54, 73, 89, 94, 105, 108, 114, 156–57, 159–160, 172, 173, 175, 188, 204, 221, 246, 249, 252, 262, 271, 273, 275, 281–282, 284; (divine): 104, 142, 161, 221, 250, 270, 272, 281

technological, 6, 17, 70, 108, 144, 146, 150–53, 166, 168, 171, 182, 198, 205, 209, 213, 218–19, 223, 228–33, 236–37, 246, 248, 283, 286
"power over power," 228–29, 231
practical reason, 96, 139, 234, 249–52
prayer, 116, 172, 281
preimplantation genetic diagnosis (PGD), 10, 182–83, 193
pre-implantation genetic haplotyping (PGH), 183
President's Council on Bioethics, 17, 21, 32, 39–42, 44, 48, 57, 62–65, 194, 258, 262–63, 265, 267–69, 292, 300, 304
presumption, xx, 88, 103, 105, 106, 162, 171–73, 176, 229, 272
procreation, 181–82, 195–96, 198, 201, 207, 209–12, 214, 217, 264, 266
procreative beneficence, xii, xix, 24, 181, 185–193, 216, 217
Progress, xvii, 6, 37, 97, 100–101, 103, 111, 142, 146, 165, 171, 229, 237, 253, 272, 276
  historical, 144, 166, 168, 227
  humanity as work-in-progress, xix, 66
  moral, 233, 256
  scientific, 54, 90, 165, 177, 193, 227, 231–32
  technological, 31, 145, 177, 219, 221, 227, 231, 233, 256, 286–87
prudence, 160, 177, 252

R

racism, 27, 55, 77–78
rationality, xvi, 22, 74, 76, 78, 81, 105–6, 117, 120, 123, 136, 147, 150, 152, 159, 256, 286–87
Ratzinger, Joseph, ix, xii–xx, 22, 72, 88, 92–101, 103–14, 115–43, 144, 146–48, 150–52, 154, 161–77, 181–82, 195, 207–12, 214–15, 217, 218, 222, 227–29, 232–34, 236–39, 241–56, 258–59, 272–84, 285–89, 291, 294, 299, 300–303, 305
  as Benedict XVI, ix, xiii, xv, 136, 162, 242–44, 272–73, 279, 291–92

Rawls, John, 19
reason
　originating, xix, 115, 117–18, 121–22
　pathology of, xix, 105, 111–12, 114, 146, 152, 181, 192, 208, 212, 286
redemption, 101, 162, 170, 233, 244, 247
relationship
　human, xix, 19, 48–52, 60, 69, 80, 130–33, 182, 201, 202, 204–5, 212–13, 217, 241, 282, 288
　with God, 126–29, 239, 243–44, 277–78
relativism, 16, 19–21, 28, 90–91, 105, 122, 140, 287
religion, 20, 26, 89, 99, 102, 103, 105–7, 119, 221, 256
remembrance, 278, 288
Remotti, Francesco, 19, 104–105, 107, 122, 137, 303
reproduction, 24, 191, 220, 223–24, 278
　sexual, 69, 130, 196
　artificial/asexual, 75, 130–31, 197, 207–12, 217, 248
　versus procreation, 182, 207, 210–12
responsibility, xv, xix, 25, 34, 57, 81, 104, 106, 107, 120, 142, 182, 198–201, 204, 217, 219, 224, 226, 249, 270, 287
　ethics of, 222–23, 228, 231–32, 236, 240–41, 253, 255–56
resurrection, 242, 276
reverence, 25, 106, 126, 129, 208, 213, 217, 243
reversibility, 204
Rhonheimer, Martin, 135, 181, 195–197, 210, 212–215, 217, 303
rights
　equal, 81, 221
　human, 59, 81–83, 86, 106, 126–27, 138, 140
　individual, 6, 53, 213, 256
　natural, 136
　negative, 220, 226
risk, 5–6, 23, 24, 34, 35, 42–44, 45, 47, 62, 69, 78, 111, 115, 137, 145–46, 183, 186, 191, 193–195, 200, 209, 225, 234–36, 244, 246, 261, 263, 268–70

Roache, Rebecca, xiii, 13, 18, 24, 29, 31–32, 34, 43, 44–50, 60–62, 292, 297
Rowland, Tracey, ix, xvi, xvii, 93, 135–136, 47, 303
Rubin, Charles, 83, 304
Russo, Maria Teresa, 74–75, 304

S

saints, 247, 252, 281
Sandberg, Anders, xiii, 12, 20, 29–35, 37–38, 50–52, 67–71, 73, 108, 115–16, 214, 293, 304
Sandel, Michael J., 17, 22, 25–26, 182, 198–200, 214, 262, 270, 304
Sarte, Jean-Paul, 254
Savulescu, Julian, xii, xix–xx, 3, 5, 10–17, 19–21, 24, 29–30, 34, 36, 39, 42, 50–56, 59, 63, 69, 77–81, 122, 145, 181, 183–93, 218–21, 223–27, 229, 231–32, 234–37, 248, 256, 285, 291, 292, 293, 294, 295, 296, 297, 298, 299, 304–5, 306
Schermer, Maartje, 46, 305
scholasticism, 79, 92–94, 135
Schönborn, Christoph, 119, 238, 305
Shulman, Carl, xiii, 305
Schumacher, Bernard, 153–55, 158–60, 162, 166–69, 171, 227, 295, 305
scientism, 92, 99, 100
secular humanism, 88, 89, 103, 113
secularization, 107, 174
　of hope (see hope, secularization of)
selection
　of children, xii, xix, 9, 181–87, 189–90, 192, 195, 197, 213–16, 217
　negative, 183–84, 189
　positive, 184, 193
selective androgen receptor modulators (SARMs), 40
selective serotonin reuptake inhibitors (SSRIs), 44, 52
serotonin, 50, 52, 56
sexuality, 75, 182
sin, 127, 128, 136, 165, 233, 244
Singer, Peter, xii, 26, 77–79, 81, 189, 305
sloth. See *acedia*

solidarity, 6, 25, 36, 80–81, 107, 125, 128, 182, 199–200
Sorgner, Stefan Lorenz, 188, 306
soul, 96, 101, 112, 124, 126, 150, 153, 156, 160, 172, 174, 207, 211, 238, 249, 271, 279
Spaemann, Robert, xiv, 21, 79–82, 112, 153, 184, 198, 201–2, 206–7, 238–41, 265, 270, 306
Sparrow, Robert, 186–87, 190, 192, 306
speciesism, 77–78
Spinoza, Baruch, 94
spirit, 138, 139, 149, 237–38, 279
  human, xv, xix, 3, 93, 111–12, 123–24, 129, 149, 151, 211, 218, 238, 248, 253, 261, 269, 273, 279, 287
  divine, 114, 133, 243, 275
Stoics, 140, 160
suffering, xvi, 4–6, 9, 17, 27, 31, 46, 48, 78, 85, 90, 93, 126–27, 224, 241–43, 259, 261–62, 269, 274, 282–83, 288
synchronization, 287

T

Tambone, Vittoradolfo, 72–73, 306
Tamburrini, Claudio, 42–43, 203, 306
Tännsjö, Torbjörn, 42–43, 203, 306
techne, xix, 98, 144, 153, 222, 232
technology, xvii, xix, 3–6, 9–12, 31–36, 44, 55, 58, 65, 69–70, 72, 74, 79, 90–92, 102, 109, 131, 144–52, 169, 177, 182, 195, 208–9, 219, 222, 225–26, 228–31, 233, 235, 241, 245–46, 248, 257, 261, 283, 286, 288
  biotechnology, xi, xii, xvii, 3, 5, 11–12, 14, 17, 25, 32, 41–42, 45–46, 53, 57, 61, 65, 70, 145, 219, 253, 266, 285–86
technological imperative. *See* imperative, technological
teleology, 112
telomerase, 63
telomere, 63–64

Temkin, Larry, 61–62, 306
terrorism, 219, 245
testosterone, 40, 50, 62
theology, xiii–xv, 93, 95, 99, 101, 102, 119, 135, 147, 166, 232, 238, 241, 273
theosis, 244, 245
therapy, xiv, 9, 14, 49, 52, 55, 63, 64, 194, 205
  versus enhancement (see enhancement, models)
Thomas Aquinas, Saint, 92–94, 108, 118, 127, 134, 154, 156, 158, 160–61, 166, 172–75, 216, 241, 250, 252, 273, 281, 291, 297, 300, 306
thou, 124, 132, 213, 238, 240–241, 277
thought, originating. *See* reason
totalitarianism, xv, 220–21
transcendence, xv, xix, xx, 65, 101–2, 104, 111, 122, 125, 128–29, 141, 144, 156, 165, 177, 202, 246, 248, 259, 270–71, 274, 276–79, 289
transcranial magnetic stimulation (TMS), 30, 32, 45
transgenesis, 10, 42, 63
transhuman, xi, 4, 7–8, 16, 286
transhumanism, xi–xv, xvii–xx, 3–6, 8–9, 11, 16–18, 22–24, 27–28, 29–30, 38–39, 43, 53–54, 56, 58, 60–61, 65, 66, 68–75, 81, 83, 86, 88–92, 102–3, 108, 113, 115, 122–23, 128–29, 131, 133, 136, 142, 144–46, 166, 173, 177, 184, 189, 192, 195, 199, 202–3, 214, 216–17, 218, 222–23, 236–237, 241, 246, 257, 258–59, 262–63, 269–70, 275, 283–84, 285–89
Transhumanist Declaration, The, xiii, 5
trust, xvii, 50, 56, 110, 142–43, 159–60, 163, 173, 175–76, 218, 227, 237, 245–46, 277, 283, 285, 287–88
truth, ix, xv, 20, 22, 90, 92–95, 97–99, 102, 104–7, 109–11, 122–23, 128–30, 133–34, 137, 139–40, 152, 155, 176, 229–30, 235, 238, 244, 247, 253–55, 263, 271, 279, 283
Twomey, D. Vincent, xiv, xv, xvi, 100, 147, 306

U

understanding. *See* knowledge
Unfit for the Future, xiii, 55, 219–21, 223–27, 231–32, 234, 237, 299
utopia, xvi, xx, 83, 97, 100–101, 164–65, 167–70, 221, 227, 233, 253, 258–59, 269, 274–76, 279, 286

V

Valera, Luca, 8, 72, 73, 74, 87, 91, 306
value discordance, 67, 69–70
vasopressin, 50–52
Vatican Council II, 93, 127, 242, 306
verification, xvii, 98, 101, 173, 286
Vico, Giambattista, 94
virtue, xviii, 35–37, 48, 54, 58, 82–83, 93, 126, 137, 154, 156, 160–65, 167, 170, 174–77, 189, 199–200, 213, 229–30, 234, 238, 243, 252–53, 259, 264, 266–67, 272, 284
Voegelin, Eric, 100–101, 306
Vulnerability, 7, 81, 91, 228, 266, 272

W

wayfarer, 162
weapons of mass destruction, 54, 219, 224
welfarist model. *See* enhancement, models
well-being, 4, 6, 13, 15–21, 28, 34, 45, 48, 59, 62, 69, 90, 116, 156, 182, 184–85, 187–88, 190–91, 287
White, Kevin, 157–58, 306
William of Occam, 102
Williams, Bernard, 77–79, 307
wisdom, 6, 68, 105, 115, 123, 134, 152, 155, 252, 259, 265, 267, 271
  of nature, 70, 71
World Transhumanist Association, xiii, 5

X

xenophobia, 56, 221, 224